STUDIES IN EAST EU

MYSTICISM AND

THE LITTMAN LIBRARY OF
JEWISH CIVILIZATION

MANAGING EDITOR
Connie Webber

Dedicated to the memory of
LOUIS THOMAS SIDNEY LITTMAN
who founded the Littman Library
for the love of God
and in memory of his father
JOSEPH AARON LITTMAN
יהא זכרם ברוך

'Get wisdom, get understanding:
Forsake her not and she shall preserve thee'
PROV. 4:5

Studies in East European Jewish Mysticism and Hasidism

◆

JOSEPH WEISS

◆

Edited by
DAVID GOLDSTEIN

With a new introduction by
JOSEPH DAN

London · Portland, Oregon
The Littman Library of Jewish Civilization
1997

The Littman Library of Jewish Civilization

Published in the United Kingdom by
Vallentine Mitchell & Co. Ltd.
Newbury House
900 Eastern Avenue
London IG2 7HH

Published in the United States and Canada
by Vallentine Mitchell & Co. Ltd.
c/o ISBS, 5804 N.E. Hassalo Street,
Portland, Oregon 97213-3644

First published in hardback in 1985
by Oxford University Press on behalf of
The Littman Library of Jewish Civilization
as Studies in Eastern European Jewish Mysticism

First issued in paperback with new title and new introduction 1997

A catalogue record for this book is available from the British Library

The Library of Congress catalogued the hardcover edition as follows:
Weiss, Joseph
Studies in Eastern European Jewish mysticism.
(Littman library of Jewish civilization)
Includes index.
1. Hasidism—History—Addresses, essays, lectures.
I. Goldstein, David, 1933–   II. Title.
III. Series: Littman library of Jewish civilization.
BM198.W43   1985   296.8'33 84-27191
ISBN 1-874774-32-3

Publishing co-ordinator: Janet Moth
Cover design: Pete Russell, Faringdon, Oxon
Printed in Great Britain on acid-free paper by
The Alden Press, Oxford

Contents

STUDIES IN EAST EUROPEAN JEWISH MYSTICISM AND HASIDISM

Note on Sources

Articles in this book that were previously published are as follows (*JJS* = *Journal of Jewish Studies*):

'A Circle of Pneumatics in Pre-Hasidism'. *JJS* 8/3–4 (1957), 199–213

'Contemplative Mysticism and "Faith" in Hasidic Piety'. *JJS* 4/1 (1953), 19–29

'Torah Study in Early Hasidism'. *Ha-Do'ar* (Heb.) (New York), 45 (1965), 615–17

'Via Passiva in Early Hasidism'. *JJS* 11/3–4 (1960), 137–55

'The Kavvanoth of Prayer in Early Hasidism'. *JJS* 9/3–4 (1958), 163–92

'Petitionary Prayer in Early Hasidism'. *Hebrew Union College Annual*, 31 (1960) 137–47

'R. Abraham Kalisker's Concept of Communion with God and Men'. *JJS* 6/2 (1955), 87–99

'The Hasidic Way of Ḥabad'. *Ha'arets* (Heb.), 13 Sept. 1946

'A Late Jewish Utopia of Religious Freedom'. 'Eine spätjüdischer Utopie religiöser Freiheit', *Eranos Jarhbuch*, xxxii (Zurich, 1964), 235–80

'Sense and Nonsense in Defining Judaism—The Strange Case of Naḥman of Brazlav'. Inaugural lecture, University College London, 29 May 1969

Note on Pronunciation

ḥ should be pronounced *ch* , as in Scottish 'loch'

ṣ should be pronounced *ts* as in 'tsar'

Introduction to the Paperback Edition

Joseph Weiss Today

JOSEPH DAN

Gershom Scholem Professor of Kabbalah, Hebrew University of Jerusalem

MOST of the studies collected in this volume were written by Joseph Weiss almost half a century ago, in the late 1940s and during the 1950s and 1960s. They are still quoted in every serious study of hasidism, and many elements in them seem to be as valid today as when they were written, some even more so. The place of Joseph Weiss in the history of hasidic research must of course be assessed in the light of current scholarship but, more than that, it must be seen in the context of new developments in hasidism itself over the last two generations.

This introduction looks at three main areas—the changing concept of hasidic history brought about by the resurgence of hasidism in the past thirty to forty years, the changing image of hasidism in non-hasidic Jewish culture and scholarship, and the development of the various schools and trends in hasidic research—and examines the place of Joseph Weiss's studies in this newly emerging scholarly landscape. The recent publication of the collection of studies *Hasidism Reappraised* (London 1996), edited by Ada Rapoport-Albert and based on lectures delivered at a conference dedicated to Weiss's memory, contains several articles surveying recent research in the field and outlining future possibilities. I will therefore concentrate here on only the most recent developments to place the present volume in a contemporary context.

I

When Joseph Weiss started his scholarly work on hasidism the phenomenon to which he had decided to dedicate his life seemed outdated and irrelevant, though it still carried a great weight of emotional significance. The world in which hasidism had grown and developed had been reduced, physically and spiritually, to smouldering ruins.

Young scholars at the Hebrew University of Jerusalem like Joseph Weiss and Isaiah Tishby, both refugees from Hungary and both students of the revered and charismatic Gershom Scholem, used to wander the old streets of Me'ah She'arim in Jerusalem during the high holidays, visiting various synagogues, mostly hasidic, comparing prayer customs and observing the few remaining hasidim carrying on their anachronistic religious lives in the capital of the newly established State of Israel. For them, as for everyone at the Hebrew University, hasidism was a spent force, a phenomenon which, after its first flowering in eastern Europe during the eighteenth century, had peaked by the start of the nineteenth and then gradually faded until being completely destroyed by a series of upheavals: the mass emigration of Jews from eastern Europe in the late nineteenth and early twentieth centuries, the great pogroms, the devastation caused by the First World War, the Bolshevik revolution and civil war in Russia and the subsequent Stalinist uprooting of Jewish culture there, and finally the Holocaust, which annihilated the communities in which hasidism had thrived.

This final catastrophe was followed by the victory of Zionism in establishing the State of Israel, which seemed to prove beyond doubt that the future of Judaism was safe in the hands of the Zionists, who alone had read correctly the forces shaping the fate of the Jewish people and come up with the right response. At the time it seemed that the hasidic congregations in Jerusalem, together with those who had succeeded in escaping war-torn Europe and had settled in New York and elsewhere, were nothing but an anachronism, a remnant of the past with no relevance to the Jewish future.

This attitude is clearly evident in Weiss's dedication of his research into hasidism to three principal areas. The first of these was the life and work of the movement's founder, Rabbi Israel Baal Shem (the Besht; 1700–60) and his circle of colleagues and disciples, one of whom, Rabbi Jacob Joseph of Polonnoye (d. 1782) preserved the Besht's teachings in his own writings. The second was the teaching, especially its mystical elements, of Rabbi Dov Baer of Mezhirech (the Maggid; 1704–72), another of the Besht's disciples and his successor to the leadership of the movement. The third was the life and works of Rabbi Naḥman of Bratslav (1772–1810), grandson of the Besht and founder of Bratslav hasidism. These three figures lived and wrote in a very brief span of time: their impact was felt and their works took shape between 1750 and 1810.

In common with his teachers and fellow scholars, Weiss regarded this as the key period for hasidism: Simon Dubnow wrote a 'History of Hasidism' which stretched all the way to 1815; Gershom Scholem hardly mentioned anything hasidic beyond Rabbi Naḥman of Bratslav; Ben-Zion Dinur wrote an extensive study of hasidism which hardly goes beyond the Besht himself; Israel Halperin wrote his first book on the hasidic immigrations of 1772 to the Land of Israel. Of Weiss's other contemporaries, Shmuel Ettinger wrote a study of the emergence of the hasidic leadership in the late eighteenth century, Chone Shmeruk studied the laws, customs, and narrative traditions of hasidism of the same period, and Rivka Schatz-Uffenheimer, a younger colleague, wrote a monograph on hasidic quietistic mysticism, using as her main source the writings of the Maggid of Mezhirech; she also published an edition of his first book, *Maggid devarav leYa'akov*, which first appeared in 1784. Students of hasidism in Britain and America, like Louis Jacobs and Samuel Dresner, took exactly the same approach as these Jerusalem-based scholars.

Neither Weiss nor any of his contemporaries could have predicted what was going to happen over the next few decades. If someone had told them in 1954 that, forty years on, hasidism would be making headlines in the *New York Times* and that journalists would regard the activities of hasidic leaders as 'hot' news they would have reacted with incredulity. The re-emergence of hasidism as a vibrant and dynamic force—probably the most vigorous spiritual phenomenon in Judaism as the new millennium approaches—is one of the most perplexing miracles of recent Jewish history.

The fact that today hasidism is a growing power—in spiritual, political, and even numerical terms—in the greatest centres of Judaism in Israel and the east coast of the United States forces us to re-evaluate hasidic history as a whole. Dubnow's approach, which sees hasidism as a meaningful and inspiring phenomenon only up to its decline in 1815, must be rejected and hasidic history reconceived in terms of centuries instead of decades. Hasidism is neither a relic nor an anachronism; it has proved that it is at home in the modern world, and there is no reason today to doubt that it will be present in the Judaism of the twenty-first century in a most significant way.

II

Do these dramatic developments mean that the scholarly work of Joseph Weiss must be re-evaluated? Should it be discarded because the hasidic movement has developed in such an unpredictable manner? My answer is that it should not: I believe that a new approach to hasidic history and thought needs to be developed, but that the serious, perceptive, and empathetic studies by Weiss and other scholars of his generation should serve as the basis for this new evaluation. Today these detailed studies on the beginnings of hasidism serve a new purpose and have wider implications and consequences than when they were written.

The best example of this is Weiss's work on Rabbi Naḥman of Bratslav. His inaugural lecture in 1969 at University College London[1] gives an overview of his approach. In this lecture Weiss forcefully presented Rabbi Naḥman's attraction to, and his simultaneous horror of, the two great heresies of his time: on the one hand Sabbatean messianism and its offshoot in the Frankist movement, and on the other the Enlightenment and its threat to draw Jews away from their ancient traditions. Weiss hinted that Rabbi Naḥman himself harboured messianic ambitions, and that some of his dreams, nightmares, and narratives should be interpreted as representing a fascination with his own redeeming role. However, he did not emphasize or develop the point in the lecture, though he made it more clearly in his Hebrew articles on Rabbi Naḥman,[2] and was even more explicit in his unpublished lectures (for example the series at the Schocken Library in Jerusalem, which I was privileged to attend). Weiss had to be careful: his presentation of the great zaddik's attraction to both the creative and heretical aspects of messianism was criticized by other scholars, including Gershom Scholem, and completely contradicted the sage-like image of Rabbi Naḥman presented by

[1] Reproduced at pp. 249–69 below.

[2] Joseph Weiss, *Meḥkarim bahasidut braslav*, ed. Mendel Piekarz (Jerusalem, 1974).

Martin Buber, whose writings on hasidism were regarded as normative at the time. I have no doubt that Weiss's concept of Rabbi Naḥman was more radical than appears from his writings.

Today the situation has changed; though controversy persists to some extent, it is commonly accepted that Rabbi Naḥman regarded himself as a messiah (though probably as a failed, tragic one whose time had not yet come), and there can be hardly any doubt that the followers of the movement, who have continued to see him as their leader and who have studied and published his writings for nearly two centuries, regard him as a messianic figure. Joseph Weiss's detailed, empathetic reading of Rabbi Naḥman's writings—the personal revelations, the dreams, the sermons, the stories, and even his speculations concerning hidden and destroyed works—has contributed in large measure to this understanding.

Recent history has given an additional meaning and importance to Rabbi Naḥman's messianism. When Weiss wrote his studies the Rabbi was an exception, a marginal, unique figure who seemed to be uncharacteristic of hasidic leadership in general. This is no longer the case: as I write there are tens of thousands of hasidim in Israel, the United States, and France who whole-heartedly believe that their dead leader was and is the messiah. Rabbi Menahem Mendel Schneersohn of Brooklyn, the leader of Habad hasidism who died in 1994, left behind a large and extremely well organized group of believers. But he died without leaving an heir, and in the absence of a live leader his disciples follow the ways of their dead rebbe; they are 'dead hasidim', just as the followers of Rabbi Naḥman were called, and they fully expect him to return and redeem them and all the people of Israel.

Rabbi Naḥman and Rabbi Menahem Mendel are as different from each other as is the Uman of the early nineteenth century from present-day New York. Schneersohn was a most capable organizer who established what Jacob Katz has called in a lecture 'the first Order in Jewish history', assembling around him scores of thousands of Jews from dozens of countries. His words were transmitted by satellite, and his sermons video-taped and distributed to Jewish communities around the world; his followers arrived at gatherings in Brooklyn by specially chartered B-747s. Rabbi Naḥman died almost alone, poor and marginalized, never having succeeded in any worldly enterprise. Yet Schneersohn's activities represent the same fundamental rebellion of a hasidic leader against the imposition of equality with other zaddikim: he was not *a* zaddik but the true zaddik, the one and only leader destined to redeem the whole people and the entire universe. It is no wonder, therefore, that what had characterized Bratslav hasidism for nearly two centuries became the mark of the Habad movement: its refusal to co-operate with other hasidic communities and leaders or to recognize their authority, even over their own followers.

The parameters used by Joseph Weiss in describing the unique personality of Rabbi Naḥman and the faith of his followers have thus become, despite the fundamental differences between the two movements, those of the contemporary Lubavitcher. It was Weiss who wrote a penetrating article presenting the Bratslav and Habad movements as polar opposites, the one emphasizing faith, the other mysticism. He could not of course have known that, in the decades following his death, they would move closer to one another, in line with his description. It was Weiss who analysed in detail the meaning of the phrase 'true zaddik' (i.e. the one and only zaddik) in Rabbi Naḥman's works; he did not live long enough to witness how the same concept would come to be utilized, on a vast scale, by the Lubavitch hasidim.

III

One of Joseph Weiss's main endeavours, amply represented in the articles in this volume, was to identify and describe the mystical element in hasidism. Gershom Scholem did this in general terms in the concluding chapter of his great survey *Major Trends in Jewish Mysticism*, but Weiss sought to create a complete and coherent picture. He was the first to apply the generally accepted methodology for the textual analysis of mystical writing to the work of several hasidic leaders, focusing particularly on Rabbi Dov Baer, the Maggid of Mezhirech, in whose writings he identified a *via passiva* type of mysticism, on Rabbi Shneur Zalman of Lyady, the founder of Lubavitch hasidism, and on the enigmatic figure of a later zaddik, Rabbi Mordecai Joseph Leiner of Izbica. His approach was influential. Several comprehensive studies have followed the outline he pioneered: Rivka Schatz-Uffenheimer's

Hasidism as Mysticism[3] focuses on the Maggid of Mezhirech and his immediate disciples and identifies quietistic elements in the teachings of these early hasidim, and Rachel Elior's *The Mystical Ascent*[4] analyses in detail the radical mysticism of the founders of the Habad movement. The historian Emmanuel Etkes's recent article 'The Besht as Mystic'[5] departs from the earlier tradition that left the study of mysticism in hasidism to Scholem's disciples. There is little doubt that Weiss's work will continue to have an impact in this area.

The perceived gulf between historians on the one hand and students of hasidic thought and mysticism on the other is embodied at the Hebrew University in the existence of two separate departments: the Department of Jewish Philosophy and Kabbalah (today the Department of Jewish Thought), which housed Gershom Scholem and his disciples, and the Department of Jewish History. For a whole generation it was thought that the two subjects were separate, that one could study ideas without history and history without ideas. Some historians even believed that it was their duty to moderate and modify the wild ideological speculations of the 'mystics', usually meaning Scholem himself, while some 'mystics' felt called upon to refute what they saw as wild historical hypotheses, such as those of Ben-Zion Dinur (it is only now that we are beginning to realize how perceptive some of Dinur's radical ideas actually were). Weiss was drawn into this tense relationship, especially when he published an extensive study of the social background of early hasidism in *Zion*, the journal of the Israeli Historical Society. Several historians felt obliged to pick holes in his arguments: a 'mystic', it was felt, should not deal with serious historical matters; he should confine himself to analysing the dreams and visions of hasidim.[6]

This separation of disciplines is now long forgotten, and today

[3] First published in Hebrew: *Haḥasidut kemistikah* (Jerusalem, 1968); English translation published by Princeton University Press, 1993.

[4] *The Mystical Ascent: The Paradox of Nothingness in HaBaD* (New York, 1993).

[5] Published in *Zion*, 61 (1996), 421–54.

[6] I well remember an occasion which expressed this tension in an extreme way. Scholem presented a lecture at the Hebrew University entitled 'The Historical Baal Shem Tov'. The title demanded that historians be present in the lecture hall, and they were. The tension in the audience was unbelievable; it was the first time that Scholem had dared present a purely historical lecture, disregarding the boundary separating the two departments. After the lecture, there was a torrent of criticism, taken (by historians) as conclusive proof

scholars from both fields co-operate (as is proven, among many other examples, by the volume *Hasidism Reappraised* mentioned above). One of the main reasons for the disappearance of this artificial boundary lies in the dual role of the zaddik. When we look at early hasidism this can be ignored or marginalized, but when we deal with the history of hasidism during the last two centuries its centrality cannot be denied. The zaddik is the embodiment of the union between history and mysticism: as the leader of the community and the one who shapes relationships between his followers and other, non-hasidic, groups, he is the focus of hasidic historical, social, and political activity; but as the linchpin between his followers and the divine world he is at the core of hasidic mysticism. The relationship between the zaddik and the divine world and the mystical connection between the soul of the zaddik and the souls of his adherents is the essence of hasidism: it is the attachment of a hasid to a zaddik that makes him a hasid.

In this new context we have every right to expect that Joseph Weiss's studies will find their appropriate place, serving both historical and ideological studies of hasidism. Again, the clearest example of this link is the relationship between Rabbi Naḥman of Bratslav and Rabbi Menahem Mendel Schneersohn. What might seem to be an abstract study of the dreams and visions of a marginalized zaddik of the early nineteenth century becomes an examination of a major historical force when the same analytical criteria are applied to subsequent developments in Brooklyn.

IV

In the last two decades the place of hasidism in Jewish culture has been completely transformed. When Weiss was writing he was confronted with a dual image of hasidism among Jewish intellectuals. On the one hand there was the historical picture, the result of the work of scholars like Dubnow, Dinur, and Scholem; on the other was the popular image of the movement found in narrative and poetic works by Y. L. Peretz, Shimshon Meltzer, and others, which presented a nostalgic, highly idealized view of hasidism. This image, which acquired a new potency after the Holocaust,

that scholars of Jewish mysticism should not deal with serious historical matters. The one exception to this rule was the Sabbatian movement, its history being studied as 'kabbalah', and almost completely ignored by the Department of Jewish History. I was then a rare exception, being a student in both departments.

disregarded the specific beliefs of hasidism such as the concept of the zaddik as redeemer and viewed it as a humanistic, socially conscious meta-Judaism, incorporating all the values seen as positive by Jews who had severed their ties with hasidic daily life but who still cherished memories of their childhood surroundings. This was the hasidism of the hasidic tales, many of them originating in non-hasidic or no-longer-hasidic circumstances, or published by non-hasidim for ex- and non-hasidim. This pseudo-hasidism (which I have elsewhere described as Frumkinian hasidism, after Michael Halevi Frumkin, the first writer and publisher of collections of hasidic tales in the 1860s) had a great impact on Hebrew and Yiddish literature; its main voice was, of course, Martin Buber.

Very seldom in history has the hasidic phenomenon expressed itself as a distinct and identifiable religious entity; the very concept of hasidism is essentially an externally applied one, much more frequently used by non-hasidim than by the hasidim themselves. It was the creators of Frumkinian hasidism who depicted the various groupings as one indivisible whole, as for example Martin Buber in his *Tales of the Hasidim*, which give equal weight to scores of zaddikim from a variety of communities and periods, something no authentic hasidic work has ever done. For the hasid, the social and religious grouping to which he belongs is a specific community led by a specific zaddik and his dynasty; other dynasties are regarded as of lower quality or, sometimes, as heretical and evil.

The gulf between hasidism as a historical phenomenon and this idealized hasidism widened from generation to generation, and scholarship has been affected by the schism separating literary image from historical reality. In fact one of the results of the dominance of the literary concept of hasidism has been the concentration of scholars on the study of early hasidism, the 'pure' period before the movement became 'contaminated'.

Since the death of Joseph Weiss this duality has become less marked, and in some cultural and political realms it already seems to have vanished entirely. Frumkinian hasidism derived its power from the weakness—real or apparent—of hasidism within twentieth-century Jewish culture. The ability to cherish warm, nostalgic feelings towards hasidism was based on the notion that as a cultural and religious force it was irrelevant to contemporary Jewish life. It has not been possible to sustain this attitude in the face of the dynamic resurgence of hasidism and its increasing power within and impact on the largest Jewish communities in the world, those of Israel and the United States. When historical hasidism proved itself a force to be reckoned with in everyday political and cultural affairs, nostalgia gave way to reality. Few today write of hasidism in idyllic terms; the re-emergence of hasidism as a powerful force in contemporary Jewish society, politics, and culture has relegated the nostalgic image to the margins of literary history.

These developments have opened up new vistas for the historian of hasidism, and made it imperative to re-examine the works of Joseph Weiss in the proper scholarly and cultural context. The most important element to emerge from such a re-examination, I believe, will be the acceptance of the hasidic doctrine of the zaddik as it really is: namely, that the zaddik is a divine leader with a messianic mission concerning his community, and that he is part of a divine dynasty destined to lead this community, materially and spiritually, for ever. In his studies of Rabbi Naḥman of Bratslav Weiss contributed probably more than any other scholar to the understanding of the zaddik's role; his analysis is applicable, with some modification, to all zaddikim, even those who have not claimed to be messianic redeemers of the whole people but who have instead limited their claims to power to their particular community. The history of hasidism as a social, religious, and political phenomenon is the study of the history of the dynasties and of the various ways in which the zaddikim have applied their divine powers to the performance of their tasks.

V

To this discussion of encouraging developments in the study of the phenomenon of hasidism I must add a cautionary note. In the last few years a new 'discipline' seems to have emerged which threatens to reintroduce confusion and incoherence to the field: the study of Jewish orthodoxy. Described by its practitioners as the study of present ultra-orthodox Jewish communities, this combines the analysis of hasidic and non-hasidic (mainly mitnagdic) groupings in various countries. The renewal of interest in these communities is understandable as the result of their increasing power and impact on contemporary Jewish life; the danger that may be inherent in the concept of such a discipline is twofold. First, it tends to separate contemporary Jewish communities from their variegated historical origins—mainly hasidic, mitnagdic, and Mediterranean—and treat them as a single contemporary phenomenon, whereas in fact their historical differences are still operating in full force, invalidating attempts at generalization. Second, such generalizations tend to obscure the vast differences between the groups' concepts of leadership. Treating them as a single phenomenon is thus both historically misleading and conceptually flawed.

A complicating factor is that the present generation has witnessed a tendency for concepts of leadership in the three main orthodox groups to converge. Leaders of Mediterranean Jewry—mainly, but not exclusively, those of North African origin—exercise a new kind of authority and exert an increasing power over their followers in ways reminiscent of the zaddikim. Heads of mitnagdic ('Lithuanian') yeshivot have assumed roles which, not long ago, were found only within hasidic communities, and there is even a tendency to accept a dynastic element in mitnagdic leadership, which was traditionally based exclusively on excellence in Torah study. As one might expect after two centuries of conflict, the old opponents of the eighteenth-century schism seem to be drawing together and assuming similar characteristics.

From the point of view of the secular observer all these groups seem to share the same superstitious adherence to their leaders. Yet historians should know better. Hasidic leadership is still radically different from that of the non-hasidic ultra-orthodox because of its complete dedication to the dynastic principle, which has neither taken root nor been given any theological basis in the other groups. There can be no doubt that the zaddik worship of hasidic communities has had a significant impact on other ultra-orthodox groups, who have sometimes adopted some of the external customs and rituals associated with it. But there is a vast difference between this copying of superficial mannerisms and the acceptance of the deep-rooted spiritual and theological components of the hasidic doctrine of the zaddik. The quest for superficial common denominators may hide now as it did in the past the true nature of the hasidic concept of the divine, redeeming messianic leader.

Joseph Weiss's studies of the nature of the Bratslav leadership were not universally accepted when they were published. Several scholars felt he identified too closely with the figure of Rabbi Naḥman and that he attributed his own concepts to the subject of his study. While Weiss's deep empathy with Rabbi Naḥman is beyond doubt, his conclusions, as I have shown, were conservative in view of later developments. Weiss suffered to some extent from his readiness to recognize, however hesitantly, the divine nature of the zaddik in hasidic life and thought. His studies should serve today as a counterweight to the attempt to disregard this crucial factor and downplay it in the context of 'orthodox studies' which group together different concepts of religious leadership.

*

In his eulogy after Joseph Weiss's death, Gershom Scholem described the conflicts within the soul of his former student and his wavering attitude towards orthodoxy and Zionism, messianism and Jewish ritual. Yet, Scholem wrote, 'he was utterly single-minded in his scholarly pursuit and commitment'.[7] This dedication to scholarship, loyalty to the texts, and insistent efforts to unravel the spiritual and historical meaning of the major phenomena in hasidism serve to preserve Weiss's studies as central and essential to every contemporary attempt at understanding this fascinating phenomenon of modern Judaism.

[7] *The Messianic Idea in Judaism and Other Essays* (New York, 1971), 177.

Editor's Introduction

THIS collection of essays and studies contains the greater part of Joseph Weiss's contribution to the study of hasidism, written in a language other than Hebrew. It is a tribute to a teacher who both commanded respect and inspired affection, and whose tragic early death robbed hasidism of one of its finest researchers and interpreters.

Joseph Weiss was born in Budapest in 1918. After specializing originally in the sciences, he enrolled at the Jewish Theological Seminary in 1937 and at the same time studied at the Department of Philosophy and Semitic Languages at the University of Budapest. In 1939 he emigrated to Palestine, where he continued his studies at the Hebrew University in Jerusalem. He came to England in 1950 and, after spending some time in research at Leeds and Oxford, joined the faculty of the Hebrew Department (now the Department of Jewish Studies) at University College London. He remained there first as Assistant Lecturer and then Reader, and was appointed Professor of Jewish Studies in 1966, which post he held until his death in 1969.

He was Director of the Institute of Jewish Studies, London, and for some time edited the *Journal of Jewish Studies*; his major written work was *Meḥkarim baḥasidut braslav* (Studies in Bratslav Hasidism) (Jerusalem, 1974).

The initial editorial work on the present volume was undertaken by Isaiah Shachar. He was engaged on it when he contracted a fatal illness, and he died in 1977 at the age of 42.

I have not attempted to add any material that did not come from Weiss's pen. The few additions to the printed studies are the author's own. A small number of editorial bibliographical references in the notes, rendered necessary by the nature of this collection, have been put in square brackets.

Weiss was always anxious about expressing himself in English, and would search for hours for the correct word. Although a number of changes were necessary to the English of his unpublished essays, I have tried to retain the original flavour of Weiss's style. I have standardized the spelling and romanization of names and technical terms.

The translations from the Hebrew of 'Torah Study in Early Hasidism' and 'The Hasidic Way of Ḥabad' are Weiss's own. I am grateful to Julia Neuberger for translating from the German 'A Late Jewish Utopia of Religious Freedom', and I acknowledge with thanks the permission of the editors of the journals mentioned in the Note on Sources to reprint the relevant articles in this volume.

My thanks also to Mrs Erna Weiss for retyping most of the studies that were in manuscript, and for compiling the Index.

DAVID GOLDSTEIN

Publisher's Note

DAVID GOLDSTEIN, whose whole life was devoted to scholarship—through his work as Curator of Hebrew Manuscripts and Printed Books at the British Library, as a lecturer at the Leo Baeck College, as a rabbi at the Liberal Jewish Synagogue before he joined the British Library, and as a participant in many other scholarly institutions and organizations—was a founding editor of the Littman Library, and he remained an editor until his death in 1987.

STUDIES IN EAST EUROPEAN JEWISH MYSTICISM AND HASIDISM

Some Notes on the Social Background of Early Hasidism

I

The Hasidic movement, which had its inception at about the middle of the eighteenth century under the impact of a few compelling charismatic leaders in Podolia and Volhynia, was in its character a Jewish revivalism. As such, it aimed at the total mobilization of emotions; Hasidism, wherever it spread, brought in its wake emotional intensification of religious life in a fashion typical of revivalist movements. From the point of view of its atmosphere, Hasidism is somewhat akin to the religious upheaval in seventeenth-century England[1] though naturally no historical connexions existed between the two.

For too long research has been concentrated mainly on the legendary biography, or occasionally also on the personality, of Israel Baalshem (1700–60), often called in both scholarly and popular literature the founder of Hasidism. In another direction Hasidism has been described as a religious movement that sprang spontaneously from the depth of an oppressed Eastern European Jewry. Sometimes the magical formula of the "mystical and rational polarity" of the Jewish soul—whatever this eloquent phrase may mean—was evoked for the understanding of Hasidism. So, too, were philosophical deliberations on the "essence" of Judaism—disregarding, in the hothouse of generalization, the historical, geographical, and sociological background out of which that particular form of Jewish piety arose.

Hasidism has also been explained as the reaction of emotional piety to the legalistic scrutinies of Talmudism and rabbinism, and by others as "the revolt of the illiterate" fighting for full religious rights within a society in which the untutored were, almost by definition, considered incapable of piety.

The varied efforts at understanding Hasidism in these terms are not totally misconceived; even if they do not appear fully satisfactory, an element of truth would seem to be inherent in some of them. And yet they persistently avoid coming to grips with the social situation in which Hasidism arose.

In an attempt to understand the social climate of nascent Hasidism, we have to consider two questions: who were the leaders, and who were those led?

It would appear that some light might be shed on the origins of this movement and its social articulation in the early phases if research could be focused more on the historical and sociological setting of scattered small marginal groups of religious enthusiasts that existed within the Eastern European Jewish communities during the first half of the eighteenth century in the geographical areas that later became the cradle of Hasidism.[2] The dim memory of these circles is still clearly discernible in the legendary literature of the movement, composed much later. But it has to be emphasized that in the historical retrospect of Hasidic sources the independence of these separate groups became very blurred, and, subsequently, leaders and members of such circles, contemporaries of Israel Baalshem and at least some of them religious charismatics similar to him, were presumed to have been his disciples rather than his colleagues, and to have propagated religious views emanating from him rather than views generally held by these groups.

As against the conventional picture of the single-handed foundation of the movement by Israel Baalshem, the historian would be inclined to venture that Hasidism did not originate with any one charismatic leader as its sole founder, but that it grew out of a number of marginal groups each harboring some charismatics, and that the group connected with the name of Israel Baalshem proved the most successful one generation later. After these groups had existed simultaneously for a time, the breakthrough of Hasidism (some two generations after the advent of Israel Baalshem) saw the gradual disappearance of the independent circles or rather their merging into the rapidly spreading Hasidic movement, with the name of the Baalshem surviving in the historical consciousness of Hasidism as that of a founder and central leader. In the reality of history the circles were less concentric.

It would be incorrect to describe those belonging to the early groups as schismatics or sectarians. It would be more correct to suggest that we find in the eighteenth century prior to the rise of Hasidism as a social movement some enthusiastic and pneumatic groups living on the periphery of established Jewish society, with religious ideals and behavior not always happily coinciding with the official atmosphere of the general Jewish community.

As to their internal social structure, these pre-Hasidic circles were apparently not all alike and to belong to one of them must have constituted a hardly definable social relationship. In some cases, as in that of the group of Kutov, about which we have some fairly reliable and more detailed information, it is hardly appropriate to speak of a permanent headship or leadership similar to the authoritarian leadership of the *Ṣaddik* in the later fully developed Hasidic community; the group patently consisted of a loose association of enthusiastic or pneumatic personalities. Connected with such groups were figures such as Phinehas of Korzecz,[3] Menaḥem Mendel of Bar,[4] Naḥman of Kosov,[5] Naḥman of Horodenka,[6] and perhaps even Menaḥem Mendel of Premyslan,[7] all contemporaries of Israel Baalshem, sharing many social and economic features of his existence. Israel Baalshem has to be understood as one of this type of enthusiast, not the teacher and master of them all. His status is not even that of a *primus inter pares*: educationally and socially he appears to have been inferior to most of them.

Israel Baalshem's persistent efforts to be accepted in one such group—apparently in that of Kutov—which can be pieced together from scattered information in the collection of legends, is a case in point. It would not appear that he ever became the head of this group—if there was a central figure there at all; it was rather the very delicate social question of his being accepted as one of the pneumatics that mattered: possession of pneumatic faculties was the crucial issue for membership, not for leadership. Conversations between members of the group, detailed quotations of which still survive in the legendary literature, show that a relationship of coordination between those belonging to the group rather than one of subordination to one leader, characterized its social structure. The pages of the collection of legends confront the reader with the vivid picture of a circle of pneumatics each one of whom is endowed with the charisma of primitive prophecy. The scope of their prophetic activities is not clearly defined in the text, but it transpires that prophesying was considered as including or even as being identical with the disclosure of secretly committed sins. The pneumatic intenseness of the group was severely reduced after a strange decision of those connected with it to renounce their prophetic powers for some reason that remains unexplained in the text.[8] Notwithstanding the self-imposed prophetic inactivity of the group, its pneumatic climate is tangible: the members of the circle fear the sudden eruption of their prophetic faculties at any moment and are determined to suppress it.

Israel Baalshem did succeed in impressing various people in the Kutov group, such as R. Moshe, the head of the rabbinical court of the townlet, and R. Juda Leb Galliner, called the *Mokhiaḥ*. After a prolonged struggle for the recognition of his pneumatic gifts, Israel was still only partly successful. There is no indication that he ever succeeded in winning over all the influential members of the group; for example, Naḥman of Kosov appears to have retained an unmitigated antagonism toward the Besht who eventually left the town, though we do not know why.

The Kutov group of pneumatics, or for that matter probably any similar group, lived in an atmosphere of continual tension with at least some parts of the general Jewish community there. The real picture was far from an idyllic harmonious congregation in which the group of pneumatics was treated with admiration or even respect by the rest of the community. The eccentric religious minority had to be always on the defensive vis-à-vis the general community, many members of which must have felt irritated by some of the more bizarre forms of piety on the part of the pneumatics whose religious extravaganzas were often exposed to ridicule. These groups of spirituals, rather than the groups of Talmudic scholars (*lomdim*) around the rabbi, were the natural area of social ascent for the Baalshem, who was certainly disqualified on scholastic grounds from acceptance in the more erudite Talmudic circles.[9]

It is not impossible that the Baalshem's marriage into the family of R. Gershon of Kutov has to be interpreted as one of his early attempts to secure status in the Kutov group. In the social environment in which this marriage was contracted and in the total absence of the ideology of love matches, marital arrangements either reflected existing social ties or indicated social aspirations. The legendary biography describes in detail how Israel Baalshem, donning the mask of the untutored and uncouth (both of which he certainly was), imposed himself by force of a betrothal contract on a family of a class that was educationally and socially certainly superior. This contract between R. Gershon's father (who acted without the knowledge of his divorced daughter, a course of action fully consistent with the general practice in that environment) and the unknown Israel Baalshem, was signed on the spur of the moment on a journey on which the two had met by chance.[10] The old man had died and some time later Israel descended on R. Gershon waving the betrothal contract, whose signature would have additional force by the very fact that one of the signatories (in this case the bride's father) was dead. R. Gershon put up a fierce struggle against his dead father's will and was anxious to prevent by every possible means the penetration into his family of Israel Baalshem, notwithstanding the fact that his sister's value in the marriage market must have been substantially lowered: she was a divorcee who would have had to put up with a second-rate candidate in any case. But Baalshem eventually succeeded in contracting this misalliance. R. Gershon yielded and thus complied with the letter of his deceased father's will, but he still proposed that his sister should divorce her new husband, which she, however, refused to do. Thus, marriage did not bring the immediate social acceptance into this eminent family and through it enhanced status within the group of pneumatics that Israel might have expected. Gershon retained his unmitigated scorn for his brother-in-law, though it would appear from the correspondence between them during the last phase of Gershon's life when he lived in Palestine that the Baalshem eventually did succeed in his ambition and was fully accepted as a pneumatic by R. Gershon, too. We no longer have the relevant facts to explain this turn for the better in their relationship. And indeed the social interpretation given here of the whole marriage story must remain of necessity inconclusive.

In a neighboring group of pre-Hasidic Hasidim, that in Miedzyborz, where Israel Baalshem eventually settled and which served as the base for multifarious journeys until his death, he also struggled for social status, and it is noticed in the hagiographical literature that his prestige with this group was low "on account of his being called a miracle-worker (*baal shem*),"[11] a clear enough indication of the difficulties he repeatedly encountered in his search for recognition.

G. Scholem has reconstructed from polemical utterances against it the picture of yet another group of enthusiasts,[12] feeling that the description of their anonymous leader, an untutored storyteller, admirably fitted Israel Baalshem. Whatever the identification of the unnamed enthusiast, it is the description of the group and its religious way of life that is important in the present context. Indeed, the group would fit perfectly well into the religious atmosphere of the mid-eighteenth century even if it were kept separate from that of Israel Baalshem.

This leads us to consider some of the personalities who appear in the pages of the hagiographical literature and who were closely connected in the legends with the Baalshem. It seems that these people should be more clearly divided into two sets: one set comprises the contemporaries of Baalshem, who belonged to the same age group and who were not his disciples but his colleagues and in some cases his rivals. Of Phinehas of Korzecz, for instance, we know that he met the Baalshem only two or three times,[13] which would hardly make this radical religious enthusiast a disciple. He was rather a colleague who shared with the Baalshem some basic ideas, such as the enthusiastic affirmation of the Divine indwelling in all things and who advocated perpetual communion with God (*devekuth*),[14] not only for a select few as the old Cabbala did, but as a religious ideal for all. In fact, demands in this central matter of *devekuth* have come down to us in traditions of at least two such contemporaries, Phinehas of Korzecz[15] and Naḥman of Kosov,[16] in a much more urgent form than in those of Baalshem. That Naḥman of Kosov was not a disciple is clear enough from a short analysis of the Kutov circle made earlier in this paper. In many respects it would appear rather that the contrary was the case and that Baalshem readily accepted or, occasionally, watered down some of the more radical religious ideas current in these circles.[17] In the course of the development of Hasidism many of these doctrines were all attributed to the Baalshem himself as their original fountainhead. So much for the colleagues.

Israel Baalshem's actual disciples are represented by Jacob Joseph of Polonnoye and, in all likelihood also Dov Baer, called the Great Maggid or the Maggid of Mesritz. Their legendary biographies describe them as intellectually fully developed Halakhic scholars when they came under the Baalshem's influence. Their encounter with him is said to have revolutionized their whole religious outlook and subjected them to the experience of a conversion to a body of ideas expounded by the Baalshem. Not merely the ideas but also the charismatic forces emanating from the personality of Israel played, no doubt, a decisive role in their development. Jacob Joseph of Polonnoye was the most important literary talent in the early Hasidic movement. Our knowledge of the great majority of Baalshem's dicta derives solely from the fact that his short sayings were duly recorded and frequently quoted in the large books written by Jacob Joseph that, on their publication, became the Bible of the movement. There is no evidence, however, that this emphatic and self-confessed disciple's literary distinction secured him automatically a leading role in the movement, particularly since the publication in print of his bulky volumes did not start until toward the end of his life,[18] when Hasidism as a social movement was already fully established with the leaders of the next generation, all of them Jacob Joseph's juniors by decades, in actual command. Indeed, it is open to serious doubt whether Hasidism prior to 1780 (the date of the publication of Jacob Joseph's first volume) developed on the basis of full knowledge of what was written down in the lengthy manuscripts of this disciple of the Baalshem who apparently possessed none of the charismatic qualities of the whole galaxy of young leaders who emerged at about the time of the death of the Maggid in 1772. Historical analysis of the development of Hasidic ideas might show that until the generation of the Maggid's disciples R. Jacob Joseph's writings (and thereby the major part of Israel

Baalshem's authentic dicta) were unknown both to the Hasidic leaders and to the Hasidic "reading public".[19] The impact of Jacob Joseph's works (including the dicta of Baalshem cited in them) is unmistakable in the books of the disciples of the Great Maggid but strangely enough not in the sermons of the Great Maggid himself.[20] In marked distiction to Jacob Joseph, Dov Baer quotes Israel Baalshem only very rarely in his sermons, which were written down later by one or two of Dov's own disciples. Nevertheless, Dov Baer too could possibly qualify for the epithet "disciple of the Baalshem," though it is remarkable how seldom he is conscious in his sermons of an indebtedness to Israel Baalshem, who seems to have been his master. While Jacob Joseph was composing his lengthy tomes in utter isolation, Dov Baer was able in hardly more than a decade after the death of Israel Baalshem in 1760 to succeed in the tremendous task of transforming scattered groups of pneumatics into a popular movement. When the Maggid died (1772), only twelve years after the death of Baalshem, Hasidism had become a serious threat to established Jewish society, and it was felt necessary to persecute it through bans and excommunication. This had never been the case before: the reaction of organized Jewry indicates that by 1772 Hasidism was a fully fledged religious movement whose further spread was acutely dreaded by the representatives of rabbinic authority. In its first generation, however, Hasidism had not been proscribed, nor had Israel Baalshem or his charismatic colleagues been seriously challenged. It was ridicule and contempt rather than organized opposition and downright persecution that were the main forms of the establishment's disagreement with the early groups of enthusiasts.[21]

II

In an attempt at a historical understanding of the origins of Hasidism, research has had recourse to an accusation that was repeated again and again in anti-Hasidic polemics. This asserted that the followers of the new movement were in some undefined way akin to the Sabbatians, the heretical Jewish sectarians of the seventeenth and eighteenth centuries.[22] This last major Jewish heresy had become, after a short period of spectacular success, a kind of religious underground movement and produced the most intricate theological doctrines in order to justify its continued existence.[23]

Sabbatianism, it will be remembered, was a messianic movement that took its name from Shabbethai Sevi, who was proclaimed Messiah by his followers, not without some ready cooperation on his own part. After a sudden eclipse of the general excitement following the apostasy of the Messiah, isolated and often rival groups of Sabbatian heretics continued to exist for some 150 years. There remained many a secret cell dispersed throughout Europe.

Scholarly examination of the Hasidic movement's sources of inspiration has shown that the accusations made by anti-Hasidic polemists were not altogether without foundation. It has been convincingly argued that indeed there existed significant contacts between the nascent Hasidic movement and the declining Sabbatian heresy. Personal lines of contact between them as well as ideological affinities, the latter possibly unnoticed by the Hasidim themselves, have recently been discovered. There were some Sabbatian sympathies on the part of the first Hasidic leaders. It has been established that secretly copied manuscripts of Sabbatian theology, though never printed, remained in the possession of Hasidic circles for many generations right up to World War II.

Certain aspects of early Hasidic teaching appear to have been derived from Sabbatian tenets. It has been suggested that the Hasidic doctrine of the descensus of the *Ṣaddik* could well be a mitigated formulation of the Sabbatian thesis of the descent of the Messiahs into the "realm of impurity."[24] Similarly, one of the central admonitions might have been modeled on the same Sabbatian doctrine.[25] Naturally in both cases the originally Sabbatian ideas underwent a solid process of re-Judaization, since the positive role of actual sin central in Sabbatian theology was replaced in Hasidism by the positive role of sinful fantasy.[26] All this gave an unexpectedly wide diffusion to religious ideas of a Sabbatian structure, though in a much-mitigated and hence more acceptable form. Nevertheless, the unconventional tone of some Hasidic teaching on the service of God in "wayward thoughts," i.e., in the fantasies of sin, is unmistakable, and was noticed as such by contemporary critics of the Hasidic camp.

The similarity of the two movements, it should be noted, is not confined to ideas; there is a striking resemblance between the social composition of the late Sabbatian elite and the early Hasidic one. In an attempt to understand the social climate of declining Sabbatianism, we have to consider a class of professional vagabonds or semivagabonds who formed an unofficial elite in the Eastern European Jewish intelligentsia. Its function was to deliver sermons and exhortations or to cast out evil spirits. Accordingly, they were known as itinerant preachers (*maggidim*), preachers of penitence (*mokhiḥim*), and exorcists (*baaleishem*). Established Jewish society was somewhat suspicious of these marginal representatives of a second-rate intelligentsia in Eastern European Jewry. The erratic way of life they led also made their moral behavior and theological outlook the object of criticism.

Anti-Sabbatian polemists of the eighteenth century observed that many propagators of the Sabbatian heresy were recruited from this mobile element, and historical research confirms that the Sabbatian underground movement was to a considerable extent organized by itinerant preachers and exorcists, at least in the Sabbatianism of the later phases, in the eighteenth century. It was significantly remarked upon by the anti-Sabbatian Jacob Emden (1697–1776) that itinerant preachers, preachers of penitence, exorcists, emissaries, etc., played an important role in the secret organization[27]; and the historian of religion may add that he often finds that a secret heterodox movement is organized by people who are professionally on the move, knowing where to turn and to which circles to bring their message. In eighteenth-century Jewry such a class of free "proletaroid" professionals who felt themselves at a disadvantage vis-à-vis the official ruling class (rabbis, dayyanim, etc.) had a natural inclination to absorb heretical teachings that, in the final analysis, would lead to the overthrow of the existing order and the complete transformation of the Jewish social hierarchy.

But the roving professionals were the social sphere not only of the leaders of the late Sabbatian movement but also of the nascent Hasidic revivalism. It is not impossible to obtain a fair picture of the social conditions of early Hasidism from the accounts in the *Shivḥei ha-Besht*, the legendary biography of

Israel Baalshem.[28] The book contains an abundance of information about the milieu in which Israel Baalshem first made his appearance. In addition to a hagiological description of the life of Israel Baalshem, the central figure, it deals extensively with his companions and disciples. The kaleidoscopic diversity of the *Shivḥei ha-Besht* mirrors these representatives of late Jewish piety wandering to and fro in Eastern Europe in the 1730s. It cannot be sheer coincidence that almost all the friends, companions, and disciples of Israel Baalshem belong to this group of itinerant religious leaders, members of a second-class elite.

Graetz, nearly a hundred years ago, was the first historian to point to this striking fact of the social composition of early Hasidic leadership.[29] What Graetz did not notice was that itinerant preachers became vocal as early as the later phases of the Sabbatian heresy, and that thus there seems to have existed a continuity between the social type of the leader who organized late Sabbatianism and that which was responsible for the rapid expansion of early Hasidism. They were charged with explosive ideas and attitudes as a carry-over from the Sabbatian period and no doubt harbored many rebellious elements, including later types of Sabbatians. Israel Baalshem himself, as he painfully noticed more than once, was a step below this social level. He was, as his name indicates, an exorcist (*baal-shem*), employing his talents among Jewish and occasionally non-Jewish villagers. In these legendary sources Israel Baalshem never appears as the teacher of a contemplative-enthusiastic piety, but consistently as the itinerant exorcist and practicing magician, a successful trader in amulets—a thriving business indeed, as is evident from the fact that he had to employ two scribes whom we know by name[30] to write them. The epithet *baal-shem* joined to his name Israel means "the master of the Divine Name," i.e., one who knows how to use the Holy Name of God efficiently (in amulets or in exorcism). This epithet, however, it must be remembered, was not coined specifically for him; Israel Baalshem was professionally not an isolated phenomenon in his environment; several other contemporary *baalei shem* are known[31]: they fulfilled an important function in the Jewish section of rural society, which needed *baalei shem* as much as did the non-Jewish population, which had its own exorcists and miracle workers.

A cursory reading of the legends about Israel Baalshem clearly shows that the sociological hinterland of his activities was identical with that of *baalei shem* in general. Though he apparently had the driving ambition to break out of his social boundaries, he was unable in his professional life to penetrate into the upper circles and was compelled to restrict himself to the traditional village areas to ply his trade. Even within the various groups among the mobile second-rate intelligentsia of itinerant preachers etc. the social reputation of the *baalei shem* was not high, still less was their profession valued in intellectually superior urban circles.[32] Starting as an assistant teacher in a village school, Israel Baalshem became the caretaker of a synagogue, and his position as a *baal shem* was the ultimate stage of a not too spectacular climb on the social ladder. He never contrived to become a *maggid*, and it seems that the body of mystical teaching that has come down in his name (and that is certainly authentic) was never preached to the customers of his trade, who, as simple villagers, would obviously not have been capable of understanding it. His short addresses were probably delivered in semiprivate conversations or at small gatherings to colleagues whose contemplative-enthusiastic piety he shared, and not to his village customers, for whom he remained merely a miracle worker. The dichotomy of his professional and his spiritual life is expressed also in the fact that hardly any relationship can be established between the figure of the Baalshem as drawn in the legend of the *Shivḥei* and the religious mind in which the bulk of the teaching of Israel Baalshem originated, as attested by the quotations of the disciples. The theory of contemplative magic found in his authentic teachings[33] reveals a puzzling discrepancy with the more primitive methods of sympathetic magic[34] he appears often to have used in his professional journeys, according to the *Shivḥei*.

III

The strain between appointed rabbis and freelance preachers reflected not only professional rivalry but also the social and economic differences in the crude facts of their material existence. The comparative stability of the rabbi[35] contrasted with the financial instability and uncertainty of the preacher.

But this needs some qualification: in some cases an itinerant preacher was not entirely dependent on gifts, but may have received a small fixed stipend from a community to which he was attached, which guaranteed him a minimum income. The rabbi, however, received a regular salary agreed upon by contract, in addition to which he also benefited from occasional gifts.

The awareness in early Hasidism of a tension between the two types of leadership is evident here and there in the collection of legends. The fame of Israel Baalshem aroused the interest of the rabbis, who could not understand how an *am ha-areṣ*, i.e., one "unlearned in the Torah," could possess Divine Spirit. Israel Baalshem was invited to the Great Synod of the four Eastern European countries to account for his activities. There he was reproached as follows: "By your whole behaviour one would think that the Holy Spirit is upon you, and yet there is the report that you are an ignoramus. Therefore let us judge by your own words whether you are learned in the law." Thereupon he was asked what the law prescribed if, on the day of the New Moon, a worshiper forgot to insert the special reference to that day, an examination question on the lowest level by any standard. He said: "The point in question is of no importance for either you or me. You will forget to say the prayer of the New Moon in spite of the strictness of the ruling, whereas I shall never forget what I must pray."[36] This is, of course, evading the question—he did not or could not answer what the law was—but the confidence of his reply implies an insistence on personal authority that the noncharismatic leaders could not claim. Both the question and the reply epitomize succinctly the whole problem of the charismatic leader's authority.

Anti-Hasidic tradition has also preserved the expression of Israel Baalshem's keen awareness of the two types of leadership. Here is the anti-Hasidic report of a situation in which rabbis learned in the law tested him. He is said to have replied to a question about dietary laws: "Why should I need to know this, since Jewry cannot exist without rabbis?"[37] Even in the above anti-Hasidic formulation of Israel Baalshem's view the charismatic and the bureaucratic type of religious authority exist side by side; criticism of the bureaucratic by the charismatic leader is radical but not destructive. The abolition of rabbinic authority is far from his mind. The function of this authority is recognized but recognized only under the rules of that office. The rabbi is rejected by the charismatic leader only as the ultimate religious authority, but his functions, such as making legal decisions, an integral and indispensable part of Jewish community life, are readily acknowledged.

There exists as yet no analysis of the social institution represented by the *maggid* (preacher) and the *mokhiaḥ* (preacher of penitence). Even for the first, provisional picture one would have to describe the position within the community of these marginal intellectuals, their lifelong wandering through the countryside, the humiliations they had to suffer in asking day after day for the warden's permission to preach in the synagogue of each of the places they visited, their insecure livelihood, which depended largely on the success of the sermon just delivered. The self-consciousness of those who had to sell their teaching in this way is clearly reflected in an exposition by Menaḥem Mendel, the Maggid of Bar, a contemporary of Israel Baalshem. This piece of information deserves special mention if only because other sources are so scanty.

> [A tradition] in the name of the saintly teacher Rabbi Mendel Bar who was in the habit of not saying words of Torah unless he was given alms; he justified this with the verse of Scripture referring to the finding of a bird's nest, where it is said: (Deut. 22:7) "You shall set the mother free but may keep the young." This means that Torah and commandments are here seen as the "young ones" and their mother is regarded as the cause through which Torah and commandments come into the world. As long as the Temple was still in existence this cause came *from above*: as in the case of the prophets . . . because at that time "the mother" had not yet become exiled and because everything of the character of the "young ones" emanated from her. But after the destruction of the Temple "the tabernacle of David" fell low, becoming material; and therefore the cause of Torah and commandments has [also] become material in character *in that itinerant preachers and preachers of repentance need a material livelihood and are dependent upon the support of the people, for which reason they are their teachers and preachers.* But since the "mother," the cause of the "young ones," had to descend [into exile] and it nevertheless says, "Thou shalt set the mother free," you must not—God forbid—make the taking of money your main task.[38]

The embarrassing economic predicament of the *maggidim* was evident to all, and their preaching was widely suspected because the need for financial support as a reward for the sermon was only too obvious. Jacob Joseph of Polonnoye cites in one of his books a popular saying to the effect that the sermons of preachers of repentance are "bitter water." He relates: "I have heard from my teacher [Israel Baalshem] the jocular saying that the reason for people not wanting to hear moral teaching from preachers is that the latter only come with the intention of making money, and it is written: '. . . and they could not drink the water,' that is the water of the moral sermon, because 'it was bitter'[39]; in other words it was offered for money."[40]

To the preachers themselves, this method of payment, in contrast to the fixed salary discreetly paid to the appointed rabbis, was a burning and painful problem, and their open material dependence upon their listeners was sometimes expressed in ideological formulations. The theory of mutual dependence of preachers and their public was often formulated in the traditional Midrashic fashion in terms of the relationship between the archetypal figures of Zebulun and Issachar: Zebulun the merchant and Issachar the scholar share as partners the common fruits of their respective endeavors.[41] However, the new Hasidic concept of interdependence necessitated often much more sophisticated ideas than the Midrashic one. It survived curiously enough in a theory of prayer as follows. The spiritual man, in accordance with his own spiritual ideal, would pray only for his spiritual necessities. His material wants thus remain unsatisfied, even if his prayer is heard. Nonspiritual persons, on the other hand, pray only for their material existence. When their prayers are heard, such an overwhelming cornucopia of material grace is poured out that even spiritual men who did not cause this material blessing to come must inevitably share in it against their wish or at least without their intention.[42]

IV

We have seen that the collection of legends, *Shivḥei ha-Besht*, describes Israel Baalshem as an itinerant exorcist, always on the roads. Had the book been "forged" just before its publication in 1815, the forgers quite unintentionally would have portrayed Israel Baalshem as the kind of *Ṣaddik* that existed in their time. But in 1815 it was no longer possible to "invent" a *Ṣaddik* that tallied with the picture given of Israel and his colleagues in these pages. The difference in terms of mobility between the early and the later *Ṣaddik* is that the latter no longer needed to travel about but could stay at home in his "court," to which people flocked in devout pilgrimages. The description of the "court" of the Great Maggid in Salomon Maimon's autobiography shows that, in some places at least, as early as the 1770s it had become the practice for the Hasidic leader to take up residence in a particular town and to enjoy a firmly settled existence.[43] This was in itself a clear indication of the stabilization of the Hasidic movement as a whole, and it became a permanent feature. The metamorphosis of the itinerant into a settled leader holding his "court" was one of the most important events in the social history of Hasidic leadership.

This change in the social conditions of Ṣaddikism is vaguely reflected in Hasidic literature. A few examples referring to Israel Baalshem himself will be sufficient to show this. Though he was in residence in Miedzyborz, a rich woman in the country beseeched her husband to send for him to drive the ghosts out of their newly built house. Israel Baalshem came immediately and exorcised the apparition. Even if this journey could possibly be explained on the grounds that magical practices can be more effective in the place concerned, nevertheless every student of Hasidism will immediately feel that not one of the Hasidim of the Great Maggid in the next generation would have dared to summon him in this fashion in a comparable situation. Instead the Hasid would have traveled to the *Ṣaddik*, explained the predicament, and been given some amulet or instruction. Another report of the *Shivḥei* mentions that on one occasion a rich man who had no children sent for Israel Baalshem to obtain his blessing for children.[44] A generation later the man would not have dared to send for the Great Maggid, but would no doubt have undertaken the journey himself, as is testified by countless stories of childless Hasidim of later generations traveling, often with their wives, to the *Ṣaddik*.

These are examples of occasional journeys made by Israel Baalshem at the invitation of individual people of wealth. It transpires, however, that his livelihood was largely dependent on such journeys. Some indication of this will be found in the following attractive story. On one of his journeys the Baalshem wished to go home and ordered his servants to make the necessary arrangements. But they refused to do this, saying: "Your Highness is a debtor at home; why go home?"[45] It is also recorded that Israel Baalshem was habitually in debt at home for large sums of money he could repay only on his return, out of the takings from his travels. The reporter in the collection of legends has this to say: "I have heard that money never rested with him for one single night. As soon as he returned from his journeys he would pay off his debts and distribute the rest as alms."[46] On one occasion he came home from a journey with "much money," paid his debts, gave to the poor, but did not give away the whole amount, and the reporter of the *Shivḥei* takes the opportunity to relate how this omission got him into trouble with the religious authorities.[47] Another story relates that, when Israel Baalshem entered the town of Radwil, "people began flocking to him in crowds in order to obtain medicines. And this [happened] everywhere, so that he brought money home."[48] Geographical mobility within the framework of the professional life led by Israel Baalshem is fully borne out in this collection of legends, which contains only a very occasional reference to "the whole world going to Israel Baalshem."[49] The vast majority of stories show that he rather than his customers traveled: he appears traveling in a cart, staying in inns or at the home of admirers, etc. The typical situation of the Baalshem in the legend is away from home, whereas the typical situation of the later *Ṣaddikim* is in their "courts."

The position of the early charismatic leader can be traced even in the theoretical literature of Hasidism. Israel Baalshem speaks in one of his dicta of people who "earn their living by wandering." He discusses this in his explanation of a passage of the Talmud that states that the Holy Land shrank marvellously beneath the sleeping Jacob while he was dreaming. A pupil of Israel Baalshem transmits in his name: "The master explained that a person earns his living by wandering from place to place because sparks of his own soul are scattered about everywhere, and it is his task to collect them and to purify them. Thus it must be understood that the Holy One, blessed be He, folded the whole of the Land of Israel under Jacob so that he could gather the sparks of his soul without having to walk from place to place to find them."[50]

This tradition of Israel Baalshem does not refer to himself or to the *Ṣaddik* in particular. Nevertheless, his theory of the sparks "belonging" to one person and yet scattered should be understood as conditioned by his own situation, and indeed it precisely reflects the predicament of the peddler in magical amulets and charms who wanders through the Jewish settlements of Eastern Europe, but dreams in Lurianic[51] terms of the possibility of earning a living in a way that would allow him to "gather up the sparks of his soul in one place," without having to move from village to village. However, these dreams of an ideal sedentary existence could not sufficiently be fulfilled in his own lifetime. The *baal-shem* (exorcist) had to become a *Ṣaddik*. Though it is not impossible that the transition to the new status had already started toward the end of Israel Baalshem's activities and that he already had a "court" in Miedzyborz on a minor scale where he received his followers, they could not have been too numerous if he was compelled to rely for his livelihood to such a great extent on traveling. His dreams were fully realized later by Dov Baer of Mesritz, and particularly in the next generation by his pupils, after Ṣaddikism had undergone a far-reaching social transformation.

R. Dov Baer is the first person whom we know to have gathered a "court"—in Mesritz—and thus become settled. In Salomon Maimon's vivid description of Dov Baer's "court"[52] no mention is made of journeys at all. But the earlier form of existence of the itinerant *Ṣaddik* did not abruptly die out. It continued sporadically for generations as is exemplified in the case of Mordecai of Czernobiel and many other minor *Ṣaddikim* right up to the eve of World War II.[53]

It is probably still the old itinerant type of charismatic leader that the anonymous writer of the following passage described: "Do not say: I shall go out to make men just; it is better that a man should stay at home and serve God and if someone visits him he shall make him just. But not that he go out to journey to other people."[54]

A clear formulation of the new settled situation of the *Ṣaddik* is to be found in the work of Jacob Joseph Hurwitz of the third Hasidic generation, that is, a disciple of a disciple of Israel Baalshem. He writes: "He who is no *Ṣaddik* has no disadvantage in travelling about, but it is a disadvantage for the *Ṣaddik* . . . for this reason the *Ṣaddik* shall remain at rest and not occupy himself by the side of the road, so that he may pray for Israel."[55]

The clash of old and new was formulated in the same third generation in the following way:

I have heard it in the name of the Baalshem Tov that the interpretation of the verse (Ps. 37:23): "The steps of a [good] man are ordered of the Lord: and he delighteth in his way" is as follows: He would say about those men, who travel into far countries in the interests of their trade and similar things, wandering far off, that God's thoughts are unlike their thoughts. They themselves imagine to be travelling to far countries merely to increase gold and silver, crushing their feet in the effort. But He, may He be blessed, does not [think] like that. He certainly knows how better to order one's affairs. Thus on occasion a man has a loaf of bread in a far country which, somehow, has to do with his spiritual character (*beḥinah*): this loaf he alone must eat just in that place and at that moment; or he has to drink his mouthful of water in that very locality. For this purpose the steps of a man are ordered so as to make him wander far off many hundreds of miles in order to bring perfection to his soul with that particular loaf of bread and with the drinking of that water, whether it is much or little.

Occasionally, it may well happen that it does not concern him, but one of his Jewish servants. If there is a morsel of bread or a cupful of water for him [the servant], and if it is not within his reach to undertake a journey to that far off place, it is this which influences the master [of the servant] to travel on his journey just to that place for the sake of his servant, enabling him in this way to fill his belly with that bread there preordained for him, or to drink of the water, which concerns him. For so God's wisdom decrees that he, who requires the perfection of his soul, should thus assemble its various elements; this is one of the ways of God. Thereto this verse alludes: "the steps of a man are ordered of the Lord"; that is to say, [when] one goes on a journey to a far-off place, everything is from God and in accordance with what His wisdom, Whose name is blessed, has decreed, for the perfection of this soul. . . .

But man does not think in this fashion, on the contrary, he merely desires to proceed on a journey concerning business, while his heart is quite oblivious that it is all from God.

One ought not to be unduly surprised at people like this, because, simply not everyone, who does much business, really becomes wise (*Avot*, 2:5) . . . But one ought to be surprised at men of Torah, who break their feet going from city to city and from country to country for their food, not resting in their home, and this is a question indeed. . . .

There are two kinds of such migrants: the party of the elect, the upright in the way, who walk in the law of the Lord in truth and without fault. Assuredly, great is their benefit and delectable. They bring about improvements by means of the paths upon which they travel. Even the very paths desire their visitation, longing for the coming of these prudent men, because they accomplish great deeds by every step of the soles of their feet. . . .

But it is not for every one, who desires to take the name, to come and take it,[56] claiming that his strength is good enough to amend the paths. Would he were in a position to rectify himself as he sits by himself alone in his house and not to seek to rectify the many, undertaking for this purpose various journeys and wandering afar off many miles. When you see a man like that, whose strength is not sufficient to rectify the many . . . yet eager to proceed on journeys from city to city in order to be [counted among] the very pious,[57] you should know that such a man is included in the mystery of "the cycle which turns in the world," included amongst the wretched and unfortunate poor people, who go from village to village and from town to town. All this comes under the mystery of "the cycle which turns in the world," this being his living apportioned to him in this particular way. In general, there is no middle way in this matter; either his journey is of a very high degree for the purpose of rectifying and uplifting holy sparks in the place of his going out and coming in as already indicated, or he is merely proceeding on a journey within the mystery of the "cycle," like a poor man and a pauper. . . .

The sum total of all that we have said above is that a man ought very much to reflect and consider, in order not to lose his lofty rank. But he ought to walk humbly, confining himself to his house, sitting alone as this has been from eternity. Let this sort of thing be a comfort to him, bodily and spiritual rest, in order that he may serve his Creator in truth and uprightly, not conducting himself according to the discreditable manner now so prevalent in this generation. . . . This is a warning to the *Ṣaddik* who desires to draw near to the holy ministry within. . . . Certainly, he should not be compelled to traverse roads and boundaries breaking his feet, going from city to city in the interests of his livelihood.[58]

This trend closes the first phase of Hasidism. The *Ṣaddik*, now secure through a kind of contract, soon became an organic part of the large Eastern European Jewish communities, and his public is no longer the rural but the urban Jewish population.

NOTES

1. The similarity of certain aspects of Hasidism to Quakerism has been interestingly argued by a contemporary partisan observer of Hasidism, see A. Rubinstein, "The MS Treatise Zimrat Am ha-Areṣ" (Heb.) *Aresheth* 3 (1961), p. 212, n. 45.

2. See Benzion Dinaburg, "The Beginnings of Hasidism" etc. (in Hebrew), *Ṣion* 8 (1943): 107–15, 117–34, 179–200; 9:39–45, 89–108, 186–97; 10:67–77, 149–96 (reprinted in his collected historical essays *Bemifne-ha-Doroth* [Jerusalem 1955], 1:81–227); J. Weiss, "The Beginnings of Hasidism" (in Hebrew), *Ṣion* 16 (1951): 46–105; G. Scholem, "The Two Earliest Testimonies on the Relations between Hasidic Groups and the Baalshem" (Hebrew). *Tarbiz* 20 (1949): 228–40; J. Katz, *Tradition and Crisis* (The Free Press of Glencoe, 1962), chapter 22, pp. 231–44.

3. See A. J. Heschel, "R. Phinehas of Korzecz" (in Hebrew), *Alei ayin, S. Z. Schocken Jubilee Volume* (Jerusalem, 1952), pp. 213–44.

4. See Weiss, "Beginnings of Hasidism," passim.

5. See S. Dubnow, *Geschichte des Chassidismus* (1931), 1:170 ff. and passim; Weiss, "Beginnings of Hasidism," p. 60 ff. and passim; and below, pp. 27–42. A. Heschel (in Hebrew) in *H. Wolfson Jubilee Volume* (Jerusalem, 1965), pp. 113–41. In this article, which is unusually rich in material collected from printed books and partly from manuscripts, the author persistently ignores the principal questions first posed by G. Scholem, which have since produced a large body of scholarly literature.

6. See Dinaburg, "Beginnings of Hasidism," 8–10: passim.

7. See my preliminary remarks below p. 114, and on R. Menaḥem Mendel's views in my article "Torah Study in Early Hasidism" (in Hebrew), *Ha-Do'ar* (New York 1965), 45:615–17 trans. below, pp. 56–68. A. Rubinstein, "Shevaḥ mi-Shivḥei ha-Besht," *Tarbiz* 35 (1966): 174–91.

8. Below, p. 30, I have suggested that this might have marked the termination of their adherence to the Sabbatian heresy, but this remains a conjecture.

9. There was no doubt some occasional overlapping between these groupings, e.g., the head of the rabbinical court belonged to the group of pneumatics in Kutov.

10. See Horodecki, ed., *Shivḥei ha-Besht* (Berlin, 1922), pp. 16–17.

11. "Since this appellation is not befitting a *Ṣaddik*" (*Shivḥei ha-Besht*, p. 25).

12. G. Scholem, "The Two Earliest Testimonies."

13. See A. J. Heschel, "R. Phinehas of Korzecz."

14. See G. Scholem, "Devekuth," etc. *Review of Religion* 14 (1950): 15–39.

15. G. Scholem, *Major Trends in Jewish Mysticism* (London, 1955), p. 378, n. 7.

16. J. Weiss, "The Beginnings of Hasidism," 60 ff.; and below, pp. 27 ff.

17. J. Weiss, "The Beginnings of Hasidism," p. 64.

18. R. Jacob Joseph must have died in 1782 or shortly after; the date, including the year, is blurred on his tombstone but the titles of three books published by him could be clearly read. See Dubnow, *Geschichte des Chassidismus*, 1:160. The books were published between 1780 and 1782. His fourth book was not printed until 1862. See my note "Is the Hasidic Book *Kethoneth Passim* a Literary Forgery?," *J.J.S.*, 9 (1958): 81–83.

19. The letters written by Meshullam Phoebus Heller of Zbaraz in 1777 make sense only if we assume that the penetration into Galicia of the handwritten copies of the Great Maggid's short sermons (which were not printed until 1784) took place only at the time of writing the letter (1777). We have similarly to assume that nothing of Jacob Joseph's ideas (or indeed Israel Baalshem's ideas as quoted in Jacob Joseph's works) on the "restoration of the wayward thoughts" was known there at the time. This was the subject that so shocked R. Meshullam Phoebus's Galician group when the scripts of the Maggid's sermons arrived there. See my remarks below, p. 122, n. 57. The breakthrough of Jacob Joseph's ideas in the Hasidic world about 1780 was most successful and presented a new basis for the development of Hasidic ideas. The teachings of virtually all disciples of Dov Baer who were active at the time of the publication of the book *Toledoth Ya'akov Yosef*, and of the other two volumes, are united in that the paradoxes of Ṣaddikology, the central doctrine of R. Jacob Joseph, are fully accepted by them as a basis for discussion. They disagree about the details but agree on the theological significance of the "fall of the *Ṣaddik*." R. Shneur Zalman is the only important case of a total defiance of Jacob Joseph's ideas that deeply attracted the disciples of the Great Maggid.

20. In my earlier study "The Beginnings of Hasidism," p. 88, I mentioned the strange fact that the common theme of the descensus of the *Ṣaddik*, a central doctrine of the generation of the Baalshem, including the Baalshem himself, is virtually absent in the sermons of the Great Maggid. My earlier interpretation of this in itself correct observation was that the Great Maggid's silence on this topic was perhaps intentional and that he suppressed this particular theme of the Hasidic doctrinal tradition because he did not like it or even opposed it in view of its theological implications. I also

considered the possibility (ibid.) that the idea of the descensus of the *Ṣaddik* did not fit into Dov Baer's more mystical system. But I must now admit that I feel a third interpretation is more likely, viz., that the Great Maggid was unaware of the descensus theme in the Baalshem traditions because Jacob Joseph's manuscript writings were not available to him, since the Maggid died in 1772, eight years before the publication of Jacob Joseph's works. The Maggid's contacts with Jacob Joseph were slender: Jacob Joseph, who quoted very willingly, mentions only a single saying of the Maggid Dov Baer. How much Dov Baer knew of Jacob Joseph's teaching one can only assess from the near total lack in his work of any echo of the religious paradoxes of descensus that dominated Jacob Joseph's world. A deep dependence of Dov Baer on the doctrines of the Baalshem would certainly have produced some discussion or reinterpretation of the descensus theme in Dov Baer's sermons, but to assume that Dov Baer depended in every subject on the Baalshem (rather than shared with him certain ideas) is *petitio principii*. It is remarkable that not only Dov Baer (died 1772), but also Phinehas of Korzecz (died 1791) and Menaḥem Mendel of Premyslan (left for Tiberias in 1764 and died there) are silent about the descensus of the *Ṣaddik*. Phinehas of Korzecz could have read Jacob Joseph's works in the last decade of his life but was probably too old to assimilate the book's ideas or was not interested in assimilating them. All these taught their Hasidism independently of the new fascination that emanated from Jacob Joseph's works from 1780 onwards—after this date there is hardly a Hasidic master (other than the founder of Ḥabad, R. Shneur Zalman) who could escape the formative influence of Jacob Joseph's version of Hasidism. I propose that the great change occurred with the publication of Jacob Joseph's works, and a radical transformation of the Hasidic atmosphere in this matter is patent to anyone who cares to compare the sermons of the Great Maggid with those of his disciples. The problem awaits detailed analysis from the point of view of the history of Hasidic ideas. In the present context I am only interested in the question from the angle of the social grouping of Hasidic teachers and their sometimes merely illusory discipleship and dependence.

21. Dubnow collected material reflecting the views of the Baalshem's contemporaries about him (*Geschichte des Chassidismus*, 1:120–28) and Scholem added much new source material and gave a new evaluation of the old material in his Hebrew article "The Historical Israel Baalshem," *Molad* 18 (1960): 335–56. On the basis of all relevant material, it must be understood that both appreciation of and opposition to the person of Israel Baalshem in his lifetime was very scant.

22. Scholem, *Major Trends* p. 330 ff., and the literature given in my article "Beginnings of Hasidism," p. 58, n. 36. A. Rubinstein "A MS Treatise" etc., pp. 210–11 and n. 39 proposed that the remarks in early anti-Hasidic polemic merely pointed to the similarity of the two movements, not to the derivation of Hasidism from Sabbatianism.

23. Scholem, *Major Trends*, pp. 287–324; see also his *magnum opus, Shabbethay Ṣevi* (in Hebrew), the first two volumes of which were published in Tel Aviv in 1957, with two further volumes—the more important ones for our investigations on the relation between Sabbatianism and Hasidism—to be published at a later date. (English translation, *Sabbatai Ṣevi* [London, 1973].)

24. The Sabbatian origin of this Hasidic doctrine was first tentatively proposed by Scholem in his essay, "Ueber die Theologie des Sabbatianismus im Lichte Cardozos," *Der Jude*, 1928 (Sonderheft zu M. Buber's 50. Geburtstag), p. 135. Reprinted in his volume of essays in German, *Judaica* (Frankfurt/Main, 1963), pp. 119–46. Subsequent research was able not only to accept Scholem's initial insight but to follow up the manifold ramifications of his thesis.

25. See my "Beginnings of Hasidism," pp. 88 ff. M. Wilenski in his Hebrew article "A Critique of the Book *Toledoth Ya'akov Yosef*", Joshua Starr Memorial Volume (New York, 1953), pp. 183–89, published a previously unknown or but partly known document from which it is clear that the practice of "restoration of wayward thoughts"

provoked weighty arguments in the anti-Hasidic camp on account of the novelty of the Hasidic teaching on this point. The document in Wilenski's paper, published two years after my article, fully endorses my conclusions that the restoration of wayward thoughts occupied a central position in early Hasidic teaching. Comtemporary public opinion in anti-Hasidic circles certainly felt so.

26. Only very occasionally does the doctrine of the *Ṣaddik's* fall imply the possibility of his actual sin. This is nevertheless always qualified in that the *Ṣaddik's* sin is committed in unavoidable circumstances, under duress, or inadvertently. The falling *Ṣaddik's* sins are always supposed to be "light" or "spiritual" in comparison with the ordinary man's "vulgar" sins.

27. Jacob Emden, *Sefer Torath ha-Kenaoth* (Lemberg, 1870), p. 70. On the early Sabbatian *baalshem* Sabbatai Raphael, see Scholem, *Sabbatai Ṣevi*, pp. 781–92.

28. On the book in general, see Dubnow, *Geschichte des Chassidismus* ("Das Buch 'die Legende des Baal Schem' sein Ursprung und seine Publicationsgeschichte"), 2:313–19; on the Yiddish variants, see A. Yaari, "Two Versions of the Shivḥei ha-Besht" (in Hebrew), *Kiryath Sefer* 39 (1964): 249–72, 394–407, 552–62. The Hebrew *Shivḥei* was edited by S. A. Horodecki (Berlin, 1922), without basically tampering with the texts, which were nevertheless rearranged under five headings, thereby dislocating the original pieces and their interrelationship. Some serious misunderstandings were created by this editorial technique. The edition by Benjamin Muentz (Tel Aviv, 1961) follows the first edition of Berditchev (1815).

29. H. Graetz, *Geschichte der Juden* (Leipzig, 1870), p. 14.

30. Horodecki, ed., *Shivḥei ha-Besht*, pp. 79, 134.

31. See *Encyclopaedia Judaica* (Berlin, 1928–34), 3, s.v. "Baal Schem."

32. Horodecki, ed. *Shivḥei*, p. 25.

33. Israel Baalshem's theory of magic has not yet been analyzed but this much is clear: it is not identical with the theories of the next Hasidic generation; see below, pp. 126–30.

34. See, e.g., Horodecki, ed., *Shivḥei ha-Besht*, pp. 69, 84, etc.

35. This did not, however, mean life appointments. The contracts of the rabbis were usually limited to three years. See Katz, *Tradition and Crisis*, p. 87.

36. Horodecki, ed., *Shivḥei ha-Besht*, p. 104. The story must be considered authentic in its essence, since it is corroborated by anti-Hasidic sources. See Dubnow, *Geschichte des Chassidismus*, 1:12–13 and ibid. n. 1.

37. Ibid., from Israel Loebel's *Sefer ha-Vikkuaḥ* (1798), p. 9.

38. *Derekh Miṣvotekha* (Poltava, 1914), 1:112b.

39. Exod. 15:23. The Yiddish original plays on the pun *vergallt* i.e., "bitter," and *far geld* i.e., "for money."

40. *Toledoth Ya'akov Yosef* (Korzecz, 1780), p. 90b. See the long excursus on the itinerant preachers, whose mind is fixed on the money they expect to make with their sermons, in R. Zeev Wolf of Zhitomir, *Or ha-Meir* (Korzecz 1798), part 1, p. 66a–67a. The vivid description reflects the generation of the Great Maggid's disciples.

41. *Genesis Rabba* 72, 4. The motif is perennial in Jewish *Musar* literature.

42. Jacob Joseph, *Ṣofenath Pa'aneaḥ* (Korzecz, 1782), p. 22, a quotation in the name of Naḥman of Horodenka.

43. Salomon Maimon, *Lebensgeschichte*, ed. Fromer (Munich, 1911), pp. 202 ff.

44. Horodecki, ed., *Shivḥei ha-Besht*, p. 73.

45. Ibid., p. 70.

46. Ibid., p. 97.

47. Ibid.

48. Ibid., p. 99.

49. Ibid., p. 105.

50. *Ben Porath Yosef*, 14a.

51. The original Lurianic doctrine does not speak of "individual" sparks belonging to one person.

52. Salomon Maimon's *Lebensgeschichte* loc. cit.

53. See S. A. Horodecki, *Ha-Ḥasiduth ve-ha-Ḥasidim*, 3:87.

54. *Likkutei Yekarim* (Lemberg, 1792), 15b. On the authorship of this anonymous collection, see below p. 122, n. 57.

55. *Zoth zikkaron*, 2b.

56. An allusion to T. B. *Berakhoth* 16b.

57. Untranslatable pun: it also means "those who travel."

58. *Or ha-Meir* (Korzecz, 1798), part. 2, p. 2b.

A Circle of Pneumatics in Pre-Hasidism

The following note aims at analyzing certain aspects of the life of "the circle of Naḥman of Kosov"[1] with a view to establishing its historical position between the late Sabbatian and early Hasidic movements. A scrutiny of a short passage in *Shivḥei ha-Besht*,[2] the legendary biography of Israel Baalshem, about the circle enables us to make the following observations:

The circle is called *Ḥavurah Kadisha*, and its members *Benei Ḥavurah Kadisha* or *Anshei ha-Ḥavurah*. Naḥman of Kosov[3] appears on the scene as a well-to-do tax farmer (*maḥzik kefar*). One may assume that this period of Naḥman's life followed in biographical sequel the one in which, according to the accusation of Rabbi Jacob Emden, he was "an illiterate and a follower of the Sabbatian sect who posed as an itinerant preacher of repentance and was received with great honours."[4] Whether the accusation was justified or was but another example of the sometimes indiscriminate heresy hunting in which Emden indulged his boundless energies cannot be decided upon owing to lack of independent evidence. But the suspicions of this ruthless enemy of all Sabbatians have often been proved surprisingly accurate, and historical research should therefore not ignore his hints.

One factual point in Emden's description of Naḥman one need not doubt, namely, that Naḥman followed the profession of those itinerant preachers who were wandering among the scattered Jewish communities of Eastern Europe in a social environment from which the later leadership of the heretical Sabbatian movement and also that of the subsequent early Hasidic movement were largely recruited.[5] No wonder, therefore, that the figures of these itinerant *Maggidim* and *Mokhiḥim* loom predominant on the pages of *Shivḥei ha-Besht*. The beginnings of Naḥman of Kosov as an itinerant preacher of penitence fit perfectly well into the same social environment. Even though he left his call as preacher to become a tax farmer, some of his spiritual activities he did not relinquish as a wealthy man. A brief analysis of what is said about him in the *Shivḥei* might contribute some details to his religious portrait and might also throw some light on the character of the whole group.

We find Naḥman[6] living in a small village near a town the name of which is not mentioned. The members of the *Ḥavurah Kadisha* to which he belongs live in this town. Geographically somewhat removed from his group he is nevertheless closely associated with it in several ways. He puts the education of his sons into the hands of a member of this circle, Rabbi Aryeh Leib, the *Mokhiaḥ*, who lives in the town near by. Naḥman's sons have their meals in the *Mokhiaḥ's* house. The father does not pay for their board but provides the tutor with corn and flour from the village—a primitive form of payment that was obviously customary in that environment.

We are told that the sons' tutor goes to call on Naḥman in the village. The official pretext for this visit is that he has not received his quota of corn and flour as agreed, but the *Mokhiaḥ* has yet another motive. Our text makes it quite clear that the circle in town had a serious complaint against the behavior of Naḥman and decided to send one of its members to discuss it with him. The *Mokhiaḥ* volunteered to undertake this mission as he wanted to discuss with him his own personal complaint about the delay in sending provisions in connection with the sons' tuition.

In the course of the conversation between the *Mokhiaḥ* and Naḥman, as reported in the *Shivḥei*, the following circumstances are revealed. The members of the circle "had agreed that no one of them should prophesy." Naḥman, according to this complaint, disregarded this agreement of self-restriction in that "he sent word to the members of the *Ḥavurah Kadisha*, to every one of them, and let them know what sins each one of them had to rectify (*le-takken*) in this world. And in everything (i.e., in specifying the sins of each person) he was right."[7]

Naḥman denies the charge: "I am not a prophet, nor the son

of a prophet." He explains in a rather lengthy discourse that he did not make use of his prophetic faculties contrary to the mutual agreement of the members of the group, but gained possession of the knowledge needed for the disclosure of his friends' hidden sins through the medium of a deceased person who died while excommunicated.

In the story related here, we are confronted with a circle of pneumatics endowed with the charisma of prophecy. The scope and tendency of the prophetic activities within the group are not clearly defined in our text. However, from the only instance of Naḥman's prophecy discussed in the text, it becomes apparent that prophesying was considered as including, or indeed even being identical with, the disclosure of secret sins. Obviously the pneumatic intenseness of this circle was severely reduced after the strange decision of its members to renounce their prophetic powers for some reason that remains unexplained in the text. Notwithstanding the self-imposed prophetic inactivity of the group, its pneumatic climate is tangible. The members of the circle fear the sudden eruption of prophetic faculties at any moment and are determined to suppress it.

Do these people fall into any clearly defined category of the religious history of eighteenth-century Judaism in Eastern Europe? The answer is that the members of the circle belong unmistakably to that pneumatic type of religious personality that was so abundantly represented in the history of the Sabbatian movement, i.e., to the type of the Sabbatian "prophet."[8] Although the prophetic scope of the ecstatic Sabbatian *navi* (prophet) embraced more than the mere divulgence of the secret sins of individuals, the "prophets" did have a strong predilection for using their prophetic faculties in this direction as part of their feverish endeavor to work for the cause of repentance, a preoccupation that followed the Sabbatian movement like a shadow.

Beyond the striking similarity between the religious phenomena of the Sabbatian prophets and of the circle to which Naḥman belongs, the fact that the pneumatic figures in both societies are called by the very same name, i.e., *navi*, suggests a historical link. The *derivata* of the root *nba* (in the form of *navi*, *nevi'ut*, *mitnabbe*) occur in the Hasidic text of the *Shivḥei* in describing the pneumatic activities of Naḥman.[9] One is tempted to suggest that he and his friends belonged to the last examples of a typically Sabbatian phenomenon in the religious history of later Judaism. G. Scholem ventured to trace back the historical origin of the Hasidic charismatic leader (*Ṣaddik*) to the Sabbatian prototype of the *navi*. In this transformation of a Sabbatian type into a Hasidic one, Naḥman and his friends, belonging as they did, perhaps only peripherally, to both movements have their place.[10]

Once it is established that the life of the circle exhibits specific features typical of certain Sabbatian groups—this is further supported by the testimony of Jacob Emden about the Sabbatian past of at least one of the members of the group, i.e., Naḥman of Kosov—we may conjecture that the reason for the mutual agreement of the members to renounce their prophetic activities might have had a theological motivation. It might have marked the termination of their adherence to the Sabbatian belief. This interpretation of their puzzling decision to eliminate the practice of prophecy would not be farfetched in view of the historical transformation of Sabbatianism into Hasidism.

The social structure of the circle can be related to the pre-Hasidic and early Hasidic environment. Dinaburg dealt with the group at some length, describing it as "the circle of Rabbi Naḥman of Kosov."[11] It would appear that this description calls for qualification. The vivid picture of the group given in the *Shivḥei* does not seem to conform with the structure of the fully developed Hasidic groups attracted by the figure of their charismatic leader, the *Ṣaddik*, as was the case since the times of the great Maggid, Dov Baer of Mesritz. Though Naḥman of Kosov clearly exhibits some personal features of the later Hasidic *Ṣaddik*—he conducts the service in the synagogue in the Sepharadi rite, in a mellifluous voice thus enchanting all,[12] etc.—he is certainly not the head of the group. The structure of a group whereby the leader lives in a village at a distance from the town where the group is centered, able to communicate with its members living there by means of notes only, would itself present an unusual picture. Furthermore, there are other indications that Naḥman was not considered the head of the group. When one examines the details of the lively conversation between Naḥman and the *Mokhiaḥ*, it becomes apparent that a relationship of coordination among the members rather than one of subordination to a leader characterizes the social structure of the group. The mutually insulting tone of Naḥman and of the *Mokhiaḥ*, however jokingly employed, calling one another "madman" (*meshugga*),[13] would hardly fit into the pattern of relations between a charismatic leader in Hasidism and his follower. One may call this group the "circle of Naḥman of Kosov" for convenience's sake, but one has to bear in mind that in this case "circle" is not used in the Hasidic sense. One could by the same right call it the circle of the *Mokhiaḥ*. The *Mokhiaḥ* and Naḥman and probably the other members of the group also are equals, and Naḥman does not even seem to be *primus inter pares*. The group consists of a loose association of spiritual personalities[14] of equal status whose relationship to one another is one of mutual agreement[15] rather than one resting on an authoritative basis in which the leader dictates and his disciples obey. The *Mokhiaḥ* comes to Naḥman in the name of the whole group and tries to enforce compliance on the part of Naḥman, who, though supposedly the head of the group, accepts their request without questioning its validity. The terms of reference in the debate are the conditions of the agreement. Naḥman's line of self-defense is that he did not commit a breach of the agreement, not that the other members lacked the authority to control the leader's behavior. It would therefore be inadequate to project our concept of the later Hasidic "circle" on to this pre-Hasidic group of pneumatic equals. Examined from the point of view of its social structure, the "circle of Rabbi Naḥman of Kosov" has a definitely non-Hasidic character.

Nevertheless, there is one distinctive facet of the religious life of the circle that was subsequently to hold a position of central importance in the Hasidic movement, i.e., the place and function of the third Sabbath meal, the *Se'udah Shelishith*. One may attempt to establish a continuity between Naḥman's circle and the Hasidic movement that we found lacking in the social sphere, by examining the character of the third Sabbath meal, as described in detail in the conversation between Naḥman and the *Mokhiaḥ* and reported in the *Shivḥei*. The most striking feature of the meal as described here is that it is not taken in the family circle, but participation in it is meant to render the meal a social occasion. It takes place in the house of Rabbi Moshe, who is the head of the rabbinical court of Kutov. The participants in this afternoon meal stay at the table long into the night. The time is devoted to discussions on religious matters. There is no light but a numinous darkness surrounds the table, though there would have been a perfectly good Halakhic way of lighting candles after nightfall.[16] It seems that the participants preferred to intensify the atmosphere by staying in darkness. This is keenly felt by a vulgar outsider, the butcher of the town, who is eager for the early termination of the meal, which had already been too prolonged for both his religious taste and material interests. He is anxious that the ritual slaughterer of the town, who is participating in the meal, should leave the table and get down to work. In order to bring the *Se'udah* to an early conclusion, the butcher bursts into the room with a candle in his hand, thus dispelling the numinous darkness and thus abruptly terminating the meal, a well-calculated act, for which he died in excommunication.[17] It was his ghost who became Naḥman's secret informer, enabling him to disclose the hidden sins of the members of the whole circle, a practice against which they protested.

The character of this meal strongly resembles, or rather foreshadows, that of the *Se'udah Shelishith* in the Hasidic environment, which from its very beginnings had a sacramental character and fulfilled a particular social function. It was the weekly highlight of communal religiosity focused on social intercourse.

Already Israel Baalshem is portrayed in the *Shivḥei* as presiding and pronouncing his teachings at gatherings of the third Sabbath meal held on a community and not a family basis. His recognition after long struggles at Miedzyborz, where his fame as an itinerant exorcist did not, at first, enhance his social reputation, was marked, according to the *Shivḥei*, by the fact that on the first Sabbath after his victory people "came to him to take *Se'udah Shelishith* with him, and he said (at the table) words of Torah."[18] When on one occasion, owing to deep contemplation, Israel Baalshem remained silent during the third meal and the customary teaching at the table was omitted, the disciples were astounded.[19]

The interminable length of the *Seʿudah Shelishit* is apparently mainly due to the words of Torah spoken by the Baalshem at dusk and continued late into the night.[20] The same phenomenon of the prolongation of the *Seʿudah Shelishith* that was mentioned in the description of the third meal of our *Ḥavurah Kadisha* is seen again here in connection with Israel Baalshem.[21]

As to the *Seʿudah Shelishith* being a Hasidic institution at least as early as the second generation of the movement, we have the independent testimony of R. Jacob Joseph of Polonnoye, the disciple of Israel Baalshem. In one of his sermons he describes the third Sabbath meal as a "gathering and joining of men."[22]

Immediately prior to this passage, in the very same discourse, R. Jacob Joseph also deals with the first two Sabbath meals, but obviously reflecting the exceptional character of the Hasidic *Seʿudah Shelishit*, he attributes the distinctive social function to the third meal only.

The colorful description by Salomon Maimon of the "court" of the Great Maggid, another disciple of Israel Baalshem, does not leave much doubt that the *Seʿudah*, probably the *Seʿudah Shelishith*, had at this time already a fully institutionalized character in the Hasidic movement.[23]

In the anti-Hasidic regulations of the Galician town Leshnev (1772) the third meal is particularly mentioned as prone to Hasidic influence.[24] The anti-Hasidic pamphlet printed upon the publication in 1780 of the book *Toledoth Yaʿakov Yosef* by R. Jacob Joseph of Polonnoye gives unequivocal testimony of the institutionalized form of the *Seʿudah Shelishith*, with pronouncement of Torah by the *Ṣaddik*. The pamphlet is probably correct in stating that the book in question came into existence during the *Seʿudah Shelishith* sessions of the sect every Sabbath.[25]

The pronouncement of Hasidic teachings by the *Ṣaddik* achieved an institutionalized form within the social framework of the *Seʿudah Shelishith*[26] instead of being preached in the synagogue or in the *Beth ha-midrash* as was the case in traditional Judaism. One can safely say that the very intimate Sabbath afternoon gathering was the birthplace of all Hasidic teaching and literature. The entire written product of Hasidism, with its short literary units and repetitious oral style, is patently conditioned by this origin. It is a bibliographical fact that nearly every Hasidic book is a collection of speeches made in Yiddish by *Ṣaddikim* at the table during the *Seʿudah Shelishith* and translated into atrocious Hebrew by inexperienced translators in a somewhat haphazard fashion on Saturday nights, a few hours after they had been pronounced.

Returning now to Naḥman of Kosov's circle for comparison, we can observe that, as one might have expected, no pronouncement of teaching by any central figure is mentioned in the text of the *Shivḥei*. As has been shown, the circle had no established leader around whom the adherents would gather and to whose teaching they would listen. Naḥman is certainly not a leader. Since there is no leading figure in the group, there is no authoritative pronouncement of Torah by a charismatic leader, only conversation and discussion among the members of the group that take up their time and make the *Seʿudah Shelishith* the prolonged session that it is.[27]

The pneumatic phenomena of the circle would point to the declining Sabbatian movement, whereas its *Seʿudah Shelishith* and some minor issues would put it into close proximity to the Hasidic group. The circle's place appears therefore to be somewhere in the historical no-man's-land between these two movements.

It appears to be possible to locate this circle geographically and identify some of its members from other stories in the *Shivḥei* about a group of "Hasidim" in Kutov which can be supposed on good grounds to be identical with our circle.

As we know, our circle gathered on the occasion of the *Seʿudah Shelishith* described above at the house of R. Moshe, the head of the rabbinical court in Kutov. This provides the clue to the identification. Several passages in the *Shivḥei* testify to the existence of a group called "Hasidim of Kutov" or "*Ḥevrah* of Hasidim of Kutov"[28] and to the fact that R. Moshe himself belonged to this group.[29] The very name *Ḥevrah shel Ḥasidim* recalls the names by which our circle was called, i.e. *Ḥavurah* and *Ḥavurah Kadisha*. It is a reasonable conjecture that the unnamed town in a village near which Naḥman is said to have lived and where the other members of the circle were to be found, was Kutov, and that these two groups of pre-Hasidim were in fact one. The role R. Moshe of Kutov plays in both sets of stories strengthens this assumption.

The *Shivḥei* reveals that the Kutov group of pre-Hasidim lived in an atmosphere of continual tension with some elements of the community at large. The picture presented is far from an idyllic one of a harmonious Jewish congregation in which a religious elite is treated with admiration or at least respect by the rest of the community. The author of the *Shivḥei* relates the story that there was in Kutov a man by the name of Tiktiner who used to disparage the circle of Hasidim (*ha-ḥevrah s̀hel Ḥasidim*). A certain R. Aaron, the brother of the famous R. Gershon of Kutov, himself the brother-in-law of Israel Baalshem, took up the cudgels against Tiktiner and in the course of the argument Tiktiner tugged at R. Aaron's beard, for which he was excommunicated by the hot-tempered R. Gershon. Soon afterwards he died in excommunication.[30]

This story, reflecting the tension between the group and its vulgar opponents, who are punished by excommunication, exhibits striking similarities to the one recorded above about the butcher of the town who came to disturb the *Seʿudah Shelishith* of the circle. It must indeed by regarded as indicative of social conditions in Kutov, and probably in other communities harboring similar groups. We also hear about a man who became a "ghost" because he derided the pre-Hasidic colony in Kutov.[31] In spite of the fact that R. Moshe, the rabbinical head of the community, was associated with the circle, the town's "*Ḥasidim*" appear to have been subjected to constant ridicule on the part of the general society of the town. These rifts must have created a turbulent atmosphere in the community. Apparently many people felt irritated by some of the bizarre forms of piety practiced by these pre-Hasidim.

The same predicament of an eccentric religious minority always on the defensive is the decisive feature of early Hasidic life too. Ridicule rather than hatred was operative there, and the writers of early Hasidism found it necessary to encourage the adherents of the new movement to remain adamant in face of the derision to which their religious extravaganza was exposed. From this aspect also the pre-Hasidic circle of Kutov anticipates the later Hasidic state of affairs.

Once the existence of the Kutov circle is established and a preliminary list of its members is drawn up, the relationship of

Israel Baalshem to the individual members of the group acquires a new significance and should be studied with reference to the group as a whole.

One thing is patent from the outset: Israel Baalshem made concerted efforts to achieve social and spiritual recognition in this circle. It seems to have been a primary ambition of his to be accepted by the Kutov circle. Even the comparatively parsimonious reports in the *Shivḥei* enable us to follow his attempts toward this end.

Israel seems to have had little success with Naḥman of Kosov whose recognition he sought as a pneumatic mindreader, i.e., in some prophetic capacity, which we have seen was the basic quality that united the members of the Kutov group. He was only too glad to be put to the test by Naḥman of Kosov, but he did not succeed in satisfying Naḥman.[32] It is very doubtful whether he ever succeeded in gaining Naḥman's recognition although the *Shivḥei* is at pains to establish a happy conclusion to such a zealous pursuit. In any event, the details of Israel's dealings with Naḥman of Kosov do not constitute a struggle for leadership in the group as Dinaburg[33] held on the basis of his assumption that Naḥman was the leader of the circle. Far from presenting a forthright challenge to wrest the leadership from Naḥman, Israel Baalshem appears on the pages of the *Shivḥei* to be humbly yet persistently requesting recognition as a pneumatic personality from a man whose own pneumatic authority is beyond doubt.

That R. Gershon of Kutov himself belonged to the circle is not so obvious, though for a while he did live in Kutov.[34] He must be pictured as the ascetic type of pre-Hasid,[35] but whether or not he was a member of the pre-Hasidic group in Kutov during his sojourn there cannot be proved conclusively. He certainly had contacts with it and had some influence on R. Moshe, whom he was able to persuade, during a visit of the young Israel Baalshem to Kutov, to put the visitor to the test by taking him to a well-known mad woman who had a reputation for prophetic faculties.[36] On the other hand, it transpires that R. Moshe and R. Gershon disagreed profoundly about the pneumatic nature of Israel Baalshem, R. Gershon dismissing him as an illiterate[37] devoid of pneumatic gifts and R. Moshe giving him help and encouragement.

Israel Baalshem's endeavor to overstep his social boundaries as an itinerant magician and to be accepted on a socially, educationally, and spiritually higher level is evident from the strange story of his marriage to the divorced sister of R. Gershon of Kutov in the teeth of the fierce opposition of the latter. This seems to have occurred rather late when R. Gershon had left Kutov and was residing in Brody as a member of the famous Cabbalistic *Beth ha-Midrash* ("*Klaus*"), a position of great honor and testifying to R. Gershon's rising fame. Though Israel Baalshem might have known his future wife from the days when she lived in Kutov, the *Shivḥei* gives us no information on this point, and the marriage is described as having been settled between the father and Israel.[38] One has to bear in mind that this happened in a cultural environment, blissfully untouched by the romantic idea of love matches,[39] in which marital arrangements generally reflected either existing social ties or social aspirations. In spite of the strong opposition of R. Gershon, the brother of the bride, Israel Baalshem managed to impose himself on this family of the spiritual upper class by force of a betrothal contract signed by R. Gershon's father, who had since died. R. Gershon, with whom the divorced sister lived, was anxious to prevent by every possible means the penetration into the family of Israel Baalshem, notwithstanding the fact that his sister's value in the marriage market was substantially deflated owing to the fact of her being a divorcee, and that he would have had to put up with a second-rate candidate in any case. Israel Baalshem eventually succeeded in contriving this marriage, which, however, did not give him the social and spiritual acceptance he might have looked for. R. Gershon tried to persuade his sister to divorce her husband and, in spite of their new family relationship, he himself did not mitigate his ruthless scorn and ridicule of Israel. Nevertheless, from his correspondence with his brother-in-law during the last phase of his life in Palestine, it would appear that eventually Israel did succeed in his ambition to be recognized by R. Gershon. But that was long after the Kutov period of R. Gershon's life.

The only member of the Kutov circle with whom Israel succeeded in establishing friendly contact was R. Moshe, the head of the rabbinical court. Furthermore, we are told that R. Moshe lent him a copy of the *Zohar* at his request.[40] This ambitious choice of reading matter only provoked the scorn of R. Gershon, but R. Moshe gave Israel his protective blessing against R. Gershon's insults and also made him a present of the book. Whatever we think of the authenticity of the details, it is certain that R. Moshe favored Israel Baalshem. According to the *Shivḥei*, Israel was able to detect by prophetic insight a faulty *mezuzah* on the doorpost of the synagogue in Kutov and this finally secured R. Moshe's recognition of his pneumatic faculties.[41]

One does not know what religious issues were discussed in the pre-Hasidic Kutov circle nor does one have the means of comparing the views of the individual members and of establishing whether they displayed that uniformity found later in the Hasidic groups. The case of Israel Baalshem would imply the contrary. Far from an authoritarian imposition by a leader of a ruling on the attitude to be taken toward Israel, we find a variety of attitudes prevailing toward him. This can only strengthen the view expressed above that the circle had no leader holding the position occupied by the *Ṣaddikim* of Hasidic groups. The dominating influence of a charismatic leader is absent here and people retain the right to personal convictions. There is thus a sharp distinction between the mental climate of this pre-Hasidic circle and that of the Hasidic ones.

It is apparent that Israel Baalshem was anxious to be accepted by pre-Hasidic circles of the time. While he met with disappointment in the Kutov group, he was more successful in Miedzyborz, where he eventually settled and where he lived until his death. This town too had a pre-Hasidic circle, two figures of which are known to us by name: R. Ze'ev Kutsis and R. David Porkes. The *Shivḥei's* hint that as an exorcist Israel did not at first command the respect of the town's pre-Hasidim[42] indicates the difficulties he met there in his endeavor to penetrate into this circle and to be recognized by it. But, unlike his parallel attempts at Kutov, his efforts were finally crowned with success.

Through the obscure hints and scattered episodes of the *Shivḥei* we can thus dimly perceive the contours of a circle of pneumatics in pre-Hasidism that was probably characteristic of the atmosphere of others that formed the background to the early career of Israel Baalshem.

NOTES

1. B Dinaburg, "The Beginnings of Hasidism," pp. 186–87; G. Scholem, "The Two Earliest Testimonies on the Relations between Hasidic Groups and Baal Shem Tov", *Tarbiṣ*, 20 (1950): 239.

2. Ed. Horodecki, pp. 56–57.

3. For his radical ideal of continuous contemplation (*devekuth*) and its technique, see my article, "The Beginnings of Hasidism," pp. 60–65. Being a wealthy tax-farmer, he could afford to pay a weekly salary to a man to be on constant attendance on him when he was among people. The man's task was to remind him with a hint of the duty of uninterrupted contemplation, a duty which he performed in a fashion characteristic of Hasidic piety, even during social intercourse, see *Toledoth Ya'akov Yosef*, p. 186a. On being asked if it was possible to occupy oneself with religious contemplation while engaged in business, Naḥman is recorded to have replied that if it was possible to concentrate on business matters during prayer in the synagogue, the reverse should be possible too (ibid., 17b). Another example of the sardonic wit of this remarkable personality, directed against attacks on the new type of religiosity, is to be found in *Toledoth* 44a, *Shivḥei* 57b.

The challenge of how to achieve *devekuth* during everyday occupations was one of the most vexed problems of early Hasidism, see G. Scholem, "Devekuth, or Communion with God," *The Review of Religion*, 15 (1950): 115 ff. and my "Beginnings of Hasidism," p. 60 ff. I wish to avail myself of this opportunity to suggest here some likely literary sources for the Hasidic ideal of *devekuth* in the course of everyday affairs. It was certainly influenced by chapters 51 and 52 of vol. 3 of *Moreh Nevukhim*, which describe the life of the Patriarchs and Moses in terms of continual *devekuth*, even while busy with profane tasks. The preoccupation of Hasidim, living not later than in the third generation, with these chapters of the *Moreh Nevukhim* can be illustrated by the fact that an anonymous Hasidic anthology bearing the title *Iggeret ha-Kodesh* (s.a.s.l.) incorporated major parts of these chapters (along with other classical texts dealing with *devekuth*, such as passages selected from *Sefer Ḥaredim*). Further, I would like to draw attention to *Shenei Luḥot ha-Berit* by Isaiah Horovitz (Amsterdam, 1698, p. 120a), which also contains a lengthy discussion on the problem to become so central in Hasidism of practicing *devekuth* in conjunction with profane work and arrives at positions similar to the Hasidic ones. Perhaps this section of Horovitz's book is the first serious deviation in Cabbalistic literature from the classical method of contemplation as a leisure-time occupation. It goes without saying that Horovitz's standard work was current in these circles and early Hasidim were no doubt acquainted with it.

4. Quoted by Dinaburg, *l.c.*, p. 187, from Emden's *Petaḥ Enayim* 14b. Emden is accusing Naḥman of Sabbatianism in *Hitavkuth* (Lemberg, 1877), p. 80b. See S. Dubnow, *Toledoth ha-Ḥasiduth*, 1 (1930), p. 102.

5. See B. Dinaburg, *loc. cit.*, p. 91, and Weiss, *loc. cit.*, pp. 49–56.

6. *Shivḥei*, p. 56.

7. הרב המפורסם ר׳ נחמן מקאסוב...: והיה שולח לעיר אל בני החבורה קדישא לכאו״א [לכל אחד ואחד] זה שצריכין לתקן בזה העולם מחטאיו והיה הכל אמת. עד שחרה להם מאד על הנביאות כי היה תנאי ביניהם שלא יתנבא שום אחד מהם, וראו לשלוח [אליו] אחד מהם לשאול מה זה (p. 56)

8. On this type of "prophet" see G. Scholem, *Major Trends in Jewish Mysticism* (1946^2), p. 334; idem, *Ha-tenuah ha-Shabtha'ith be-Polin*, in the volume "*Beth Israel be-Polin*," p. 49; idem, The Two Earliest Testimonies etc., pp. 238–40; and *Sabbatai Ṣevi* (London, 1973). See index, s.v. "Prophecy."

9. The term occurs throughout the anti-Hasidic polemical literature in which the *Ṣaddikim* are ironically called *nevi'im* (prophets) or contemptuously *nevi'ei sheker* (false prophets). Dinaburg in *Ṣion*, 10 (1945): 155–56 (*Be-mifneh ha-Doroth*, pp. 187–88) has

collected many such instances to which one could add more, e.g. in the text of *Shever Posh'im* as emended and quoted by S. Dubnow, *Toledoth ha-Ḥasiduth*, 3:356, or the expression *nevi sheker* in the ban of Vilna (1772) as applied to R. Issar, correctly translated by Jost, *Geschichte des Judenthums und seiner Sekten*, 3:(1859): 193: "ein Gelehrter, der sich als Prophet geberdete." The conspicuous absence of any reference to this term in the Hasidic literature is no doubt due to the bad reputation of the word *navi* and has to be regarded as apologetical silence.

10. The author of the *Shivḥei* himself notes (p. 7) as a typical feature of the Sabbatian movement the prevalence of ecstatics (*meshugga'im*) who torture themselves during the reading of the Torah, and "reveal to the people their sins and state about themselves their own past sins and for which sin they are in transmigration." The approach of the Hasidic writer to the Sabbatian movement in this context is most remarkable. The author complains about the decline of miracles, which he connects with the decline of faith (*emunah*), a word which, if taken as a technical term, stands for the Sabbatian heresy itself! Far from complaining about the heresy itself, the author is looking at his own generation rather with pity, because it is not privileged to witness the admirable fruits of great faith. The writer appears not in the least embarrassed by the fact that this high tide of faith was connected—in his own opinion too—with the heresy of Sabbatianism. His admiration of and positive attitude to at least the Sabbatian period, if not to Sabbatianism itself—a kind of "those were the days!" attitude—becomes here surprisingly patent. See the expressions:

"וגם אני נתתי אל לבי כי מאז הייתי לאיש ועד זקנה קרוב לשיבה שאני רואה בעו"ה [בעוונותינו הרבים] מדי יום ביום נתמעטו הניסים ונסתלקו המופתים. כי בימים קדמונים אירע לפעמים etc. והיה בעת שהתעוררו כת שבתי צבי ימ"ש [ימח שמו] ... וגם בימיו היו משוגעים שהיו מקיזים א"ע [את עצמם] באבנים בשעת קריאת התורה והיו מגלים לאנשים חטאם והיו אומרים על נפשם חטאם באיזה חטא הם בכף הקלע .etc ומחמת כל אלו דברים היו רבים חוזרים בתשובה והאמונה היתה מתחזקת בלב כל איש ישראל. ועכשיו בעוה"ר נתמעטו הצדיקים וחשכו הרואות בארובות. ובעו"ה נפלה האמונה עד מאוד וכמה מינות נזרקה בעולם."

One wonders what contemporary heresy the author of the *Shivḥei* has in mind after having called the times of Shabbetai Ṣevi the days of great faith. Note that except for the obligatory formula **ימ"ש** after the name of Shabbetai Ṣevi, he makes no derogatory remarks about the Sabbatian heresy. See Scholem *Shetei Iggaroth me-Ereṣ Yisrael* in *Tarbiṣ*, 25 (1956): 438, n. 35.

11. *Ṣion* 9:187 (*Bemifneh*, etc., p. 161):

"רבי נחמן מקוסוב שעמד בראשה של חבורה קדישא"

12. *Shivḥei*, p. 57:

וכששמעו הדבורים היוצאים מפיו היו מתוקים מדבש ונופת צופים היו נהנים ושותקים... ולאחר קדיש דרבנן התחיל הודו קודם ברוך שאמר

This order of prayers is indicative of the Sepharadi rite. Similarly the hymn *Ha-adereth ve-ha-emunah*, which in the Ashkenazi rite is sung only on the High Festivals, was sung by Naḥman on Sabbath morning in accordance with the Sepharadi rite. His enthusiastic manner of praying (*Shivḥei*, p. 57) foreshadows the Hasidic practice, but is also in the tradition of Sabbatian groups. See Scholem, *Beth Israel*, p. 64; idem, The Two Earliest Testimonies etc., pp. 237–38.

13. Ibid.: ואמר המוכיח אליו [אל ר' נחמן] בזה"ל [בזה הלשון] משוגע ר' נחמן... והשיב לו ר' נחמן אתה המשוגע

Naḥman does not appear to be happy about the epithet *meshugga*, which might have been originally given to him for his ecstatic nature; see G. Scholem, ibid., p. 239.

14. Among them R. Moshe, the head of the rabbinical court at Kutov and the ritual slaughterer (*shoḥet*) who remains unnamed.

15. *Shivḥei*, ibid.: היה תנאי ביניהם

16. One of the participants could have recited the evening prayer and kindled the light. This is the accepted practice in synagogues on the termination of the Sabbath, and

on this must have rested the much later Galician type of *Se'udah Shelishith* as described by T. Ysander, *Studien zum Beštschen Hasidismus* (Uppsala, 1933), p. 316: "Das Torasagen . . . findet beim Belzer Rebben zweimal bei der dritten Mahlzeit statt, nach dem Einbruch der Dunkelheit und nach dem Anzünden des Lichtes. Man spricht auch von der dunklen und der hellen Tora."

17. *Shivḥei*, ibid.

שאתה יודע המעשה שישבתי סעודה שלישית אצל הרב ר׳ משה אב״ד דק״ק קוטיב והיו מאחרים בתוך הלילה והשוחט היה מאנשי החבורה וישב ג״כ שם. ובא קצב אחד ושמו ליב המכונה ליב גליץ וקרא להשוחט לשחוט פעם אחת ושתים ושלש ולא רצה השוחט לילך כי תאב לשמע דברי אלהים חיים. וזה הי׳ תמיד שיחתם איך לעבוד ה׳. וכשראה הקצב שהשוחט אינו רוצה לילך ולהפרד משם, אמר בלבו אבא ואבלבל אותם ויתפללו ערבית. וילך השוחט לשחוט, וכן עשה. וכשהביא נר כעס עליו הרב והחרים אותו ומת הקצב.

18. P. 26: מיד באותו שבת באו אליו לסעודה שלישית ואמר תורה זו

19. P. 111: פעם אחת ישב הרב הבעש״ט בסעודה שלישית והיה טרוד מאד בעמקות המחשבה ולא אמר תורה בסעודה שלישית כלל, מה שהיה לפלא בעיני התלמידים.

The expression טרוד מאד בעמקות המחשבה indicates in the *Shivḥei* deep contemplation, see p. 108. והנה הבעש״ט מהלך בחצר בהכ״נ [בית הכנסת] אנה ואנה וטרוד מאד בעמקות המחשבה.

Similarly p. 18: פעם אחת נכנס בעומק ההתבוננות: והיה הולך אל ההרים . . . וכשראו אותו מרחוק שהוא הולך לסוף ההר בעומק המחשבה, אמרו . . .

20. *Shivḥei*, p. 108.

פעם א׳ בסעודת ג׳ אמר הרב [בעל שם] דברי תורה ונתעכבו כמה שעות בלילה.

21. In all these instances I assume, of course, that the *Shivḥei* is not a late fabrication invented just before its publication in 1815, but that it reflects essentially the way of life of the Hasidic movement during the lifetime of its founder.

22. *Toledoth Ya'akov Yosef* (1780 ed.), p. 10b. Only if we assume that the communal nature of the third meal had already been firmly established could he have written the following words.

כוונת האסיפת אנשים והחיבור בסעודה ג׳ שיתחברו וילוו עלי ליחד ג׳ בחי׳ הנ״ל שהיא עלי בסוד אז תתענג על ה׳ והבן . . . כי ע״י הזווג נמשך השפע להשפיע משא״כ [מה שאין כן] כשיושב בסעודה זו בפ״ע [בפני עצמו] אז עשה שבתך חול וכו׳.

23. S Maimon, *Lebensgeschichte*, ed. Fromer (1911), pp. 202 ff. The meal described by Maimon was held on the Sabbath day and not on Friday night; Dubnow, *Toledoth*, 1:86, says it was probably the third meal.

24. See *Ẓemir 'Ariṣim ve-ḥarbot Ṣurim* (1772), last page: בנידון שלש סעודות בשבת, וגם שארי סעודות שעושין לעצמם כל בני הקהלה, חלילה להזמין אליהן מן אנשי הכת:

25. In the manuscript copy of *Shever Posh'im* in Dubnow, *Toledoth ha-Ḥasidut*, 1:96, n. 3: מוסרים וחדושים שדורשים [החסידים]לפי דרכם בתורה בכל פרשה בסעודה שלישית בשבת.

26. See Dubnow, ibid., 3:353 and 362–64. See also T. Ysander, *Studien*, p. 321: "In gewisser Hinsicht ist das Torasagen der Höhepunkt der Mahlzeit"; p. 322: "Sowohl durch den Inhalt als auch durch den traditiongebundenen Platz bei den Mahlzeiten gehört das Torasagen zu den Gebräuchen, die in der religionsgeschichtlichen Charakteristik des Hasidismus beachtet werden müssen." In the later developments of Hasidism the third meal lost its exclusive function as the only time for Torah.

27. *Shivḥei*, p. 56: ולא רצה... לילך, כי תאב לשמוע דברי אלהים חיים, וזה הי׳ תמיד שיחתם איך לעבוד ה׳.

28. Ibid., pp. 22–23, 123.

29. Ibid., p. 22. A. Heschel, "R. Gershon Kutover", *HUCA* 23 (1950–51), part 2, p. 18, makes him the leader of the group.

30. Ibid., p. 123.

31. Ibid., p. 23.

32. Ibid., p. 55. See Weiss, *Ṣion*, loc. cit.

33. *Ṣion*, loc. cit.

34. On this figure see I. Halpern, *Ha-Aliyoth ha-Rishonoth shel ha-Ḥasidim le-Ereṣ Yisrael* (Jerusalem–Tel Aviv, 1946), pp. 11–16; A. Heschel, loc. cit., pp. 17–71, G. Scholem, *Shetei Iggaroth* etc. in *Tarbiṣ* 25 (1956): 429–33.

35. I Halpern, *Ha-Aliyoth*, pp. 11–12. On ascetic figures among the pre-Hasidim see Scholem, *MTJM*, 1946^2, p. 331.

36. *Shivḥei*, p. 22.

37. Curiously enough, Heschel seems to take the story of the *Shivḥei* about Israel Baalshem's "hiding" his great erudition at its face value (loc. cit., p. 20).

38. *Shivḥei*, pp. 16–17.

39. See J. Katz, "Marriage and Sex-life in the Late Middle Ages," (Hebrew) *Ṣion* 10:21 ff.

40. *Shivḥei*, p. 24.

41. Ibid. An elaborated parallel to this story with the scene transferred to Brody is to be found in *Shivḥei*, p. 20. In this novelistic version R. Gershon appears as the head of the rabbinical court in Brody, which he never was (as proved by Halpern, *Ha-Aliyoth*, p. 13, notes 13 and 15), while the other rabbinic figure, corresponding to R. Moshe of the Kutov version, remains an anonymous "rabbi of the community."

42. Ibid., p. 25.

Contemplative Mysticism and "Faith" in Hasidic Piety*

To the memory of Julius Guttmann

The general structure of Hasidism is usually seen by the student of Jewish mysticism as a uniform pattern. Nothing mars the uniformity of the picture of this last religious revival in eighteenth-century Judaism in Eastern Europe; at the most, only slight differences within the same movement are distinguished, differences that may be described as "various paths in the same worship," which diverge from the central unity without breaking the unity and the uniformity of the movement itself. Almost all research presupposes the theory of the unity and uniformity of Hasidism—the theory that the whole Hasidic religious outlook is dominated by an essential unity, which cannot be called in question.

It seems to me that this general view of Hasidism is open to serious doubt.

A certain degree of uniformity can be seen in the realm of folklore and in some forms of religious life. A common frame is to be found in the ecstatic prayers or in other customs shared by all the trends of Hasidism. But it is obvious that such matters are not sufficient to argue a unity of ideas. Both from the theological point of view and as far as religious values are concerned, this standardization of the Hasidic schools and their doctrines must be rejected. The postulated artificial unity and uniformity disappear when we look for their verification in the theoretical literature of Hasidic authors.

* This paper is a revised version of the lecture delivered by the author in August 1947 at the Congress of Jewish Studies convened by the Hebrew University in Jerusalem.

I shall attempt here to describe two trends of the Hasidic movement, which have assumed a clear and distinctive outline. The two trends are diametrically opposed to each other. Even in the controversies of the "Ṣaddikim" (the Hasidic spiritual leaders), which seem to have a personal basis, the theoretical motifs can be often clearly discerned.

The aim of this study is to trace the two different types of piety that are to be found in Hasidism—the mystical, contemplative piety and the piety of faith. On the distinction between these two general types of piety is based some of the finest of the German *Religionswissenschaft*, such as Heiler's book *Das Gebet.*[1] These two types of piety not only *differ* from each other, but are *opposed* to each other; they form two distinct categories of religious phenomena and as such are of great value for the understanding of Hasidism.

The present inquiry will not be concerned with the origins of the two types; it will be a study of the contrast in their main features. It is worth mentioning that the Hasidic literature itself contains remarks that illustrate the characteristics of the various schools and trends of Hasidism in terms of this contrast.

It seems correct to say that these two types of piety are not represented merely by two classical examples in the theoretical literature of Hasidism, but that the entire Hasidic literature, as far as theory is concerned, may be divided into two clear-cut types—the mystical, contemplative Hasidism and the Hasidism of faith, of *emunah*. It is not my intention to trace the historical development of the two types within the Hasidic thought, but to describe both sectors, each type as exemplified by an extreme case. Mystical, contemplative Hasidism will be illustrated by a description of the teaching of Rabbi Dov Baer (the "Great Maggid of Mesritz") and of his disciple, who developed the master's system, Rabbi Shneur Zalman of Ladi, the founder of the Ḥabad movement. The second type, the Hasidic piety of faith, of *emunah*, will be illustrated by the teaching of Rabbi Naḥman of Brazlav.

It is important to remember that Rabbi Dov Baer and Rabbi Naḥman of Brazlav are extreme examples and representatives of whole schools or trends. This is what makes them "typical." The characteristic features of Hasidism of the mystical, contemplative type will, thus, be found not only in the teachings of the

Great Maggid and Ḥabad, but also in some central ideas of Baalshem Tov, the founder of Hasidism. This accounts for the fact that the mystical, contemplative type predominates in Hasidic thought. On the other hand, I have chosen R. Nahman of Brazlav as typical of the other type of piety, because of his keen penetration into problems of *emunah*, faith. Other representatives of this type are Rabbi Menaḥem Mendel of Rimanov, R. Menaḥem Mendel of Kotzk, R. Alexander Susskind Ha-Kohen,[2] and R. Zevi Elimelekh of Dinov. In confining this study to the representative examples of the Great Maggid of Mesritz and Rabbi Naḥman of Brazlav, I scarcely need say that they are not pure types—such in fact do not exist; or that they do not exhaust the complex variety of historical phenomena.

1. When we consider the concept of deity in the two systems of the Great Maggid and Rabbi Naḥman, the difference between them at once becomes clear. This difference can be defined as the contrast between an impersonal pantheistic concept of deity (the Great Maggid) and a concept of a personal and voluntaristic God (Brazlav).

The scholarly controversy of the last quarter of a century concerning the pantheistic character of the Hasidic teaching is well known. Some scholars tried to mitigate the pantheism of the early Hasidic texts by explaining it as pan-entheism. It must be asked, however, whether there actually exists a Hasidic doctrine that teaches the existence of God *in* the world. Is it not rather, according to Hasidic teaching, that not God himself but only His divine power emanates into the world? This particular aspect of the problem is beyond the scope of the present study. It can only be solved by an exact analysis of the various Hasidic systems, since the character of the pantheistic doctrine in each of them differs very largely from one another. The pantheistic attitude of Hasidic thought cannot, however, be denied, and is actually generally accepted; the Ḥabad system, for instance, is very close to a-cosmism,[3] the denial of the reality of the cosmos.

The conception of God's immanence in the world is to be found, however, only in the mystical-contemplative type of Hasidism. God is conceived here not only as present *in* the world, but as impersonal too. These two facets of the concept, though not necessarily connected in the various forms of contemplative mysticism, are generally linked together. They form the characteristic feature of the mystical-contemplative Hasidism, as of many mystical philosophies. The theology of the mystic Rabbi Dov of Mesritz, the Great Maggid, is not based on the three moments of Creation, Revelation on Mount Sinai, and Redemption by the Messiah. His experience of God is based on the perception of the divine essence which is present in, and pervades, all things. R. Dov's God is not the Creator *ex nihilo* whose historical Revelation is unique and whose Redemption will come in the messianic period—such conception of God is not prominent in the Great Maggid's mystical piety. It seems to me unnecessary to point out that this position implies no dogmatic denial of those principles of Jewish faith. While not denying the personality of God, the contemplative mystic experiences, not a personal God, but that "dynamic essence" (*hiyyuth*), that "divine spark" (*niṣṣoṣ elohi*) which dwell in all worlds and in all beings, in a real ontological sense. This conception is not identical with that of the Talmudic-Midrashic *Shekhinah*, which is divine immanence of a personal character.[4] The Hasidic *hiyyuth* has in the school of the Great Maggid the definite sense of dynamic pantheism, expressed through the originally neoplatonic, later Cabbalistic, doctrine of emanation. Even if some traces of a personal conception can still be found in the process of emanation, it is quite clear that the result of emanation, the divine, *hiyyuth*, which is the object of the religious experience, is definitely impersonal. In the Ḥabad system the "impersonality" of God becomes even more accentuated.

If the mystical theology of the Great Maggid and of Ḥabad can be formulated in a series of terms such as: immanence, pantheism (pan-entheism), impersonal God, emanation; the theology of Brazlav can be expressed in a series of almost opposite terms such as: irrational or rather antirational theism, transcendence of God, and a personal and voluntaristic God who leads the world towards Redemption in a paradoxical way according to His absolute Will. While the basic experience of Rabbi Dov is that of God as the very essence of the world and the ontological source of it, the basic experience of Brazlav is that of a voluntaristic God whose will is anti-rational, and sometimes even antinomian. Hence the full concept of a personal God becomes the basic characteristic of Rabbi Naḥman of Brazlav.

The whole relation of God to the world changes fundamentally as soon as God is conceived not as dwelling in the world, as pantheism does, but as ruling it from above by absolute will. God's relation to the world is that of a sovereign creator who rules His creation absolutely. According to Brazlav God's power is unlimited and He bequeaths life to all being, whereas to the contemplative mystic God is the hidden life of all being. According to Brazlav God's decrees and deeds excite but wonder and amazement in man. As against this the Ḥabad motto is characteristically "the divine thing is very close to you." In the mystical, contemplative conception the frontiers remain open between the "above" and the "below," whereas in the school of Brazlav there is no such mystical "confusion." God is God, the world is the world, and neither kingdom invades its neighbor.

2. Such are the differing conceptions of God which derive from a pantheistic view on the one hand, and from a paradoxical theism on the other. Other, no less important, consequences follow from these contrasting positions. Pantheistic mysticism is intrinsically monistic. If the whole universe is full of God, the realm of the metaphysical evil, the realm of impurity and *kelipah* has no place in it. The strong monistic tendencies in R. Dov's doctrine are not the accidental result of historic development; they are consequential and self-consistent. Indeed, the extreme monism of the Ḥabad doctrine extinguishes all dualistic tendencies in its religious world-picture. The changes that have occurred in Hasidism as compared with the mystical Lurianic world picture, are easily recognisable, since the frame of the Lurianic Cabbala with its sharp dualistic tendencies was retained, as the formal medium of thought and expression, in the Hasidic theory. But in the latter, the Lurianic terminology has changed its meaning; in the course of this semantic change the Lurianic concepts have lost all their dualistic poignancy.[5]

Let us take, for example, the Lurianic concept of *Ṣimṣum*, or the "self-withdrawal" of God. This concept, originally formulated in order to avoid even the remotest possibility of a pantheistic view, became in Hasidism, through a new interpretation given to it by the Great Maggid, the very floodgate for pantheism. In the Lurianic Cabbala *Ṣimṣum* originally indicated God's withdrawal from the universe,[6] while in the world picture of the Great Maggid, it indicates God's dwelling within the universe. Furthermore, in the Lurianic Cabbala, with its dualistic tendencies, evil as a metaphysical reality has its own realm, whereas in the pantheistic monism of the Great Maggid the reality of evil is totally annulled. Good and evil, holiness and unholiness are no more diametrically opposed to each other, but become "degrees" of being in the one world of divine emanation. Evil is but the lowest degree of the "good," and sin may become the throne of "excellence."

It is altogether different in the Brazlav system. In it the dualism of the Cabbala, and especially of the Lurianic Cabbala, becomes again alive with even greater intensity and vitality. The evil powers carve out for themselves an autonomous demonic realm. The anonymous demonic powers of the Lurianic Cabbala find now in Brazlav a point of reference, the Devil, who is conceived as a living personality, full of reality, not as the personification of anonymous, evil powers.

3. The further point of this analysis of the two Hasidic trends deals with the problem of the relation between God and man. This problem is concerned with the "what," and with the "how" of this relation.

Regarding the "what" of this relation, the crucial question is: What is in the scale of religious values the supreme value which determines man's life? The contemplative, mystical systems of Hasidism answer this question by the concepts of contemplation, *devekuth* and ecstasy *bittul ha-yesh* (Baalshem, the Maggid and Ḥabad). In the system of Brazlav faith, *emunah* is placed at the summit of all religious values. The mystical way of contemplation and ecstasy, and the life of faith, are two different and even opposite categories of religious existence and religious consciousness. They seldom mix with each other as the history of religions clearly shows, except in the ordinary unreflecting religious life when they appear as supplementary to each other.

Ecstasy, as well as contemplation, has at its basic assumption the consciousness of a special nearness of God to man. I have already mentioned that this nearness is theologically established in the systems of the Great Maggid and of Ḥabad. The very act of contemplation and of ectasy following upon it are based on a direct experience of the Divine. There is no gulf between God and man. On the contrary: a direct bridge unites them.

The main characteristic of faith, *emunah*, is an "indirect" way in a special sense. The open gulf between the believer and the object of his belief is overcome, according to Brazlav, by "faith" in dangerous paradoxes. The gulf between the divine and the human realms appears not only in the ontological transcendence of God (He is not "within" the world), but also in His "logical" transcendence (He is paradoxical), and these two kinds of transcendence are by no means identical. The Brazlav school puts thus its highest religious value, *emunah*, faith, on the edge of a knife: faith is paradoxical and the believer must hold to it, not by an intellectual act of understanding, but by the sacrifice of his intellect; this amounts to an "existential" struggle and a permanent logical crisis, since man is confronted with the paradoxical God and the paradoxical *Ṣaddik*.[7]

It is not surprising that subtle discussions as to the genuineness of ecstasy should predominate in the Ḥabad system, and that faith became almost to be considered a biological fact.[8] Such discussions turn round the criterion of the "divine" ecstasy, as opposed to the artificially stimulated "devilish" ecstasy. All this is characteristic of the special interest which mystics of all ages and all religions take in their inner life and the analysis of their ecstatic experiences. It is therefore not accidental, but a corollary of their underlying ideas, that the crucial problem in the Ḥabad school is the certainty of the mystical experience and in the Brazlav school, the certainty of faith.

4. The other radical difference between the contemplative and ecstatic way of the mystics and the way of faith comes to light in the "how" of the relation between God and man. In the spiritual exercises of the Great Maggid and his school the personal relationship with God is lacking. The Divine is conceived as something impersonal. The divine essence, the *hiyyuth*, which dwells in all things is a-personal. Indeed, the contemplative mystic renounces even his own personality, since he aims through the complicated technique of contemplation at attaining a state of ecstasy in which the "extinction of existence," *bittul ha-yesh*, the extinction of personality in the self-annihilation of consciousness, is achieved.

"Faith" in the Brazlav school is opposed to this impersonal way. "Faith" is here considered as the relation of one personality to another. The assertion of the personality on the human as well as on the divine side is carried to its extreme. Not only the duty of "faith" in God, but also, and even more so, the duty of "faith" in the *Ṣaddik* is inculcated. Such "faith" is by definition essentially personal. This personal character of faith reaches its peak with the demand for a paradoxical faith in the "true *Ṣaddik*" (*Ṣaddik ha-emeth*), Rabbi Naḥman himself. The religious life in the Brazlav school is thus built upon the "life in faith," upon the relation between "I" and "Thou." The lack of this "I-Thou" relation and, indeed, its extirpation, characterises the opposite mystical contemplative trend.

5. The essential difference of attitude in the two trends of Hasidism is fully reflected in the opposing conception of the function of prayer. The essence of a religious attitude can be generally found in prayer. In the school of the Great Maggid and Ḥabad, prayer serves as an occasion for, and as the means of, contemplation and ecstasy. Prayer becomes here a kind of special vehicle of the main contents of the contemplative life.

In the Brazlav school prayer is conceived, to the contrary, as a "dialogue between creature and Creator" (*siḥah veno le-ven kono*)—a dialogue between a personal human being and a personal divine being. It is no longer an occasion for ecstasy leading to self-annihilation. The Brazlav prayerbook[9] bears witness in all its details to this conception of the nature and the function of prayer.

The difference between the two schools is even more accentuated in the contents of prayer which display the antagonism between the personal and impersonal attitudes on a new level. According to the theory of the Great Maggid which originated in some sayings of Baalshem Tov, and further back in the Cabbala, no one should pray for his own particular, personal needs. The abolition of the worshiper's personality begins thus in the very act of contemplative prayer from which all reference to personal needs is eliminated, and reaches its culminating point in the ecstasy when the personal consciousness becomes totally annihilated. The worshiper's desire to annul his personality and to disregard his private needs, is typical of all contemplative mystics. The contemplative, mystical school of Hasidism demands the elimination of the worshiper's personality in a twofold way—the extinction of personal consciousness in ecstasy, and the elimination of all reference to personal needs.

When the worshiper prays, not for his own needs, nor for the needs of the community, but "for the needs of the divine *Shekhinah*"—a closed circle, not an arc, of relation is thus established between him who speaks and Him who listens.

In the Brazlav school, on the contrary, the worshiper asks in his prayer for God's deliberate intervention in the world; he asks for miracles, both "hidden" and "visible." The Brazlav prayer, therefore, always originates from a given situation and refers to a concrete state of misery: the personal note is never eliminated. All private matters may become the subject of prayer. In the "dialogue between creature and Creator" the personal wish is not submerged in the higher, divine pattern.

6. The antagonism between the two conceptions comes also to light in the theoretical sphere dealing with the nature of man and his power. An optimistic anthropology, a positive assessment of man's powers and his metaphysical situation as to the possibilities available for him for perfection and holiness stand against a pessimistic anthropology and a negative assessment of man's metaphysical situation. The contemplative, mystical conception of the Great Maggid overestimates man; the anthropological despair of the Brazlav school underestimates man's powers. There is in some of R. Naḥman's allegories a striking expression of the fallen metaphysical state of man.[10] We find in them, as it were, an echo of modern polemics between the philosophical anthropology of idealism and that of dialectical theology.

The metaphysical remoteness of man from the divine proclaimed by the Brazlav school is derived from its theological conception of the extreme transcendence of God. The theological conception and the anthropological conception represent the two sides of one and the same coin. The essential human remoteness from the divine characterises man's status and is the result of his original sin. No deeper difference in religious consciousness could be conceived than that between the optimistic atmosphere of the Great Maggid's and the Ḥabad schools concerning man's high possibilities (his "divine soul" becomes the dwelling place of the *Shekhinah* in the act of ecstasy), and the atmosphere of pessimistic teachings of the Brazlav school in regard to the fallen nature of man. Far from asserting that the human soul is divine, the highest conception the

Brazlavic anthropology has reached is represented by the notion that there are some "good points," *nekudoth tovoth*, in every man.

7. The problem of man's status in the world leads directly to the problem of the nature of sin. The mystic, contemplative trend dilutes the nature of sin in a general idealistic frame. In Hasidic mysticism, sin has lost its depth from the moment that it is admitted that religious enthusiasm is but the transformation of the "will to evil" (*yeṣer ha-ra*).[11] It is very instructive to compare the dilution of sin achieved in the mystic, contemplative school with the tragic conception of sin in the Brazlav school. According to the latter school, every sin committed by man is an echo of the fathomless primordial sin, which dwells in man owing to his very existence as a human being.[12] The specific antagonism between enthusiastic idealism and theology of crisis reveals itself again in the concepts of sin of the Great Maggid and the Brazlav schools.

8. The opposition of the two schools can be clearly seen in their different attitude to the essential Hasidic phenomenon, the personality of the *Ṣaddik*, and, in general, to the institution of charismatic leadership. While the school of the Great Maggid, and especially Ḥabad, does not overstress the function of the *Ṣaddik* and of his status as an extraordinary being, we find in Brazlav a special theory of the *Ṣaddik* and his vocation. According to this theory there is but one *Ṣaddik*, the exceptional personality, the unique hidden leader of the universe, who is the "paradoxical" Messiah and in whose hands are the keys of the whole cosmos. This is Rabbi Naḥman himself. The esoteric doctrines of Brazlav teachings have not yet been made public by their followers, but it seems that they contain the doctrine of the divine nature of the *Ṣaddik*-Messiah. The "paradoxical" belief in the *Ṣaddik* is by its nature indirect, in contrast with the direct relation prevailing in the ecstatic experience of the contemplative mystic. The direct ecstatic experience of God in the contemplative mystical trend of Hasidism leaves, in fact, no room for the function of the *Ṣaddik*. But in the Brazlav teaching which admits no ecstatic experience, the theory of Ṣaddikism appears in the shape of a theory of mediation.

9. The last point of our analysis of these two Hasidic trends concerns the problem of eschatology, that is, the expectation of the Messianic redemption. Again, the differences between the

two trends are very poignant. The contemplative, mystical trend abolishes the intense interest in the Messiah and his collective redemption. No Messianic yearning exists in the mystical tenets of the Maggid. This is a necessary corollary of his original attitude: the contemplative religious experience—the central point of this type of piety—is a personal, private experience and it is not connected with history. Since the mystical experience is not essentially based on the historical event called Revelation on Mount Sinai, it is not related either to the post-historical event called Redemption. The well-attested mystical indifference to all history is fully confirmed by the contemplative, mystical trend of Hasidism. The lack of all Messianic tension is a characteristic feature of its contemplative piety.

In the Brazlav school, on the contrary, the main emphasis is laid on the paradoxical ways of Redemption. Rabbi Naḥman himself thought that his own soul was the soul of the Messiah, and he hoped at one time that the final Redemption would come during his lifetime. This is the point of crystallisation of the two basic categories of Brazlavic existence: "faith" born from despair converges at the eschatological point with the "hope" born from despair. Both categories tend toward Messianic redemption; no one should despair to see the final redemption, even now in a state which is beyond despair.

The picture of the future redeemed world is again consistent in both schools. The Great Maggid and Ḥabad are extremely parsimonious in giving details of the changes that will take place in the days of the Messiah, and there is in their teachings no trace of a revolutionary conception of the Messianic future. This contemplative mystical school does not, of course, deny the Messianic redemption in a dogmatic sense, but it never describes Redemption as something fundamentally different from the present state of the world.

On the other hand, the school of Rabbi Naḥman hopes for radical change in the future, which will fulfil the most intimate yearnings of the believer. In the present world, faith is opposed to reason, but in the "world to come," in the Messianic era, faith will become reason. There will be complete identity between them. In the present world we do believe despite all evidence, but in the next world rational evidence will support the believer.

The world of faith will become the world of reason, and the paradoxical faith of today the rationalism of the Messianic tomorrow. There can be no other expectation for those who, like the followers of the Brazlav school, feed their faith on a religious paradox.

We may sum up the results of this brief survey of Hasidism thus: there is in it no conformity of ideas on any basic religious question. There is, on the contrary, a dichotomy of directions that find expression in two theoretical systems: one direction is that of the mystical, contemplative type with an idealistic and semipantheistic outlook. The other is that of the piety of faith, which lives in an atmosphere of "existentialism."

No difference more fundamental than that between these two schools of thought can exist within a religious movement. To present Hasidism as a uniform movement is to take no account of the vital differences that exist in it.

NOTES

1. Publ., 1918; 5th ed., Munich, 1923. Translated into English by Samuel McComb with the assistance of J. Edgar Park, Oxford and New York, 1932. See also K. Beth, *Froemmigkeit der Mystik und des Glaubens* (1927); H. E. Weber, *Glaube und Mystik* (1927); H. E. Brunner, *Die Mystik und das Wort* (1928); there are also fine remarks in the first chapter of J. Guttmann, *Philosophies of Judaism* (1964), pp. 9 ff. On the relationship between mystical piety and the piety of faith, see R. Otto, *Sünde und Urschuld* (Munich, 1932), chapter 11.

2. I made a preliminary attempt to analyze some ideas of this unknown but profound thinker in a Hebrew essay in the *Literary Supplement* of *Ha-aretz* of September 14, 1945.

3. See G. Scholem, *Major Trends in Jewish Mysticism*, 2nd ed. (1946), p. 341. As to the exact meaning of Baal Shem's allegedly pantheistic allegory of the king's palace, see my Hebrew article, "Beginnings of Hasidism," *Ṣion* 16 (1951): 97 ff.

4. See J. Abelson, *The Immanence of God in Rabbinical Literature* (London, 1912), passim.

5. The first attempt to analyze this semantic process was made by M. Teitelbaum, *Ha-Rav mi-Ladi* (1913), 2:3 ff.

6. The original Lurianic concept of *Ṣimṣum* is discussed by Scholem, *Major Trends*, pp. 260–65; and Is. Tishby, *Torath ha-Ra*, etc. (Jerusalem, 1942).

7. See my Hebrew essay on the Brazlavic concept of paradoxical faith, in *Schocken Festschrift, Alei Ayin* (Jerusalem, 1947–52), pp. 245–91. Further research has convinced me that the theory of the paradox is much more centred round the person of the "true Ṣaddik"—R. Naḥman himself—than I had thought at the time of writing this article.

8. See R. Dov Baer's Preface to his *Kunteres ha-Hithpa'aluth*.

9. R. Nathan Sternherz, *Likkutei Tefilloth* (Brazlav, 1822).

10. One of R. Naḥman's allegories has been compared to Kafka's short stories. This is the only valuable remark in E. Steinman's otherwise worthless introduction to his

selections from R. Naḥman's writings, *Kitvei R. Naḥman mi-Brazlav* (Tel Aviv, 1951), p. 23.

11. On the romantic psychology of religious enthusiasm in early Hasidism, see my "Beginnings of Hasidism," p. 88.

12. The tragic sin of the *Ṣaddik* lies in his necessarily antinomian destiny as Restorer and Redeemer.

Torah Study in Early Hasidism

The new position occupied by the *miṣvah* of Torah study (*Talmud Torah*) with the rise of Hasidism has been discussed by scholars under headings such as "Judaism of the emotions as opposed to Judaism of the intellect" and so on. It has been called by some "the revolt of the people," a thing far removed from the truth. Nevertheless, these attempts at categorization are on the right track in that they indicate the poor status of Torah learning at the beginning of the movement (but not from the first half of the nineteenth century onward, when a decisive change took place). The lack of the light of Torah learning has been noted by modern historians, as it was indeed by the "opponents" (*mithnaggedim*) of the time, who talked of the contempt for the Torah in the Hasidic camp.[1] And this is, in fact, a historical phenomenon that needs to be explained. The problem may be clarified by a look at some of the criteria involved.

The question of the method of Torah learning in the new religious movement was important for the daily conduct of every one of its adherents who was affected by the Hasidic notion of "the fear of Heaven," since Torah study was considered incumbent upon every Jew. The differences between the complex of values in classical Judaism and those of Hasidism sorely troubled the first Hasidim when they came to establish their life pattern, because they advocated constant *devekuth* (spiritual adherence), an activity that is contemplative, and perhaps emotional, but is certainly not merely intellectual.

The basic works of Jewish mysticism already note a discrepancy between Torah study as a supreme value and the imposition of *devekuth*. *Devekuth* is not an invention of Hasidism but is derived with some changes of meaning from the Cabbala.[2] By way of generalization, it can be said that medieval cabbalists resolved the contradiction between *devekuth* and Torah study by imposing a strict separation between the periods of time that had to be devoted to *devekuth* and those which were for Torah study. The time scale was measured in hours, on the basis of the well-known *mishnah* about the early Hasidim, who would wait one hour before praying (Mishnah, *Berakhoth* 5, 1), a fundamental text. The cabbalist manuals explain this delay as an expression of *devekuth*. The timetable of the particularly pious mystics could be then divided into large areas of *devekuth* and prayer, with only the time remaining devoted to Torah study. During *devekuth* one would be occupied with nothing else—with neither Torah nor prayer.

This regulated system collapsed with the coming of the Hasidic concept of *devekuth*. This concept differs from that of classical Cabbala in three respects: (*a*) it has a considerably increased emotional load; (*b*) it pervades every moment of daily life, which the cabbalistic notion of *devekuth* did not touch; (*c*) it is a religious obligation incumbent not only on the specially pious as the cabbalists would have it but on everyone. These changes generated by Hasidism—such as the promotion of *devekuth* to a supreme religious and almost exclusive value, with a concomitant denigration of Torah study, and the above-mentioned changes of emphasis—brought in their wake alterations in the contemplative technical apparatus of *devekuth*. We find that Israel Baalshem Tov had a different behavior pattern from that of the classical cabbalists. Whether from the historical point of view this behavior pattern was original to the Baalshem Tov or whether he borrowed from unknown sources is a question that cannot as yet be resolved, though a clarification of this matter is one of the principal tasks of the historian of Hasidism.

The main thing about this new pattern of behavior is that one can perform two *miṣvoth* at the same time: that of *devekuth* and that of Torah study. There are not two separate times for these activities according to Israel Baalshem Tov: on the contrary, the two form a perfect synthesis. Here we have the essence of the Baalshem Tov's system: to combine and synthesize the contemplative ideal with the action performed at the very same time, whether it appertains to *miṣvoth* or not.[3] Action and *devekuth* are not mutually exclusive, but interpenetrate when performed at the same time. This technique, not easy even when an action is performed automatically, is considerably more difficult when the student is concentrating on the details of halakhic discussion. In any case, we must understand that the contemplative technique of study involved in *devekuth* is not isolated from the totality of the Baalshem Tov's approach, but is a detail that fits into the complex of the contemplative system adopted by the Baalshem Tov during the performance of *miṣvoth*, both in physical act, and in Torah study.

As for the terms used to indicate this synthesized activity of study and *devekuth*, the Baalshem Tov found the traditional concept of studying "Torah for its own sake," with the stress on "for its own sake," a most useful indicator for his new method of study, that is, study with *devekuth*. "Torah for its own sake," mentioned in the Talmud and in ethical literature, is according to Israel Baalshem Tov's interpretation "study for the letter,"[4] study in which the letters of the holy words of the Torah become the focal point of the contemplative concentration of the student. Understanding the letters, which is the basis of this technique, is Platonic or neo-Platonic in essence. The letters have come down from their source in the upper world. It is, therefore, incumbent upon the student to return and "affix" these external shapes of letters to their spiritual originals and to bind them to their forms in their highest sphere, where they originated. As the student "affixes" the letters of the Torah, which is learned through them, so he himself becomes affixed to those higher forms. This is *devekuth* through study according to the system of the Baalshem Tov, and is what he calls "Torah for its own sake." All the stories and traditions pertaining to R. Israel Baalshem Tov bear witness to this.

The state of the sources that have come down to us concerning the traditions of the Baalshem Tov is complex, and it is not possible in a short article to give a detailed presentation of the different formulae that express the Baalshem Tov's doctrine concerning study with *devekuth*. These formulae appear in the works of his disciples, were analyzed in the works of *their* disciples, and were adapted and reformulated until they became one of the central preoccupations in the Hasidism that moved the heart for generations—not just in the Hasidic camp either, but among their "opponents" too, who, with all their criticism of the very idea of study with *devekuth*, were still influenced to a certain extent by this doctrine.

We shall content ourselves with one or two quotations from the Baalshem Tov that clearly reflect his position. R. Jacob Joseph writes on several occasions that he learned from his teacher, the Besht, that during Torah and prayer, one should look at the letters (apparently of the open book), so as to be affixed to the "light of the infinite" that emanates from the letters: "I learned from my teacher the Besht that the principal thing in Torah and prayer is to affix oneself to the innerness and spirituality of the light of the infinite within the letters."[5] It is already apparent from this quotation how traditional Torah study became a contemplative exercise for the Hasid (and similarly with prayer).

This tradition on the Besht recurs several times in the works of R. Jacob Joseph, as well as in R. Ephraim of Sudylkow's *Degel Maḥaneh Efraim* (R. Ephraim was a grandson of the Besht) and in other sources, so that there can be no doubt of its authenticity. The same or similar tradition is found in R. Meir Harif Margoliouth's book, *Sod Yachin u-Voaz*. The position of the Besht with regard to Torah study is also confirmed in the words of his second great pupil, R. Dov Baer of Mesritz, and is echoed in his sermons as well: Torah study should come from an emotional awakening of the attachment of the student's soul to the creator: this is the spiritual meaning of "Torah for its own sake." The traditional concept of Torah for its own sake, one of the basic concepts accepted by all Jewry, was thus invested with a new spiritual meaning. In the usage of the first Hasidim, "Torah for its own sake" no longer means Torah alone without any desire for benefit, whether of money, status, or anything else. The Hasidic meaning of "Torah for its own sake" is "Torah for the sake of the letter that is being learned, through contemplation of the light of the infinite that is within the letters of the Holy Scripture." Torah study and *devekuth* should be simultaneous, and Torah study is the right occasion for contemplation and *devekuth*.

Almost complete unanimity prevails in the different traditions regarding the psychological possibility of combining Torah study with contemplation of the letters of the book that is being studied. This ability is not one to be taken for granted. The cabbalists preceding the Besht made a clear distinction between study and *devekuth*; so it seems that we have here an original concept of the Besht regarding the technique of attaching Torah study to *devekuth*.

The preacher of Mesritz, although formulating the matter differently, does not, in the main, move from his teacher's position. In his words, one should engage in *Talmud Torah* by looking for the "vitality" in the letters of the book being studied. Only the form changes, but not the original doctrine. And there is no need to point out that the Besht's doctrine was accepted by R. Jacob Joseph of Polonnoye, his literary pupil, who wrote down his sermons in his four books, which are full of the Besht's doctrines and are, indeed, interwoven with reliable traditions of his utterances. Although the Besht's opinions on Torah study for its own sake (that is, with *devekuth*) were certainly handed down in Hasidic circles as oral traditions even before they were published in R. Jacob Joseph's works, there is no doubt that the enormous publicity given to his ideas in this matter started in 1780, when R. Jacob Joseph's books began to appear. From that year onward, the new significance given by the Besht to the concept of Torah study "for its own sake" was disseminated very widely, and these traditions, as formulated and published in this work, became guiding principles for many Hasidim, and for their "opponents" too.

It must be stressed again and again that the Besht's position regarding Torah study was a moderate one, because his desire to synthesize Torah and *devekuth* precluded any possible extreme opposition, in the name of *devekuth*, to the *miṣvah* of Torah study. This new behavior pattern of Torah study through *devekuth* led to a more emotional approach than the purely intellectual one that had been adopted over the centuries. The status of study was automatically lowered, and its center of gravity was moved from the realms of Halakhah to that of Cabbala and Musar literature. But the Besht's words do not contain the slightest hint of any opposition in principle to Torah study or any specific instruction to reduce the time devoted to Torah study. The opposite is the case. The two concepts, Torah and prayer, that the Besht combines in *devekuth* signify that he did not seek to abolish or curtail Torah study through *devekuth*, but that he aspired to imbue prayer with *devekuth* (and it is, of course, unthinkable that the Besht was opposed to prayer, or that he wanted to reduce the time devoted to it).

It is clear, however, that this manner of studying the Torah through *devekuth* does not lead to an intellectual concentration on the text, but to a contemplative, emotional concentration. The lights that shine in the holy texts are of doubtful value to the student searching for intellectual understanding. From the purely academic point of view, it is clear that we have here, rather than an aid to study, the introduction of ecstatic elements, which are foreign to learning *qua* learning, and which are in fact liable to hinder learning in the traditional sense. The Hasidic system of study, which is seen only as a means to *devekuth*, was certainly not ideal for distinguished scholars, and it is difficult to determine whether this method of study was the cause of the decline of Torah study in Hasidic circles, or whether this whole emotional, contemplative system of study could only have grown in a spiritual climate where Torah study was already weak. It is certainly easier to learn Aggadah than Halakhah according to the rules established by the Besht, and perhaps it is no coincidence that we find R. Israel studying the book *En Ya'akov* with great love.[6]

On some points of doctrine, including the problem of Torah study and *devekuth*, two different trends were established in Hasidism. The conflict between them was known to their original authors, but it was forgotten or blurred in the course of time, and must be brought to light again by the historian. There was one branch of the Hasidic camp that did not agree with the Besht's combination of *devekuth* and study, but insisted on the classical distinction between Torah and *devekuth*. Anyone who glances at the small pamphlet called *Darkhei Yesharim*; *Hanhagoth Yesharoth* by R. Menaḥem Mendel of Premyslan will clearly discern the main points of view of the author who was the head of this branch. The ideal of *devekuth* is still completely dominant in R. Mendel's philosophy as in that of the other early Hasidim; and it could be said that this ideal is even more intensive in him than in the Besht. But it is obvious nevertheless that Dubnow exaggerated when he wrote that R. Mendel, in this pamphlet and in that which is quoted in his name in *Likkutim Yekarim*, repeats what the Besht had said.[7] Regarding Torah study, there is here a completely opposite view, one that does not adopt the Besht's interpretation of the concept "Torah for its own sake."

The basic assumption of the teaching that we find in this pamphlet is that Torah study and exercises in *devekuth* do not go together and cannot exist simultaneously. In contrast to the Besht's method, *devekuth* and Torah study are separate from one another, because the two ideals are apparently contradictory, the ideal of *devekuth* being preferable. So R. Mendel's method is not a sequel to that of the Besht, nor a logical conclusion of it.[8] R. Mendel is more extreme than the Besht and his pamphlet is severe, but his view (regarding the relationship of study to *devekuth*) is not a radicalization of the Besht's. It suggests a method that is technically opposed to that of the Besht. What was possible for, and perhaps even came easily to, the Besht and to R. Dov Baer of Mesritz was impossible for R. Mendel. There is in his work a complete abandonment of the attempt to bridge the gulf between study and *devekuth*; it is taken for granted that the value of *devekuth* grows, whereas that of study becomes very limited.

R. Mendel of Premyslan restricts the time that should be devoted to study in a manner that does not accord with Jewish tradition, according to which Torah study is one of those things that has no limit. In the view of R. Mendel, it is obligatory to reduce Torah study, that is, the time appointed for studying. The possibility of a complete renunciation of study does arise for him, but is dismissed. In all, his advice is to reduce the time devoted to Torah study in favor of that devoted to *devekuth*. This is the general purport of his pamphlet.

R. Mendel attempts to resolve the contradiction between his teaching and the holy status of Torah study in Jewish tradition by making a distinction between the "early generations" and the "later generations"—a distinction that occurs occasionally in Jewish traditional, including halakhic literature. "In our generation, there is no room for extensive Torah study, as time is needed for a more important religious requirement," i.e., *devekuth*. There is yet another rule, namely, not to study overmuch, because in the early generations, when their intellect was powerful, and they studied with supreme and great holiness, they did not have to worry about awe (*yir'ah*). Awe was constantly with them, and they were able to study extensively. "But we, whose intellect is small, if we divert our attention from *devekuth* to the blessed Name, and study a lot, we will forget the awe of the Lord.[9] Awe is the main thing; awe of the Lord is His treasury, as is written 'the beginning of wisdom (is the fear of the Lord).' Therefore we should study little and constantly think of the greatness of the blessed Creator, in order to love and fear Him. And one should think not many thoughts, but one thought."[10]

This is to say that the psychological assumption at the basis of R. Mendel's extreme view is that there is no possibility of carrying out the Besht's advice, and of practicing *devekuth* during Torah study. "Torah for its own sake," in the Besht's contemplative sense, is not feasible, in R. Mendel's opinion. We have here not the outburst of a popular enthusiast, renouncing the holy ideal of Torah study, but a conservatism tempered by the revolutionary idea of separating *devekuth* from Torah study. By separating the periods of time to be devoted to these two things, R. Mendel returned to the classic view of *devekuth*. But as to the practical conclusion of displacing Torah study by *devekuth*, this is something new not only in the history of the Jewish spirit but also in the world of Hasidism, and the author of *Darkkei Yesharim* represents perhaps the most extreme standpoint of all.

That central assumption of R. Mendel that Torah study and *devekuth* should be temporally isolated from one another finds clear expression in the practical advice given by the author regarding the timing of Torah study. He writes: "When one learns one should rest a little every so often so as to affix oneself to the blessed One."[11] That is to say that one should make a break in Torah study at appointed times, so as to allow during those breaks the hegemony of *devekuth*. He also says: "Although during study it is impossible to affix oneself to the blessed Creator, the Torah refines the soul and is a tree of life to those who abide by it, and if a man does not learn, his *devekuth* is void."[12] That is to say that much learning is indeed damaging because we have not sufficient strength in our poor generation to bear it or the concentration demanded by it. Nor do we have "the fear of Heaven." But, on the other hand, study is necessary because it can prepare one for "the fear of Heaven."

What argument does R. Mendel use to delimit Torah study?

Torah study is not demanded here in the absolute, neither as one of the most important Torah *miṣvoth*, nor as a metaphysical basis on which the existence of heaven and earth depends. Torah study is presented here as a preparation, as a peripheral action leading to achievement of *devekuth*. Torah study "refines" the soul, and makes it fit for its highest task, which is *devekuth*.

The lower status that R. Mendel ascribes to Torah study clearly emerges from the following words in the pamphlet. After the author establishes that, if a man has not learned, his *devekuth* is void, i.e., that study is a condition of *devekuth* (though study and *devekuth* do not go together), and that, in any case, by separating study from *devekuth*, the time spent learning, from the religious point of view, is also barren, the author comforts the reader thus: "He should think that just as during sleep he cannot achieve communion, nor when his mind is empty, so time spent in study is no worse than these, and since learning is void during *devekuth*, we will have none of it."[13] This formulation comparing *Talmud Torah* to sleep and emptiness of mind follows from the two general assumptions of R. Mendel: (*a*) that it is impossible to use time spent in study for *devekuth*, and (*b*) that only *devekuth* has genuine religious value, whereas *Talmud Torah* has no religious importance. Study is necessary marginally, but has no value in itself.

It should be emphasized that the declared position of R. Mendel concerning the value of study is not anti-intellectual, and the historian should be cautious in interpreting his ideas. In general, R. Mendel returns, in large measure, to the classical assumptions regarding the ideal conditions of *devekuth*. The classical theoreticians of *devekuth* did indeed distinguish between the time for *devekuth* and the time for Torah study. But they did not regard the two as rivals, but rather as two complementary values. And so they did not conclude that the time spent in studying Torah should be reduced. R. Mendel did conclude from the rival position of the two that one should prefer *devekuth* to Torah study. He does this on the basis of the comparison that he makes between *devekuth* and awe: if a choice must be made between Torah study and awe, it is clear to him that awe i.e., *devekuth*, should take precedence.

R. Mendel holds that there are ideal conditions for inducing *devekuth*, and that one of them is silence. Here he abandons the usual attitude of the Besht and his followers, who encouraged an atmosphere of intermingling with the people,[14] even with the masses, and of engaging in light conversation with them, so as to influence them. The conflict between the ideal of mystic isolation and the Hasidic ideal of social intercourse, including light conversation, left its mark on the most important theoretical struggles of the new movement in its early stages. R. Mendel's pamphlet values silence as a principal condition of *devekuth*. The right environment ideally for *devekuth* is an atmosphere of undisturbed silence. Since Torah study in its traditional form, especially the public teaching of Torah, was done aloud, and since this prevented in R. Mendel's view the invocation of *devekuth*, he was forced to take up his extreme position. He who talks a lot causes sin, i.e., a lack. Even when one speaks to people about the wisdom of the Torah, it is better that one should be silent. The reason is that one can contemplate God's greatness better in silence, and can tie oneself to Him better than during speech.[15]

Throughout the pamphlet, there is a marked tendency to base the invocation of *devekuth* on the contemplative concentration of man through his mystical withdrawal from society, and through cessation of all other occupation, even prayer. We have here a very narrow view of *devekuth*, a view that regards all other activity, including study and even prayer, as a distraction. The author writes in this connection: "And this is a great rule; sometimes he should stand in prayer and affix himself to the blessed Creator very closely, and not speak because of *devekuth*; and afterwards he should say some words, and do this several times in one prayer."[16] Not only do we have here a concept of *devekuth* that is so severe that even prayer is regarded as a distraction and a disturbance, but we have the same contemplative approach to the value of prayer as to that of study: cessation of study or prayer makes *devekuth* possible, and it exists just during those moments of cessation.

When the pamphlets and anthologies of R. Mendel and his followers began to appear, the different tendencies were much blurred (because those of the second group pretended to be followers of the Besht, although they differed from him on a number of matters). The names of the Besht and R. Dov Baer of

Mesritz were always displayed in one form or another on the title pages of books that reflected the opinions of the other group. The basic differences between the doctrine of the Besht and his followers and that of R. Mendel and his followers with regard to Torah study (as in other matters) were not mentioned, and were perhaps even not recognized. When an anthology called *Likkutim Yekarim* appeared in Lvov in the year 1792 (which contained, according to the title page, the doctrines of the Besht and of R. Dov Baer of the mainstream, and those of R. Mendel and R. Yehiel Michel of Zloczów), it is very doubtful whether any reader noticed the contradictions between the doctrines of the first two and the last two.

The extreme position of R. Mendel, which advocated separating Torah study from *devekuth*, was not isolated in early Hasidism. R. Phinehas of Korzecz, the pupil of the Besht (though not literally), adopted a stand similar to that of R. Mendel. In the writings of R. Phinehas there occurs an extreme idea, the like of which is hard to find elsewhere in Hasidic literature: "In this generation one is not occupied with Torah as in early generations. For now great awe has spread throughout the world. But in early times there was not such great awe; so they occupied themselves with Torah. There are a few places that learn; there is no awe there."[17] It seems that this daring utterance of R. Phinehas belongs originally to that branch of early Hasidism to which R. Mendel's works belong. The fact that R. Phinehas uses the term *awe* as distinct from study also gives him an affinity with R. Mendel, who identified awe with *devekuth* and opposed it to study. Also the distinction between "the early days" and "this generation" in R. Phinehas is completely parallel to the distinction that R. Mendel made in his *Darkhei Yesharim* between the "early generations" and "us." It could be that R. Phinehas read R. Mendel's pamphlet in manuscript or heard the words orally. But there is an outstanding similarity, from another point of view, between these two great representatives of early Hasidism. We hear extreme declarations from R. Phinehas with regard to *devekuth*, such as that wonderful dictum whose literary source we have in the original language, "one should always go in God,"[18] and it seems that R. Phinehas went even beyond R. Mendel's position in some respects in his demands for religious *devekuth*. A. Y.

Heschel has followed the career of R. Phinehas's second dictum, which commends awe as against study, and has demonstrated how this statement was buried in different collections of dicta named after him. A similar fate befell R. Mendel's extremist essays, which stress the separation of study from *devekuth*, and prefer *devekuth* to study, which he says should be diminished. When the editor of the pamphlet that included the Baalshem Tov's will made his selection from a variety of sources (including R. Mendel's pamphlet),[19] he did not include in his collection those essays which preferred *devekuth* to Torah study, because they were liable to bewilder or annoy the reader.

This was the natural development of Hasidism, which rejected the extreme enthusiastic elements and overcame them, and so became a recognizable part of Eastern European Jewry instead of an extreme sect. The problem of study versus *devekuth* continued to trouble people both in the Hasidic and in the opposite camps, but the battleground moved. In the mainstream of the Besht's followers the Hasidic argument turned not so much against actual Torah study, as against the students who were overproud of their learning. This argument of the Hasidim disarms criticism in that it does not attack such a hallowed tradition in Judaism as Torah study, but is directed against the personalities who uphold the ideal. In any case, we must distinguish between this and the argument against Torah study. The argument against the students for their pride is widespread in the works of R. Jacob Joseph of Polonnoye (who was himself a distinguished scholar, as can be seen from every page of his work) and left an impression on the comments of the Besht's second pupil, R. Dov Baer. This Hasidic argument, which shifted the attack from the theoretical to the personal plane; and thus lost some of its penetration, has still not been fully described.

NOTES

This article is based on a lecture delivered at the Third Congress of Jewish studies in Jerusalem.

1. A. Rubinstein, in his Hebrew essay, "The MS Treatise 'Zimrat Am ha-Areṣ' " in *Aresheth* (Jerusalem, 1961), 3:204–7, cites a number of examples in support of this argument from the works of the *mithnaggedim*.

2. See G. Scholem, *Major Trends in Jewish Mysticism*, Index, s.v. *devekuth*, and his essay "Devekuth," *Review of Religion* 15 (1950): 115 ff.

3. See my essay "The Beginnings of Hasidism" (Hebrew), *Ṣion* 16 (1962), especially from p. 65.

4. *Toledoth Ya'akov Yosef* (Korzecz, 1780), 3b.

5. Ibid., 25a.

6. See below, p. 118 and also G. Scholem, "The Historical Figure of the Baal Shemtov" (Hebrew), *Molad* 144/145 (1960): 353.

7. *Geschichte des Chassidismus* 1 (1930): 104.

8. G. Scholem, "Devekuth," p. 127.

9. In the special terminology of the author, "awe" equals *devekuth*, as can be gathered from the context. The contrast between Torah study and awe is based on T. B. *Shabbat* 31a, where the possibility of opposition between Torah and awe is mentioned in another sense.

10. *Darkhei Yesharim* (Zhitomir, 1805), f. 4a.

11. Ibid., f. 3b.

12. Ibid.

13. Ibid.

14. Ibid., 9b.

15. I will cite here just one passage from the *Toledoth* in this connection that was, as is known, an issue between the Hasidim and the *mithnaggedim*: "When the higher sign, which is mercy, comes so that it can mingle with people and [help him] to pronounce the unity (of the divine name) in recounting matters with them . . . and (even though) he will not be studying constantly, but will just mingle with people, even then the fear of the Lord will be upon him, so that he observes the tenet 'I have set the Lord constantly before me': even when it appears to be the opposite: the negation of Torah and prayer." (*Toledoth*, f. 24b.)

16. *Darkhei Yesharim*, f. 8b.

17. A. Y. Heschel, "Le-toledoth R. Pinḥas mi-Koreṣ," *Alei Ayin Schocken Jubilee Volume* (Jerusalem, 1948–52), p. 216.

18. *Likkutei Shoshanim* (1876), p. 17, quoted by Scholem, *Major Trends in Jewish Mysticism*, p. 378, n. 7.

19. Hence we talk of the relationship between "the *Darkhei Yesharim* and the will of the Ribash" and not vice versa, although the will of the Ribash appeared in print before the *Darkhei Yesharim*. The internal structure of the Ribash's will seems to indicate that it is dependent upon the *Darkhei Yesharim*. See A. M. Habermann, *Sefer ha-Besht* (Jerusalem, 1960), p. 40. Habermann regards the will of the Baalshem Tov as a primary source, adducing the bibliographical considerations of Yizhak Raphael, published in *Ha-Aretz* of 31 May 1960. It seems to me that the dates of the publication of the first editions are not the decisive factor, since these selections were widespread in manuscript copies, and would be used, copied, and rearranged, with things omitted, before appearing in printed form.

Via Passiva in Early Hasidism

That the human soul must conduct itself in a mode of passive receptivity whilst God takes the active part is said to be one of the fundamental principles of mysticism. Indeed, it is claimed that this particular quality of consciousness is a permanent postulate of all mystical experience. One of the most prominent students of medieval mysticism wrote: "Mystiker wollen reines Passivum sein."[1]

This point, the mystic's craving for quietude and passivity, seems to be one of those rare instances where there is general agreement between the theologian of mysticism and the student of the history of religion. Just as speculative mysticism is nearly always associated with pantheistic leanings,[2] so one is justified in considering practice and teaching as to the passivity of the soul to be another, hardly less characteristic mark of religious experience of the mystical type: the requirement of passiveness is as closely connected with mysticism at the practical level as is pantheism on the theoretical plane. Statements of passivity are made both in the works of formal theologians of mysticism and in the description of historians and phenomenologists.

One will find in the literature of the mystics ardent recommendations of complete passivity. All mystical writers use a common language in regard to the question of passiveness and appear, in this respect, to live in the same spiritual climate.[3] Indeed, Miss Underhill echoed the great chorus of mystics, theologians, and historians of religion when she wrote (in her eloquent book *Practical Mysticism*) about passivity as follows:

> This unmistakable experience has been achieved by the mystics of every religion, and when we read their statements, we know that all are speaking of the same thing. . . . They are the passive objects upon which *it* works.[4]

This being so the basic texts of early Hasidism, and in

particular the texts of the Great Maggid, will now be examined, in an endeavor to determine to what extent they conform to the pattern described above.

The claim is that passivity is conducive to ecstasy, and indeed instrumental in attaining it; and it is this that I shall attempt to trace in the literature of early Hasidism. If the mystical spirit is present in that literature, as I believe it to be in abundance, Hasidism will show affinities to all other mystical trends and the aspect of passivity will not be lacking.

In this study of the passive conduct of the early Hasidic mystic I shall not be able to lean to any extent on the work of students of Hasidism; this particular aspect has not, so far, been accorded any attention at all. On the contrary, the very possibility that an attitude of mystical passivity might have existed in Hasidism has been denied by such a distinguished writer as Martin Buber, when contrasting Hasidism with the phenomena of medieval German mysticism.[5]

I shall now attempt to show that this view is open to question and that in fact the opposite may be confidently affirmed. The whole impulse toward mystical self-negation as expressed in medieval German mysticism finds its closest parallel in Hasidism. Of course, there is no suggestion of any literary dependence on the grounds that the Great Maggid might somehow or other have known the works of Eckhart; the intention is rather to indicate that early Hasidic mystics give expression to the same type of religious experience.

Whereas students of early Hasidism have, surprisingly, overlooked this fascinating aspect of Hasidic piety,[6] a contemporary source of no scholarly pretensions, the *Autobiography* of Salomon Maimon, included it in a particularly vivid description of the state of Hasidism and its essential tenets at the time of the Great Maggid. As far as I am aware Maimon, writing in 1792, remains the only person who has drawn attention to the part played by the tenet of passivity in the mystical teaching of early Hasidism and in its way of life, and who emphasised its pivotal importance. In describing his visit to the court of R. Dov Baer in Mesritz he writes: "I observed that their ingenious exegesis (sc. that of the Hasidim) . . . was limited strictly to their own extravagant principles, such as the doctrine of self-annihilation."[7]

This seems to mean that in Maimon's view, a considerable part of the talk in the Maggid's circle revolved around the "extravagant principle" of mystical self-annihilation. Indeed, one of the three homilies that Maimon heard from the Maggid, and which he noted down in his *Autobiography*, is concerned with this very *motif*—a clear indication of the importance Maimon felt that the Maggid attributed to this facet of his teaching. Perhaps it is not surprising that the doctrine of passive bearing impressed itself on Maimon as so vital an element in Hasidism. His insight into this aspect was all the more sharply focused because of his own position in the intellectual world of his time. Maimon belonged to the philosophical school of German Idealism, the development of which he helped to further toward Fichte and Schelling. It was this philosophical movement which was to discover in medieval German mysticism a fertile and positive spiritual force.[8] Maimon's vision is perhaps on this account too sharply accentuated, but it is by no means misconceived. My aim here is to follow up the line of investigation first pointed out by Maimon.

I

The reason I begin by analyzing the recommendation of passivity proclaimed by the Maggid Baer of Mesritz[9] as quoted in Maimon's autobiography, in spite of its being but a secondary source, is that this particular formulation of the homily is an obvious starting point for discussion because of its extreme brevity and pregnancy:

> "*When the minstrel played, the spirit of God came upon him*" (2 Kings 3:15). This is explained in the following way. As long as a man is self-active, he is incapable of receiving the influence of the Holy Ghost; for this purpose he must hold himself like an instrument in a purely passive state. The meaning of the passage is therefore this. When the minstrel (*ha-menaggen*, the servant of God), becomes like his instrument (*ke-naggen*), then the Spirit of God comes upon him.[10]

In this Hasidic *locus classicus* of the doctrine of mystical passivity, the Maggid's comparison of a man to a musical instrument on which the spirit of God plays happens to be one of the great motifs on the subject of ecstatic passiveness.[11] It is to this numerous group of expressions that the saying of the

Maggid clearly belongs in his assertion of the instrumental passivity of the mystic.

The shofar is referred to in early Hasidic literature as the favorite variation for the harp in the previous image. The Maggid himself made use of it:

> Let him consider (*yaḥshov*) that the "World of Speech" (*Olam ha-Dibbur*) speaks within him and that without it speech would be impossible, as it is written "*O Lord, open thou my lips*" (Ps. 51 : 17) . . . so that he is merely like a shofar, for it produces merely the sound that is blown into it; and if he who blows departs from it, then it can produce no sound. Similarly in His absence, blessed be He, one is not able either to speak or think.[12]

Man's speech and thought come from God; but man's action is here quite deliberately excluded from the sphere of God's activity. Every student is aware of the trilogy "Thought, Speech and Action"[13] found in abundance in Cabbalistic and Hasidic literature. The meticulous avoidance by the Great Maggid of the obvious third member of the phrase, "action," in the above-cited passage (and in all parallel passages) cannot be fortuitous. The Maggid clearly excluded "action" from the sphere of human passivity. It was probably on dogmatic grounds that he refused to attribute man's actions to Divine activity.[14]

R. Hayyim Haika of Amdura, another disciple of the Great Maggid, repeats the trope of the shofar of Dov Baer, though without acknowledgment. But the combination of motifs leaves no shadow of doubt that he is expounding the doctrine of his teacher, the Great Maggid:

> *Like the shofar raise up thy voice* (Isa. 58 : 1), that is to say: just as the sound of the shofar issues from the person who blows it and not from the shofar itself, so man should see to it that the speech that issues from him is no more than the sound of the shofar, and that it is of the Holy One, blessed be He.[15]

The shofar motif must have had a strong appeal in Hasidic circles since its diffusion was considerable and we find it, with many variations, throughout early Hasidic literature. It appears in the body of teaching of R. Elimelekh of Lizensk, a disciple of the Great Maggid. R. Kalonymos Kalman of Cracow, a disciple of R. Elimelekh, testifies to having heard the shofar allegory from his master:

> As I have heard from my master, teacher and Rabbi, the man of God our sainted Rabbi Elimelekh, on the verse *Raise up thy voice like the shofar*—his

explanation being that just as the shofar does not exult in the sound that comes from it, if it should be fair and pleasant, so the expositor and he who raises his voice to preach chastisement and ethics does not at all exult [namely, in his eloquence].[16]

It is clear that the essential theme here is that of the Maggid spun out, however, into this somewhat complex formula. The passivity spoken of here is not of the pure instrumental type, but has the habitual moralistic tone of admonition against pride; and this application of the theme is indeed to be found in the formulations of the Great Maggid himself. A decisive difference represented by the above passage lies in the fact that the homily here does not presuppose a contemplating or a praying Ḥasid, but a preaching *Ṣaddik* or admonishing *mokhiaḥ*. This aspect of the doctrine of instrumental passivity will interest us at a later stage.

R. Abraham Hayyim of Zloczów, a pupil of the Great Maggid, quotes the simile in the name of his teacher; but he introduces it in a somewhat radicalized form, which aims at including within the realm of instrumental passivity more than the relatively harmless sphere of speech and thought:

I have heard in the name of the Rabbi, that holy light, our teacher Dov Baer, may his memory be for an eternal blessing, the interpretation of the verse *And like the shofar raise up thy voice*: that is to say, man must consider himself as nothing (*laḥashov eth aṣmo ke-'ayin*), as having no merit or good deed, and even if he performs *miṣvoth* and good deeds it is not he who performs them, but he does them through the power of God, and by virtue of the intelligence, the love, and the goodness, which He has graciously bestowed upon him. . . . And likewise in his prayer let him consider that the "World of Speech" (*Olam ha-dibbur*) speaks within him, and that his thought is the "World of Thought" (*Olam ha-maḥashavah*), and that he is like a *shofar* which has within it no sound but only that which is blown into it. And this is the meaning of that text of Scripture *like the shofar raise up thy voice.*[17]

All essential features of the shofar motif are here assembled. Closer examination of the passage, comparing it with the shofar passages of the Maggid, makes it patent that R. Abraham Hayyim slightly overstated his teacher's tradition in the direction of his own radical views. It was rather his own than the Great Maggid's view that God and not man is responsible for all meritorious human actions.[18] An important ramification of the doctrine of instrumental passivity is the idea of R. Abraham Hayyim that the principle, if applied to the work of *miṣvoth*, would exclude the possibility of free will and would open up problems in connection with the doctrine of divine reward which must be firmly based on the assumption of the autonomy of human action. Consistent in his denial of human activity, R. Abraham Hayyim allocates divine reward as an act of grace for man's meritorious will only—which is free—but not for man's actions, which are, in his view, carried out if not by God, at least by divine power.[19] These ramifications of the problem definitely lie outside the Great Maggid's religious orbit and belong to the subsequent development within hasidic thought of the Maggid's thesis on human passivity.

But harp and shofar are not the only symbols in the Maggid's teaching on mystical passiveness. He reiterates his doctrine untiringly, in a variety of images.:

> Let him consider himself as nought, for he is only like an organ (*magrefah*) made of leather in which there are holes, and it is through these holes that the instrument produces its music; and should the leather vessel pride itself that melody proceeds from it? So also the human being. "Thought" and "Speech" and all qualities dwell in him as in an instrument (*keli*). And wherefore should he exult? Is he not in himself nothing?[20]

This wording is once again couched in the form of an hortatory expression of the instrumental doctrine: against pride. But a parallel passage shows the Maggid expounding the pure instrumentality of the mystic in his non-separate state from God:

> Let us consider that one is merely as a craftsman's tool. Just as a craftsman beats the hammer upon the stone at his own desire and not by the desire of the hammer which actually strikes the stone: for were that so, the hammer would be separate from the man who wields it. Thus it is just like the *Kadmuth ha-Sekhel*[21] which emanates to *Binah*. And all one's limbs are but vessels.[22]

Shofar, harp, hammer, and craftsman's tool—these are the great images of the instrumental doctrine representing the fundamental feature of mystical passivity.

II

We have seen that there is a tendency in the mystic to feel that in all that he does he is the object rather than the subject of his action, in other words, that he feels himself placed in a state of utter passivity. From this he will draw the conclusion that, in whatever he does, the mystic's own doing is unreal or fictitious in view of the all-inclusive activity of the Divine.

Israel Baalshem—though not in connection with the practice of instrumental passivity or self-annihilation, which play no part in his religious world—did entertain such ideas, in a manner that has no air of caution or reticence about it. His disciple R. Jacob Joseph writes in the name of Israel Baalshem: "while one is engaged in *Torah* and *miṣvoth* one should not think in one's heart that he himself is doing it, but that the *Shekhinah* is doing it."[23]

And in a more elaborate form, the same teaching of Israel Baalshem is attested by the same disciple: "I have heard from my master that he who did a great *miṣvah* or learned much *Torah* or prayed with devotion, (such a man) must not induce any pride into his heart that he has done all that. But *Malkhuth* which is called '*I*' has done that."[24]

It should be borne in mind, of course, that Israel Baalshem was not interested mainly in the pure metaphysical form of the principle that God and not man is agent in human actions, but rather in its practical, i.e., moralistic, application. The above formulation is intended as an admonition to humility—a basic quality of the mystic, which may or may not reveal a mystical-passive aspect. Israel Baalshem's exhortation could be summed up like this: "Do not be proud of your religious achievements, since you do not play an active part in the fulfilment of your religious duties. The active part is played by God." As the teaching stands, it amounts mainly to a warning against every kind of religious self-confidence or self-complacency; but it also implies a wider religious principle, that of the exclusive divine activity in all religious actions of man.

More reluctance and, above all, more caution can be observed on this particular point in the atmosphere surrounding the Great Maggid.[25] Salomon Maimon, who knew the teaching of the Great Maggid partly from firsthand knowledge he acquired during his visit to Mesritz and partly from reliable information given him by the Maggid's disciples, as noted above, is not sufficiently exact on this particular point. Describing the divine service of the Hasidim, Maimon writes:

> Their worship[26] consisted in a voluntary elevation above the body, that is, in an abstraction of the thoughts from all created things, even from the

individual self, and in union with God. By this means a kind of self-denial arose among them, which led them to ascribe, not to themselves but to God alone, all the actions undertaken in this state.[27]

As this passage is found in the context of the author's description of Hasidic prayer, it would appear that the principle of attributing all actions to divine activity was limited to actions (or gestures?) during ecstatic prayer.

It would seem that the Maggid's doctrine of passivity, in the positive formulation of which God becomes the sole subject of man's activity, is applicable to the time of prayer only and has no general validity in regard to human actions as such. Maimon does not state this explicitly, but it is apparent from the fact that he discusses the doctrine and its practice when describing the prayer life of the Great Maggid's Hasidim. On the mere basis of Maimon's evidence, it could hardly be contended that the application of the doctrine went beyond these rather narrow limits.

Has the internal Hasidic literary tradition of the Great Maggid's teaching anything to say regarding the narrower application of this doctrine? There is nothing in Hasidic literature written in Hebrew that would contradict this qualified interpretation of the Maggid's teaching and practice as derived from Maimon. The reverse is true: inner Hasidic tradition would corroborate this interpretation.

All salient passages of the Great Maggid's authentic teaching would corroborate the narrow interpretation given above, that it is during ecstatic prayer that the divine is supposed to take hold of man and govern his speech. Ps. 51 : 17; "O Lord, open thou my lips" is referred to repeatedly in the most pertinent passages of the doctrine of passive speech. There can be little doubt that this verse—the opening phrase of the *Amidah*—indicates the *Sitz im Leben* in which the doctrine of mystical passivity becomes operative:

When one commences praying, as soon as one says *O Lord, open thou my lips* (Ps. 51 : 17), the *Shekhinah* is enveloped [*mithlabbesheth*] in one and says these words.[28] And when one believes that it is the *Shekhinah* which says it, fear will descend upon one, and the Holy One, blessed be He, will contract Himself and will dwell with him.[29]

A further passage also illustrates the *mise-en-scène* of instrumental passivity in the state of ecstatic prayer:

Since we say *O Lord, open thou my lips*, meaning the *Shekhinah*, that is the "World of Speech." If this is not enveloped [*mithlabbesheth*] in the lip, the lip cannot speak. But the wicked man says *our lips are with us* (Ps. 12:5), that is, he speaks by himself. . . . One's speech is from the "World of Speech" and one's thought is from the "World of Thought."[30]

Another parallel:

The *Shekhinah*, as it were [*kiveyakhol*] contracts itself and dwells in the speech as is found in the *Book of Creation*, "He fixed them [the letters] in the mouth," and it is written *O Lord open thou my lips* (Ps. 51:17) meaning the *Shekhinah*.[31] If one's evil urge [*yeṣer ha-ra*] entices one, God forbid, [saying] "How do you know that?" one should answer: "Did not Moses our teacher, peace be upon him, say 'I am the Lord thy God' (Lev. 18:2)[32] and certainly it was the Holy One Himself, blessed be He, who said this.[33]

A third variation on the theme of automatic speech does not quote Ps. 51:17, which constitutes the preamble to the *Amidah*. Nevertheless, it is an admirable description of the atmosphere of early Hasidic prayer life:

Sometimes the holy spark of the *Shekhinah* which dwells in one's soul spreads and then She [i.e., the *Shekhinah*] actually speaks the words [that come forth] from one's mouth. It seems as if one is not speaking, that the words come forth from one's mouth of their own accord. This is an elevated rank. We can see similar things on the evil side with mad people.[34]

It will be appropriate to mention in this connection that certain apparently radical dicta of the Great Maggid on our subject are, in fact, less radical than their phrasing would lead one to suppose.

"Your God is a priest"[35]: that means, one only worships God, blessed be He, by means of the power which He has given [both] in thought and speech [through] the World of Thought and the World of Speech. Consequently it is because of Him that one worships Him [*me-ḥamatho ovedim otho*]. What is meant by "your God is a priest" is that He Himself, as it were, worships Himself [*she-oved kiveyakhol eth ąsmo*].[36]

The use here of the qualifying *kiveyakhol*, "as it were" which is a traditional expression to tone down an extravagant statement regarding the Deity, clearly indicates that the pronounced doctrine was considered (either by its author or by the scribe) a daring one; but there is still no explicit statement that God is active in man's performance of *miṣvoth*. I believe that the above passage where *avodah* is described as the activity of God rather than of man, refers to the "worship" of God in a limited sense, that is to say, in prayer[37] and not to worship in general, that is to say, in the performance of *mișvoth*. The passage describing God as a priest worshiping Himself thus would refer but to the prayer life of the Hasid, who is supposed to receive his enthusiastic prayer from God and who in turn offers his *oratio infusa* to God, thereby closing the circle.

III

Where the fixed Hebrew formula of prayer is concerned, it is not difficult to assume that its utterance has been brought about by God, but it is far less easy to assume divine infusion in the case of a sermon delivered in the Yiddish vernacular, where there is no set text to follow. And yet the doctrine of passive speech was applied in early Hasidism also to the *darshan* delivering his *derashah* or *derush*. The requirement of abolute passivity having been extended to this field of speech too the preaching *Ṣaddik* was expected to break into improvised doggerel when in a quasi-ecstatic state. The speaker must have no power over his diction, which bursts forth from him uncontrolled and impulsive. Thus his speaking is not a voluntary act; rather than being the free architect of his own speech, he feels himself compelled to utter words that are infused into him. His duty is not to preach but rather to withdraw, by mystically annihilating himself, and allow God to make use of his lips. The sermon is thus considered a piece of inspired improvisation. This does not mean vague and inarticulate intuition for which the preacher himself must find words, but rather a precise verbal infusion—it is not merely the theme of his speech of which he is the recipient, but the entire sermon, as it were, verbatim. If, consequently, it is not only the general idea of the sermon which is supposed to be inspired, the actual phrases that fall from the lips of the preacher must be considered the *ipsissima verba* of the Divine.

It is by conducting himself with the utmost passivity that the preacher is "carried away" in a radically theological sense, and becomes merely the "instrument" of speech. Powerless, he feels that some divine force speaks through him. Unlike the well-known phenomenon of glossolalia, the early Hasidic sermon does not consist of short disconnected phrases that subsequently require interpretation. In the early phase of this revivalist movement we have what can be defined as involuntary speech, which differs from glossolalia in that it is coherent where the other is incoherent, and in that it is well developed where the other is fragmentary. The Sabbatian movement exhibited phenomena closer to the glossolalia pattern than did the Hasidic. It must remain an open question whether there is any historical bridge between the Sabbatian and Hasidic forms of involuntary speech.

Incidentally, there is available the testimony of a reliable eyewitness showing how the Great Maggid himself put his ideas on instrumental passivity into practice: R. Ze'ev Wolf one of the highly original disciples of the Great Maggid, writes:

> Once I heard the Maggid of blessed memory state explicitly "I will teach you the best way of pronouncing Torah, which is as follows—not to be aware of oneself [*eyno margish eth aṣmo*] but as an ear hearkening to the way in which the 'World of Speech' speaks within one. It is not he himself who speaks. As soon as he hears his own words, let him stop!" On many occasions I have seen him [the Maggid] with my own eyes, I myself, when he opened his mouth to speak the words of Torah; he appeared to everyone as if he were not in this world at all, but as if the *Shekhinah* were speaking from his throat.[38] And sometimes, even in the middle of a subject or in the middle of . . . a word he would stop and wait for a while.[39]

The sermon of which the Hasidic *Ṣaddik* is the passive agent is improvised, in contradistinction to the carefully prepared discourse given by the rabbi in a non-Hasidic environment. The ideal of utmost spontaneity in delivering sermons is but the natural corollary of the doctrine of passivity. The short units of early Hasidic sermons, in contrast to the long and elaborate *derashah* of the traditional Jewish type, may be conditioned by the theory and practice of passive speech.[40] The test of whether or not a sermon is dictated from above is its involuntary character. It is this which indicates that its content has not been conceived by the intellect of the preacher but springs from that upper region described as the "World of Speech" (*Olam ha-dibbur*).

Contemporary records on this aspect of Hasidic life written by non-Hasidic or even anti-Hasidic authors, depict scenes that tally well with one another and also with what we know of the doctrine of infused sermon from the Maggid and his disciples.

The dependence of the ideal of the infused sermon on the

theory of ultimate passivity in self-annihilation was acutely recognized by Salomon Maimon. In his *Autobiography* he wrote:

Their sermons and moral teachings were not, as these things commonly are, thought over and arranged in an orderly manner beforehand. This method is proper only to the man who regards himself apart from God. But the superiors of this sect hold that their teachings are divine and therefore infallible only when they are the result of self-annihilation before God, that is, when they are suggested to them *ex tempore*, by the exigence of circumstances, without their contributing anything themselves.[41]

The particular forms of improvisation in preaching become clear from Maimon's description of the general setting of the Hasidic sermon. This is delivered on Saturday afternoon at dusk or after nightfall, usually within the framework of the *se'udah shelishith*, the traditional "third meal" of the Sabbath.[42] In order to emphasize the impromptu character of the address, the preacher invites the people present to provide him with several random verses from sacred texts, biblical or otherwise, and it is of these unrelated threads that the texture of his sermon is woven. He is not unlike the popular magician who prefers to use articles proferred him by the audience in order to emphasize the authenticity of his performance:

Every newcomer . . . recited, as he was called, some verse of the Holy Scriptures. Thereupon the superior[43] began to deliver a sermon for which the verses recited served as a text, so that although they were disconnected verses taken from different parts of the Holy Scriptures they were combined with as much skill as if they had formed a single whole.[44]

The opponents of Hasidism, though unappreciative of the outbursts of these private revelational inundations, described them in a fashion which matches the picture of the Hasidim themselves or of Maimon as far as the phenomena are concerned, though not, of course, their evaluation. In *Sefer Vikkuaḥ* (*The Book of Contention*) by R. Loebel[45] a description is to be found which, while independent of Maimon's, corroborates it.

They trod a new path in that at the *se'udah shelishith* the chief of them would pronounce Torah as it came to him [*mah she-yavo le-yado*] and anyone [*sic*] on a biblical verse or a midrash about which he was asked. Does not the Zohar proclaim about those who pronounce Torah and are not harnessed to the truth that the Devil goes to meet such [men] and kills them? And so said R. Simeon to the Holy Assembly, "I pray you, do not say a word which you do not know and have not heard from Big Trees,[46] so that that will not be the cause of death of people." And they said "God forbid that we do it." So far the Zohar.[47] In any case supposing that he does not pose as a prophet and has no Holy Spirit, why should he involve himself[48] . . . and boast that he is cleaving to God, blessed be He and that He gives him Torah and speaks from his throat. How does one know whether God gives it him? From his teaching it looks as if the thing did not come from God, for their teaching is like the jingle of the jester in which though the ending of the second rhyme is like that of the first nevertheless there is no connection between the two. . . . Moreover, I testify that there is no Holy Spirit in them: and I was told by the great scholar R. Me'ir of Biala who attended a *se'udah shelishith* in Praga[49] at the house of a very great *ṣaddik*. They quoted to him [a verse][50] from the [pentateuchal] portion of *Ṣav* and he expounded it. And later he said that it [the explanation] had been very sweet and true. So the above-mentioned scholar answered. "If it were stated in that verse *le-kaddesho* you could have said it was true [i.e., the explanation of the verse]. But since this word does not occur in that passage, how can it be true?"[51]

The author of this pamphlet, a violent opponent of Hasidism, then reports another instance of a passage misquoted by a highly respected Hasidic leader and remonstrates against the theory of divine infusion of sermons: "They want to show their piety by saying that God granted them Torah."[52]

He concludes by indicating the theory—which he attacks—of the stammering of enthusiastic speakers:

Have you no spare time to develop thoughts so that the thing may be well established. . . . I find this behaviour bad in the extreme. I can find no excuse for it. Either you think that they [i.e. the *ṣaddikim*] speak with the Holy Spirit. . . . This is disproved, as I have explained. It is patent that your aim is that you should be given the title of prophets.[53]

Here the anti-Hasidic polemist develops a lengthy argument against what he calls prophetic behavior. Although Hasidic literature meticulously avoided making use of the nomenclature *navi* and *nevu'ah*[54] in describing ecstatic preaching and praying or in agitating for its cultivation, ecstatic experiences were regarded as manifestations of an overwhelming divine power that came upon the Hasidim mainly at the time of prayer and of sermons, and induced them to make improvised utterances. These experiences constituted a determining element in the religious life of early Hasidism. The theory that the "World of Speech" takes control of man's utterances in ecstasy sums up adequately the thrilling sense of the real presence of this divine power, abundantly experienced in the revivalist phenomena of early Hasidism. The atmosphere surrounding the delivery of the sermon was no less revivalist than the atmosphere of its prayer life. Both testify to the intense sensation shared by the members of the sect, and to their vivid feeling that a divine power of speech actually does take possession of man and work within him in his ecstatic experience.

IV

The metaphors mentioned in section I are accompanied by a note of admonition, "let him consider himself as nought." This becomes the practical program of a specific kind of contemplation. What we are presented with here is not, for the most part, an abstract account of the nature of man, or even of the nature of the mystic, but rather practical advice on contemplative procedure. Rather than constituting a comment, in the style of mystical anthropology, on the essential nothingness of man, it is a practical guiding principle as to how to reach experimentally one's true nature, which is nonexistence. The human being begins fulfilling his merely passive role in the moment when he recognizes his own *nihilitudo*: he is empty and immobile, activated only by the power of God within him. His sole task is to understand that he is no more than a passive instrument and mentally to prostrate himself in repudiation of all selfhood. This "ascetic" effort is not guaranteed in all the texts to lead to the promised inflow of the divine that the mystic awaits. The Maggid does not actually specify that an ecstatic state will arise as the result of the instrumental passivity of the mystic. On many occasions he omits altogether to mention this second, ecstatic, stage. But his remarkable homily on the musician is enough to prove that passiveness is not merely one of the general requirements of ascetism, but rather a preparatory phase of a precise contemplative technique aimed at the attainment of ecstasy. Contemplative exercises centered on the nature of human instrumentality are the best possible means whereby the instrumentality appreciated by the mystic in contemplation may become actualized within the ecstatic experience.

Contemplation of this kind is not focused on the "greatness of God" or the "greatness of His creation." Likewise, it can be said that the way to ecstasy described here is not the gradual ascent of the soul from "world" to "world", remounting the path of emanation—although the Maggid does indeed, in a different context, advocate this latter type of contemplation. But the technique for achieving ecstasy in self-annihilation is the searching penetration of the contemplative mystic turned inwards into the very depths of his own soul, in scrutiny of his own essential nature.

The mystic's contemplation here means a specialization in his mental activity, and its simplification by narrowing down the field of consciousness and thus intensifying the activity of thinking. In other words, it means thinking more and more about less and less. The content of this intensified thinking is very limited: it is the passivity or the nullity of the human being. The way is that of self-knowledge, achieved by a mystical introspection which amounts to recognition of the instrumental character of man in a very specific respect, namely, of oneself. By thinking of oneself in a repeated contemplative way—whether in the image of the shofar, the hammer, or the harp—one comes to accept the nature of God as the sole agent not only in the world, but even more emphatically, within oneself. One has then reached the stage at which the objective consideration of the exclusive activity of God and the radical passivity of man becomes a subjective reality, in the form of the ecstatic experience. But in the Maggid's view the recognition by the mystic of his own nothingness in his *via passiva*, and his preparatory evacuation of selfhood, are in themselves a kind of "ascetic" discipline of inestimable spiritual benefit, even if they are not followed by ecstasy.[55]

APPENDIX[56]

Notwithstanding the predominance of the idea of human inertness in the Great Maggid's outlook, the theory of the instrumental character of the human being in his relation to God still implies, or at least allows for, a doctrine of man that is in some measure positive.

The most radical form of negative self-awareness in the Great Maggid's thought is the denial of personal existence itself. The mystic looks into himself and finds himself to be nothing. In this way he discovers not only that he is a passive instrument in God's hand; he also comprehends his own absolute nothingness.

There seem to be two conceptions of the nature of the mystic's ecstatic experience of self-negation. In one concept the mystic becomes an instrument on which God exercises His exclusive activity. In the other concept the mystic undergoes total self-annihilation. Whereas there is implicit in the first form a doctrine of man that is still in some measure assertive, the second and more radical form of the negation of man's capacity is tantamount to the denial of personal existence altogether.

In each case the psychological method of approaching the goal by way of contemplation is conditioned by the goal itself. In the first case, in the instrumental experience, man is required to reflect on his actions as nothing but the work of God through him as a medium—a work in which man has no share. The Maggid's advice to the mystic is that he should make himself unceasingly aware of this insight into the nature of man in order to intensify that increased consciousness of human passivity which leads eventually to ecstasy.

In the second case the object of contemplation, in accordance with the final aim, is not man's passiveness, but his virtual nonexistence. The two lines of thought are not always clearly differentiated in the Hasidic texts themselves. The advice "consider yourself as nothing" is used by the Great Maggid in both contexts, although, strictly speaking, one would not expect it to be used as a substitute for "consider yourself as an instrument" (*keli*). The different aspects that analytic investigation can distinguish are inseparably interwoven in the texts themselves. Indeed, they are but variations on the same theme.

Which of the traditional values of nonmystical Judaism is likely to retain its force in the mystical-contemplative climate of early Hasidism? It is clear that it will not be any of the assertive values of biblical religion, such as the impassioned pursuit of truth or of justice and the human endeavor to realize them on earth.[57] Likewise, the gravest sin will not be falsehood or injustice or any similar evil. In fact, early Hasidic texts, and in particular those of the Great Maggid, clearly exhibit humility as the supreme religious value (apart, of course, from *devekuth*, communion with God). This is not fortuitous; the corollary to the establishment of contemplation as the highest ideal is obviously the supreme importance attributed to the passive virtues.

The focus of early Hasidic mystical religion is indeed the emotional concentration of all mental powers on the achievement of a state of total humility. The idea of human abjectness, that is, of man being but "dust and ashes," operates in early Hasidism not as a means of inducing a numinous atmosphere as in biblical religion, but as the essential prerequisite to the state of mystical ecstasy.[58] Many basic doctrines of the Great Maggid in this respect are summarized in an undoubtedly authentic tradition contained in the work *Degel Maḥaneh Efrayim* of R. Ephraim of Sudylkow: "Someone asked the Maggid of blessed memory, 'How do we achieve a state of enthusiasm [*hithlahavuth*] toward the Holy One, be He blessed?' And he answered him, 'He who requires fire, let him search among the ashes!'"[59]

"Ashes" stands for the total nullity of the human being and the advice of the Maggid seems to be that the contemplative process should start with that mystical humility which subsequently passes over into religious enthusiasm. This interpretation of the above-quoted words of the Maggid is confirmed by other teachings of his, as will be seen later.

When humility, as the first step in the mystical path, was discussed by two disciples of the Great Maggid, the Maggid's opinion was requested. The question on which the debate seems to have turned was the correct technique of contemplation: should it start with mystical humility achieved by introspection or with the apprehension of the greatness of God? R. Gedaliah of Linitz noted down the course of the discussion and the position taken by the Maggid:

> I have heard from the mouth of the deceased saint, our teacher R. Zusha of Annopol, that once upon a time he was arguing with his famous brother, R. Elimelekh of Lizensk: one of them maintained that above all things a man must be humble in the extreme so that from the greatness of his self-abasement he comes thereafter to apprehend the greatness of the Creator, be He blessed; and the other maintained that on the contrary he should first give heed to the greatness of the Creator, blessed be He, and thereby he would come to a correct recognition of his own humble status. And they asked the Maggid, may the memory of the righteous and sainted one be blessed, that he should decide with whom the truth lay. And the words of both of them were right in his sight, and he pronounced that indeed both these and these are the words of the living God. But that condition which begins with self-abasement is the greater of the two.[60]

There were evidently differences of view among the disciples of the Great Maggid. Unfortunately we do not know which point of view was held by the one disciple and which by the other. The nonmystic will find it hard to grasp the implications of the difference between the two points of view, and will consider the argument an example of some sort of mystical casuistry. In mystical practice, however, there is a radical difference between the two methods. Both the introverted negation of self and the extroverted enthusiasm for the greatness of the Creator are tangible realities for the mystic, and they are for him psychologically different realities. The significance of the quotation above lies in the fact that the Maggid himself inclined toward the negation of the human subject and stressed nothingness as a contemplative means to the attainment of ecstatic enthusiasm. The other technique of contemplation here hinted at must have been some kind of ecstatic method that began with the contemplative appreciation of the Creator's greatness unfolding in the expanding circles of emanation, the method Rudolf Otto described as the "way of unifying vision."

What is humility? In its primary meaning it is to be understood as operative in relationships between human beings. It becomes more sophisticated when transmuted into the religious category of the human awe of God: in this sense it is used in both philosophical and mystical moralizing tractates. The Hasidic use of humility as an ecstatic device goes one step beyond this.

Humility is the chief virtue in the Maggid's teaching and pride is therefore the chief sin. He repeats untiringly—following the example of Israel Baalshem—that pride is the root of all sins. The Maggid has, of course, a long tradition of moralizing literature behind him, attributing to pride the same central position. All the voluminous criticism directed at the camp of the *Mithnaggedim* can be resolved into a ubiqitous allegation of pride.[61]

But sometimes a new note enters into the words of the Maggid when he says that pride is the great hindrance, and indeed, the sole hindrance to God's indwelling in man. The Maggid here speaks of the dialectics of pride that can transform even an act of repentance into a sin:

> There are two kinds of sins: one which occurs when a man transgresses the precept of the Holy One, blessed be He, and the second when one takes pride in one's service of God, blessed be He. And it is said that for the first sin he may do repentance when his conscience is aroused, but when he suffers from pride, then even when he is stirred to repentance, he only increases the degree of his pride. And this thing disqualifies a man from all service of God whatever. . . . The man [of this kind] says to himself when he begins to learn that he will become a great scholar and a great man of piety, and since he has this spark of pride he shows that he and I cannot dwell in the same place.[62]

The last phrase, of course, points to the passage in the *Gemara* on the subject of pride that reads, "Everyone who prides himself, of him the Holy One, blessed be He, says that he and I cannot dwell [together] in the world."[63] The Talmudic passage originally reflected a belief that certain sins, notably that of pride, caused the *Shekhinah* to depart from the place in which the sinner dwelt.[64] But in the Talmud there was no doctrine of God's indwelling in man. In later Cabbala this saying received a personal significance—the *Shekhinah* is there described as avoiding the sinner and not merely his immediate environment.[65] In early Hasidism the idea has a much more vital implication. Ecstasy was the culmination of religious experience and was conceived of as the ingress and the indwelling of the divine spirit in man. Thus the sin of pride, by shutting out God, would exclude ecstasy.

An examination of the precise nature of this negative mystical experience will reveal that ecstasy in early Hasidism never led to the deification of the mystic: all the texts are unanimous in describing the twofold mystical experience of the Hasid as (*a*) the *via negativa* of the self-annihilation of man and (*b*) the consequent infusion of the Divine into man and its indwelling in him. It is never said that the mystic becomes, even momentarily, God or Godlike. The Hasidic type of ecstasy conceives of man as the mere vessel into which the Divine flows—he never actually merges with the Divine. The idea of the absorption of man into the Divine is barely mentioned in texts from this earliest period of Hasidism, even though the concept does develop somewhat later. Nor is the soul to be visualized in early Hasidism as being shriveled up like a moth in a flame. Needless to say, all radical expressions of "identity-mysticism" (*Identitäts-mystik*), such as those found in Islamic mysticism, where the mystic states, "I am God and God is me," have no place at all in Hasidic literature.

There is hardly any trace in early Hasidism of a conception of *unio mystica* as the coalescence of human existence into the divine existence, similar to the absorption of a drop of water by the waters of the ocean. In the genuinely Maggidic texts the process moves strictly in one direction only: God invades the human frame and dwells within it.

There is also no question of the soul's ascent or return to the divine soul whence it sprang. The idea of a return that is so widespread in descriptions of ecstasy in non-Jewish mystical literature is conspicuously absent. The function of asceticism is not to volatilize the soul for its heavenly journey. The ascent of the soul heavenwards does not play any part at all in the mystical experience. Ecstasy does not signify the passage of the soul from the body. The soul remains motionless waiting for the Divine to take possession of it following its self-annihilation. The meaning of the unitive experience is quite unequivocal. It can be best illustrated by the image of water flowing into a jar emptied of its contents, although the Maggid himself never uses this comparison.

The mystical aim of the annihilation of self is clearly not the annihilation of the soul. The soul is considered to be of Divine origin or character and even a "particle of God from above." What is required is to eradicate the self-assertive impulses of the human ego and the possessive claims of the self. Selfhood in its various expressions, ranging from pride to the very awareness of separate existence, is to be extinguished, if the ecstatic experience is to take place.

A more radical type of mystical union is represented by R. Yehiel Michel of Zloczów of the second generation. His teachings come closer to the ideas of the pure mystic than do those of the Great Maggid, with whom he is at variance in such important matters as the treatment of wayward thoughts during prayer or contemplation. In his view, as opposed to the view of the Great Maggid, self-annihilation should lead to that type of ecstasy in which the human personality will be absorbed and lose itself in a fusion with God. In a language with strongly pantheistic overtones, he propounds the mystery of self-extinction leading to deification as the fruit of communion with God. The essential oneness of man with God is expressed by means of the simile of the relationship of a branch to the root of a tree and the final experience is compared to that of the drop absorbed in the waters of the sea. The Divine and the human are no longer distinct entities within the mystical experience but they are of one and the same substance: water and water, wood and wood:

And this is the content of his words—writes R. Meshullam Phoebus of Zbaraz—that the purpose of the creation of the world was the pleasure and delight that God, blessed be He, would receive from it, the great pleasure He would receive from emanating the souls of Israel which would come down through many thousands and tens of thousands of worlds until they reached this world, where they would take a material shape and from which, from a great distance, they would purify themselves in order to approach Him and cleave to Him in their thoughts and in their love of Him. They would be attached to Him with cleaving, desire and wish. And they would consider themselves to be nought [*ayin*], understanding that truly without the power of the Creator, blessed be His Name, who created them and who keeps them in existence, they are nought just as before the creation; consequently there is nothing in the world but the Creator, blessed be He. And he said accordingly that it is the opposite of what men imagine: when they are not attached to the Creator, blessed be His Name, but to earthly things, they think that they themselves exist [*yesh*] and are important and great in their own eyes. And can they be great when one night they exist and the next they are lost? Their days are as passing shadows and even in their lives they are vanity. Thus if they think that they exist then they certainly do not. This is not so if they think that they are nought because of their attachment to the Creator. Consequently they cleave with all their mental powers to God and thus they are very great since the branch [of the tree] came to the root and is one with the root. And the root is *En-Sof*. Therefore the branch is also *En-Sof* because it has lost its existence [*nithbattel ba-meṣiuth*] like a drop which has fallen into the great sea and has come to its root and therefore it is one with the waters of the sea and it is not possible to recognise it as a separate thing [*bifnei aṣmah*] at all.[66]

Radical features the absence of which we have noticed in Maggidic mysticism come strongly to the fore in this passage. They are the deification of the human being and his transformation into the divine substance in terms of absorption into the Deity. Man is capable of becoming divine in the mystical experience because he was always essentially divine.

Was this passage perhaps conceived within the radius of Ḥabadic influence? There are certain terminological usages that would suggest this; they may have crept in later, however, when the above dictum acquired its written form from the pen of R. Yehiel Michel's disciple.

Though Ḥabad represents Hasidism at both its most academic and refined, nevertheless this school was unrestrained in its experience of deification and also abandoned all reticence in its description of this experience. The Ḥabadic mystics went much further in exploring in their scholastic fashion the intricacies of mystical self-annihilation by drawing subtle distinctions among the various mystical states. R. Dov Baer, the son of R. Shneur Zalman, concentrated his analytical powers on defining the double aspect of Ḥabadic ecstasy. He differentiated between two aspects of the ecstatic experience which he called respectively self-annihilation (*bittul aṣmo*) and self-integration into the higher light (*hithkalleluth le-or ha-elyon*).

A novel feature in the Ḥabadic concept of self-annihilation relates to the external circumstances in which the mystical experience occurs: the time for ecstatic self-effacement during the course of the daily prayers has altered. In the Great Maggid's practice, the *Amidah* prayer of the Eighteen Benedictions—the central prayer of Jewish liturgy—was the supreme occasion for self-annihilation; in the Ḥabadic school this prayer and the other important feature of the traditional daily service, the recital of the *Shema*, have only a preparatory function, and the climax of self-annihilation takes place during *Taḥanun*, a prayer traditionally uttered immediately after the *Amidah*, while the worshiper is in a condition of prostration.

Probably the symbolic interpretation of the prescribed bodily positions of the worshiper during these prayers was decisive in moving the climax of ecstasy to *Taḥanun*. Apart from the obvious suitability of a prayer uttered while the body is prostrate for an experience of self-effacement, there is a precedent in Lurianic Cabbala for the elevation of *Taḥanun* to a most prominent place in the liturgy. Here, too, the bodily position of prostration was considered a symbolic expression of the spiritual state of the worshiper. Whereas in Lurianic Cabbala prostration was the occasion for the contemplative *descensus ad inferos*, in Ḥabadic Hasidism the prayer served as an opportunity for contemplative self-annihilation. So much for the new location of the highest stages of ecstasy in the course of the daily service.

A second novel feature, and one of more fundamental significance, is the incisive distinction made in the Ḥabadic texts between two types of self-annihilation. There are two stages in the mystic's process, each of which corresponds to a different degree of ecstasy. The lower degree of self-annihilation includes the suspension of the senses and amounts to the loss of personal existence. Confusion and incapacity to use one's intellectual qualities are the main symptoms of the first stage of self-annihilation, which still leaves man separate and as yet not absorbed into the Godhead.

This absorption into and inclusion within the divine life is the accomplishment of the second, higher grade of self-annihilation. At this degree of mystical experience man ceases to exist as a separate being and is totally integrated and absorbed into the Divine.

NOTES

1. Joseph Bernhard, "Zur Soziologie der Mystik," *Süddeutsche Monatshefte* 1 (1928): 27.

2. Bibliographical references on this point would run into legion; I note here only W. R. Inge, *Christian Mysticism* (London, 1912), pp. 117–22.

3. W. R. Inge, *Mysticism in Religion* (London, n.d.), p. 28.

4. *Practical Mysticism* (London and Toronto, 1914), pp. 133–34, see also pp. 128–30.

5. Sein [des Chassidismus] Kern ist eine höchst gotterfüllte und höchst realistische Anleitung zur Ekstase als zu dem Gipfel des Daseins. Aber die Ekstase ist hier nicht, wie etwa bei der deutschen Mystik, ein 'Entwerden'; nicht die sich beschränkende und entäussernde sondern die sich vollendende Seele mündet ins Unbedingte" (*Die jüdische Mystik*, in *Die Chassidischen Bücher*, p. 14). Perhaps it is unfair to Buber to quote such an early formulation of his (written originally in 1906 in the introduction to his German translation of Rabbi Naḥman's parables). The formal distinction between the two types of ecstasy is certainly legitimate; see, e.g., the very same distinction between Plotinus and Philo: "The Plotinian ecstasy, unlike the Philonic . . . is presented less as the abnegation of the self-hood than as the supreme self-realization," E. R. Dodds, "Parmenides and the Neoplatonic 'One,'" *The Classical Quarterly* 22 (1928): 142.

6. A short analysis of it is given below, pp. 156–7.

7. *Solomon Maimons Lebensgeschichte*, herausgegeben von Dr. Jakob Fromer (Munich, 1911), p. 204. An English translation by J. Clark Murray was published in 1888 (new edition, 1944), p. 169.

8. The link between the philosophy of German idealism and the German mysticism of the Middle Ages is well known. For a great mass of detail, including the question of

self-annihilation, see the bulky albeit shallow study by E. von Bracken, *Meister Eckhart und Fichte* (Würzburg, 1943). On the question of self-annihilation in the philosophy of idealism, see Fichte's memorable words in his short mystical treatise *Anweisung zum seligen Leben* ed. Medicus (Leipzig, 1910), p. 128: "Solange der Mensch noch irgend etwas selbst zu sein begehrt, kommt Gott nicht zu ihm, denn kein Mensch kann Gott werden. Sobald er sich aber rein, ganz und bis in die Wurzel vernichtet, bleibt allein Gott übrig, und ist alles im allem. Der Mensch kann sich keinen Gott erzeugen; aber sich selbst, als die eigentliche Negation, kann er vernichten, und sodann versinket er in Gott."

9. The identity of the *Ṣaddik* called by Maimon "B. from M." is obvious.

10. *Lebensgeschichte*, p. 200; *Autobiography*, p. 166. A but slightly different rendering of this homily is to be found in the book *Tifereth Uzziel* by R. Uzziel Meisels, a disciple of the Maggid, who reformulated the originally mystical wording of the Maggid in an ethical rather than mystical tone. "What I have also heard from my teacher and Master Dov Baer . . . on the verse *and it was when the minstrel played that the spirit of God came upon him*, it is apparent to anyone that one who plays well upon an instrument has ulterior motives (*peniyyoth*) and his chief object is pride in his own voice. This is not so of the instrument whereon he plays. For it is inanimate and certainly lacks any ability to have ulterior motives. And this is the meaning of the verse *and it was when the minstrel played*, i.e., if the minstrel, that is to say the human being, is as that which is played,—in other words if he is like the instrument on which music is produced, so that he too has no ulterior motives, like an instrument which has none either—then the spirit of God will come upon him." (*Tifereth Uzziel* [Warsaw 1862], p. 39b). This formulation of the teaching expresses the idea of passive conduct with emphasis upon humility (see my note on the two variants, "A Hasidic Homily by the Maggid of Mesritz [Hebrew], *Ṣion*, 12:97). The self-annihilation counseled in R. Uzziel's version is in fact the annihilation of individual pride, a feature with which we cannot deal fully in this paper. R. Ephraim of Sudylkow, a grandson of the Baalshem, adopts the above-cited verse and also its exegesis, in incidental fashion and without mentioning the Maggid's name as his authority; but it is perfectly obvious that he quotes the same tradition. See his *Degel Maḥaneh Efrayim* (Korzecz, 1810), p. 99a, in the homily for *Shabbath Teshuvah*.

11. In European tradition this kind of image is as early as the fifth oracle of Montanus, who compared man in ecstasy to a harp upon which the divinity plays; see P. de Labriolle, *La Crise Montaniste* (Paris, 1913), p. 45. This author collected in a footnote all the parallels on the theme of "instrumental" human passivity he had succeeded in finding. But there is much material that might be added. On further parallels in medieval mysticism, see, e.g., the posthumous work of H. S. Denifle, *Die Deutschen Mystiker des 14-ten Jahrhunderts* (Freiburg in der Schweiz, 1951), pp. 98, 163.

12. *Or ha-emeth* (1900), p. 3b.

13. *Maḥashavah, dibbur, u-ma'aseh.*

14. On this point, see below.

15. *Ḥayyim va-ḥesed* (Warsaw, 1891), p. 34a.

16. *Ma'or va-shemesh* (Satmar, 1942), part 1, p. 44a.

17. *Oraḥ le-ḥayyim* (*s.a.s.l.* Lemberg?) 5th part, p. 26b.

18. Very occasionally the Maggid too, although in principle excluding action from the realm of direct Divine instigation, would state that "all comes from thee, and we do for thee what is thine." (*Or Torah* [Korzecz, 1804], in the section on *Psalms* without pagination ([p. 94a-b]), but unlike the teaching of R. Abraham Hayyim, no further theological conclusions are drawn from this, except that in spite of this God takes pride in man (ibid.) "Thou takest pride in us as if what we do comes from our own strength." By implication, this must mean meritorious deeds only, and not all actions indiscriminately. There are hardly any instances to be found in Hasidic literature in which God is made responsible or coresponsible, on account of His exclusive activity, for human sins. Perhaps in popular Hasidism with its subliterary and oral forms of transmission (as to the

existence of which, see my remarks below, p. 121, n. 45), which made possible the maintenance of unusually radical and enthusiastic views, the coresponsibility of God with man in man's sinful acts was entertained. A vague statement to this effect by R. Phinehas of Korzecz is briefly recorded in *Ḥayyei Moharan* (Jerusalem, 1947], *Hashmatoth* added at the end of the volume, § 3. It may be symptomatic, however, that the particular saying does not occur in any of the various collections of R. Phinehas' dicta or in the rich material contained in A. Heschel's article on R. Phinehas in *Alei Ayin*, Jubilee Volume in honor of S. Z. Schocken (1947–52), pp. 213–44. Of course, his historical relationship to Israel Baalshem is in need of clarification. One wonders whether he was a disciple of Israel Baalshem, as later Hasidism described him or rather a colleague of his. Phinehas visited Israel Baalshem once or twice (see A. Heschel, p. 218), but his teaching does not seem to be derived from Israel Baalshem. He appears rather to be one of a number of exponents of a wild popular pantheism current in the Ukraine. Among these comparatively illiterate or semiliterate charismatics Israel Baalshem was not necessarily chronologically the first though clearly the most successful. To understand the figure of Israel Baalshem in the context of a group of itinerant enthusiasts of popular pantheism is one of the urgent tasks of historical research.

19. *Oraḥ le-ḥayyim*, part 2, p. 34b: "In all acts of worship man does nothing at all. . . . So we see that it is God that does and completes every act of worship and every commandment; but through His grace He rewards man for his will and desire to do the commandment, as if [man himself] performed it. Thine, O Lord, is grace, for Thou dost repay man according to his deeds, that is to say, as if he himself had performed them."

20. *Or ha-emeth* (1900), p. 8a, in *mashal lifnei ha-teki'oth* i.e., in the context the passage is connected with the shofar and has to be considered as a variation on the shofar motif. On the organ (*magrefah*), see T.B. *Arakhin* 10b.

21. On *Kadmuth ha-Sekhel*, see G. Scholem, "Ha-Bilti muda' u-musag Kadmuth ha-Sekhel ba-sifruth ha-ḥasidith," *Haguth*, 1944, pp. 145 ff.

22. *Or ha-emeth* (1900), p. 86.

23. *Ṣofenath Pa'aneaḥ* (1782), p. 16b.

24. *Ben Porath Yosef* (1781), p. 60a. This passage is identical in content with the previous one. *Malkhuth* is nothing but the tenth *Sefirah*, which has several names in Cabbalistic literature. The most usual among them are *Shekhinah* and *Malkhuth*. Likewise *Ani*, the Divine *I*, is one of the names of the last *Sefirah*. An almost identical formulation, also in the name of Israel Baalshem, is to be found in the same author's *Toledoth Ya'akov Yosef* (1780), p. 143b.

25. See above, p. 72.

26. In the original German text, *Gottesdienst*.

27. *Lebensgeschichte*, p. 195; *Autobiography*, p. 160–61.

28. I.e., the words of the *Amidah* prayer.

29. *Or Torah* (Korzecz, 1804), p. [136b] in the section on Aggadoth of the volume that has no pagination. Zolkiew ed. (1850), p. 40b.

30. Ibid., Korzecz [115a], in the section on Selected Verses. Zolkiew (1850), p. 24b. Also *Or ha-emeth*, p. 12b.

31. In Cabbalistic nomenclature *Adonai*, Lord, stands for the last *Sefirah*, otherwise termed *Shekhinah*.

32. The whole passage reads as follows: "And the Lord spoke unto Moses, saying: Speak unto the children of Israel and say unto them, I am the Lord thy God. (Lev. 18:1–2).

33. *Or ha-emeth*, p. 32.

34. Ibid., p. 68b.

35. T. B. *Sanhedrin*, 39a.

36. *Or Torah* (1804), p. [132a]. Also *Or ha-emeth*, p. 4a.

37. In accordance with the Talmudic definition of prayer as the "service of the heart," *avodah she-ba-lev* (T.B. *Ta'anith* 2 b).

38. The expression "the *Shekhinah* speaks from his throat" (*Shekhinah medabbereth mittokh gerono*) is not to be found in the Talmud or Midrash, and it seems to have been coined later, see A. Hyman, *Oṣar divrei ḥakhamim* (Tel-Aviv, 1947), p. 524. Already Goldziher, when investigating the Islamic ramifications of the dictum, had to admit regarding the Hebrew formula: "Die Quelle kann ich leider nicht angeben; ebenso wenig ist es mehreren, in den rabbinischen Schriften belesenen Gelehrten gelungen, die Stelle dieses Spruches, dessen Vorhandensein jeder der Befragten zugestand, nachzuweisen" (*Abhandlungen zur arabischen Philologie*, 1:195); idem, La Notion de la Sakîna, p. 12.

39. *Or ha-meir*, (Korzecz, 1798), part *Rimzei Vayikra*, p. 2b. R. Ze'ev Wolf himself was no advocate of ecstasy and *via passiva*, as his voluminous book clearly indicates.

40. The long *derashoth* of R. Jacob Joseph of Polonnoye are in this respect not representative of the early Hasidic sermon; their author is patently no ecstatic.

41. *Lebensgeschichte*, p. 199; *Autobiography*, p. 164.

42. See my remarks above pp. 000–00.

43. In the German original: *der hohe Obere*, meaning, of course, the *Ṣaddik*.

44. *Lebensgeschichte*, p. 203; *Autobiography*, p. 168.

45. On the man and his polemical writings see G. Scholem in *Ṣion* 20 (1955): 153–62.

46. I.e., great authorities.

47. Vol. I, p. 5a.

48. Here the text seems to be corrupt.

49. In Poland, near Warsaw.

50. The verse was misquoted by the Hasidim, as becomes clear in the course of the story.

51. *Sefer Vikkuaḥ* (Warsaw, 1798), p. 19b–20a.

52. "*she-ha-Shem yithbarakh mizdammen* (=*mezammen*) *lahem Torah*," ibid., p. 20a.

53. Ibid.

54. Probably as a kind of internal apologetic censorship, see above, p. 39, n. 9.

55. The radically quietistic attitude of R. Hayyim Haika of Amdura, epitomized in the demand of "slaughtering one's own will": "when they bring to Thee sacrifice of will [freewill sacrifice], i.e., when a man wishes to offer [sacrifice] himself to the Holy One, blessed be He, he sacrifices his own will" (*Ḥayyim va-ḥesed* [Warsaw, 1891], p. 31b), lies outside the narrow limits of the present enquiry. R. Hayyim's aim is not ecstasy, but *unio per voluntatem*.

56. [J. W. apparently intended this to be added to section II of the foregoing. It seems, however, to be unfinished.]

57. The religious ideas of the early *Ṣaddik* Rafael of Berszada, a pupil of R. Phinehas of Korzecz, are quite isolated in the general stream of Hasidism, being crystalized round the ideal of truth (*emeth*). Accordingly, his system lacks the mystical-contemplative values of other early masters of Hasidism. Indeed R. Rafael's connections with Hasidism seem to have been more environmental than doctrinal. The work *Pe'er la-yesharim* (Jerusalem, 1921) contains much material from R. Rafael and would merit a full analysis.

58. The connection between humility and ecstasy in early Hasidism has been correctly understood by Ysander. See *Studien*, p. 244.

59. *Degel Maḥaneh Efrayim* (Korzecz, 1810), f. 56b (beginning of section *ṣav*).

60. *Teshu'oth ḥen* (Berdyczów, 1816), f. 31b.

61. It is impossible to recount here the history of the accusation of pride leveled by the Hasidim against the *Mithnaggedim* in the earlier period of the movement, before the advent of the later charges. I can only bring one characteristic extract from the Great Maggid to illustrate this standardized condemnation of their opponents: "These are the servants of God who stand in the house of God" (Ps. 135:1–2). The meaning is: there are

two classes of men who come to take lodgings with an important man; one class says that they too are important people and that when they come to the important man, they maintain that that person should be exceedingly honored by their coming. But the other class are in their own account as *nothing*, and when they come to reside with the great man, they have a strong sense of privilege, for [they ask] in what have they deserved that they should come and stand in his courtyard? So is this matter. There are men who learn a little and say that He, blessed be He, is honored in them, which is what we mean by saying that they are self-important and that they do not find it natural to subordinate themselves. But there is another class of modest folk whose element and temper are like the dust which is trampled underfoot by all and who humble themselves and wonder by what merit they stand in the courtyards of the Holy One, blessed be He." (*Or Torah* [Lublin, 1884], p. 9). The use of the word *lomedim* (scholars) makes it quite clear that the proud ones to whom he refers are the Talmudic scholars, notoriously the archenemies of Hasidism. Prima facie, the pride of which one would expect a scholar to be accused by his revivalist opponent is social pride: the scholar congratulating himself on his intellectual superiority over the illiterates. It is interesting to note that it is not this kind of pride of which the Maggid accused the *Mithnaggedim*, but pride in the face of God. The shift of the scope of humility from the social to the religious context of the relationship between man and God is paralleled by the same shift in the concept of its antithesis, pride. This by no means implies, of course, that the concepts of humility and pride in their conventional social meaning are altogether absent in Hasidic writings.

62. [*Or Torah* (Lublin, 1884), p. 70.]
63. [T. B. *Sotah*, 5a.]
64. See J. Abelson, *The Immanence of God in Rabbinical Literature* (London, 1912), p. 112.
65. See *Reshith Ḥokhmah*, *Sha'ar ha-anavah* (Munkácz, n.d.), chap. 3, f. 220.
66. [*Yosher Divrei Emeth* (Munkácz, 1905), f. 15b.]

The Kavvanoth of Prayer in Early Hasidism

The mind of the Cabbalist at prayer confronts not the God of traditional religion, but the whole Sefirotic universe. As he progresses through the fixed prayers, the utterance of each and every word or phrase is expected to cause a particular zone on the Sefirotic map to flash into his contemplative consciousness. Moreover, this system of *Kavvanoth*, particularly in its Lurianic version, has a strong magical flavor[1] arising from the assumption that human contemplative recollection of Sefirotic processes taking place in the Divine realm is capable of contributing to, and is indeed instrumental in, activating the very same Divine processes.

The Cabbalist's contemplative journey through the zones in the Sefirotic world is not left to the wanton choice of the contemplative traveller but requires extreme discipline and follows clearly charted routes. The strict progression of the *Kavvanoth* is the very opposite of religious anarchism. The mystic's contemplative thought is not allowed to float indiscriminately or in an irresponsible, arbitrary and capricious way, but is supposed to follow an exact chart directing every movement of the contemplative mind during prayer.

From the situation described a problem inevitably arises: The fixed texts of the traditional Jewish prayers reflect the religious world of Judaism in the first centuries C.E., the time of their formulation. They were left unchanged by the Cabbalists, along with all other Jews, in deference to the well-known conservative tendencies of Jewish mystics.[2] Nevertheless, while the Cabbalist uttered the prayers in their traditional wording, his contemplative mind would be at large in an entirely different religious landscape. He had to reinterpret all the elements of a religious conception he had left behind in terms of his Cabbalistic piety revolving round the Sefirotic system and its emanative or copulative intricacies. In other words: it is not the original concern of the petitionary prayer that was at the forefront of his contemplative interest, but the new religious fascination of Sefiroth[3]; their emanations and re-emanations, the descent and ascent of the "upper worlds" or the holy copulation between the male and female aspects of the Sefirotic universe.

But the Cabbalist had to pay a high price for the retention of the traditional formulations of his prayers. It was the price of a certain divorce between the text of the prayer he was uttering and its contemplative meaning. The psychology behind the technique of *Kavvanoth* during prayer is still a riddle to the student of Cabbala. Was mind completely separated from lips except insofar as the spoken word of prayer acted as a springboard for the contemplative journey to the "corresponding" Sefirotic realities? The coordination between the minute literary units of the prayer text and their corresponding meditations was certainly such as to exclude the primary meaning of the text from the threshold of the contemplative mind—at least in terms of normal, everyday-life psychology. But did this exclude the literal meaning of the prayer from the mind of the Cabbalist who lived in a state of consciousness more complex than the normal? Can one assume that there were two levels in the mental activity of the Cabbalist working simultaneously, a dichotomy of mind that enabled him to follow on a conscious level—though not on a contemplative one—the thread of the text and at the same time to pursue, on a contemplative level, his rapidly shifting mental concentrations? I would be inclined toward the latter interpretation and assume rather that the coexistence of the two levels is the main clue to the psychology of *Kavvanoth*. This would explain why it is reported to be so extraordinarily difficult to acquire the meditative technique of prayer with *Kavvanoth* and become a well-trained practitioner of this art.

The Cabbalistic method of *Kavvanoth* is founded on the "paradox of solitude and community." It is an aristocratic art practiced by the Cabbalists within the praying community of simple, plebeian worshipers of the non-Cabbalistic fashion. The usual setting of the Cabbalistic *Kavvanoth* is thus in the solitary practice of the exceptional individual who is outwardly embedded in the prayer life of his community. The large gathering of the synagogue would never be capable of reciting the prayers with meditative perfection; this is why the Cabbalist, even though praying in a synagogue and thus participating in corporate worship, will practice the *Kavvanoth* in a climate of mental isolation—to say nothing about the unavoidable time lag between the community praying at a nonmeditative pace and himself enveloped in lingering *Kavvanoth*.

However, the solitary meditations of the Lurianic system of *Kavvanoth* were put into practice in a communal setting in a small Jerusalem group called Beth El. It was founded by the great Yemenite Cabbalist R. Shalom Sharabi in the eighteenth century. Today it consists of about thirty members of a Cabbalistic elite centered round a synagogue which used to be in the Old City of Jerusalem before the Arab-Israeli war. Its members are called *Mekhavvenim*, i.e., those who pray with meditation. The "holy order" endeavored from its inception to remove the method of *Kavvanoth* from the original setting of aristocrats meditating among ordinary worshipers and transformed the whole practice of *Kavvanoth* into a corporate reality among the select group with their three daily prayers conducted in long sessions of several hours each. As we know from the vivid description of a son of one of the members of this order, Ariel Bension,[4] this predominantly Sephardi community of the *Mekhavvenim* used to practice the art of meditation during prayer rapt in complete silence and only later was cantillation introduced to accompany the silent *Kavvanoth* of the members.

Another congregation of meditating Cabbalists, near in both time and place to the rise of Hasidism, was the famous Klaus of Brody.[5] Its members were also called "Hasidim" but in an older meaning of the word. The members of this group, like the members of Beth El in Jerusalem, were Cabbalists of the highest repute, and to belong to their Beth Midrash was a hallmark of profound Cabbalistic learning. This community provided a fertile soil for the fine intricacies of corporate meditative prayer. The members of the Klaus were explicitly exempt from the ban pronounced against Hasidim in Brody in 1772. In the text of the ban, the Cabbalists of the Klaus are characterized, in contrast to the new Hasidim, as "learned in both the exoteric and esoteric teachings, their main preoccupation being the exoteric[6] . . . famed for their piety, [people] who know their Master and who direct themselves in the way of truth, מפורסמים בחסידות, יודעים רבונם ומכוונים על דרך האמת."[7]

In the first part of this passage, "famed for their piety," etc., the word *piety* (*ḥasiduth*) is certainly not a vague expression thrown up carelessly, but chosen deliberately to hint at the association of this Cabbalistic aristocracy with the type of "true" Hasidim, that religious type of ascetics who largely constituted pre-Hasidic Hasidism.[8] Similarly, the closing part, "and they direct themselves in the way of truth," has a technical meaning. The "way of truth" (*derekh ha-emeth*) is a widely used circumlocution for Cabbala. One did not need to be a Cabbalist accustomed to eliciting hidden allusions in order to understand the formula in this sense. It was a commonly used reference to scores of Cabbalistic commentaries described as being "'*al derekh ha-emeth*." Similarly, the expression *mekhavvenim* seems to be used in its Cabbalistic technical sense meaning not simply "directing themselves" or "intending" but "meditating" or "practicing *Kavvanoth*." Thus the concluding passage of the sentence, in which the mainly Yiddish text of the ban falls back on Hebrew, characterizes the Cabbalistic circle of the Klaus of Brody as true Hasidim who meditate in Cabbalistic fashion. This is in emphasized contrast to the common Hasidim, against whom the ban is directed, and who are obviously considered not to be doing so. It is not stated that the meditations in question which the true Hasidim practiced, and which the new Hasidim, by implication, did not, were meditations of prayer and not, for instance, meditations during the practice of *miṣvoth* (*kavvanoth ha-miṣvoth*). But since the ban deals at length with habits of prayer among Hasidim and is motivated by an attempt to wipe out certain peculiarities pertaining to them, e.g., their lack of respect for the prayer times laid down by the Halakhah, etc., and since the phrase in question appears in such a context, its interpretation in the sense of meditations of prayer rather than meditations accompanying *miṣvoth* is beyond doubt. By implication, it would appear that the Hasidim in 1772 did not practice *Kavvanoth* of prayer, a result that will be corroborated by the analysis of the relevant Hasidic texts.

Already before the sudden collapse of the practice of the *Kavvanoth* in the early phases of Hasidism, the elaborate Lurianic system of meditation during prayer suffered a severe crisis in the Sabbatian movement of the seventeenth century. Nathan of Gaza, the first theologian of this heresy, abolished the whole system of Lurianic *Kavvanoth* in 1666, basing his abrogation on the claim that a system of *Kavvanoth* which had been worked out for pre-Messianic times was utterly unsuitable, even impermissible, at the dawn of the Messianic epoch. Anyone practicing such a system was compared by him to "someone doing weekday work on the Sabbath."

One may say that the latent revolutionary attitude of Sabbatian religious thought exhibits a more radical break with tradition in the question of the *Kavvanoth* than in any other field. Certainly, the Halakhic system of commandments and prohibitions was not thrown overboard at this comparatively early phase of the Sabbatian movement. But the radical abolition of *Kavvanoth* in prayer was an expression of the latent revolutionary forces in Sabbatianism, which scored a full victory at this point of least resistance in the texture of traditional Judaism. The *Kavvanoth* of prayer, the ripe fruits of meditative prayer life according to the Lurianic Cabbala, fell first victim to the Sabbatian sensation of a new epoch.[9] The Hasidic movement witnessed a somewhat similar abrogation of this meditative practice. Since the motives which led the Hasidim to eliminate the *Kavvanoth* were entirely different from those which had brought Sabbatianism to the same result, there is hardly any need to point out that no historical connection existed between the two parallel phenomena.

In any event, the Lurianic tradition of *Kavvanoth* was not wiped out suddenly when Hasidism emerged in the history of Jewish mysticism. The *Siddur ha-Ari*, the great prayerbook of Isaac Luria containing the *Kavvanoth*, was reprinted in Hasidic circles. The famous prayerbook of Shabbethai of Raszkow, who perhaps did not belong to Hasidism yet had close personal contact with Israel Baalshem (quoted several times in his commentary on the prayerbook), was in essence but a reproduction of the Lurianic *Siddur* with the traditional *Kavvanoth*.[10]

One cannot find any clear-cut statement or declaration of principle on the question of the *Kavvanoth* of prayer from the earliest days of the Hasidic movement.[11] Indeed, the position of Israel Baalshem himself concerning the practical question of *Kavvanoth* during prayer is rather obscure. He did not explicitly oppose *Kavvanoth* of prayer. On the other hand, we do not know whether he practiced them himself. I have already called the Cabbalistic prayer meditations an aristocratic art. The practice of the elaborate technique of the Lurianic *Kavvanoth* was by necessity confined to the limited number of a spiritual elite who could cope with the immense intellectual task of countless contemplative flying visits to precisely charted points of the Sefirotic universe, the mental map of which was at the fingertips of every well-trained Cabbalist.

It is very doubtful whether Israel Baalshem himself was fully qualified as a Cabbalist to become one of those initiated into the mysteries of meditative prayer life. Both his Cabbalistic and Talmudic knowledge seems to have consisted of some bare elements drawn from the secondary sources of the then popular anthologies. His Talmudic education appears to have been based mainly on *En Ya'akov*, an anthology of the Haggadic passages of the Talmud collected by the sixteenth-century Italian Talmudist R. Jacob Ibn Ḥabib, which had become a standard work for the untutored with good intentions.[12] Similarly his scanty Cabbalistic knowledge was possibly drawn from widely read Cabbalistic anthologies. People with so limited a knowledge were certainly not considered well equiped for the rather involved meditative art of *Kavvanoth* during prayer.

In what follows we shall have to consider two different kinds of testimony about Israel Baalshem's position regarding the *Kavvanoth* of prayer. Both of them are derived from secondary sources. The first source is the legendary biography of Israel Baalshem, published 1815, over half a century after its hero's death. Despite this time-lag we have in it a fairly reliable source for the life and *millieu* of the founder of Hasidism, and not a late fabrication projecting contemporary problems and attitudes into an earlier period. The second and more direct body of sources of information is a number of scattered passages in the writings of his disciples, who either quote his teachings verbatim or describe behavior reflecting his views. The scarcity of material compels one to make use also of certain fragmentary and clumsy traditions. From all this analysis no consistent concept of *Kavvanoth* of prayer seems to appear and the picture of Israel Baalshem's views and practice that emerges is somewhat vague. The evidence predominantly suggests that he had abandoned *Kavvanoth* as a method of meditation in the strict Cabbalistic sense, or rather never practiced them at all.

There is no vast amount of biographical testimony that could be collected and from which some preliminary conclusions could be drawn. The most important passage of the *Shivḥei ha-Besht* regarding the place of the *Kavvanoth* in the prayer life of Israel Baalshem is the following:

> I have heard from R. Falk that when R. Gershon of Kutov came abroad from Palestine to marry off his son, he said incidentally: "thank Heavens, I crossed the sea, let me go to my brother-in-law the Baalshem Tov." He arrived there on Friday. The Baalshem stood up and was [engaged] in the afternoon prayer and he prolonged his prayer until stars came out.[13] R. Gershon also prayed from a prayer book of R. I. Luria.[14] Afterwards [R. Gershon] read the [weekly] portion twice with translation,[15] then he asked for cushions which were brought, and he lay down to rest. On Friday night during the meal R. Gershon asked his brother-in-law the Baalshem Tov: "Why did you prolong the prayer so much? I too prayed with *Kavvanoth* and read the [weekly] portion twice with the translation, then I had to lie down to rest while you were standing and trembling and making gestures!" For he [R. Gershon] wanted to elicit some statement from him. But the Baalshem remained silent and answered him nothing. And he asked him repeatedly. So the Baalshem Tov replied: When I come to the words "He revives the dead" . . . and I meditate the *Kavvanah* of *Yiḥudim*, then the souls of the dead come in their thousands and in their tens of thousands, and I have to discuss with each one of them why he was cast out of his heavenly place.[16] And I effect a *Tikkun* for him, pray for him and uplift him. . . . And they are so numerous, that if I wished to uplift them all, I would have to stand in the *Shemoneh Esreh* prayer for three years.[17]

In its further development, the story proves to be describing one of those situations recurrent in the legendary biography in which representatives of higher Halakhic or Cabbalistic knowledge put Israel Baalshem to the test. In these circumstances it is apparent, at least in the opinion of the *Shivḥei's* author, that R. Gershon's remark "I too prayed with *Kavvanoth*" was an ironical jibe at Israel Baalshem's assumed incapacity to meditate due to his scanty knowledge of Cabbala. Israel Baalshem at first ignored the question,[18] but eventually betrayed that it was not the Lurianic *Kavvanoth* of prayer that kept him so long in prayer. He rather busied himself with some highly individual meditative operations of his own devising that he was willing to put at the disposal of his brother-in-law.[19]

A second example of prolonged meditative prayer on the part of the Baalshem Tov without *Kavvanoth* is the following, reported similarly in the *Shivḥei*:

> I have heard in the name of R. Eliyyahu of Sokolwka[20]: When he was still a youngster, living in Miedzyborz,[21] he heard once that the Baalshem Tov said, "He who wishes his prayer to reach Heaven, let him pray with me word for word!" And R. Eliyyahu did so. When the Baalshem Tov said "*Adon*," he said so too, and when he said "*Olam*," he too said, "*Olam*,"[22] until the whole prayer was ended. And they did so for a long time. Once the Baalshem Tov reached in the *Pesukei de-zimra*[23] the verse "false is the horse for deliverance" (Ps. 33:17) and he repeated it several times, lingering over it for a long time. [R. Eliyyahu] said it with him the first time and afterwards wondered what he was meditating upon in this verse. So he looked up the book *Mishnath Ḥasidim*,[24] but there were no *Kavvanoth* [for this verse]. So he ceased to pray with him. One day he came to the Baalshem Tov's house. The Baalshem saw him and said to him: "Eliyyahu, you have ceased to pray with me!" He told him that it was because he said that verse several times. He replied: "it happened that a Jew on the highway on Friday could not reach a village before the Sabbath and spent the Sabbath in a field. It became known to a robber that a Jew was spending the Sabbath in a field, and he rode on a horse to find and kill him. By saying this [verse] I put him off the track so that he would not find him."[25]

Here the Baalshem is confronted not by a Cabbalist of high standing who does not deem him qualified to pray with *Kavvanoth* as on the previous occasion, but by a young boy who naturally expects the lengthy prayer of Israel Baalshem to result from the use of Lurianic *Kavvanoth*. But the Baalshem disappoints him. The sequel to the story reveals a similar state of affairs as above. The Baalshem turns out to have been engaged in meditations but decidedly not of the Lurianic type. While repeating the verse "false is the horse for deliverance," he was deeply involved in an experience of clairvoyance concentrated on saving a Jew. Here again the Baalshem is caught in an improvised method of meditation during prayer while the outward appearance of lengthy prayer would convey to the onlooker an impression of adherence to the Lurianic *Kavvanoth*, from which the Baalshem was in fact far removed.

Thus far the legendary material about the Baalshem, many details of which are open to doubt but which is nevertheless authentic in its core.[26] In neither case is Israel Baalshem explicit in denouncing the Lurianic method of meditation, but in practice he is clearly interested in more individual meditations directed at more concrete and proximate aims than the Sefirotic ones of the Lurianic *Kavvanoth*.

The highest degree of authenticity can be accredited to traditions of Israel Baalshem written down by his disciple R. Jacob Joseph of Polonnoye. What can one learn on our subject from the teachings transmitted in his name by this disciple? The following tradition is quite unequivocal. In it, as in the legendary biography, Israel Baalshem is not abrogating the Lurianic method of *Kavvanoth* but is rather silently discarding it in favor of a more emotional and direct, though less disciplined and less complex meditative prayer life.

I have heard from my teacher [Israel Baalshem] that R. Neḥunya ben ha-Kanah, even after he knew all the *Kavvanoth*, used to pray like a one-day-old child, etc.[27] And my teacher explained that in the matter of prayer and the worship of God there were two aspects: (a) the "left" [i.e.] that the Holy One, blessed be He, repels one and (b) that God's "right" hand draws one close. And the matter is expounded in *Tur Oraḥ Ḥayyim*, ch. 5, where the author wrote that one should have in mind [*yekhavven*] the name of God as it is pronounced *Adonai*, meaning that He is the Master of all, and one should have in mind [*yekhavven*] the name of God as it is written *YHVH*, meaning that He was, He is and will be, and keeps in existence (*mehavveh*] all the worlds. Therefore, when a man says with an understanding heart "Blessed art Thou", then God is face to face with him. And as to the interpretation of the Tetragrammaton, its meaning is that He was, is and will be and keeps in existence [*mehavveh*] all the worlds and gives life to all souls, through the mentioning of this [Divine] name. Is there an enjoyment superior to this, speaking with the King, King of the universe, face to face? As it is written (*Cant.* 1:2], "Let Him kiss me with the kisses of His mouth," and then this state [*beḥinah*] is called "His [God's] right hand will embrace me" [ibid. 2:6]. This is not the case if one's sins separate one from one's Maker, in which case when saying "Blessed art Thou" a wayward thought [*maḥashavah zarah*] interposes itself between oneself and one's God, and the thought irritates him with the vanities of his dealings in this world and he cannot concentrate [*le-khavven*] and he is deprived of the marvellous enjoyment of "Let Him kiss me with the kisses of His mouth." Then this state [*beḥinah*] is called "the left hand of the Holy One, blessed be He." . . . Thus there are two states, "right" and "left," and the wise man has eyes in his head to understand and realize whether the time is appropriate to concentrate [*le-khavven*] within the inner mystery, and to enjoy it as mentioned above. This is good. But if he sees that he is within the mystery of littleness [*katnuth*][28] and he cannot concentrate [*le-khavven*] because wayward thoughts overwhelm him, then he should pray like a one-day-old child from a written text [*kethav*] as my teacher testified about himself: that for a while he had been in a "foreign country" [*ereṣ aḥereth*] in this respect; that the above-mentioned [high state of concentration] had left him; and that he used to attach himself to the letters [*ve-hayah*[29] *medabbek aṣmo el ha-othiyyoth*]. And he said that when he was praying from the written text and was attaching himself to the letters, he would uplift the *Asiyyah.*[30] . . . And so he ordered a person to do this until he returned to his high level.[31]

This certainly reliable tradition in the name of Israel Baalshem starts with the statement that Rabbi Neḥunya ben ha-Kanah after having learned all the *Kavvanoth* did not make use of them in prayer. In other words the *Kavvanoth* of prayer, an outstanding feature of Cabbalistic tradition, existed for Israel Baalshem on paper only. His special method, a technique he developed for use during both prayer and study,[32] is called "attachment of oneself to the letters." Its core is an extreme atomization of the text of prayer or study into its ultimate elements, i.e. (in Hebrew), the consonants. The technique of meditation consists in gazing rapt upon each letter. Atomized letters of the Hebrew alphabet are highly capable of serving as the medium of meditation, because for the traditional Jew the alphabet of the holy language is of metaphysical origin and importance.

In this atomization the literal meaning of the sentence evaporates, and the letters that constitute the words and sentences after becoming meaningless through atomization are a psychologically effective inducement to the performance of meditative exercises. This method is a patently visual one and the Baalshem Tov explicitly recommends the use of a visual inducement in the form of a printed text by the aid of which one performs the meditative exercises. In structure this method is not far from the medieval technique of Abraham Abulafia, who recommended the even more sacred four letters of the Tetragrammaton in its various vocalized forms for the purpose of meditation.[33] The method of the Baalshem is somewhat clumsier. The differently vocalized forms of the Tetragrammaton are meaningless in themselves, whereas the texts on which Israel Baalshem would perform his exercises have first to be deprived of their literal meaning in order to become the abstract vehicle needed for the meditative movements of the soul. But we must realize that the Baalshem's method is far removed from the Cabbalistic doctrine of *Kavvanoth* during prayer, particularly from its Lurianic version.

The interesting thing is that this much advertised method of prayer is considered by Israel Baalshem himself to be an inferior one. It is the method of prayer in the state of mind called *katnuth* which amounts to anything from lack of concentration to deep depression.

A second fully authentic tradition from the pen of the same disciple:

> I have heard in the name of my teacher on the matter of prayer and its *Kavvanah* and the *Yiḥudim*, by means of which man must attach himself.[34] And it is known that he [i.e., man] is a microcosm and through the awakening below awakening above is brought about. And "abundance" [*shefa*, divine emanation] will be sent down to the level of the man who concentrates [*mekhavven*] on it, and he receives the "abundance."[35]

In this passage the precise nature of *Kavvanah* in prayer is left undefined. On the face of it, Baalshem could mean the Lurianic *Kavvanoth.* The magical aspect of the Lurianic concept is certainly present, though rather than affecting the Sefirotic world the *Kavvanoth* act in this case upon the real world of the worshiper. One thing is clear: *Kavvanah* has become a vehicle of the central Hasidic virtue of *devekuth.*

Rather surprisingly, another completely isolated tradition makes Israel Baalshem advocate the practice of the Lurianic *Kavvanoth*, though perhaps not wholeheartedly: "The Baalshem of blessed memory saw that it was necessary to pray with *Kavvanoth* and found only the *Kavvanoth* of R. Isaac Luria, and so they prayed of necessity according to those *Kavvanoth.*"[36]

Although this collection of traditions originating from the circle of R. Rafael of Berszada contains some authentic traditions of the Baalshem, a critical evaluation of this particular piece could hardly lead one to defend its genuineness. The doubtful character of the tradition seems to be indicated not only by its complete isolation in presenting Israel Baalshem as a protagonist of the Lurianic *Kavvanoth* but also by the fact that it is quoted in order to support the claim for superiority of certain editions of the prayer book. For the text continues: "Therefore one must only pray from the *nosaḥ* of the prayerbook of Luria in the Lemberg edition or in the prayer book of R. Shabbethai [of Raszkow],[37] not from other *noshaoth* which are in the new prayerbooks."[38]

In the body of writings that have come down in the name of the Great Maggid R. Dov Baer, there are some pertinent expressions reflecting the new evaluation of *Kavvanoth* during prayer. Occasionally he implies the possibility and legitimacy of both ways of prayer with or without *Kavvanoth*:

כשמתפלל בפשוטה אז התיבות אינם חיים, רק מחיה אותם. למשל כשאומר ברוך אתה ה׳ אין החיות רק אח״כ כשמזכיר את השם. אבל כשמתפלל עד״ה (ר״ת על דרך הסוד) אז כל התיבה שם בפ״ע כי הוא עולם הדיבור.

Or ha-emeth (Zhitomir, 1900), 25a. And yet with him started the virulent campaign against the *Kavvanoth* of prayer in their original Cabbalistic form. This disintegration of the old meaning of *Kavvanoth* and the emergence of a new concept based on the emotional values of a revivalist movement can be traced back to two statements of the Great Maggid that exercised a paramount influence on the question in Hasidism. The first statement is in the literary form of a parable. Its tendency is self-evident, in spite of the clumsy formulation and the somewhat confused symbols:

> This resembles [*mashal*] a door which one opens with something which can break iron. Thus the ancients [*kadmonim*] employed in meditation the *Kavvanah* [*hayu mekhavvenim kavvanah*] suitable for each thing. [But] now that we have no *Kavvanah*, only the breaking of the heart will open [the door] to everything.[39]

The division between the "ancient ones" and "we" does not imply any revolutionary consciousness of time as one might have inferred. It is utterly different from the deep sensation of the renewal of time found in the Sabbatian repudiation of *Kavvanoth* where there is a consciousness of a caesura in history, while here it is merely a literary form subordinate to the need to justify the abandonment of old ways. The formula itself has a long history in Halakhic thought and was occasionally used also in early Hasidism to overthrow practices that, though recommended by great authorities of earlier generations, were now thought to stand in the way of piety.[40]

The second statement by the Great Maggid against *Kavvanoth* does not employ the argument of new times, but advocates the new values of *devekuth* and enthusiasm as superseding and indeed embracing the old ones. The magical implications of *Kavvanoth*, which greatly faded in Hasidism, are still discernable in the new concept of *Kavvanoth* of prayer as put forward by the Great Maggid:

> He who meditates [*mekhavven*] in prayer on all the *Kavvanoth* knows he can do no more than meditate on those *Kavvanoth* which are known to him. But when

he says each word [of the prayer] with great attachment [*hithkashruth*] all the *Kavvanoth* are by that very fact [*me-aṣman u-me-alehen*] included since each and every letter is an entire world. When he utters the word with great attachment, surely those upper worlds are awakened, and thus he accomplishes great operations [*pe'ulloth gedoloth*]. Therefore, a man should see to it that he prays with great attachment and enthusiasm [*be-hithkashruth u-ve-hithlahavuth gedolah*].[41] Then surely he will accomplish great operations in the upper worlds for each letter awakens [things which are] above.[42]

The metamorphosis that took place in the meaning of *Kavvanoth* at the advent of Hasidism, and more explicitly after the Great Maggid, consists in this—that an originally intellectual effort of meditation and contemplation has become an intensely emotional and highly enthusiastic act. The changes in the meaning and function of *devekuth* that occurred in Hasidism are parallel to the changes to which the *Kavvanoth* of prayer were subject in the same movement. If, as Scholem put it, in Hasidism thought was transformed into emotion, one is justified in saying that similarly in Hasidism *Kavvanoth* were deintellectualized: they lost the intrinsic meaning they had had in Cabbala, i.e., that of a series of highly specialized, technically focused, and singularly intentional acts of the contemplative mind. Their intellectual character thus lost, they have become but one of the various synonyms of *devekuth*, that ubiquitous and multifarious Hasidic concept. This is small wonder, since Hasidism did its best to amalgamate all ideals of religious psychology into its central obsession with *devekuth*. All religious passion of the mind in early Hasidism was concentrated on this single aspect of mental communion with God, while all other aspects of religious life were either shown to be identical with *devekuth* or simply ignored altogether in the intense heat of *devekuth* piety. Just as faith (*emunah*) was deprived in early Hasidism of its special psychological and religious physiognomy and became equated with *devekuth*,[43] so was the fate of Cabbalistic *Kavvanoth*. With all religious energies canalized in one compelling direction, *Kavvanoth* of prayer were interpreted—one might well say, were interpreted away—as *devekuth*.

Indeed, there was no other way for Hasidism but this. The metaphysical map of the *Sefiroth* of the Cabbalists had become blurred for them. Not only could its details not be seen with accuracy, but the whole Sefirotic world had lost its original significance and could consequently not serve as an object of religious meditation during prayer. With the fading of the "gnostic" aspect of the Sefirotic universe from the mind and heart of the Cabbalist, the original *Kavvanoth* became meaningless and their disintegration was inevitable. This may be one of the reasons why the Hasidim reshaped and remotivated the concept of *Kavvanoth* in such a way that it was changed beyond recognition.

In conclusion, I propose to discuss one isolated tradition in the name of Israel Baalshem that would attribute to him an outspokenly negative attitude to *Kavvanoth*. This tradition was written down by R. Ze'ev Wolf of Zytomierz, a disciple of the Great Maggid, in his work *Or ha-Me'ir*. I did not refer to it in discussing Israel Baalshem's views as I surmise that it reflects later opinion:

> I heard in the name of the Baalshem Tov, may his memory be blessed in life everlasting, that he related on this [i.e., the practice of *Kavvanoth*] the following parable: A man wants to eat and he craves for certain foods which please him. He then sees lying in a high place the food he likes but his hand cannot reach it, hence in imagination he pretends to himself that he is eating it [*mekhavven ke-illu okhel*].[44] It turns out that his pretense [*kavvanah*] does not help him, for the more he pretends [*mekhavven*] the hungrier he becomes. Similar are those men who employ in meditation grand and lofty *Kavvanoth* [*mekhavvenim kavvanoth nora'oth ve-ramim*]. . . . For their mind cannot reach there, since they are so remote from the meditation [*kavvanah*]. Thus what did it avail him? It is much better for him to refrain from intruding into a place too high for his rung and ability [*erko ve-hassaghatho*].[45]

This unequivocal and radical rejection of the practice of *Kavvanoth* has no parallel in those traditions of Israel Baalshem which are certainly authentic. On the other hand, it has many parallels in the sayings of the Great Maggid and his disciples. R. Ze'ev Wolf bases Israel Baalshem's objection to *Kavvanoth* on the incapability of the worshiper to use them—an argument that was current, as we have seen above, in a slightly different version in the Great Maggid's circles. Unless very considerable argument can be advanced for concluding that the tradition in question is genuine after all, we have all reason to cast serious doubt on its authenticity as emanating from the Baalshem. Embedded as it is in a long discussion in the book *Or ha-Me'ir* on the uselessness of *Kavvanoth*, the tradition seems rather to reflect the climate of opinion in circles deriving their inspiration from the Great Maggid than to represent Israel Baalshem's own view.

As a practical measure of gradually building up and consuming the emotional resources of prayer life, a regime of rationing of emotion and devotion was devised in early Hasidism which aimed at the careful planning of the emotional ebb and flow during prayer, thus controlling the devotional energy so that the worshiper was not exhausted by losing too much devotion on the preparatory phases before reaching the peak of his daily prayer.

> I have heard it from my master [Israel Baalshem] . . . that one ought to fortify oneself before prayers in order that one may have mind [*moḥin*] for prayer. . . . And this by means of Psalms and Torah with which one should occupy oneself at the commencement. Consequently, when one stands up to pray, one has a mind for it. . . . There is, however, the case when one multiplies reciting Psalms or Torah before prayers and, as a result, has no mind for prayers. This, then, is the significance of what was said "it is all one whether a man does much or little, if only he directs his heart towards Heaven," i.e., that he has a mind for prayers.[46]

The aim of this planning of a devotional curve can be described as the coincidence in time of the emotional climax of the worshiping individual with his utterance of that section of the prayer which is considered the holiest. The advice is still more unequivocally formulated in the *Ṣavva'ah* about the technique of economizing in emotion in order to "save strength" and attain the high tide of sense of *devekuth* at the right place of the prayer:

> Let a man not recite many Psalms before the prayer in order that he may not weaken his body and find himself unable to recite the most important prayer, relative to the duty of the day, i.e., the hymns and the *Shema* and the prayer [of *Amidah*] with great attachment, because he had spent his strength before the prayer on other things. . . . [Similarly,] on the Day of Atonement, before the *Ne'ilah* prayers, one ought to recite the *Maḥzor* in littleness [of emotion] in order that afterwards he may be able to say his prayers with attachment.[47]

By contrast, R. Ze'ev Wolf seems to care little for curbing his radically subjective approach to matters of prayer. He has no interest in carefully calculating and correctly timing the worshiper's mounting emotion in prayer. Its sudden eruption in the course of the prayer is welcome at any time. As against the background of the more sober views of Israel Baalshem and the *Ṣavva'ah*, the following passage in *Or ha-Me'ir* appears as the recommendation of subjective abandonment in prayer and of immersion in the abysmal depths of emotional orgies:

And behold the Men of the Great Synagogue, by the magnitude of their enlightenment, established for us the matters of the order of prayer in accordance with the emanation of the Worlds, *Aṣiluth*, *Beri'ah*, *Yeṣirah*, *Asiyyah*, corresponding to which there are four sections of prayer . . . , as indicated in the *Kavvanoth* of R. Isaac Luria. . . . So also their lofty wisdom demanded with regard to the order of the totality of the rungs [*madregoth*]. Thus they arranged . . . unifications and copulations [*yiḥudim ve-zivvugim*] of prayer, each one in its proper place: in the verse, *Shema*, unification [*yiḥud*] as shown in the [Lurianic] *Kavvanoth* while afterwards the three first benedictions [of the *Amidah*] with their proper *Kavvanoth* belonging there; then the twelve middle [benedictions of the *Amidah*] with their proper *Kavvanoth* followed by the mystery of prostration. Thus demanded their lofty wisdom, because they were sages, who comprised the totality of the generations after them until the coming of our Messiah soon and in our days. Now, however, in our generation, with our diminished hearts, none possesses knowledge of the quality of the *Kavvanoth* properly, to be able to harmonize his own feelings [*middothav*] by a stirring up and enthusiasm [*hith'oreruth vehithlahavuth*] in prayer so that each *Kavvanah* of the prayer finds itself in its proper place. At times he will awaken his heart with such great enthusiasm as almost to make his soul depart and become oblivious to any movement in the world, and he is attached [*mekushar*] with both his 248 members and 365 veins to Him Who is blessed. And he should know that just then is the real unification which is due in the verse "Hear, O Israel"; to him it happens immediately at the commencement of prayer, or occasionally in the middle of it or at the end. However, when [reciting the prayer] he reaches the mystery of unification of "Hear, O Israel," he may not yet feel the high tide [of emotion]. Since the high tide [of emotion] may come to him at the end of prayer or by chance at the commencement of prayer, and when he comes to the verse "Hear, O Israel," this tide may have already come to an end and finished. The general rule is that he, who desires to approach the service of the heart which is prayer,[48] let his heart be perfect with God in order to meditate with the strength of his understanding so as to feel the high tides at any place in the prayers, at the beginning or in the middle or at the end, when enthusiasm falls upon him; when he utters words with fear and love to attain the departure of his soul, there is the real point of unification of his prayer in his individual way [*le-erko*], and there the high tide comes to an end, wherefore he says the remainder of his prayers not with due exertion as before; that is to say, the main aspect of his unification incumbent upon him had come to an end for him. But all this depends on the individual character of every one of Israel and on where the place of his soul is in the upper worlds. Although according to the order of the rungs the unification should be with abandon of soul in the *Shema*, this is [only] in the generality of all the worlds and in the generality of all generations. But as far as a particular soul of the House of Israel is concerned the aspect of his unification depends upon his [own] high tides, whether these are strong or weak and where the place of his soul is. Accordingly the unification of his prayer occurs when he is awakened with enthusiasm for God with fear and love . . .[49]

R. Ze'ev Wolf fulminates against the unjustified use by the

unworthy of *Kavvanoth* of prayer. The use of these must have persisted sporadically in Hasidic circles, although R. Ze'ev Wolf does not specify the location of the abuse, whether in circles of Hasidim or of Mithnaggedim. From his general approach however it clearly transpires that his criticism is directed against hasidic circles as he was one of the first *Ṣaddikim* to transfer their target of criticism from the Mithnaggedim to their own flock.[50] His most pertinent passage against *Kavvanoth* is perhaps this:

> For indeed he, who has not bent his neck in divine service even though he be a learned scholar having perfect knowledge of all the *Kavvanoth*, he should know that he has not tasted yet the taste of prayer. . . . Because he has failed to grasp the difference between his right hand and his left, viz., the nature of the *Kavvanah*. Certainly the Men of the Great Synagogue did not intend this, while he with his small perception and comprehension imagines that he meditates the *Kavvanoth* of Luria: "Wherefore is there a price in the hand of a fool to get wisdom, seeing he hath no heart to it."[51] I vouch for it that had he but a rudiment of the fear of Heaven, he would most certainly be afraid for himself to seek and to look into the *Kavvanoth*, which reach heaven, while he himself stands below, ignorant of even one single word concerning the *Kavvanoth* of R. Isaac Luria, and if the Lord will, we shall yet speak in the following chapters on this subject to rebuke them to their face, those who consider themselves also to have a hand and a name among the great ones and to recite their prayers from the prayer-book of Luria . . . and to meditate *Kavvanoth*. It would be good for them, if they merely recited the prayers according to the simple meaning of the words and not give occasion for alien meanings to meddle with the combination of their letters and words, which they utter in a perfunctory way. Then it would indeed be well with them.[52]

Instead of the complex method of intellectual concentration involved in the Cabbalistic *Kavvanoth*, R. Ze'ev Wolf himself advocates a simplified emotional method based on the predominant religious mood of each unit of the prayer:

> He whom God endowed with understanding will know that the essential *Kavvanah* [*ikkar ha-kavvanah*] is only the one which a man derives for himself [*lokeaḥ le-aṣmo*] from the meaning of the verse [*kavvanoth ha-pasuk*]. Thus he induces in himself the Love of God or the Fear of God according to the meaning [of the verse]. Then in the next verse he concentrates on another *Kavvanah* and derives for himself another aspect to arouse his heart to utter his words before God "in Love and Fear"; consequently he will pray with fervor and enthusiasm.[53]

This patently amounts to a new concept of *Kavvanoth* of prayer. It is a further development of the emotional concept of *Kavvanoth* first put forward by the Great Maggid. In the Great

Maggid's view *Kavvanoth* became a vague emotional state of the worshiper, the precise nature of which was not specified. This indeterminate flood of emotion is now forced by turns into the two main channels of traditional religious emotion, love and fear. The alternating moods of the worshiper will now be determined by the meaning of the verse uttered by him at each particular moment of the divine service. The worshiper may no longer indulge in emotional excesses independent of the text on his lips. The emotional anarchy that had followed in Hasidism the systematic discipline of Cabbalistic *Kavvanah* is curtailed in R. Ze'ev Wolf's method. The worshiper is once more bound to his text.

A strikingly similar method is advocated by the anonymous author of the minor tractate *Darkhei Ṣedek* by a disciple of R. Elimelech of Lizensk.[54] His method makes provision for three basic religious emotions instead of two: in addition to love and fear, it recognizes joy (*simḥah*). In other respects it prescribes the same procedure as R. Ze'ev Wolf: the worshiper has to derive the flow of his religious moods from the changing emotional implications of his prayer text.

> All *Kavvanoth* of prayer are [designed] to serve Him with love in a verse that speaks of love and with fear in a verse that speaks of fear, and similarly with joy. Even though the whole prayer requires [the emotions of both] love and fear, only during a verse that speaks of love must there be a predominance of love over fear and joy, and so on.[55]

R. Meshullam Phoebus of Zbaraz occupies a special place in the school of the Great Maggid for several reasons. His outspoken stand against the early Hasidic technique of 'uplifting the strange and wayward thoughts' secures for him an important position in the history of Hasidic ideas. Although he defeated the Great Maggid on this issue[56], he undoubtedly belongs to the school of the Great Maggid as regards the question of *Kavvanoth* of prayer.

In his most important second epistle, written in 1777,[57] after giving some advice on *Kavvanoth* to be used in a ritual bath or during necessary ablutions, he admonishes his addressee:

> But you must learn and revise this *Kavvanah* several times with some good friend until it is fixed in your mind so that you are able to meditate with facility. This is the way with all the *Kavvanoth* which must be very firmly fixed in the mind [ready] to meditate in a moment. For our mind is limited and

cannot comprise all that one must meditate upon. And the real *Kavvanah* [*ikkar ha-kavvanah*] is cleaving [*devekuth*] to God, blessed be He. And if we meditate on the *Kavvanoth* of the Divine Names we are not able to meditate on what is really necessary [i.e., *devekuth*]. This is why the *Kavvanah* must be fixed [and ready] in a moment. The real *Kavvanah* in truth is upon God, blessed be He, who tries the reins and the heart, when [the worshiper] truly attaches himself to God without ulterior motives [*peniyyoth*], God forbid. Therefore one must revise many times the above mentioned *Kavvanoth* of Divine Names. And truly, the real *Kavvanah* is the breaking of the heart in humility and cleaving [*devekuth*] to God, blessed be He. There is a simile on this matter in the writings under the name of Rabbi Baer that there is a key to every lock, a key that opens it precisely, and the key is fitted [*mekhuvvan*] according to the lock. But there are thieves who open without a key, that is to say, they break the lock. Thus is this matter: to every hidden thing there is a key, which is the *Kavvanah*, fitted to it [*mekhuvveneth*, also "to be meditated"].[58] The real key is like a thief who breaks everything—breaking the heart well in great humility so that the barrier above is broken. . . .[59]

And, indeed, you know that I learned some *Kavvanoth* in childhood, but I do not meditate upon them at all, for the real *Kavvanah* is the breaking of the heart as mentioned above, with love and fear, simplicity . . . as mentioned above. And were we granted this, we could easily meditate all the *Kavvanoth* of Rabbi Isaac Luria of blessed memory; for these were indeed not intended but for men of his stature, or of a little lower standing, whose heart was already pure from all dregs. . . . But we are afflicted from top to toe, and all our heads are ill and our hearts ailing. Our hearts are not purified from physical desires at all, how much less from refined desires, as we take pleasure and delight in being praised and exalted, and hate being scorned. Because of this we are far from God, blessed be He, and we are not able to meditate the high meditations. Therefore I have chosen to meditate on one *Kavvanah*: to direct the heart [*le-khavven ha-lev*] as much as possible to God, blessed be He, [and] to the meaning of the words [*kavannath ha-tevoth ve-ha-milloth*] (of the prayer) as far as possible. And in spite of this, if I can meditate in an instant some easy *Kavvanah*, that is to say, a Divine Name which does not give trouble and does not distract from the true *Kavvanah* as mentioned above—that is good.

But during the performance of *miṣvoth* such as *tefillin*, *sukkah*, *lulav* or *shofar*, it is good to meditate on the *Kavvanoth* of Divine Names. For there there is no speech, only action. But in speech like prayer there are directives [*Kavvanoth*] to concentrate [*le-khavven*] the heart on what is being said because it is almost impossible to speak unless with great effort. And how can one proceed [*la-ṣeth*] from the literal meaning to the *Kavvanah*? Nevertheless, it is very good to learn the *Kavvanoth* of all the prayers, for by this means the soul awakens when it knows how far these things go—[namely] that [the words of the prayer] bring about a great achievement above, very fearful. By means of this a great stirring will come about so that we may direct our minds, and mouth and heart may agree [when we pray][60] in love and fear. By means of this God, blessed be He, will receive our prayer and He Himself will take the necessary action. Although we do not know what we are doing, He establishes upon us the work of our hands. . . .

> All this I wrote for your knowledge as I heard it from the holy mouth of my teacher Menaḥem Mendel of Premyslan. But let every one do as he will if he but do it for the sake of Heaven, and you yourself will choose.[61]

This view contains the two crucial points of the Hasidic position: (*a*) the abrogation of the Lurianic *Kavvanoth* on the basis of our spiritual "inability", and (*b*) the presentation of the fullness of the heart in *devekuth* as the real meaning of *Kavvanoth* during prayer.

In his intimate note R. Meshullam Phoebus testifies that he gave up *Kavvanoth* of prayer under the influence of R. Menaḥem Mendel of Premyslan, one of his four teachers, whom he mentions frequently in his epistle. We have no direct information about R. Menaḥem Mendel's views on the practice of *Kavvanoth*, but it transpires from this account of the disciple that he too was opposed to *Kavvanoth* of prayer, as were most of the contemporary Hasidic teachers. R. Meshullam Phoebus's expression of his view in the above passage should not necessarily be read as an exact replica of R. Menaḥem Mendel's ideas. The disciple may have adapted them and infused them with certain elements of his own experience. Moreover R. Meshullam Phoebus appears to have had too much respect for the time-hallowed Cabbalistic practice to reject it outright. He is well aware that a radical simplification of the method of prayer is essential and advocates it wholeheartedly, but at the same time he is not quite resolute on the question of total rejection of *Kavvanoth* of prayer and therefore suggests occasional recourse to them. But it is worth noting that he only mentions the comparatively "easy" *Kavvanoth* of the Divine Names in this connection and not the full apparatus of the Lurianic *Kavvanoth*.

He makes a careful distinction between the *Kavvanoth* of prayer and the *Kavvanoth* of *miṣvoth*. In the epistle from which the above passage is quoted this distinction emerges naturally in the course of a description of the *Kavvanoth* to be practiced during immersion in a ritual bath. He transcribed these meditations from a document deriving from the Baalshem Tov with which R. Meshullam Phoebus finds himself in complete agreement. Indeed, he expressly states in the passage under discussion that the *Kavvanoth* of the Divine Names during the performance of *miṣvoth* are to be encouraged. While there is no reason to object to them where they can accompany actions without impairing their quality, this is not the case, in his opinion, with the *Kavvanoth* of prayer.

The author is faced with the following problem: The classical *Kavvanoth* of the Lurianic system, which was the only system of reference available to the Hasidim, had strong activistic and functional implications. The *Kavvanoth* had a job to perform in the Sefirotic universe. They were responsible for bringing about certain fruitful conjunctions between the *Sefiroth*. In principle, R. Meshullam Phoebus does not challenge this activist doctrine of *Kavvanoth*, but in practice he is not perturbed by the gap left in the machinery of the heavenly mechanism by omitting the *Kavvanoth*. With little regret, he delegates the responsibility for the smooth working of these Sefirotic processes to God Himself, who, he is confident, will reharness the energy of sincere and devout prayer and dispense it to the *Sefiroth* in order that they may function as efficiently as under the influence of the great praying Cabbalists' *Kavvanoth*.

Though giving up the practice of *Kavvanoth* of prayer, he still has enough regard for them to encourage the study of them. The motive for this advice is that the knowledge of the high metaphysical potency of the *Kavvanoth*, for whose use we are not qualified will at least give us the inspiration to approach sincere prayer, which is within our reach, with the necessary enthusiasm. The infusing of the soul with fervour and the intensification of the inner qualities of prayer have now become the chief end of all religious activity. *Kavvanoth* are beneficial for the soul but no longer serve an objective purpose. This shift of interest from objective processes in the universe to intimate psychological experience is perfectly in tune with the Hasidic tendency to turn the gaze inward, from the metaphysical to the psychological.

Indeed, R. Meshullam Phoebus's advice on replacing *Kavvanoth* by what he calls "directing one's mind to God" is within the orbit of the standard Hasidic directive. His avowed reason for this new policy is that because of our sensual desires we are unworthy to aspire to prayer with *Kavvanoth*. This is but a slightly elaborated form of the reason given by the Great Maggid. R. Phoebus maintains that the system of Lurianic *Kavvanoth* was evolved not for general use but for people of Luria's own high spiritual standing. So much for the declared motive for abandoning Lurianic *Kavvanoth*. But indirectly from an analysis of the text in question, another line of reasoning, which seems to have carried more weight with him, can be discerned. It would appear that in the author's view the chief ideal of prayer is meticulous attention to the literal meaning of the text of the prayer, so that mouth and heart are in accord. As we have seen, a worshiper concentrating on *Kavvanoth* is always in danger of letting the literal meaning of the text slip from his mind. It is for this reason, then, that R. Meshullam rejected *Kavvanoth*, and for this too that he was more lenient towards *Kavvanoth* of *miṣvoth*, because *miṣvoth*, unlike prayer, are actions and the practice of accompanying *Kavvanoth* would not interfere with them.

His practice in detail is the following: (*a*) concentrating on God as a general theme, (*b*) concentrating on the literal meaning of the text of the prayer, and (*c*) an occasional short and "easy" *Kavvanah* of a Divine Name on the spur of the moment, provided it does not prevent one from following the thread of the literal meaning of the prayer. Thus the author reluctantly retains a limited application of the old *Kavvanoth* which are to be used in a haphazard way. In this way he completely reverses the character of the *Kavvanoth*, making them arbitrary, irregular, and erratic. R. Meshullam Phoebus is not the most radical exponent of the new Hasidic attitude to the Cabbalistic method of praying with *Kavvanoth*. The hesitations and compromises apparent in his writing reflect an endeavor to bridge the gap between the old and the new. But there can be no doubt that he belongs to the new school.

Moreover, R. Meshullam's hesitancy was of historical importance. The defeat of the old method of *Kavvanoth* was final. Whether one turns to R. Elimelech of Lizensk or to other disciples of the Great Maggid or to the Brazlav school, one finds the new approach universally prevailing.

The argument of new times found another exponent in the person of R. Kalonymus Kalman Epstein of Cracow. His testimony as to the practice of his teacher R. Elimelech of Lizensk reads as follows:

> There are several people who pray with the Divine Names [*be-khavvanath ha-shemoth*] but in these generations they do not need to do this. And so I have heard from my master and teacher, the holy light, Rabbi Elimelech, may his

memory be for a blessing, who said that he did not pray with *Kavvanoth*. And if he prays from the prayerbook of Luria, it is only because the Divine Name is written there in a clear script [*kethivah tammah*] and it [the prayerbook] is big. And to understand this well [one must know that] meditation on the Divine Names depends mainly on their vocalisation. The Divine Name vocalized in one way signifies one thing and the Divine Name vocalized in another way signifies another thing. For it is well known from the holy books that the vowels are the souls of the letters, and the cantillation signs and the coronets [*taggim*] are the spirit and the *neshamah*, as it is written in the *Tikkunim*. Consequently if a man puts together his soul, spirit, and *neshamah* . . . and unifies them by uttering the letters and words of the prayer, then the Divine Name which he utters with his whole soul and spirit and *neshamah* . . . will receive vowels and cantillation signs and coronets, which point to the soul and the spirit and the *neshamah* of the letters as mentioned above. And this *Kavvanah* is superior to any *Kavvanoth*.[62]

NOTES

1. G. Scholem, *Major Trends in Jewish Mysticism* (1955²), p. 277: "That the doctrine of Kawwanah in prayer was capable of being interpreted as a certain kind of magic seems clear to me; that it involved the problem of magical practices is beyond any doubt." Both an orthodox scholar of the type of A. Berliner (*Randbemerkungen zum täglichen Gebetbuche*, 1909) and a protagonist of reform such as H. G. Enelow (in his valuable though not exhaustive survey: "Kawwanah: the Struggle for Inwardness in Judaism," *Studies in Jewish Literature in Honor of Kaufmann Kohler* [Berlin, 1913], pp. 82–107) appear to be irritated by the magical implications of the Cabbalistic *Kavvanoth* of prayer. For a historical understanding of the doctrine of *Kavvanoth* in Cabbalah see G. Scholem, "Der Begriff der Kawwanah in der alten Kabbala," *MGWJ* 78 (1934): 492–518, *Enc. Jud.*, vol. 9, coll. 714–17 and in his *MTJM*, passim, see Index, s.v. *Kawwanah*; idem, *Ursprung und Anfänge der Kabbala* (1962) passim, see *Register*, s.v. *Kawwana*, particularly pp. 172, 214–48, 367–73. See Z. Werblowsky in his review of Tishby's *Mishnath ha-Zohar* (Tarbiṣ 34:205). *Kavvanah* in the sense of Cabbalistic meditation is omitted altogether in Ben Yehuda's *Thesaurus*, 5:2301–2. In view of the fact that this specific technical sense of the term certainly overshadowed in later Hebrew usage all other meanings of the word, the omission is rather baffling and I can make no suggestion that could explain it.

2. Scholem, *MTJM²*, p. 29, and idem, "Religiöse Autorität und Mystik," *Eranos Jahrbuch*, 1957, pp. 246 ff.

3. There is a great deal of truth in what is quoted in Luria's name: דאיתא בהאר"י זלה"ה אם האדם אינו מכוון כוונת התפלה ע"ד האמת כל עוד שמכוון יותר שואל פרס מרבו יותר (Ze'ev Wolf of Zytomierz, *Or ha-Me'ir*, 1798, 1:7a). The petitionary character of the statutory prayers is repeatedly stated by the same author: הגם שכן סדרו לנו בסדר תפלתינו כתבנו בספר פרנסה כתבנו בספר סליחה ומחילה וכדומה, הנראה שכל עצמה של השאלה רק לצורך הגשמי, וכיון שכן כל עוד שיכוין בתפלתו יותר אזי שואל פרס יותר (ibid., 3:34b). "*Gashmi*" in this context obviously stands not merely for "material" but for "human," i.e., anything for the benefit of man, whether material as *parnasah* or spiritual as *seliḥah* and *meḥilah*.

4. *The Zohar in Moslem and Christian Spain* (London, 1932), pp. 245–46. See also the description of the synagogue in *Iggeroth ha-Rabh Kook*, 2:68–70 (No. 414).

5. See Scholem, *MTJM*², p. 328. N. Gelber, *Toledoth Yehudei Brod* (Jerusalem, 1955), p. 62 ff.

6. In contradistinction to the Hasidim who were ill-famed for their neglect of the study of the Talmud.

7. *Ẓemir Ariṣim*, end.

8. Scholem, *MTJM*², p. 331.

9. See G. Scholem, *Shabbethai Ṣebhi*, 1:225–26; 2:412–14. Only two years later, in 1668, the abrogation of the whole Halakhic system was advanced precisely with the same argumentation of weekdays—Sabbath, see ibid., 2:704.

10. Printed for the first time by the Hasidic printer in Korzecz in 1797.

11. I have not been able to rely to any extent on previous work in the field of Hasidism. No treatment of the subject of *Kavvanoth* of prayer in Hasidism exists. M. Buber's essay "Kawwana: von der Ausrichtung" (*Die chassidischen Bücher* [Berlin] pp. 149–56) does not touch on the subject of *Kavvanoth* of prayer. Even the thorough analysis in T. Ysander's *Studien zum Bestschen Hasidismus* (Uppsala, 1933), pp. 177–85 deals with the concept of *Kavvanah* as the devotion of prayer only, but does not differentiate between the devotional and the meditative aspects of Hasidic prayer and thus the whole Cabbalistic background of the meditative method of prayer and its subsequent Hasidic overthrow, the basic thesis of the present study, remain unnoticed.

12. In spite of A. Heschel's remark (*HUCA* 23 (1950–51), part 2, p. 20) implying the acceptance by him of the legendary idea of Israel Baalshem's hiding his great knowledge from his brother-in-law, I think that there can be little doubt about the relative illiteracy of this charismatic figure. I should go further and venture to describe him as what was popularly called "*En Ya'akov Yid.*" His scope of education emerges fairly clearly from what his legendary biography describes were his reading habits. There is a striking consistency in the implications of the various stories. On a journey his companions read passages to him from a book they had with them on the journey and which was, as our text says, "either *Mishnayoth* or *En Ya'akov* or the *Ẓohar*" (*Shivḥei*, p. 59). On Saturday night a relative of Israel Baalshem reads to him from *En Ya'akov* (ibid., pp. 84–85). The course of education of a Hasidic *am-ha-areṣ*, according to the detailed description of the *Shivḥei* (p. 124), contained the following stages: *Mishnayoth*, *En Ya'akov*, *Musar*-books and the *Ẓohar*. But this is almost identical with the reading matter of Israel Baalshem himself. The *Shivḥei* relates that his secretary, Zevi, read the *Ẓohar* to him and Israel Baalshem repeated it with great enthusiasm (p. 79). A noticeable feature of these descriptions is that Israel Baalshem does not study the books himself but others read aloud to him from the books, a habit certainly not inducive to great intellectual absorption and no doubt outside the traditional pattern of study of the contemporary Talmudic scholar. The *Shivḥei's* Hebrew expression for this intellectual activity is not to "study" or "learn" (*lilemod*) but to "say" a particular text (*lomar Ẓohar, lomar En Ya'akov*, in Yiddish: *zogen*). It is of course a perfectly adequate form of reading for pneumatic purposes, as indeed it is indicated in the various passages of the *Shivḥei* the purpose of the reading was (particularly p. 59, also pp. 84–85), but one has to emphasize that this was certainly not the way in which the traditional *talmid ḥakham* would engage in study. The other important point that emerges is the fact that the Haggadic anthology *En Ya'akov* figures predominantly on the short list of books with which the founder of Hasidism would occupy himself. It is not without significance in this connection that nearly every Talmudic citation that occurs in Israel Baalshem's dicta occurs also in *En Ya'akov* and could have been drawn from this secondary source instead of from the Talmud itself. That Israel knew his Talmudic passages not from a detailed study of the Talmud but rather from this famous anthology becomes more probable in view of the fact that sometimes when a Talmudic text in *En Ya'akov* differs from that of the Talmud itself, Israel Baalshem quotes the Talmud according to the *En Ya'akov* version.

13. A remark designed to give authority to the Hasidic custom of very late *Minḥah*?

There is no other evidence that the custom was established as early as the lifetime of the founder of Hasidism, but there is no evidence to the contrary either.

14. I.e., a prayerbook with the Lurianic *Kavvanoth.*

15. It is a religious duty to read twice on every Sabbath the weekly portion of the Law and the traditional Aramaic version of Onkelos, see *Shulḥan Arukh*, *Oraḥ Ḥayyim*, chapter 285.

16. We can observe in Hasidic circles a curious fascination with the secrets of one's own soul and its spiritual vicissitudes. This inquisitiveness is articulated in three questions: (*a*) what is the "root" of one's soul; (*b*) what was one's crucial sin during the preceding phase of the transmigration of one's soul; or (*c*) which is one's sin in the present phase, a sin that, if unattended, will cause the soul to transmigrate further. This psychological interest came down to Hasidism from earlier generations brought up on the Lurianic version of the doctrine of metempsychosis. The Maggid of R. Joseph Caro promises to reveal to him the *Gilgulim* of all the members of his family and also of his friends (see *Maggid Mesharim*, similarly M. C. Luzatto, *Iggaroth*, p. 19). In Hasidism this interest exuberated and was connected with the institution of Ṣaddikism, as it was the *Ṣaddik* who was able to satisfy it. This is well illustrated by Isaac Emter's satire *Gilgul ha-Nefesh* in his *Ha-Ṣofeh le-Veth Yisrael*, ed. Letteris (Vienna, 1858 and 1864). For the Lurianic antecedents, see G. Scholem, "Seelenwanderung und Sympathie der Seelen in der jüdischen Mystik", *Eranos-Jahrbuch*, 14 (1956): 55 ff. and the passage from Moses Zacuto quoted by R. J. Z. Werblowsky, "Das Gewissen in jüdischer Sicht," *Das Gewissen* (Studien aus dem Jung-Institut Zurich 7), p. 113. For the phenomenon in Hasidism, see the instructive passage in *Or ha-Meir*, 2:58b–59a; see also *Shivḥei ha-Besht*, pp. 7, 56, 59, 64. I hope to discuss this subject in greater detail on some future occasion.

17. *Shivḥei*, p. 64–65. Note the irreverence in the behavior and expression of R. Gershon toward Israel Baalshem, which the Hasidic writer does not conceal though the whole affair is supposed to have taken place after R. Gershon's *aliyah* to Palestine, i.e., long after his alleged acceptance of Israel Baalshem's spiritual authority. See my remarks on Israel Baalshem and R. Gershon, above, pp. 36–37. From the text of the *Shivḥei* quoted above, it is plain that its author did not consider R. Gershon "converted" to Israel Baalshem as late as his journey from Palestine to his previous home. As to chronology of this journey, see A. Heschel, *HUCA* 23 (1950–51), part 2, p. 41 but see G. Scholem, *Shetei 'Iggaroth*, *Tarbiṣ*, 25 (1956): 430–31, n. 4.

18. A parallel situation is to be found in *Shivḥei*, p. 104, where he is asked by Rabbi Abraham Abba to answer Halakic questions, but evaded the demands of the questioner just as he does here. As to the identity of the questioner, see I. Halpern, *Pinkas va'ad arba araṣoth* (Jerusalem, 1945), p. 531.

19. The same R. Gershon persisted in dismissing Israel Baalshem's pneumatic claims on the grounds of the latter's not being sufficiently educated, see above, p. 36.

20. In the county of Brazlav.

21. The town in which Israel Baalshem settled and died.

22. The morning prayer (*Shaḥarith*) commences with the words *Adon Olam.*

23. A series of Psalms in the first part of the morning prayer.

24. Written by the Italian Cabbalist Emmanuel Hai Ricchi, who belonged to the Lurianic school. His book is a summary of the Lurianic Cabbala. The part called *Mafteaḥ ha-kavvanoth* (Amsterdam, 1740, pp. 34 ff.) is a most elementary *vademecum* for prayer with *Kavvanoth.*

25. *Shivḥei*, p. 100.

26. I have restricted myself here to examples of *Kavvanoth* of prayer only. There is ample evidence in the *Shivḥei* concerning other *Kavvanoth* being employed by Israel Baalshem. See pp. 16, 101.

27. The enigma of this fantastic quotation, which, naturally, does not occur anywhere in Talmudic or Midrashic literature, was solved by R. Shimeon Menaḥem Mendel

Wandek in his valuable though uncritical collection of Israel Baalshem's "complete" dicta, both authentic and apocryphal (*Sefer Baalshem Tov*, 2 vols. [Lodz, 1938], 1 : 180, n. 126), where the author suggests that R. Neḥunya ben ha-Kanah is erroneously substituted for R. Samson of Chinon, who is quoted by R. Solomon Luria (*Responsa* No. 98) to the same effect. This identification is certainly correct. It would be of some value to decide whether the mistake was made by Israel Baalshem or whether he found it already in his sources.

28. On this psychological term and its meaning, see G. Scholem, "*Devekuth*," *Journal of Religion*, 15 (1950): 130–34 and below, pp. 155–69, especially pp. 159–60.

29. I emended *yihyeh* of the printed text to *ve-hayah.*

30. The last of the four "worlds" of emanation.

31. *Kethoneth Passim*, p. 43, a–b.

32. On contemplation during study, see G. Scholem, "*Devekuth*," pp. 123 ff.

33. See G. Scholem, *MTJM*², pp. 132 ff.

34. *She-ṣarikh le-kasher eth-aṣmo ba-hem*, i.e., by which man accomplishes *devekuth*; the other possibility of translation, "to which he must attach himself," would also make sense. In this case it would be a construction like "*le-dabbek* (*aṣmo*) *el ha-othiyyoth.*" The idiom *le-kasher aṣmo* is widely used in early Hasidic texts and is synonymous with *le-dabbek aṣmo.* So far no attention has been paid to the fact that *devekuth* and its derivations are not the only technical term for contemplation employed by Hasidic writers. *Hithkashruth, le-kasher aṣmo* etc. are used almost as frequently. Whereas *devekuth* is an old-established term going back to the philosophical translators of the Middle Ages, *hithkashruth* seems to be a more recent coinage.

35. *Toledoth*, 90b.

36. *Pe'er la-Yesharim* (Jerusalem, 1921), p. 19a, § 211.

37. A Kabbalistic prayer book with Lurianic *Kavvanoth.* It contains several traditions of Israel Baalshem's religious customs but none from the sphere of *Kavvanoth.*

38. *Pe'er la-Yesharim*, ibid. Another dubious source would appear to present Israel Baalshem as opposed to the *Kavvanoth* of prayer. The following tradition is somewhat obscure and as it stands perhaps self-contradictory, and certainly open to various interpretations. I dare not say what its exact tendency is but nevertheless wish to call attention to it. "In the month of Elul a man must prepare himself for Rosh Hashanah. Rabbi Shmeril of blessed memory said in the name of Rabbi Naḥman [of Horodenka?] that in Elul he [R. Naḥman] used to pray every day with *Kavvanoth.* The Baalshem Tov sent word to him to stop doing so, for one did not know whether one should pray with those *Kavvanoth*, because the war was God's; nevertheless one must prepare oneself, for one must not rely on a miracle." (M. J. Gutman, *Torath R. Pinḥas mi-Korzec* [Bilgoraj, 1931], p. 18). The "war" referred to is probably the "war" with the wayward thoughts (*maḥashavoth zaroth*). A rapidly changing strategy is needed in dealing with these, see *Toledoth*, p. 172a. Does the Baalshem mean to say in this tradition that *Kavvanoth* depend greatly on a special frame of mind, i.e., on the changing mood of the worshiper? This impressionist concept of *Kavvanoth* is patently not in tune with the Lurianic teaching.

39. *Or ha-emeth*, 14a. A variant of this parable in a more elaborate form is quoted by R. Meshullam Phoebus in his epistle printed in *Likkutei Yekarim* (Lemberg, 1792), p. 27b, also in *Kether Shem Tov*, toward the end of vol. 1. (For a translation, see below, p. 112). A variant of the parable is quoted by R. Benjamin of Zaloscie in his *Turei Zahav* (Mohilew, 1816), p. 57b. "In the name of the preacher of the community of Miedzyrzecz our teacher Dov. There are people who open the lock with a key, but he who has no key must break the door and the lock with something strong which can break iron. Thus the ancients [*rishonim*] used to open all the gates which have been closed since the destruction of the Temple with keys, i.e. with special *Kavvanoth* for every single gate. This is not so in later generations when the power of the *Kavvanoth* is not in our hands, and we must break all the locks without keys but only with the breaking of our evil hearts."

40. The apology stating that the present generation is weak and incapable of great mental effort has in Hasidism well nigh become a literary idiom that covers up the departure from established practice. It comprises, for example, the argument of a later generation of Hasidim against the early Hasidic practice of reintegrating wayward thoughts (*maḥashavoth zaroth*) into the stream of contemplation, see *Likkutei Yekarim* (Lemberg, 1792), p. 21b. The same formal argument was used in the little tractate *Darkhei Yesharim* by R. Menaḥem Mendel of Premyslan for justifying a reduction of the time given to the study of the Torah for the sake of practicing *devekuth*.

41. For *hithkashruth*, see above, note 34. Note the juxtaposition of *hithkashruth* and *hithlahavuth* in the text.

42. *Or ha-emeth*, 64a. See the noncommittal passage ibid. 25a.

43. האמנה הוא דביקות, *Toledoth* 129a, 195b; *Ṣofenath Pa'aneaḥ*, 94a.

44. The reader will realize that I have rendered the Hebrew *le-khavven* and *kavvanah* here and in other passages given in English translation, by several English words, e.g., to have in mind, concentrate, meditate, pretend, etc., according to the context. That this should be necessary, and indeed possible, is a clear indication of the fact that the character of the word as a technical term disintegrated in the hands of the Hasidic writers.

45. (Korzecz, 1798), p. 12a. All bibliographical questions relating to the early editions of *Or ha-Meir* have been dealt with in an exemplary fashion by A. Tauber, *Defusei Koreṣ*, *Kiryath Sefer*, 2:221–23 and 4:286. I give references according to what Tauber's paper proved to be the first edition. He did not, however, discuss the question of authorship. The book consists of homilies delivered by R. Ze'ev Wolf in oral form and arranged according to the weekly portions. The circumstances of the composition of the book are not quite clear. The *haskamoth* only mention that the book originated in the author's sermons and the printer had the permission of the author's heirs to publish the material, but on the literary formation of the manuscript (date of the colophon and, according to Tauber, date of completion by the author: 1796) they remain silent. Only R. Lev ben Joseph, *av beth din* in Dzydlow, uses the expression *ḥibber* in connection with R. Ze'ev Wolf.(ס' אור המאיר,אשר חיבר...מוהה"ר זאב וואלף). This would indicate a clear literary authorship in the usual sense, i.e., that the author himself committed to writing in Hebrew his sermons either before or after delivering them in Yiddish. On the other hand, it is possible that a disciple or disciples of the author were responsible for translating the sermons from the original Yiddish into Hebrew and editing them as was customary in early Hasidic circles. See my preliminary remarks on this custom above, p. 33. One receives the impression that the book is a literary document of uniformity of style. Its verbosity is not indicative of short notes taken down by disciples. Expressions like the following would hardly be suitable for a disciple merely recording his master's teachings: וכמו שאני עתיד לבאר את זה לקמן אי"ה (ii: 11a); וכבר רמזתי בהקדמות הקודמות (ii: 36b); ... עיין שם לשונו כי כתבתי תוכן הכוונה ...; (3:49a) והדברים עתיקים ולית מי להבין עכ"ז לא מנעתי מלכתוב כמו ששמעתי (2:36a) this last passage does not refer to the text of *Or ha-Meir* itself but to a quotation within it. Moreover, some expressions permit conclusions as to the literary personality of the author. Though he probably made use of his sermons, nevertheless he wrote the work as one literary unit, and considered it as such, as can be seen particularly from the extensive system of accurate cross-references. This does not mean, of course, that everything was written down exactly in the order in which we have it in print, e.g. 2:18a כאשר הארכנו נזה בדרוש שבועות and *Derush shavu'oth* is 2:62b ff. A. Walden, *Shem ha-gedolim*, s.v. *Or ha-Me'ir* quotes Isaac Jehuda Yehiel Safrin of Komarno, who expressed his doubts about the genesis of the book. According to the latter's *Nethiv Miṣvotekha* (Jerusalem, 1947), pp. 100–101, the book was written down by an anonymous *shoḥet* and not by R. Ze'ev Wolf himself. I. Y. Safrin also quotes his father-in-law R. Abraham Mordekhai of Pinczow, who was an eyewitness of the

author's dissatisfaction with the *shoḥet's* work, when this was brought to him for inspection. S. Dubnow, *Toledoth ha-Ḥasiduth*, 2:203, n. 4, quotes Walden and mentions that a similar Hasidic tradition was recorded by E. S. Zweifel in his *Shalom 'al Yisrael*, 1:50. In fact, Zweifel's tradition is in all probability not an independent one but drawn from Walden's *Shem ha-gedolim*, which was published in 1864, several years prior to the publication of Zweifel's work (1868), and Zweifel was no doubt acquainted with it. Since Walden derived his information from Safrin, ultimately all doubt about R. Ze'ev Wolf's authorship goes back to that single passage in Safrin's *Nethiv Miṣvothekha*. But Safrin's testimony should be considered against the background of the malicious bibliographical gossip scattered over all the works of this prolific writer and vitriolic critic. Very many of his bibliographical remarks are intended to discredit famous Cabbalistic and Hasidic works or parts thereof. Safrin's pneumatic methods of literary criticism on questions of authorship need not concern us here; on the other hand I would not like to commit myself as to whether events which Safrin says he had witnessed himself or about which he relates the evidence of eye-witnesses are in fact reliable, and so it is in the case under discussion. I would not suggest that Safrin made up the story of the *shoḥet* handing over the manuscript of the book to R. Ze'ev Wolf; but the circumstances might have been much simpler, e.g. that R. Ze'ev Wolf had his own manuscript copied by the *shoḥet* and was dissatisfied with the work done; Safrin, preoccupied as he was with exposing literary forgeries, immediately drew serious bibliographical conclusions on hearing a second-hand account of this in itself perhaps trivial story. It is obvious that one would wish to learn of the exact circumstances in which the book came into existence, particularly since it contains a great number of quotations from Israel Baalshem and the Great Maggid.

46. *Toledoth* 83a, see parallel passage ibid. 145b. The quotation "It is all one" etc. is from *Mishnah Menaḥoth* 13:2; *B. Berakhoth* 5b.

47. *Ṣavva'ath ha-Ribhash*, beginning.

48. *B. Ta'anith*, 2a.

49. *Or ha-Me'ir*, 2:109b.

50. See, e.g., 1:5a, 1:60b his criticism of the view held by what he calls vulgar masses that movements of the body during prayer drive out wayward thoughts. Such pieces of criticism by both Hasidic and anti-Hasidic authors are relevant to the historian: research will have to reconstruct on this basis the features of a popular Hasidism. By this I do not mean popularized Hasidism but a body of teachings, tenets, and practices of anonymous provenance which had a subliterary and oral existence among the Hasidic masses. These teachings were never expressed in adequate literary media by the *Ṣaddikim* or recorded by their literarily minded disciples. Neverthless, the existence of popular Hasidism can be inferred from references to it in the literary works of the movement. This popular Hasidism comprised widely held views and practices based on or derived from genuine Hasidic doctrines or attitudes and also many religious views too radical for survival in the more disciplined and more responsible "upper" literature of Hasidism. Research in an amorphous body of teachings, the existence of which can only be deduced from the implied or overt criticism of it in Hasidic literature and in anti-Hasidic polemic, must obviously be tentative.

51. Prov. 17:16.

52. *Or ha-Me'ir*, 2:34a.

53. *Or ha-Me'ir*, 1:12a.

54. Probably R. Zechariah Mendel of Jaroslaw.

55. *Darkhei Ṣedek* (Lemberg, 1796), p. 9a.

56. See above, p. 106 and n. 40.

57. The date of the epistle is not mentioned in the anonymously printed *Likkutei Yekarim* (Lemberg, 1792) in which the epistle is incorporated (also anonymously), but the date is given in the new edition of the author's writings, including the two epistles,

under the title *Yosher Divrei Emeth* (Munkácz, 1905), p. 10b. The editor, Samson Heller of Kolymyja, a descendant of R. Meshullam Phoebus, used a manuscript that contained the date of the first epistle: Tuesday, 19th Sivan 5537 (1777). The second epistle containing the passage on *Kavvanoth* does not bear a date but must have been written during the *yamim nora'im* (see Munkácz, ed. 35a, *akhshav ba-yamim ha-nora'im*) of the year 5538 (1777) since the *aliya* of R. Menaḥem Mendel of Vitebsk, R. Israel of Płock, R. Abraham of Kalisk, and their followers is clearly alluded to as a recent event (p. 24b): אבל כעת כפי הנראה והנשמע מהנסיעה שנוסעים לארץ הקדושה רבים וכן שלימים וכן נגוזו ועברו והשלימים שעברו הם המפורסמים מאד בעלי רוה"ק וגדולים בתורה בנגלה ובנסתר ועמהם רבים מעניי הצאן קדשים. The time of this *aliya* was Adar 5537, see Dubnow, *Toledoth ha-Ḥasiduth*, 1:134; I. Halpern, *Ha-aliyoth ha-rishonoth shel ha-Ḥasidim* (Jerusalem–Tel Aviv, 1947), p. 20. Since from internal evidence it is clear that the second epistle was written after the first, we may safely date the second epistle in the following autumn (*yamim nora'im* of 5538). I should like to take this opportunity to mention that the book *Likkutei Yekarim* printed anonymously in 1792 must have been edited by R. Meshullam Phoebus himself, or at least with his permission. He was still alive in 1792, the year of the edition, since according to family tradition (published in the book *Zerizutha de-Avraham* of his brother R. Abraham Noah Heller [Lemberg, 1900], p. [4]) he died on Kislev 20th, 5555 (1795). He probably used the mask of anonymity for reasons of religious self-effacement. Dubnow in his *Toledoth ha-Ḥasiduth*, 2:323, n. 5, correctly suggested the name of R. Meshullam Phoebus in connection with the anonymity surrounding *Likkutei Yekarim*; he did so partly at the inspiration of A. Walden, *Shem ha-Gedolim he-Ḥadash*, partly on bibliographical considerations. The Munkácz edition of *Yosher Divrei Emeth*, which could have settled the problem definitely, was unknown to Dubnow. In any event, Dubnow is too vague regarding the role he would assign to R. Meshullam; he identifies R. Meshullam as the author of the two epistles, but he mentions a "circle" in whose editorial work R. Meshullam participated; thus the anthology would be the result of collective editorship. Things become much simpler if we assume that R. Meshullam alone was the compiler and editor of the anthology (no "circle" is ever mentioned in the work), smuggling his own two epistles anonymously into the anthology that he prepared for a similarly anonymous publication. The question of editorship has far-reaching implications. If R. Meshullam Phoebus's concealed editorial function in the anthology *Likkutei Yekarim* can be established conclusively, as I believe to be possible on philological grounds, then the tendentious composition of the anthology becomes self-evident. The choice and arrangement of the various Hasidic texts were anything but random. The anthology is a highly partisan selection of early Hasidic texts. We possess unexpectedly good information about the editor's religious tendencies: in his second epistle he set out the principles of a radical revision of Hasidic teaching and practice concerning the "uplifting and restoration of wayward thoughts." R. Meshullam Phoebus advocates the restriction of this paradoxical technique of early Hasidism to persons of extremely high spiritual standards only (a proviso that certainly did not exist in the early Hasidic formulations of the same technique); for all practical purposes this proviso was paramount to abandoning the admittedly not only paradoxical, but also dangerous involvement with *maḥashavoth zaroth*. If the author of the epistles and the editor of the anthology are the same, the criterion for the selection of early Hasidic texts for an anthology was obviously the same declared policy of doing away with the practice of dealing with *maḥashavoth zaroth*. The compiler of the anthology may be expected to have selected from earlier Hasidic literature only such passages as he deemed most fitting for his clearly stated purpose. Once we suppose that R. Meshullam Phoebus himself was behind the anthology, it is not surprising that he did not include in the anthology the hundreds of passages of early Hasidic literature dealing with the "uplifting and restoration of wayward thoughts," a favorite topic of early Hasidism; for he wished the whole theme to become practically obsolete. Obviously the inclusion of any such passages in this anthology would have frustrated its purpose. Moreover combined with his epistles, in which he expressly fought against the technique of restoration of *maḥashavoth zaroth*, R. Meshullam made the entire collection of *Likkutei Yekarim* the vehicle of a powerful appeal in the interests of his reformed Hasidism. Far from being an innocent compiler of a nonpartisan anthology chosen *sine ira*, and, as it were, at random from the body of Hasidic texts available at his time, the compiler, identified as R. Meshullam, emerges as a propagandist of his own ideas. An analysis of the material chosen for *Likkutei Yekarim* would show a clear policy of discrimination against those aspects of early Hasidism which indulge in the exotic meditative cult of "uplifting the *maḥashavoth zaroth*." While our anthology carefully eliminates the dark and chthonic aspects so prevalent in the teachings of the first two Hasidic generations, it throws into calculated prominence the pure mystical side of Hasidism with its radiant serenity of plain, nonparadoxical *devekuth*. The same is true of the early tractate on contemplation, *Hanhagoth Yesharoth* (also called *Darkhei Yesharim*), by R. Menaḥem Mendel of Premyslan, one of R. Meshullam Phoebus's masters. R. Meshullam drew heavily on this tractate in compiling the anthology. The so-called *Ṣavva'ath ha-Ribhash* also contains tendentious material. The partisanship of the latter two is more veiled, but the polemical tendency against the old views of Hasidism and propaganda for the new ones could nevertheless be shown to exist in both. Much scholarly work on Hasidism (Dubnow, Horodetzky, Ysander) is invalidated on account of taking these three books, and particularly the *Ṣavva'ah*, not as exponents of a reform of original Hasidism but straightforward Hasidic teaching. In a short hint in my paper on the "Beginnings of Hasidism" (p. 104) I still thought that the book *Likkutei Yekarim* was the watershed between old and new in Hasidism, but in view of the fact that in the short tractate *Darkhei Yesharim* the germs of the reform can be discovered, it now seems to me that rather R. Menaḥem Mendel of Premyslan was the first to develop an antagonism against the technique of re-integration of the wayward thoughts into the stream of contemplation and that R. Meshullam Phoebus was thus not an innovator but merely continued his master's tradition and formulated it more explicitly. A full inquiry into the various and often contradictory techniques of dealing with *maḥashavoth zaroth* in early Hasidism is an urgent desideratum.

58. The author is obviously playing on the various meanings of the verb *le-khavven*, meaning "to meditate" and, particularly in non-Cabbalistic texts, "to fit," and on *le-khavven ha-lev*, "to direct one's heart." See also n. 44.

59. A variant on this parable has been dealt with above, p. 106. The present version is reproduced in *Kether Shem Tov*, vol. 1, toward the end.

60. "*Pinu ve-libbenu shavim.*" This idiomatic expression (*Mishnah Terumoth* 3, 8, *B. Pesaḥim* 63a, *B. Nazir* 2b, etc.) originally indicated sincerity of speech in a vow or consecration of a sacrificial animal with no reference to prayer. R. Meshullam, while adopting this idiom as referring to prayer, lends it a different sense. I hardly believe that he was the first to use the idiom in this sense; he probably imitates usage found in *Musar* literature. In the present context the expression implies concentration of mind on the literal meaning of the prayer uttered by the lips, in contradistinction to the Cabbalistic practice of busying the mind with *Sefiroth* and the upper worlds while the lips pronounce the traditional text of the prayers. The insistence of R. Meshullam Phoebus on this attachment to the simple meaning of the prayer text is apparent from another passage in the same epistle (*Yosher Divrei Emeth*, p. 32b): ". . . and surely you know yourself of the holy custom of my teacher R. Menaḥem of Premyslan . . . that on a holy day such as this [namely, the High Festivals] a man must surrender himself entirely to the meaning of the words and letters (*le-khavvanath ha-tevoth ve-othiyyoth*), as is well known and as I have written above." *Kavvanah* is explained as the attachment to the simple meaning of the prayer in another letter by R. Meshullam (*Yosher*, p. 39a): "Concerning the thought accompanying prayer, do you not know that all unanimously say that the essence of

prayer is to train oneself to pray with attention to the meaning of the words (*le-hithpallel be-kavvanath perush ha-milloth*), that is to say, that one should not think of anything except the letters of the words one utters."

61. *Yosher Divrei Emeth*, p. 21a.

62. *Ma'or va-shemesh* (Satmar, 1942), 2:51a.

Petitionary Prayer in Early Hasidism

Both historians and philosophers of religion have stated as an iron rule that mystical prayer is never petitionary.[1] The naïve prayer of the unsophisticated worshiper for help and deliverance appears to the mystic as a demonstration of vulgar egotism. Augustine's advice, *nolite aliquid a Deo quaerere nisi Deum*, expresses the genuine attitude of the mystic who despises petitionary prayer. Consistent mysticism refrains from addressing supplication to God, since this would be the expression of wish and desire, and the mystical ideal insists on the pursuit of desirelessness as an integral factor in the extermination of selfhood. The attitude of early Hasidism to petitionary prayer will now be examined in the light of this position.

If Hasidism did not wish to be divorced from Jewish tradition—as it patently did not—the statutory prayers of Jewish liturgy, which are all of nonmystical origin and character, could not be tampered with textually. But the communal prayers had to be reinterpreted in private contemplation in order to suit the mystic's stern spiritual requirements.[2]

Israel Baalshem was not an extremist in this matter and his position of balanced compromise became the unchanging legacy of many a Hasidic master. His basic view was that unambiguously egotistic tendencies in prayer are to be avoided, and he made no differentiation between private and congregational prayer in this respect. Nevertheless, if it were possible to subsume the private necessity under a higher, more universal, and indeed Divine necessity and to see the private need *sub specie Divinitatis*, by tracing any need in oneself to its origin in a corresponding need in the *Shekhinah*, then prayer should concentrate on the Divine and not the personal aspect of this particular need.

With much reluctance, R. Jacob Joseph of Polonnoye gives the following summary of Israel Baalshem's comments on a certain passage from the *Zohar* (vol. 3, f. 240a). The disciple is obviously hesitant to commit himself by a verbatim report of his teacher's words, possibly because of their strong leaning toward pantheism:

And I have already heard my master's explanation of this [*Zoharic*] passage and it is a basic principle in the service of God. But at the moment I have forgotten it all. Nevertheless it is fitting to put [in writing] a little bit. And I do not know whether this is the meaning of his words or not. May God protect us from error.

The thing is, as has already been mentioned, that all man's prayers should be for the benefit of the *Shekhinah*—who is also called *Tefillah* [Prayer] since She asks and prays her Beloved[3] to supply Her wants. And everything man lacks is due to the [corresponding] lack of the *Shekhinah*. And man must pray for Her wants to be filled. And reparation above is naturally followed by [reparation] below, because [what is below] is also a limb of the *Shekhinah* for His [God's] Kingdom ruleth over all (Ps. 103:19) and there is no place void of Her [the *Shekhinah*].[4]

The same disciple also quotes another formulation of this doctrine of unselfish prayer, which is, however, free of the pantheistic implication of the previous extract. Probably this is why he can write without hesitancy and without disclaiming his teacher's responsibility for the view expressed:

I have heard from my master, that the *Shekhinah* is called *Tefillah* [Prayer] as we find in the Lurianic writings, where it is explained that one should set one's face, in prayer, toward the *Shekhinah* . . . and not aim at one's own benefit, lest, heaven forbid, the verse be applied to his prayer "The Lord hath delivered me into their hands, from whom I am not able to rise up" (Lam. 1:15). And my master of blessed memory explained the matter further in this way, namely: If a man directs his prayer to his own material benefit, hoping to be answered to his material advantage, then a dividing curtain arises [between him and God] through his having introduced the material into the spiritual realm, for then he cannot be answered at all.[5]

Pantheistic views concerning the divine character of the human being can be eminently useful in shaping a climate of petitionary prayer that does not fall into the trap of selfishness, as is shown by the former of these two quotations. Early Hasidic masters, who included the Great Maggid, were quite vague in stating how far the Divine is indwelling in man and how far man, in his essential nature, is separate from God. The student of these texts will perceive that there is a certain inconsistency in the passages that deal with this point. Some imply the habitual indwelling of God within man and this determines man's very nature and metaphysical status; in other passages man's Divine bond does not seem to be a permanent feature of the human structure but rather the ultimate goal of a contemplative life. The student of Hasidism will gain nothing by an attempt to harmonize the two views. Obviously Israel Baalshem or the Great Maggid, with their main interest focused upon the practical problems of contemplation, were not concerned about inconsistencies that would worry the mind of the metaphysician more than the mind of a practicing mystic.

The mystical conception of man as part or particle of the Divine can be made use of most conveniently in formulating the paradox of a petitionary prayer purged of all egotism. Obviously if the petitionary prayers of the statutory service are not ruled out altogether, thus reducing the life of prayer to mere hymnistic adoration of the Divine, the danger either of pantheism or of egotism must be faced: to escape egotism by merging oneself and one's needs with the Divine, is to be caught in the pantheistic trap. No wonder that Hasidism with its preeminently mystical leanings preferred the pantheistic to the egotistic solution.

It is worth noting that the Hasidim did not adopt the solution that would have been ready to hand in any nonmystical climate. Rather than integration of personal needs into the Divine need, their integration into the communal need, which has a long tradition in Judaism, could have served equally well as a means of circumventing selfish formulations in prayer. No doubt a religious community more concerned with man's relationship to man than with his relationship to God would have developed a technique of circumvention of petitionary prayer on the lines of the Talmudic view[6] "He who prays for his fellow when he himself is in need of the same help, will be answered first [i.e., his own need will be supplied first]."

The self-identification of the individual with another individual or with the community at large is the social equivalent of the pantheistic subsumption of petitionary prayer. Had theoretical thinking in the Hasidic movement been imbued with the immense social concern that Buber believes to have been the main feature of the personal life of its members, this would have been the preferred way of extracting the egotistical sting from petitionary prayer.

The Great Maggid added little that was new and his views on the subject of unselfish prayer clearly echo the statements of his teacher, Israel Baalshem. The pantheistic flavor of the teacher's advice is also present and is the core of his argument. Specific personal requests must not be sought in prayer unless they can be seen in the perspective of Divine necessity. The pantheistic concept of man is openly declared to be the key: man, as a divine particle, recognizes his personal need as a reflection of Divine needs. The duty of the mystic is to treat his own wants as merely indications of higher needs beyond. He writes: "One should not stand up in prayer save with heaviness of the head [i.e., in a sober mood]."[7] The sense is: Do not pray for something that you lack, for then your prayer will not be answered. But, when praying, you should pray for "heaviness of the head," meaning the heaviness or deficiency in the Head, i.e., in the *Shekhinah*, for what you lack is also lacking in the *Shekhinah*. Since man is a particle of the Divine and that which is lacking in the part is necessarily lacking in the whole; and, moreover, the whole feels the deficiency that is in the part, let your prayer therefore be for that which is lacking in the whole.[8] "This thought is to be carefully understood," concludes the Great Maggid.

The mystical demand to raise oneself above personal needs necessitates arduous contemplative efforts. The danger of spiritual self-deception, which lies in the possible incongruity between the mystic's disciplined contemplative thought and his unconquerably egotistic motivation, is only too clear to the sensitive religious mind. Menaḥem Mendel of Bar, a personality of less pronounced mystical tendencies than Israel Baalshem or the Great Maggid (if such a conclusion is permissible on the basis of the few extant fragments of his teaching), was well aware of the potential insincerity inherent in the contemplative practice recommended by Israel Baalshem. Jacob Joseph of Polonnoye, after describing Israel Baalshem's advice on the abolition of selfishness by raising one's wants in contemplation to the divine level, continues in a sad, understanding spirit:

> Nevertheless, the heart knows the bitterness of the soul, for the spiritual state of man is not always the same. Now, it may happen, God forbid, that a person is afflicted with a great sorrow, and he prays for his own deliverance without

bearing in mind that his personal sorrow is contained within the *Shekhinah* and that he ought to pray rather for the sorrow of the *Shekhinah* in which everything is contained. It is also possible that in the midst of his praying he remembers that he ought to leave his own self out of account and pray instead for the *Shekhinah*, only he finds that he is unable to contain himself with regard to his own sorrow. Now if he pretends that he is praying for the *Shekhinah*—and the Searcher of hearts knows that this be untrue—then it is possible, God forbid, that he may be rejected altogether.

Consequently it is better that he should pray simply according to his state of mind at the time, for the main thing is that his mouth and his heart should be one, for "he that telleth lies shall not tarry in my sight" (Ps. 101:7). This I heard explicitly from the mouth of the preacher R. Menaḥem Mendel.[9]

This small example of the controversy illustrates the practical problems encountered by mystical prayer in its early Hasidic phase.

NOTES

1. On the nonpetitionary character of mystical prayer, see F. Heiler, *Prayer*, trans. S. McComb and J. E. Park (Oxford and New York, 1932).
2. On some basic problems of traditional prayers in a Cabbalistic climate, see above, pp. 95 ff.
3. [*Tiferet.*]
4. *Toledoth* 91a. See my remarks on the last phrase and its Hasidic interpretation in "Beginnings of Hasidism," p. 98.
5. *Ṣofnath Pa'aneaḥ*, 1a.
6. [T. B. *Baba Kamma* 92a.]
7. Mishnah, *Berakhot*, 5:1.
8. [*Or Torah* (Korzecz, 1804), portion *Aggadah*, sig. 39, f. 2b.]
9. *Toledoth* 91a.

Contemplation as Solitude

The author of the *Darkhei Yesharim* holds a particular view with regard to such a central theme of Hasidism as the ideological background of devotion. What is the spiritual precondition for devotion, and what are the general rules by which it is conducted? As a first assumption, everyone admits that the contemplative life must be organized in such a way as to bring about the soul's communion with God. For it is universally accepted that communion as such (*devekuth*) is no regular and spontaneous expression of our nature: it depends upon exercises, persistence, concentration of the soul upon its task, and the removal of all spiritual distractions and disturbances. The limitation of social intercourse was always considered an important device for inducing *devekuth*, or as an important precondition for its achievement. Just as there is a whole array of positive regulations designed for the attainment of *devekuth*, so there is an array of negative restrictions—that is to say, a catalogue of things, the avoidance of which liberates the human being for his contemplative task; and the limitation of speech, or to put it in more positive terms, silence is one of those very significant commands. Idle or unnecessary talk arising from the obligations of social intercourse prejudice what may be called the higher functions of the soul. This fact is taught by every mystic from his own personal experience. Speech swallows strength and powers of concentration that are needed elsewhere. The solitary life of a desert hermitage or of a monastery present the ideal pattern of contemplative existence or, to be more exact, the ideal conditions for it. Solitude, being the sociological expression of the habit of silence, serves to limit the external hindrances to the attainment of *devekuth*. It is no wonder then that the exponents of the contemplative way (whether Jewish or non-Jewish) have always emphasized the important principle of solitude and its corollary, silence. Solitude and silence are the chosen climate of those who lead the life of contemplation. The deeper and more comprehensive the silence, the better the prospects of success in the contemplative way.

What novel departure does the manual *Darkhei Yesharim* make in the history of Hasidic contemplation? We must understand the paradoxical nature of R. Israel Baalshem's position on this question. His claim that *devekuth* was possible *precisely* among the trivialities of social intercourse had been intended as a thrust at the accepted order and convention, just as his words on the subject of "worship by material means" had in them something of a polemical impudence. How impertinently satirical by implication are some of the traditions noted by R. Jacob Joseph from his master, R. Israel Besht. We quote three relevant passages:

(1) "As I have heard in the name of my teacher who used to closet himself with the sister of the Matronitha to indulge in earthly storytelling."[1]

(2) "And men of understanding know how to achieve a state of union [*yiḥud*] even by means of exchanging tales with their friends, as I have heard from my teacher [commenting on the saying][2] 'hearing a woman's voice is indecency,' etc."[3]

A third tradition preserved by the same disciple quotes overwhelming evidence for R. Israel's view that "conversation with one's friend in the street" equals in merit learned discussion of Torah or prayer as factors in bringing about states of contemplative union:

(3) "As I have heard from my teacher, of blessed memory, there may be states of union in talking of Torah and in prayer, or else in speaking with one's friend in the marketplace, since one may join a man [to God] and cause him to ascend, every man according to his [spiritual] rank, whether by means of speech of holiness, or whether by profane conversation, wherein are the twenty-two letters [of the alphabet]. Moreover, I have heard in his name, may his memory be blessed for life everlasting, that if a man is obliged to talk with his fellow or to listen to idle talk from him, he may sublimate it [literally, "cause it to ascend"] by due attention; for the act of hearing is an act of the soul which is part of God above."[4]

It is clear that the two distinct traditions noted in the third passage agree in describing trivial talk between friends as a background for contemplative ascent of the soul. But there is a difference between them. The first tradition R. Jacob had apparently heard directly from his teacher. The second appears to be of a lower degree of authenticity, for he had heard it only "in his name." (There is, of course, the possibility that the same tradition may be mentioned in one book as "heard from my teacher" while another book, or the same book in a different place, uses the formula "As I have heard in my teacher's name." In this present instance, however, the fact that the two traditions are differentiated in one and the same passage entitles us to conclude that one was truly heard by the author from his teacher's mouth, while the other was merely reported to him.)

The first tradition in passage (3) encourages the promotion of the spiritual ascent (*ha'ala'ah*) of one's fellow. It implies that mundane talk may be *necessary* in order to provide for the ascent of someone of lower-ranking spirituality, and that this state may be termed *yiḥud*. All speech, whether of sacred matters or of everyday concerns, is articulated by means of the twenty-two letters of the Hebrew alphabet. Speech is therefore fit to serve as an instrument of ascent, and there is no essential difference between the holy and the profane use of speech. One employs one or the other according to the particular spiritual rank of the person concerned. According to this doctrine, it is not the letters themselves that are made to ascend, but the person to whom the words are addressed.

The second tradition noted in passage (3) is more cautious in its formulation. If it is necessary to speak or hear trivial matters, we may yet cause such speeches to "ascend" by being attentive to their religious possibilities. The content of the contemplative act that proceeds during idle talk is a meditation on the divine character of the soul that had made it possible to hear and participate in that particular conversation.

The astonishing lengths to which the Baalshem Tov went in his positive attitude to ordinary discourse can be gauged from a further report in the writings of the same disciple. Here a different technique is proposed from those we have considered so far: sublimation is to be achieved not by means of a contemplative act proceeding simultaneously with the idle talk itself, but by a perception of the heavenly origin of the twenty-two component letters of the discourse after its completion and during their reuse in Torah study:

> I further heard from my teacher that all slanderous talk [*leshon ha-ra*] is accomplished by articulating and pronouncing the twenty-two letters of the Torah, etc. Similarly when one speaks of indifferent matters and afterwards learns [Torah] making use of [the same] twenty-two letters, then one causes the twenty-two letters of idle conversation to ascend.[5]

This is a far-reaching theory indeed. To be sure, the doctrine as expressed here does not actually approve the practice of slanderous talk and evil gossip. But it provides a simple way of remedying such sins after they are committed, and one can hardly imagine anything easier than rectifying the twenty-two letters of slanderous talk by means of the twenty-two letters of subsequent Torah study. It is not surprising, therefore, that the Maggid, R. Dov Baer of Mesritz, utters a shrill protest against the unlimited possibilities implied in this doctrine. In contrast to the way of the Baalshem Tov, the Maggid inveighs against the sublimation (*ha'ala'ah*) and rectification (*tikkun*) of idle talk, and declares this prohibition to be binding not only on those who indulge in such talk but even on those who merely hear it:

> And lo it is known that "the lower waters weep"[6]—which refers to the letters of the words composing the utterance of speech, i.e., the words of Torah and prayer which an intelligent man may elevate [to their divine origin] *when he hears them*: and thereby he raises the [fallen] sparks of holiness which are the alphabetical letters, and gives satisfaction to his Maker. But it is known that it is forbidden to utter "words of nought" (*devarim betelim*) such as slander, tale-bearing, mockery and the like; and note that they are called "words of nought" *because a man should not say I will go and raise these letters back to their origin*: God forbid that a man should say so, for such words [of nought] are the subject of a [biblical] prohibition. And let no one be anxious lest the letters concerned remain in their shattered [i.e., fallen] state. As it is known, once the three drops have dripped from the vessel, there is no need to be particular about the rest [of the contents] for they have become ownerless.[7]

The expression "Let no one be anxious," etc., provides overwhelming evidence of the fact that, according to some extreme views held in the Hasidic camp, it was a holy duty to apply the principle of *tikkun* to idle words. The Great Maggid clearly combats the view in the text quoted and arms himself with an opposing theory based on the etymology of the word *betelim*, and likewise draws on the analogy of the Rabbinic law regarding the vessel whose contents become ownerless (*hefker*), after the first three drops have been removed. The Maggid clearly seeks to overthrow the whole principle of *tikkun* as applied to the twenty-two letters composing "idle words." In his view, the principle of "rectifying" the alphabet of discourse is applicable solely to the letters of Torah study and prayer, which, if uttered without due devotion (*kavvanah*) or concentration, are susceptible of rehabilitation. The concept of *devarim betelim*, in the Maggid's terminology, is hardly that of common usage, i.e., idle or indifferent speech. *Devarim betelim* for him denotes forbidden speech, i.e., slander, tale-bearing, and mockery. As for these, no theory of *tikkun* can avail, for speeches that carry with them the flavor of illegality are not to be redeemed after the manner taught by the Besht. On the other hand, it needs to be said that these types of discourse *do not require tikkun*, since, in the view of the Maggid, they are "automatically made null and void." According to him, the general theory of the fallen sparks does not fit this special case.

The Maggid's distinct strand of polemics is revealed in the phrase "Let no one be anxious"—which means, "One should pay no heed to those who say that a man must rectify everything; i.e., all discourse whether of piety or of sinful matters such as slander, etc." According to the Maggid, those who would rectify the letters composing slanderous speech profess a misleading doctrine, since there is no need to seek *tikkun* for these "letter-sparks." Being automatically canceled, they demand neither *tikkun* nor *ha'ala'ah.* And yet this false doctrine which the Maggid seeks to discount is none other than the teaching of his master, the Baalshem, as we have seen above.

The position of the Maggid is therefore clear. Forbidden speech is not subject to *tikkun*. Speech that belongs to the sphere of *miṣvah* (i.e., religious duty), such as Torah study and prayer, is susceptible of *tikkun.* The letters making up such speech seek their *tikkun* "with tears." The actual situation visualized is, as the passage goes on to say, the rectifying of the words of Torah study and prayer "when they are heard," that is to say, the Hasid who hears negligent and ill-managed speech may, and in truth must, rectify and raise the twenty-two component letters thereof.

The theory of the twenty-two letters is indeed a two-edged

weapon. It is possible to use it as a technique of contemplation aimed at causing the reascent of the component letters of any discourse whatever, sacred or profane. The Maggid only opposes the use of the theory as a means of redeeming "words of nought, slander and tale-bearing." It must be admitted, however, that the theory is, in its essential nature, a comprehensive one, designed to serve for all cases; and yet, as we have seen, the Maggid impugns its validity in the case of any profane discourse that contains a suggestion of sin.

The general theory of the twenty-two letters is retained by the Maggid as good Hasidic doctrine in cases where no clear contravention of biblical law occurs, i.e., in indifferent speeches between one man and another. In such instances he would admit, and even enjoin, the procedure of *tikkun*. In a long exegesis on the verse that is central to the whole practice of communion in Judaism, viz., Deuteronomy 11:22, "To cleave [*u-le-dovkah*] to Him," the Maggid distinguishes two degrees of *devekuth*. The higher degree is "the worship of God with intense devotion [*hithlahavuth*] and this is total communion [*devekuth*] with Him, be He blessed." The ecstatic and direct communion with God Himself is in the Maggid's view necessarily not constant or sustained at the same pitch, but rather is it interrupted for longer or shorter periods. In such intervals, a communion of a different and more humble sort applies, and this operates by using the theory of the twenty-two letters. After the height of ecstasy comes a period of silent contemplation wherein the contemplative subject pictures in his mind the letters of the alphabet. Conversing with one's fellowmen does not necessarily disturb this silent contemplation, for all such conversation is articulated by means of these letters and therefore there exists the possibility and, in very truth, the obligation, of using the component letters of such discourse as the material for contemplation.

And this is the force of the question posed in the *Gemara*,[8] "and is He not a 'consuming fire'?"—meaning that the state of transport is interrupted and comes to you in alternating waves. "So how is it possible to cleave to Him, blessed be He?" The answer is given [in the *Gemara*]—"Cleave to His attributes." And the meaning of that is, [cleave] to His garments, viz., to the alphabetical letters; for a man can always engage his thoughts by considering the letters of the Torah, and the Torah is the garment of the Lord, blessed be He. And even in coversing with one's fellowman, let one consider only the letters composing those words [of common discourse], for they also belong to the twenty-two letters of the Torah.[9]

The Maggid's essentially positive attitude to the question of discourse with one's fellowmen and the possibilities of divine worship arising out of such discourse is expounded with great clarity in one of his homilies dealing with the modes of worship. Of these he distinguishes two: a safe and a perilous one. The sublimation of ordinary speech is the perilous one, but even so is apparently regarded as a true mode of worship.

For behold, it is known that the term *derekh* is applied to a beaten road and the term *oraḥ* to an unbeaten path, from which it is sometimes possible to lose one's way and stray into a place of danger, which does not occur on a beaten road from which we are unlikely to stray. So a man has these two possibilities. There is a beaten path of divine worship whence—if he faithfully follows it—he will certainly not stray. This is the case with a man who has separated himself from all [earthly] matters and concerns, and occupies himself solely with the Torah day and night, and *only speaks when speech is unavoidable*, but not otherwise. And there is an unbeaten path termed *oraḥ* which applies when a man talks to his fellow in a speech intended for the sake of Heaven, namely, when one speaks those things from which some moral or some [stimulus to the] love or fear of God might be derived, and the like; or when a man [speaks] who knows how to cause the ascent of speech in holiness which is a faculty known to many. It follows that such speech is certainly permissible. *But there is danger in these words*, for he will possibly stray from the path of good and begin to utter words of nought also, as is the way of the multitude; for without His special help, blessed be He, a man may easily stray from his path. Therefore a man must needs pray strenuously [literally, gird his loins in prayer] not to fall into the snare of sin, which Heaven forbid.[10]

The intention of the passage is clear. In spite of the danger in following the path (*oraḥ*) that is liable to lead to words of nought—those which belong in his view to the category of strictly prohibited speech—the Maggid does not prohibit this path to his followers. On the contrary, he sees its value enhanced by the danger it involves, and his aim is to caution those venturing on this path in order that they may pray for the gracious aid of God in a daring undertaking so close to the very heart of Hasidism. After all, there are those who know how to extract some heavenly meaning from the trivialities of everyday conversation.

One may appropriately examine in this context the position of R. Meshullam Phoebus. He strongly recommends that common discourse be restricted to a minimum. This is almost identical with the position of the author of *Darkhei Yesharim*, who likewise recommended the policy of limiting discourse and even suppressing it altogether. But R. Meshullam knows very well that his position implies a deviation from the views of both the Besht and the Great Maggid. He explains the difference between the line taken by him and that of his predecessors in the same way as he explains their difference on the subject of the sublimation of "strange thoughts" and their "rectification." There is no one left today, he claims, whose spiritual stature is great enough to permit him to indulge in mundane discourse. R. Meshullam, therefore, issues a warning against making use of the principles of the Besht and the Maggid that acknowledge various possibilities of discourse, and, like the author of *Darkhei Yesharim*, he bids his disciples observe a restriction of speech. The words of R. Meshullam Phoebus hinge on two homilies of the Great Maggid found in those "texts" (*ketavim*), as he calls them. One of these homilies can be identified and completed from the printed version of the Maggid's sayings, while the second, unfortunately, seems not to have survived, unless it is possible to identify it from other sources. This is the line of attack developed by R. Meshullam:

And you should understand that the above-mentioned texts all speak of an absolutely holy man, as the *Rav* of blessed memory has expressed it in his writings . . . on that *Mishnah*[11] [which reads]: "The sons go out with laces [literally 'with bonds'] and true sons of kings with bells." And this applies to the generality of men. But the sages spoke about the custom of their own day. He explained that those called "sons" who have degrees of soul supplementary to that of the [ordinary] soul and spirit that is within them, and who are bound in their thought to the Creator, blessed by His Name—they are permitted to go out even into the street from time to time, if need be, since they are greatly "bound" to their Creator, be He blessed: nor will the passersby interrupt such a one in his devotion. This is the meaning of the saying "the sons go out with bonds"—which means to say, with bonds linking them mentally to the Creator. But the King's sons who have merely [the normal allowance of] soul and spirit and who are called the sons of the King because they come from the [dark] side of the heavenly kingdom, they go with bells; which means to say that such a one must not go unoccupied but must be like a bell which gives out a tinkling sound. Thus he sends out his voice at all times with words of Torah, and prayer, and piety, and does not put his trust in his [capacity for] mental devotion, for the passersby will interrupt him, Heaven forbid, since his *devekuth* is weak. "And this applies to the generality of men"—which means that in this matter everyone is equal and *there is hardly anyone in existence who is in the rank of those "sons who go out with bonds."* What the sages say about the "sons who go out with bonds" refers to their own day; it is according to what men were then. They spoke mainly of themselves, not about others [who might come after them].[12]

All that needs to be noted here is that the decisive words, "there is hardly anyone in existence who is in the rank of those sons," etc., are not in the source passage in the Maggid's works as we have it. It is clear that these words reflect the view of R. Meshullam rather than of the Maggid.

In a subsequent passage R. Meshullam writes,

Furthermore he wrote there [evidently referring to the writings of the Maggid] on the verse ([Eccles. 5:1), "Be not rash [*tevahel*] with thy mouth, and let not thy heart be hasty to utter a word before God [for God is in heaven and thou upon the earth; therefore let thy words be few]". In [*Reshith Ḥokhmah*], *The Gate of Holiness* [chapter 10] there is a forced explanation of this. What does it say afterwards? "Therefore let thy words be few." And he, be his memory blessed, has written in his own saintly fashion that in truth he who clings to the Lord, be He blessed, in the proper way by believing that the whole world is full of His glory . . . and who attains Love and Fear, and communion with the Creator, blessed be He—can in truth [permit himself to] speak many words. For as he cleaves fast to holiness, he is able to raise profane words into the sphere of holiness. He will also be able to achieve this by possessing the skill of the concatenation of letters as known to the divine early master, the Besht—may he be remembered for life everlasting—and his inspired pupils who drank of his waters. . . . And this should not be a matter of surprise because we are bound to admit *that there exists a wisdom of this kind.* For do we not find in the *Aggadoth* of the *Gemara* many things which seem to be words of nought. But the *Tanna'im* were men inspired by the holy spirit and possessed this skill of the concatenation of letters in perfection and spoke all things in the spirit of their holiness; and these are the mysteries of the Torah. And they succeeded in doing all this because of their *devekuth* with the supreme [sphere of] Holiness by virtue of their piety and simplicity, and their great and continual reverence for the name of God, blessed be He. On this subject the saintly rabbi and teacher Menaḥem Mendel of blessed memory has said—and I heard this from his holy mouth, may his merit protect us, in the name of the Besht of blessed memory—that this is the meaning of the *Mishnah*,[13] "He who occupies himself with Torah for her own sake, merits many things"—and by "Torah for her own sake" he means, as I have said earlier, *devekuth* with the Creator, blessed be He, and by saying "he merits [*zokheh*] many things" he means, "he can then purify [*zakekh*] even many profane words"—for why are they called "words of nought [*betelim*]," because they are as it were void of life, seeing that they are not words of Torah. But he who cleaves to the name of God is able to purify them and give them vitality by means of his *devekuth* and his higher wisdom, *of which it is however impossible for us to form any conception, for we do not in any way occupy such a position. How, then, might we know its place and value except that by faith we may believe it to be so*; by which is meant, faith in the sages, i.e., by believing that they possessed this wisdom as we have seen in reference to the *Gemara* mentioned above. And all this applies to such a one as is capable of continually thinking of God as of Him whose glory fills the world, and who conducts himself with modesty, shame, and humility before God, blessed be His name, as though He sees him [continually]. All of which does not apply to one who thinks of God as being in heaven above whilst he himself is on the earth below as the majority of people think. Such a person is indeed compelled to reduce the number of his words as much as possible, for he is not in a position to remedy any profane speech; [hence] let him only speak words of Torah continually. This is the meaning of the verse (Eccles. 5:1) "For [*ki*] God is in heaven and thou upon earth." . . . If it [*ki*] is in your mind that God is in heaven . . . and you do not cleave to Him with that kind of faith which considers Him always as the God whose glory fills the earth, then let your words be few, for in this case it is impossible for you to remedy any [profane] speech whatever. In this way you will walk in safety.[14]

This very important extract teaches a number of things. First of all, it is possible to attempt the reconstruction of an extremely daring doctrine of the Great Maggid that apparently has not come down to us in any other source. It is true that R. Meshullam Phoebus interrupts the quotation from the Maggid in order to add his own qualifying remarks; nevertheless, the character of the Maggid's homily on which these notes turn is clear enough. As was his wont, the Maggid stipulated the qualifications that have to be observed in the paradoxical procedure discussed in this chapter. It is certain that he does not draw the same conclusions as did R. Meshullam; and it is equally clear that R. Meshullam does not mean to attribute his own extreme conclusion ("We do not in any way occupy such a position," etc.) to the Maggid.

NOTES

1. [*Toledoth Ya'akov Yosef* (Korzecz, 1780), f. 36a, beginning of *parashah Shemot*.]
2. T. B. *Berakhot* 24a.
3. [Source untraced.]
4. [*Keter Shem Tov* (Tel-Aviv, 1960), p. 84.]
5. [Source untraced.]
6. [*Tikkunei ha-Zohar* (Jerusalem, 1978), f. 19b.]
7. [*Maggid Devarav le-Ya'akov*, ed. Rivka Schatz-Uffenheimer (Jerusalem, 1976), pp. 110–11, no. 66.]
8. T. B. *Sotah* 14a.
9. [*Or Torah* (Lublin, 1884), p. 61.]

10. [*Or Torah*, p. 85.]

11. *Shabbat* 6:9. [See *Or Torah*, p. 129.]

12. [*Yosher Divrei Emeth*, no. 19, in *Likkutim Yekarim* (Jerusalem, 1974), f. 120a.]

13. *Avot* 6:1.

14. [*Yosher Divrei Emeth*, no. 19. See *Maggid Devarav le-Ya'akov*, p. 247, no. 146, and *Or Torah*, p. 106.]

Contemplation as Self-Abandonment in the Writings of Hayyim Haika of Amdura

Hayyim Haika of Amdura takes his place in the history of Hasidism as the disciple of the Great Maggid Dov Baer of Mesritz. Indeed, his teaching is dependent to no small extent on that of his master. However, there are new tones in the doctrine of Hayyim Haika that have no parallel in the works of the Great Maggid or indeed in the entire history of Jewish mysticism, including Hasidism.

What is the nature of these new tones and how are they to be defined in terms of the science of religion? The peculiar climate of Hayyim's teaching cannot be mapped without resort to the concept of quietistic mysticism; in many respects Hayyim may himself be termed the quietist par excellence of Hasidism. In Hayyim's scale of values the supreme religious task is no longer contemplation in its two basic forms, i.e., the cleaving of the soul to God, and the elevation and transformation (toward God) of one's human qualities as they are expressed in wayward thoughts.[1]

In Hayyim's teaching man approaches God with the human will as his vehicle rather than emotion or intellect. The annihilation of human will in face of the Divine Will, in the famous saying of Rabban Gamaliel, the son of Judah the Prince (*Avot* 2:4), contains the most elementary features of a quietistic standpoint. Although the pure form of the doctrine was not reached in that rabbinic maxim, the scholar Dean Inge was nevertheless right in his book on Christian mysticism[2] to quote the words of Rabban Gamaliel in his exposition of that approach to religion which finds the basis of the worship of God in complete surrender and abrogation of the will. In fact, however, Hayyim of Amdura lends the idea a greater complexity, a more religious basis, than does the simple moralist Rabban Gamaliel.

Hayyim developed a doctrine of quietism. The long list of his exhortations on the subject of will begins with general statements such as may apparently be found in every Jewish religious system, and yet they suggest a very specific climate of religious thought: "It is necessary to direct oneself solely to perform the service of the Holy One blessed be He" (*Ḥayyim va-Ḥesed* [Warsaw, 1891], f. 62b), or "One should desire to do solely the Will of the Creator without regard to one's own needs" (63a). Expressions such as these obviously prove nothing in the way of special quietistic mysticism in Hayyim's teaching.

The quietistic character of his thought is more prominent in expressions such as the following, to which Hayyim reverts again and again:

"Man must raise himself above material things by annulling his will before that of the *En-Sof*, blessed be He" (8b). "He equated his will with that of the Will of God" (ibid.). "It is necessary to do the Will of the Creator and this is the meaning of that rabbinic axiom: Be as careful in a light commandment as in a severe one for there is no difference between 'light' and 'heavy' in respect of the Will of the Creator" (ibid.).

"He who does not put his heart in subjection before that of the Will of God, blessed be He, his heart is brought into subjection through poverty" (22b).

There is an abundance of sayings of this kind. In the book *Ḥayyim va-Ḥesed*, the supreme task of the annulment of the will is given many different forms, as for instance: "Now also when we desire to serve in the City of the Lord of Hosts, i.e., in the 'stirring-up' of the Lord of Hosts, which means when we desire to subject all our wills [note the plural form] beneath His Will, and therefore is He called the Lord of Hosts because He is the Will of wills" (71a).

The most radical expression of enthusiastic quietism is to be found in his comment on the Mussaf prayer for *Rosh Ḥodesh*: "'When they offer before you sacrifices of favour [*Raṣon*]'; when one wishes to offer oneself to God one should slaughter one's own will" (31b).

The image of slaughter expressing the surrender of the human will is characteristic of religious quietism wherever it occurs. This need not be due to literary cross-fertilization, but rather to a basic unity of religious experience that suggests that particular image in this context.

The primary problem concerning the doctrine of will is the problem of individual volition. Whence does man's self-will come? The general answer is that the source of human will is in the Divine Will:

"[God says:] 'Return unto me' (Malachi 3:7) in your thought, and we reply, 'Turn thou us unto thee, O Lord, and we shall be turned' (Lamentations 5:21). For you are Infinity [*En-Sof*], but our will is but little. And it is necessary to know that it [our will] comes from God" (9a).

The idea that the origin of human will is in the Divine Will occurs time and again, in different formulations throughout the book; and it is precisely this idea which creates the difficulty: Self-will is inconsistent with the Divine Will. This is proved by the very fact that self-will must be annulled and *offered as a sacrifice*. How, then, can we account for this inconsistency which occurs despite the initial unity of the wills? A deliberate willful act is required from man to bend his own will to the Will of God. But how is human self-will at all possible?

Hayyim's answer inevitably introduces duality into the Divine Will. Without this duality, it would be impossible to explain the abundant psychological phenomena of autonomous human wills that are, by their very definition, inconsistent with the Divine Will. Any voluntaristic metaphysics must acknowledge this divine duality. Hayyim primarily intends to explain man's "other" will, not as resulting from his defiance of God's will, but rather as providing him with the possibility of religious subjection. Duality is inherent in the Divine Will: It is the absolute will, but at the same time it contains our own autonomous wills:

> It is written, What is the purpose of *Keter*? Because within the Divine Will are depicted our own wills as well. The meaning of this is that He willed us to will other things. This is free will. And it is the will of the Holy One blessed be He that we should bend our will to His own (28b)[3].

The divine duality plays a religious role, for it enables man to exercise free will. In order to resolve the difficulty arising from this duality, the author stresses in several parallel passages that the "other" will, man's self-will, does not oppose God's will, but rather, God Himself had willed this "other" will into being. (This, of course, does not resolve the problem of duality, it only disguises its existence.)

A parallel attempt at explaining the existence of self-will occurs elsewhere in the book, where the author "solves" the problem, not from the human angle, i.e., by presenting it as providing the opportunity for man to exercise free will, but from the divine angle. He finds the reason for the existence of autonomous human will, and for the tension between this self-will and the Divine Will, in the need to create an opportunity for divine *pleasure*—an important, one might even say, central concept in the teachings of the Great Maggid of Mesritz: "Surely, it was His will that we should have another will [than His own], and that we should bend our will to His will. For, otherwise, what pleasure has He? Therefore, *Will also has an obverse aspect*" (45b). The Divine Will and human will constitute, as it were, two sides of the same coin, the position of the human will remaining here the same as in the passage quoted above. Man's "other" will is contained in the Divine Will. This is Hayyim's opinion in yet another passage:

> In the Will of the Holy One, blessed be He, are contained two kinds of will. For, [first] it was His Will that His life-force [*Ḥiyyut*] should be returned unto its root. . . . Subsequently it was His Will that we should have another will. And it is His pleasure that we should bend our will (50a).

The position of human will seems to alter slightly in another teaching, where Hayyim speaks, not of the representation of human will within the Divine Will as its "other side," but literally of the *creation* of man's self-will by God: "It is known that the Holy One blessed be He has created in us another will, so that we might bend our will before His Will. And *through this He derives His pleasure*, which He could not have done if we *had no 'other' will*" (57a). In this passage our individual volition is deprived of its ontological position, in the sense that the creation of our wills is not conceived of as their representation within the Divine Will, but rather as their existence within the human soul. However, the motivation remains unaltered: the reason for the duality is divine pleasure.

Another attempt to deal with the question of independent will is to be found in a long section of the book *Ḥayyim va-Ḥesed*. Here there is a double motivation. One motive is that the self-subordination of His servants makes the divine sovereignty stand out all the more and this subjection of our will is only possible if we have in fact a separate will of our own that may be overcome or broken for the sake of the Divine Will. Hence it follows that the independent human will is essential to the establishment of divine sovereignty. "Another reason why the Holy One blessed be He created in us a separate will is because He wanted us to become His servants so that He might be called King; and if there was only one single will, the quality of sovereignty would not be recognized. But since we have in us another will, and since we nonetheless are prepared to subject ourselves to His Will, then the quality of sovereignty is made manifest" (67a).

The second motive to be found in this passage tries to deal with the relationship between the Divine Will and this other will.

Behold there are in human thought the categories *Ḥokhmah*, *Binah Da'at* which signify [a representative, respectively] from the right and from the left and from the center [of the Sefirotic system] for *Ḥokhmah* teaches man continually how to cleave to the Holy One blessed be He, and *Binah* has creative power and sometimes works its effects on the body also, which means things that the body has need of, and *Da'at* is at the center, i.e., [it operates] both in thought and act. There is also *Ahavah*, which is *Ḥesed* and comes from the same side as *Ḥokhmah*, and *Gevurah*, which comes from the side of *Binah*, and *Tiferet*, which comes from the side of *Da'at* and this is both in potency and in action. There is also *Neṣah*, *Hod* and *Yesod*, the connecting link. And this is three included in three, the three which belong to the realm of thought included in the three which belong to the realm of potency. And the three which belong to the realm of potency are included in the three which belong to the realm of act. And with us who proceed upward from below it is thus, because we conquer ourselves and give thanks to God and join ourselves to God. Then the Holy One, blessed be He, loves us and opposes our opponents and glorifies Himself with us. And afterwards there falls upon us the "marrowfatnesses" which are the reasons of the commandments and which are also called "three included in three." And behold it is proper that every man's will should be one with God. But nevertheless it is necessary to transcend one's nature until one attains this [state] because man is compounded with his body; therefore did He make with us a separate will so as not, Heaven forbid, to take the Will of the Creator [directly] and to join it to the body. Only when one transcends one's nature and beats down [literally, "smashes"] all the powers of the body, is one able to attain the Will of the Creator so that both He and the indirect effects of His work should become one. And this is the meaning of that saying [T. B. *Ḥagigah* 12a] "The light which He made use of . . . in the days of the Creation. And He saw that the whole world was not worthy of it because they were joined to the corporeal, therefore He hid it for the righteous in the world to come." The interpretation is that this refers to one who has come to this state after having overcome all his [lower] nature and is joined to the Holy One, blessed be He . . . .

And behold the sovereignty of the Holy One is termed the *Name* of the Holy One. And how did He create in us another will? By virtue of the quality of *Binah*, which designed the Creation of this world as it was needful, and this is "that *Binah* nestling in the calyx," which is as much as to say that the Will of God is concealed for we have another will, and this latter is the world of created things, and creation [*Beri'ah*] has the meaning of observation since He observed how this world needed to be made. And this is the meaning of the verse (Isaiah 43:7), "Every one that is called [by My name, and whom I have created for My glory, I have formed him, yea, I have made him]," meaning, whenever a separate will occurs. And calling has the sense of designation, that is, "by My Name," so that He might be called King. "[And whom I have created] for My Glory" so that I might be magnified, reverenced and exalted over the world, and that is, "whom I have created"—at all events the world of "creation" was necessary. "I have formed it," it was necessary also to form and to bind in us a vital element from the Holy One blessed be He, because, seeing that *Binah* nestles in the calyx, which is as good as to say that the Will of the Creator is concealed from us, therefore did the Holy One blessed be He create in us a Divine element of vitality and by this means are we enabled to join ourselves [to Him] and to attain the Will of God, and this is why it was necessary for Him to form [it] in us. And the meaning of the phrase "Yea I have made him" is "because I wanted also the world of action," and if the Will had been a single unit, the grafting would have been in vain. Therefore He created in us a separate will and on this account He was obliged to form and to join His vitality to us so that by this means we might be able to attain the Will of the Creator.

And behold when we reach the Will [of God], it may be said that the three are included in the three and the interpretation of this is because one conquers oneself and gives thanks [to Him]. Of a certainty one has not thereby reached the reason of the Commandments for had one reached the reason one would not be required to conquer oneself and to give thanks and to join oneself to the Holy One blessed be He; and it is certain that when one needs to join [oneself]—this indicates that one does not yet attain the reason for the Commandments. But afterwards one attains *Ahavah* [love] because on account of the Love of God one's own loves are nullified and one is strengthened by this thing; and because of this He is strengthened because of a certain glory. And afterwards one attains "the marrowfatnesses" which are the reasons of the Commandments and that is the "field of apples." Because *Neṣaḥ, Hod* and *Yesod* are termed a field awaiting sowing and apples is the term for *Gedulah, Gevurah, Tiferet.* For just as an apple has many colors, red, green, and other colors, so these three above-mentioned virtues have likewise, for each virtue is a color in itself. And afterwards they are termed the sacred "marrowfatnesses" which are separate, and behold *Neṣaḥ, Hod* and *Yesod* are termed three men and this is the meaning of that saying of the Rabbis "The feet of a man. They are the habits of a man." And this *Neṣaḥ*, *Hod*, *Yesod*, which a man should accustom himself to attain, they are sureties [or "sweetnesses" by paronomasia], which is as good as to say that they guarantee to a man whatever he desires, for by their means he may attain even the marrowfatnesses, and hence that saying "to the place where one desires to go, thither do they lead him." [T. B. *Sukkah*, 53a].

And this is the meaning of the verse in connection with Abraham, "And behold, three men were standing over against him" (Genesis 18:2) on which we may remark, how can standing be used in reference to three men? And this is why they [*Neṣaḥ*, *Hod*, *Yesod*] are called "feet" since they may be easily joined to the body. And this is the meaning of the verse "Send out men for thyself" (Numbers 13:2), which means that you send them from before you, which means that you should not take those men, i.e., *Neṣaḥ*, *Hod*, *Yesod* for yourself, but you should join them to the Holy One blessed be He. And by this means "They may spy out the land of Canaan," which means that you should be able to loosen, i.e., open the knot from the body and that is Canaan, so that you might be subordinate [*nikhna*], and subordinate the body to the Holy One blessed be He, in subjection to the Will of the Holy One blessed be He" (67a–67b).

The doctrine of the creation of separate human wills opposed to the Will of God naturally has lurking within it weighty antinomian dangers. But this explosive material is not liable to be touched off in the quietistic context of Hayyim's teaching. It is not surprising that everything of this kind in his work is merely verbal, as for instance: "And behold when we are made void of reality we are joined with the Hidden One and that is the meaning of the verse 'and He and His substitute [shall be holy] [Leviticus 27:10, 33], which is as good as to say that when he should be joined to Him who is hidden, then His substitute also, i.e., even our separate will which is called substitute [*temurah*], which is opposition to God, shall become holy because all its affairs shall be directed to the name of Heaven" (59a). One cannot accuse him of exploiting the antinomian possibilities contained in his doctrine. In this respect, he falls below his colleagues. This should not occasion surprise. The explanation is, as I have already indicated, that quietism is not conducive to antinomianism. Sin itself, as it were, receives a new dimension in depth, for it is the realization and fruit of what was already sin before it was acted out, viz., our individual will itself. Hence it follows that the essential function of repentance is not to wipe out the sin or the blemish the sin has produced in the higher worlds, as in the case of other Jewish mystical systems, but its essential function is conceived—again in this startlingly quietistic formula, as the annihilation of the will. "Man should see to it that he destroys a sinful soul, which means that he should kill *that will* [i.e. the human will] *in which sin resides*" (35a). In this direction and not in the direction of antinomianism the pattern of religious quietism is worked out with absolute consistency.

The most striking contradiction to Hayyim's quietistic doctrine is his theory of the magical capacity of the human being. The teaching of his master, the Great Maggid, evolved a radical theory as to human power, or rather the specific power of the *Şaddik* (the distinction matters little in the present instance), which consisted in effecting "mutation" of a thaumaturgic character. This tradition of the magical powers of man is inherited by Hayyim from the Maggid as a doctrine that was still potent. What does the pupil make of this doctrine? Does he accept it as it stands? It would be superfluous to emphasize the essential antinomy between a quietistic and a magical point of view: the former hands over, as it were, all power and enterprise to God, while the latter places such power in the hands of men. From the religious standpoint there can be no greater opposition, in fact, than that between quietism and thaumaturgy.

Students of religion have truly observed that the exponents of quietistic mysticism refrained from all petitionary prayer because of what was felt to be the magical or quasimagical implications of such activity. The content of quietistic prayer, on the other hand, as Heiler defines it in his book on prayer is merely the "transference of all volition into the hand of God, the absolute surrender [*Hingabe*] to His Will and the offering up of the individual."[4] All petition must be removed from the contents of prayer, and, from the quietistic point of view, it is irrelevant whether such petition is directed toward favors of a material or spiritual kind. The remark of Madame Guyon in her confession before Bishop Bossuet is well known: she felt unable in her prayers to make any request at all of God.

There is no evidence in those sayings of Hayyim which have come down to us to suggest that he drew such radical conclusions as these regarding the content of prayer. There is no admonition in his writing against the use of petitionary formulae. Even more surprising is the fact that in his teaching he continues the magical doctrine of the Great Maggid. Of course, teachings of a magical tendency are very infrequent in his book *Ḥayyim va-Ḥesed* as compared with those of his master. But at any rate they are there, and it may well be asked what form does the magical doctrine of the Maggid take in the writings of his pupil? The essential feature of the Maggid's theory of magic was the metaphysical category of the *Ayin* (nothingness). This may be defined as that supreme ontological sphere where all contradictions are annihilated by means of a sort of *coincidentia oppositorum*. As far as the Maggid was concerned, the *Ayin* was mainly identified with the Cabbalistic *Sefirah Ḥokhmah*, because "the *Ḥokhmah* is the *Ayin*"; whereas in the metaphysical chart of Hayyim, the supreme *Sefirah* is the region of the Will, which he considers to be the "Nothingness," and also identifiable with *Keter*. *Ḥokhmah*, for its part, comes second to Will. Although his words do not reveal complete consistency in this complicated matter of identification between the *Sefirot* and the spiritual regions in general, he has at any rate departed from the more striking novelty introduced by the Maggid, according to which *Ayin* = *Ḥokhmah*. Hayyim, indeed, returns to the standard Cabbalistic equation that asserts that *Ḥokhmah springs from Ayin*. The latter is nothing other than *Keter* or, in the terminology adopted by Hayyim, *Raṣon*. This *Raṣon* (will) serves the same function as the *Ayin* of the Maggid, and rightly so, for in Hayyim's work it is also called *Ayin*, a factor that makes it possible formally to transfer the functions of the Maggid's *Ḥokhmah* to his own *Raṣon*.

What is the specific theory of magic that Hayyim held? Put simply, cleaving to the Divine Will enables the human being (or the *Ṣaddik*) to effect change.

> And behold it is written "Thy sons have seen Thy Kingdom" [*Prayer Book*, Evening Service], which may be taken to mean that they have seen merely the attribute of sovereignty [*Malkhut*]; "He cleaves the sea before Moses" [ibid.] and thus the sea was merely cleft before Moses, *because Moses was closely attached to the Raṣon and therefore he was able to draw out change* (literally, "renovation"] *from the sphere of Raṣon so as to alter nature*, so that the sea might be split, and this is the meaning of the saying: "The righteous who perform His Will [*reṣono*]" and it is not written "who perform His Word [*devaro*]" because the *Ṣaddikim* are bound up to a region higher than that of speech [*Dibbur*] and therefore they are able to overthrow the *Dibbur* of the Holy One blessed be He and so alter the nature of the physical universe (49b).

This is tantamount to saying that there exists a basic

possibility of altering the spoken will (*Dibbur*) of the Lord since the *Ṣaddikim* have a connection with some region above it, that is to say, with the region of *Raṣon* or Will proper. At the same time, the *Ṣaddik* does not effect change within the sphere of *Raṣon* but draws out or attracts the "renovation" from the area of Divine Will. This interpretation of magical activity naturally limits its magical character, and that indeed is the general tendency in Hayyim.

There is also another way in which this limitation on the character of magical operation is effected. Of course, the *Ṣaddikim* are thought to change the *Dibbur* of the Holy One, but this is only possible for the *Ṣaddik* because he is so conveniently connected with the higher Will (*Raṣon*) and is thus beyond the restrictions of the practical or spoken Will (*Dibbur*). The essential qualification of the magical character of his practice is achieved through a new definition of the nature of the Divine *Raṣon*, or higher Will. To our great surprise, we discover that the *Raṣon* is not a region of absolute divine determination, of final decisions, so to speak, but it is, more precisely, the region of all hypothetical possibilities. Therefore we do not here have to reckon with real change, but with a new choice between possibilities of equal standing, as it were.

> Lo, we say "that the righteous perform Thy Will" and not "who perform His Word" [*Devaro*] because it is the Will of the Holy One blessed be He to which the righteous are bound in consequence of which they are able to change the "word" [*Dibbur* or *Davar*] of the Holy One blessed be He. And behold the *Raṣon* is termed *Ethan* [strength] because it conducts the *Ḥokhmah* and it is also termed *Tenai* [condition], which has the same letters as *Ethan*. This is to say that *whilst it is in the state of Raṣon it is still doubtful whether or not it will issue into practice* (50a)

The aspect of potentiality here given to the sphere of *Raṣon* helps Hayyim in his obvious inclination to reduce the magical impact of the *Ṣaddik's* practice. He does not so much change the Divine *Raṣon*; rather, he *exchanges* one *Raṣon* for another ("Since he is able to join himself to the *Raṣon* and can thus draw thence another will" (ibid.).

Firm opposition to the idea that the *Ṣaddik* can overthrow the Divine Will is strongly expressed in another saying of a pragmatic kind that has come down to us. Because of its fragmentary character and its obscurity of language this saying is not altogether clear but the magical activity is evidently associated with *Ḥokhmah* and not with *Raṣon*; that is to say, it coincides with the thesis of the Great Maggid. In any event, Hayyim's essential point is that there is no complete overthrow achieved by the adept, but rather a drawing out from the *Raṣon* of something in keeping with the *Raṣon* itself. This is emphasized with great force: "As our sages have taught 'My sons have conquered me' (T. B. *Baba Meṣia*, 59b), which means that the Holy One has given to us the attribute of conquest so as to enable us, so to speak, to conquer Him! *But this is merely His Will*, which is as good as to say that we do not overthrow, Heaven forbid, the [divine] volitions but draw out [a particular] impulse into the world as the Will of God" (26a). The drawing out of this new impulse is thus *itself* the Will of God.

We must attempt to analyze another saying of the same kind as the passage cited above. The terminology of this saying is unusual in that it features the concept of "the annihilation of reason"—a matter that needs consideration. The joining of the practitioner to the Divine *Raṣon*, which we recognize as the method of achieving magical effects, makes its appearance here in close conjunction with what is termed "our self-concealment in the annihilation of [our] reason." This concealment or "veiling" has two complexions depending on whether it is for a shorter or a longer period. This in turn depends upon the varying function of the concealment.

And when we join ourselves in firm connection with Him and we attain to the state where we clothe ourselves in the Divine vestments, we can be conjoined thereby with the *Raṣon* itself by means of two kinds of choice: (*a*) when we desire to know the reason of something which has already been introduced [as a novelty] into the world, then we require to veil ourselves in the annihilation of reason [*afisath ha-sekhel*] for a little time so as to sweeten the reason of a thing, and this is what is termed the minor *Keter*. And (*b*) When we desire to draw out an original thing into the world such as was not there previously, and this is that to which the sages refer when they say: "the righteous convert the quality of judgment to the quality of mercy" (T. B. *Sukkah* 14a]—which is to introduce what was not there previously, then we need to veil ourselves in the annihilation of reason for a greater period so as to bring in this new event and this is termed simply *Keter*. This is the meaning of the verse "He performs the will of those who fear Him" [Psalm 145:19], which means to say that the *Ṣaddik* is bound up in the *Raṣon* and is thus able to draw out into performance the new thing, and behold in the *annihilation of reason is the Will*. (26b).

This is not the place to analyze the concept of "annihilation" or "extinction of reason" in Hayyim's theory. It is a phrase encountered rarely enough, and indeed seems to occur about three times altogether in the book *Ḥayyim va-Ḥesed.* In general, it may be said that we are dealing here with an extremely exalted ontological area. The text cited above concludes by unambiguously identifying the "annihilation of reason" with *Raṣon.* This identification is apparently not based upon the irrational and arbitrary character of *Raṣon*, as if *Raṣon* were essentially of a purely voluntaristic and nonrational character; rather, this identification is based upon the aspect which *Raṣon* presents from the human angle. Human intelligence is extinguished in that area; it is, as it were, annihilated. I do not wish to affirm too dogmatically that Hayyim's intention is to point to some ecstatic experience in this annihilation of reason. But one thing is clear: in accordance with his emphatic pronouncement elsewhere, a human being cannot possibly remain continually in the state of "annihilation of the reason"; this is possible only "at intervals," an indication perhaps of the transient, ecstatic nature of man's experience of the annihilation of reason.

> It is necessary to raise up these loves to the Holy One blessed be He Who is their Head. And lo there is one other level which is when one is continually in the annihilation of reason, but this thing is impossible except at intervals, for if the human being were to be there continually, the human frame could not endure, God forbid, for one might collapse, and this is what is meant by the saying "it is forbidden to remain with hands outspread on high for more than three hours" (43b) [See *Sefer ha-Bahir*, end of chapter 49].

If the "annihilation of reason" in the above passage is equivalent to *Raṣon*, and if it is elsewhere termed *Ayin*, this should not worry us. In Hayyim's terminology *Ayin* is very often the same as *Raṣon.* It is in this sense that we may understand the following remark, which establishes the ontological layers with great directness and clarity: *Ḥokhmah*, *Kadmut ha-Sekhel* (literally, "the original intellect"), and *Maskil* (the intellectual) are all terms used to refer to a very high ontological area, but not to the highest. Above them is the *Ayin*, which is equivalent to the "extinction of the reason":

> Behold there is *Maskil*, and it is [also] called *Kadmut ha-Sekhel*, and it is the *Ḥokhmah* and it is *Porath* [literally, "the fertile one"], because from it there flow intellectual ideas in abundance to men . . . and a man is able to draw out from

the *Maskil* new thoughts which are [suggested by] the permutations of letters [of Scripture] so that he may gather himself together by this means prior [to embarking] upon the annihilation of reason, which is termed *Ayin*. And he should know that in the whole world there is only that power which acts upon [preexistent] matter, as the seed which is sown and is lost, and then sprouts forth afterwards (6a).

The annihilation or extinction of reason in its double meaning—the metaphysical and the psychological—constitutes, as it were, an additional level above that of the *Kadmut ha-Sekhel*.

NOTES

[This article, with the preceding one, were meant to be part of a book on Hasidic contemplation.]

1. See above, pp. 123–4.

2. [W. R. Inge, *Christian Mysticism* (London, 1899), p. 223.]

3. The key to the understanding of this passage is the supposition that the Divine Will is identical with the first *Sefirah*, *Keter*. For the exact location of Will on the ontological map, see below. The following is a parallel teaching that fixes, though somewhat ambiguously, the relation between the Divine and human wills: "The letter *kaf* [of the Hebrew alphabet] is *Keter*, and the reason for this is that in the will of the Creator our own will is included. . . . And the second reason is that all wills bend to His will. The letter *kaf* stands for 'bent' [*kefufah*], and this is [indicated in the verse] 'They shall bear thee up in their hands' (Ps. 91 : 12; the name of the letter *kaf* is also the Hebrew for 'hand'), which means that I shall bear you up, above all wills, for each will bends another thing" (64b).

4. [F. Heiler, *Das Gebet* (Munich, 1918), trans. *Prayer* (New York, 1932), p. 343.]

R. Abraham Kalisker's Concept of Communion with God and Men

The figure of R. Abraham Kalisker (d. 1810) emerges in Hasidic tradition as that of a revivalist *enfant terrible* whose wild behavior scandalized practically everybody and evoked revulsion and anger even among Hasidim, to say nothing of their opponents, the Mithnaggedim. According to R. Shneur Zalman of Ladi, the Maggid of Mesritz rebuked his disciple R. Abraham in the strongest terms for his and his followers' conduct.[1] Hasidic tradition speaks of the "*Talk* Hasidim," the group connected with R. Abraham, as a kind of religious anarchists.[2]

Very little is known of his teaching. He wrote no book, neither were his homilies noted down and collected by disciples. Some sayings of his appear at the end of *Sefer Ḥesed Le-Avraham*,[3] but these contain little that is new or of interest to the student of the doctrinal history of Hasidism. In many respects, e.g., in his emphasis on *emunah* (faith), he is evidently under the influence of his older friend to whom, in a letter, he refers as his master, viz., R. Menaḥem Mendel of Vitebsk.

The letters, however, written by R. Abraham from Palestine, where he had emigrated (1777), together with R. Menaḥem Mendel,[4] are full of interest in many respects. During the latter's lifetime, R. Abraham would add only a few lines to R. Menaḥem's long letters. When he died (1788), R. Abraham himself wrote long epistles containing much information concerning the life of the small Hasidic community and its relations with those around it. The epistles abound with unceasing complaints of the high and ever-rising cost of living.

Fortunately these letters comprise not only historical but also doctrinal material that both in content and literary form surpass what is otherwise extant of his teaching and homilies. Moreover, here we do not have secondhand notes made by some clumsy-handed disciple, but authentic letters of R. Abraham himself, although most probably these (like R. Menaḥem Mendel's letters) were dictated to a scribe.

It is intended in this article to analyze one of R. Abraham's letters[5]—which is unfortunately undated—dealing mainly with *devekuth*, the ideal way of life in Hasidic theory and practice.[6]

The letter is clearly divisible in two. The first part analyzes the concept and practice of *devekuth* proper, while the second part analyzes a secondary state of *devekuth*, namely, those phases in which, through lack of spiritual concentration, *devekuth* proper is not attainable. Both parts of the letter hold surprises for the student of the theory of Hasidic *devekuth*, as R. Abraham's doctrines on the subject contain much that is novel.

1. The epistle opens with an introduction on how to attain *ayin* (the mystical nihil). This doctrine R. Abraham had taken over from the Great Maggid R. Dov Baer of Mesritz, who had developed it in two clearly distinguishable, though often intermingled, forms.

One formulation of the *ayin* doctrine by the Maggid urges a mystical *anavah*, that is, humility and self-abasement before God. It is practiced in contemplative exercises leading to the mystical annihilation of self. As the contemplative Hasid annihilates himself, viz., his individual consciousness, the vacuum thus created within his soul is immediately filled by a new content. His soul is invaded by God., viz., the Divine *Shekhinah*. The withdrawal of the human ego from his individual consciousness conduces to the entry of the divine ego. In this process the *Shekhinah* or God takes the place of the human ego that has been converted to *ayin*. According to the Maggid this process is not an act of grace but is almost as natural as if a law of spiritual *horror vacui* were at work. The expulsion of the human ego is the only necessary requirement for the soul's attaining to its divine nature. The ways of self-annihilation, well known to mystics of all ages, thus form an important element in the teaching of the Great Maggid. To him *anavah* is not so much social humility but a mystic-contemplative self-abasement of man before his Maker. The technique of self-annihilation and of the passive retreat of the soul possesses unmistakable marks of ecstasy; the ecstatic atmosphere so clearly noticeable throughout the writings of the Maggid is partly due to them. But the Maggid speaks also of *anavah* as humility in its accepted moralistic connotation, i.e., as a quality of conduct between man and man. It is clear that the latter kind of *anavah* contains no ecstatic elements. It implies the deliberate weighing of the merits of one's fellow man against one's own, with a view to recognizing one's own deficiencies as greater and graver.

It is characteristic of R. Abraham of Kalisk that when he speaks of attaining the state of *ayin*, he thinks of it not in its ecstatic meaning but as an attitude of social humility plain and simple. He makes use of all the terminology of his teacher, the Great Maggid, but evades all its ecstatic implications. By *ayin* he does not mean the mystical *ayin* and by *anavah* he does not mean ecstatic self-abasement. In his own words:

> The final aim of Torah and *Ḥokhmah* . . . is to attain the perfect *ayin*, wherefore a man should render his self nonexistent; the very source of Wisdom is *ayin*. *Ayin* is its very root and from this root grow humility and lowliness, even as our sages said: "The Torah is fulfilled only by him who makes himself like the desert," free to poor and rich alike, and who regards himself as no greater than his fellowman, but feels "nonexistent" before him. In this way they [man and his fellow man] are integrated [*mithkalelim*] one into the other, for *ayin* combines a thing and its opposite, and therefrom results the straight line which encompasses peace and blessing.

It is worth noting how formulae and expressions that in the works of the Maggid are reserved for the realm of mystic and ecstatic *ayin* are applied by the writer to the context of social humility. *Hassagath ha-ayin* "the attainment of *ayin*," a characteristic expression of the Maggid denoting ecstatic self-annihilation, is divested by R. Abraham of its mystical sense and is used of self-annihilation in terms of human relationships. R. Dov Baer's frequent exhortation "to render oneself *ayin*" and his use of the scriptural verse *ve-ha-Ḥokhmah me-ayin timaṣe*—"Wisdom comes from *ayin*"—(Job 28:12) are now understood in a moralistic sense. The Maggid's term *battel ba-mṣi'uth*, "non-existent," denoting the state of mystical ecstasy or "annihilation," is employed by R. Abraham in the sense of practicing social humility. Here the Maggid's most cherished mystical concept is converted into a nonmystical virtue. This clearly points to a nonmystical, at least nonecstatic tendency of R. Abraham. To the Maggid, *ayin* is one of the supreme metaphysical principles—that of the peaceful *coincidentia oppositorum*. To R. Abraham it is, characteristically, the principle of reciprocal humility that conduces to peace in human relationships.[7]

2. The second section of the epistle deals with *emunah* (faith) as the alpha and omega of all religious values. The highest duty is the pursuit after simple things "and Faith is the simplest thing, and equally obtainable by every person." "Faith has no limits: with it man begins, with it he ends." What R. Abraham says in this letter is in full accord with what he says elsewhere. He insists most emphatically on the primacy of Faith. "Great is Faith . . . in that it supersedes human reasoning."[8]

3. The writer proceeds to urge the shunning of jealousy as an objectionable form of human relationships, and points with great emphasis to the fact that Hillel the Elder declared the verse "Love thy neighbor as thyself" to be the principal commandment of the Torah. The relationship between man and man is the pivot round which the thoughts of R. Abraham revolve; time and again he comes back to this theme, which seems to hold him in a spell. Without apparent logical transition he then proceeds to give an exposition of the concept of *devekuth*.

4. *Devekuth* denotes for R. Abraham man's emotional relationship with God. One of his frequent expressions is "The sense of Love and Fear (of God) which flows down upon us is the *devekuth* between ourselves and Him, blessed be He." It indicates that for him *devekuth* is not an active but a passive state. This interesting point is further borne out by what follows. Simultaneous and commensurate with man's self-discipline in *devekuth* is the Divine help that complements it. Here R. Abraham passes on to the mainspring of his theory. "The truth of the matter is that Divine Providence is in accordance with the *devekuth* that exists between ourselves and Him, blessed be He, and commensurate with man's own *devekuth* is the exercise of Providence towards the person who never withdraws his thought and *devekuth* from Him. Should anyone allow his thoughts to turn away from Him for a time, then during that period Providence will recede from that person."

This is a new idea in the history of Hasidic *devekuth*. *Devekuth* and *hashgaḥah* (Providence) are correlated here for the first time: God's Providence toward an individual depends on that individual's *devekuth*. It is only a deduction from this principle that "if a person who, as a rule, is spiritually perfect happens to be affected by adverse circumstances, the reason must be sought in temporary *shikheḥah* (forgetfulness, nonawareness, insensibility of the Divine) and cessation of *devekuth*. . . . According to the measure of his forgetfulness and the length of time it persists will be the duration of the adverse conditions from which may God preserve us."

This theory of R. Abraham is new, indeed revolutionary in the history of Hasidic *devekuth*, which had not previously known this combination.[9] Outside Hasidism it is, of course, as old as Maimonides' *Guide*, to whose conception of Providence (*Guide*, part 3, chapter 51) R. Abraham's doctrine bears a strong resemblance. In fact, the almost slavish dependence of R. Abraham on Maimonides, both as regards the theory and its formulation, is apparent from a comparison of the texts concerned.[10]

5. However, after this rather slavish following of the *Moreh*, the surprising originality of our author becomes apparent when he goes on to describe the spiritual state known in Hasidic literature as *katnuth* (literally, "littleness"). From R. Israel Baalshem onwards, *devekuth* was understood in empiric, psychological terms as occurring in alternations of exaltation and lowness, high and low tide, climax and anticlimax of the spiritual life. The low tide was usually termed *katnuth* and the high tide *gadluth* (literally, "greatness"). Dissipation of the spirit and lack of spiritual concentration are the marks of the former, even as intensive concentration of the soul upon God is the mark of the latter, which is considered throughout Hasidic literature as the ideal state. Various theories developed in Hasidism concerning the role of this lowness of spirit in which *devekuth* diminishes or ceases altogether as a consequence of the great spiritual effort preceding it.

Now R. Abraham too recognizes this state and also calls it *katnuth*, i.e., a state of lower value. But the role he assigns to this state is one unthought of by his Hasidic predecessors. According to him the phase of *katnuth*, occurring at a time when the emotional concentration upon God is not possible, offers the leisure time necessary for emotional concentration of the soul upon one's fellowman. *Katnuth*, in R. Abraham's view, is not simply an emotional desert but the choicest opportunity for "loving one's neighbor," and one should wholeheartedly avail oneself of this opportunity. In its ideal form *katnuth* has a positive function and constitutes "*devekuth* with the neighbor." Whenever the supreme form of *devekuth*, that with God, is impossible of attainment, it should be taken up in a modified form in which it can be realized, namely, in the human or social context. Here again the object of *devekuth* is not God but man.

Just because there is no man who is never subject to *katnuth* of his intellect or to a cessation of *devekuth* with God, He clearly commanded us in His Torah "Love thy neighbor as thyself"; for love brings about *devekuth*—the clinging together of many as one man. Similarly there is no person who does not at one time or another experience the influx of true *devekuth* while his fellowman is idle [in *devekuth*]. When they regard themselves as one, it [i.e., the *devekuth*] can be gained by him through the *devekuth* of his companion and through the latter's cleaving to God.

Here we have a community of contemplative individuals cleaving to God and also bound one to another. Gone is the isolation that the individual suffers while in a state of *katnuth*, when he is estranged from God. Through the new human bond a new sense of belonging is created.

6. The most important aspect of *devekuth* with one's fellowman is that it is calculated to lead, albeit in a roundabout manner, back to the same security as *devekuth* with God. This security is guaranteed because one is in *devekuth* with one's fellowman who in turn is (or, at any rate, should be) in *devekuth* with God himself. To be isolated means to be unprotected. Joining a human relationship offers the unprotected individual a new, this time human, shelter which is still under Divine Providence. From the context in R. Abraham's dissertation it is not quite clear whether the ideal *devekuth* in the phase of *katnuth* is just a matter between two individuals, one cleaving to the other and the other cleaving to God, or whether it is a matter of collective *devekuth* in which a whole group participates, in that some members are cleaving to God and some to each other.

For all the members of the body receive Divine Providence through being connected with the brain and heart and these receive more Divine Providence and protection than all the other parts of the body since they are closer to the life-essence (*ḥiyyuth*) and to the attachment and to the *devekuth*. Nevertheless, by way of these all other parts of the body are also recipients of Providence.

What exactly is the sociological situation implied in this theory? For a moment it seems as if R. Abraham, in the above passage, had in mind the relation of Hasidim to the *Ṣaddik* (the brain and heart of the allegory), the latter constituting *devekuth* in his own person and all of them receiving a share of Providence through *devekuth* with the *Ṣaddik*. "The saying of our teachers," writes R. Abraham, "'A *miṣvah* brings a *miṣvah* in its train, and a transgression brings a transgression in its train' has been said not necessarily of one person, but of all who cleave to a perfect man. Is it not reasonable that anyone attached to him is the more readily drawn—by reason of being bound to him—to holy deeds and, similarly, to transgressions? It is indeed clearly taught in our teachings: 'When it is well with the righteous man, it is well with his neighbor, etc.'"

This is clearly enough an allusion to the *Ṣaddik*, but soon this theory of *devekuth* between man and perfect man proves to be a special case within the general theory of *dibbuk ḥaverim*, i.e., close association of friends of equal status. In a description that follows immediately on the foregoing passage in his letter he writes: ". . . and thus within the *dibbuk ḥaverim* who hearken intently to the voice of God, *miṣvah* and Torah are certainly extended and continued through *devekuth* with men who are themselves cleaving (*devukim*) to God." The use here of the expression *dibbuk ḥaverim* and of the plural *anashim* ("men") implies that R. Abraham does not refer to the *devekuth* of Hasidim with their *Ṣaddik*, but rather to mutual *devekuth* among men. And indeed *dibbuk ḥaverim* is the keyword in R. Abraham's system, whereas the *Ṣaddik* plays a very unimportant role in it. One would be tempted to formulate it this way: Ṣaddikism, to R. Abraham, is but one form in the varieties of *dibbuk ḥaverim*. What R. Abraham has in mind in the above passage is something like a closely knit group of companions in a state of *devekuth* with God. It is the first time in the history of Hasidism that clear expression is given to the idea of the value of the Hasidic community per se as distinct from its dependence on the *Ṣaddik*. What comes to the fore here is the autonomous value of *dibbuk ḥaverim* as such.[11]

7. This social significance of the contemplative community which is, in principle, independent of the *Ṣaddik*, is apparent from a piece of practical advice given by R. Abraham in the

course of the same letter. Discussing the needs of the individual, R. Abraham refers to the aforementioned theory that harm comes to a person only when there is a weakening on his part in his *devekuth* with God. From this it follows that all that is necessary in order to escape harm is the strengthening of the individual's attachment to the contemplative community whose members are bound together by love in the fulfilment of the commandment "Love thy neighbor as thyself." The integration of the individual in this emotional community will, of itself, effect the extension of Divine Providence also to him. Despite his temporary inability to participate directly in the members' *devekuth* with God, he yet does, through membership of the group, become part of them.

It is a wonderful boon for the individual to have continuously the advantage of Divine Providence through his associates who are attached in *devekuth* with God, and to be eligible for all good things and success in the uplift of body and soul; and it is possible that this is the meaning of the saying "A person to whom a misfortune has happened—heaven forbid—should inform others [*rabbim*, literally "the many"] of his suffering, those others being persons who seek Heaven's mercy on his behalf." The Rabbis did not say the others "should seek" [*yevakkeshu*] mercy for him but that they do—as a matter of course—seek [*mevakkeshim*] mercy. Evidently this dictum speaks of someone who conducts himself in accordance with Torah and its central principle, namely, the *miṣvah* "Love thy neighbor as thyself." Now if some misfortune befall him, at a time such as has been described, all he needs to do is to make his misfortune known to the many with whom he is in a relationship of *devekuth* and who are themselves protected by Divine Providence from suffering and distress by the abundance of their *devekuth* with God. Thus those who are in trouble live under the divine protection which shields them [i.e., through those in full *devekuth*]. In order that the perfect ones might suffer neither pain nor grief, he, too, will have Divine Providence extended to him when they become aware of his grief. Thus [the communication of one's distress to the contemplative colony] in itself constitutes a seeking of mercy. For this reason the Rabbis did not say "they should seek" but "they seek." This is, too, what Scripture means when it says "that redeemed my soul with peace" (Psalms 55:19), that is to say, the attachment of love and peace to the many has redeemed my soul "from such as advanced upon me," i.e., from troublemakers—Heaven forbid—whether they menace the body or the soul. "That saved my soul," thanks to "the many who were with me" [*ki ve-rabbim hayu imadi*], that is through the many seeking divine mercy for me.

R. Abraham sums up his advice, which almost amounts to an early attempt at group therapy, with these words:

What it all comes to is this: that which brings about Divine Protection and

Providence whereby one may be rescued from misfortunes, is the abundance of the sense of man's love and fear of his Maker. Protection against what may happen in the future at a time when man is in a state of *katnuth* and experiences a cessation of *devekuth* consists in a common bond, love and true peace found in *dibbuk ḥaverim*. When man is without either [*devekuth* or *dibbuk ḥaverim*] he is one from whom the Divine Countenance is hidden, may God save us from being in such a state.

Indeed, it is advisable to be in a state of *devekuth* with close friends. When one of the circle falls out of *devekuth* with God into a state of *katnuth*, he then cleaves to his associates. The contemplative colony can assure all its members a fair amount of security, since the Divine Providence is guaranteed to the whole fellowship through those members who are, at the time concerned, fortunate enough to be in complete *devekuth* with God. The portion of Providence is to be shared by all members.

8. The letter ends with a salutation and an exhortation to foster good relations between men; cleaving to God is not even mentioned. The reader of R. Abraham's letter gets the impression that although in R. Abraham's view *dibbuk ḥaverim* is no more than a helpful remedy in moments of *katnuth*, he really is more interested in the formulation of the emotional values of *dibbuk ḥaverim* than in the formulation of the contemplative values of *devekuth* proper with the Maker:

And now children come hearken unto me. . . . Whoever is smitten by his conscience let him, for the sake of God and for his own sake, act as follows: Let him seek peace and fortify it . . . and if, Heaven forbid, his heart urges [literally, "hustles"] him to separate himself from the fellowship of men, let him hasten swiftly to his spiritually stronger brethren who truly and intently obey the voice of God, and say to them, "My brethren-in-soul, save me and let me hear the word of God that He may heal my broken heart." Moreover, let this man school himself to fill his heart with love for his fellows even if it should lead to the departure of the soul. Let him persevere in this until his soul and the soul of his brethren cleave together. And when they have all become as one, God will dwell in their midst, and they will receive from Him an abundance of salvation and consolation.

Behind this florid style it is not difficult to discover the whole theory of R. Abraham concerning *dibbuk ḥaverim* as a fundamental value that comes into play whenever man is unable to maintain a state of *devekuth* with God. Actually, however, *devekuth* with God is not mentioned at all in the closing exhortation. This is surely significant. For although *devekuth* with God is discussed in the course of R. Abraham's letter, it yet seems as if for all practical purposes *devekuth* with one's fellow has replaced *devekuth* with God. The difficulties of complete *devekuth* with God are fully recognised, if not to say taken for granted. Instead of exhortations to return to *devekuth* with God, it is hoped that the atomistic solitude of the individual, alienated from God in his state of *katnuth*, will be broken if and when he tries to find new human bonds into which he can integrate himself. The myth of the small contemplative group creates for him hope and the security of an intimate sheltering community. R. Abraham's exhortations for peace among *ḥaverim* are not merely the traditional clichés of Hebrew idiom in praise of the pursuit of peace. They give expression to a new value: that of the contemplative community whose members are bound together by the emotional values of sympathy and brotherhood, in the manner of revivalist communities whose members are held together by the binding power of intense emotional loyalty.

It should be noted that, according to the above, the emotional reintegration of the isolated and unprotected individual is not to be achieved by means of the traditional concept of the Community of Israel (*Kelal Yisrael*), semitranscendental as it is and certainly devoid of any concrete social meaning. *Kelal Yisrael* would be a self-inviting, almost natural contemplative refuge for the alienated individual.[12] R. Abraham, however, proposes an emotional integration within a small but concrete group (*dibbuk ḥaverim*) and not within the vague, sociologically abstract entity of *Kelal Yisrael*. It is precisely the belonging to such a small but closely knit group which gives, in R. Abraham's opinion, a distinctive sense of security of existence.

9. From the abstract theories in the epistle we have, so far, reconstructed the picture of an emotional group in which the psychological forces inherent in all group activity come into play. This picture is fully confirmed by a piece of practical advice given by R. Menaḥem of Vitebsk in one of his epistles which, incidentally, also fills some gaps left by his other writings. The letter in question, which is undated, is addressed to the *kehillah* of Bieshika and is published in part 2 of *Likkutei Amarim* (attributed to R. Menaḥem Mendel of Vitebsk), p. 5.[13] After direction and advice on a study schedule (which in itself would deserve detailed analysis), the writer proceeds to lay down rules

of conduct in *dibbuk ḥaverim*. We learn to our great surprise that one of the acts demanded is individual confession between friends. The exclusive tradition of collective confession in general terms, so characteristic of Judaism, is here breached. True enough, there had been previous attempts in that direction, as, for instance, by the Cabbalists of Safed, who developed a form of confession by the individual to a small group, not dissimilar to what R. Menaḥem is advocating. It is unnecessary to point out that the obvious likeness notwithstanding, there is no direct historical connection between the experiment of the sixteenth-century Safed Cabbalists and that of the Tiberias Hasidim of the eighteenth century. Both are the expression of specific psychological needs which demanded satisfaction in the one instance as in the other. In the words of the epistle:

> Let also every person see to it that he has close attachment with kindred persons [*dibbuk ḥaverim*] who are chosen with discrimination as being in sympathy with one's own mental and spiritual nature, men who seek only truth and who also desire to rid themselves of lust, insincerity, and falsehood. Then let him hold converse with them every day for about half an hour, and engage in self-reproof for the evil ways he sees in himself. His companion should do likewise. When he has accustomed himself to doing this, it will be found that when a person will see in a friend something wrong or objectionable and reprove him, he will not feel self-conscious before the other and will confess to the truth. Thus falsehood will fall and truth will begin to shine.

If we were to go more closely into R. Menaḥem's wording and observe that he sometimes uses the plural and in other cases the singular, we should deduce that the social setup envisaged is, apparently, the following: There is a group of intimate friends, "kindred persons chosen with discrimination," who form the body of the emotional brotherhood. Perhaps the reciprocal confession is not carried out openly in a gathering of all members, but remains an individual confession between two companions. Such private conversation between two friends is also described in a letter written from Tiberias by R. Menaḥem Mendel.[14] The writer quotes the authority of R. Jacob Emden to the effect that real love of one's fellow(אהבת חברים),profounder even than all moral exhortations, manifests itself when "a man speaks to another and tells him what is in his heart, even the counsel of his evil inclination (יצר) within him, for then the very speaking works salvation (הנה הדיבור בעצמו פועל ישועות). Then the evil inclination is forced out, for the 'two are better than the one,' the two *ḥaverim* are superior to the one [i.e. the lonely]. That which the two will confirm with the counsel of God is that which will endure." This fine perception of the therapeutic value of such unihibited talking leaves no room for doubting that this custom was actually in vogue in the Hasidic circles in Tiberias among the followers of R. Menaḥem Mendel Vitebsker and R. Abraham Kalisker. Although there is no decisive evidence to show whether these intimate talks took place between two companions or (less likely) in the presence of more than two, it is clear that both R. Menaḥem and R. Abraham refer to one and the same practice.

10. Most striking of all in this context is the fact that the important Hasidic notion of the *Ṣaddik* as the charismatic leader is not mentioned at all in our texts. There is no doubt that the confession of which we read was *not* a confession before the *Ṣaddik*, but rather an exchange of confessing between people of equal status. The custom of confession before the *Ṣaddik* is to be found in the Hasidic movement only sporadically. But more surprising than the fact that it is found at all is the fact that it is not found in far greater measure and force in an atmosphere so heavily charged with emotion and in a geographical environment in which the Christian practice of confession prevailed throughout. True enough, the Bratzlav Hasidim were popularly dubbed *widduynikkes* on account of their custom of confessing to the *Ṣaddik*.[16] This custom was undoubtedly more widespread, and one cannot infer from the fact that this name was applied to the Bratzlav Hasidim that confession before the *Ṣaddik* was an essential and distinctive mark of this sect alone. R. Abigdor, the notorious opponent of R. Shneor Zalman of Ladi, mentioned in the official document of complaint against the Hasidim which he sent to the Russian government, that the *Ṣaddikim* regularly instruct those who wish to join them to confess before them.[17] Here, as with the Bratzlav usage, the confession is clearly part of the initiation rite. The practice recommended in the letters of R. Menaḥem Mendel or R. Abraham is confession not before the *Ṣaddik*, but as between equals; neither is it part of an initiation ceremonial but a daily custom with the time to be spent thereon specifically recommended.

The psychological significance of *dibbuk ḥaverim* in the Tiberias circle becomes apparent if we consider the specific function of this exchange of confession between "close friends." The emotional pattern of the Tiberias circle is clearly different from that of, for example, the various religious groups within Italian–Jewish society of the same period. The nineteenth-century *Musar* movement too apparently evaded the seductive possibilities of reciprocal confession that might easily have become part of its method. The practice of confession must have provided for the members of the Tiberias group that profound sense of belonging to a closed circle (with its concomitant feelings of satisfaction and security) that constitutes the psychological power of a group over its members. There is, of course, an attraction in the secret sweetness of exchanged confessions that may well have been an important psychological factor in the development of the Hasidic concept of *dibbuk ḥaverim*. The emotional attachment to the group is greatly enhanced by the relief that is effected through such confessions, and its emotional tension gains new strength. Our texts make use of rather clumsy circumlocutions in defining the aims of these confessions (making possible the administration of reproach by one's fellowman, etc.) Nevertheless, it is evident that to the participants themselves "the very speaking works salvation." The deeper motive seems to be the feeling of gratitude and relief that results from the confession or, to be more exact, from the attitude that could be confidently expected of the one who listened to it. For what was hoped for in the Tiberias circle, no less than in the Oxford Group, was not so much a statement as a personal attitude of *ego te absolvo*.

NOTES

1. See S. Dubnow, *Toledoth ha-Ḥasiduth* (Tel Aviv, 1930), 1:112–3; G. Scholem, *Major Trends in Jewish Mysticism* (London, 1955), pp. 344–45.

2. M. Wilensky, in *Kiryath Sefer* 1 (1926): 240; W. Rabinowitsch, *Der Karliner Chassidismus* (Tel Aviv, 1935), p. 33.

3. ס׳ חסד לאברהם פי שנים ודרושים על התורה, האחד ... ר׳ אברהם המלאך ... והשני ... מו״ה אברהם קאליסקער. [Cernovitz] תר״א.

4. See I. Halpern, *Ha-Aliyyot ha-Rishonot shel ha-Ḥasidim le-Ereṣ Yisrael* (Jerusalem–Tel Aviv, 1946).

5. It is published among the letters that form the Appendix of the book *Pri ha-Areṣ* by R. Menaḥem Mendel, of Vitebsk (Kopyst, 1814). Some copies of this edition do not contain the Appendix.

6. See G. Scholem, "Devekuth in early Hassidism," *Review of Religion* 15 (1950): 115–39.

7. One understands how R. Abraham's *social* concept of *ayin* developed out of certain formulations of the metaphysical *ayin* in the teaching of the Maggid, e.g.:

... ועינינו רואים שהחכמה מקשרת יחד ומתווכת שלום. אפי׳ בין ב׳ דברים הפכיים כמו היסודות שאילו לא היה החכמה שביניהם לא היו יכולים אש ומים לדור יחד ואעפ״כ אנו רואים שהם מורכבים יחד והכל מפני שהחכמה ביניהם וכל אחד רואה האי״ן שבחכמה ע״כ אינו מתגבר על חבירו כי הוא רואה שהאי״ן הוא חיותו ...

(*Or Torah* [Korzecz, 1804], f. [140a].)
For the Maggid *ayin* is identical with *Ḥokhmah*, whereas for R. Abraham *ayin* is the source of *Ḥokhmah* (as generally in Cabbalistic symbolism). The basic difference between the Maggid and R. Abraham is that the principle of peaceful coexistence of the opposite elements in the physical structure of the world was transformed into the principle of social coexistence.

8. *Likkutei Amarim*, by R. Menaḥem Mendel, of Vitebsk (Lemberg, 1911), pt. 2, p. 41b. Every student of Hasidism will see at a glance that only the second part of this book contains material emanating from R. Menaḥem and R. Abraham; the first part is clearly a collection of homilies of the Great Maggid.

9. There is some resemblance to it in the theory expounded by another disciple of the Great Maggid, R. Hayyim Haika of Amdura. See his *Ḥayyim va-Ḥesed* (Warsaw, 1929), 38b, s.v. *ha-Ḥodesh*.

10. This has been noted by Zweifel in his apologetical but by no means valueless *Shalom al Yisrael* (Wilna, 1873), 3:17–18.

11. A later variation on the same idea is to be found in *Maor va-Shemesh*, by R. Kalonymus Kalman, of Cracow.

"... ונראה לפרש הענין כך כי בהתאסף עדרי צאן קדושים אל הצדיק ... וכל אחד ואחד ישמע לחברו ויהיה קטן בעיני עצמו ויהי רוצה לשמוע איזהו דבר מחבירו איזהו בחינה האיך לעבוד את השי״ת והיאך למצוא את השי״ת וכן כולם יהיו כך וממילא שהאסיפה היא על זה הכוונה אזי ממילא יותר מה שהעגל רוצה לינק הפרה רוצה להניק ממילא הקב״ה מקרב עצמו אליהם ונמצא עמהם ונפתח להם ממילא כל הישועות ... ממקור הרחמים ... וחסדים טובים.. נמשך על כנסת ישראל ... ומפרש הפסוק ושמעו בני יעקב פי׳ שאתם בני יעקב שמעו עצמיכם זה לזה כדכתיב גבי מלאכין ומקבלין דין מן דין ..." (פר׳ ויחי ד״ה הקבצו). Here the *Ṣaddik* does not seem to have any function at all.

12. This advice for the emotional reintegration of the faithless individual within *Kelal Yisrael* has been given, e.g., by a contemporary *Ṣaddik*, R. Ahron Roth, of Jerusalem, in his *Mevakkesh Emunah* (Jerusalem, 1942).

13. The letter is in a fragmentary state; the beginning, the end, and the signature are missing. It is written probably by R. Menaḥem Mendel, along with the bulk of the epistles duly signed by him. The only other possible author is R. Abraham.

14. *Likkutei Amarim*, part 2, p. 16a.

(דברים נחמדים מהרב ... מנחם מענדיל ... מק״ק וויטעפסק ... והשני ... מוה׳ אברהם ז״ל מקאליסקא והשלישי ... מוה׳ חיים חייקל מק״ק המדורא ... ועוד הנהגות ישרות מן הרב ... מוה׳ אלימלך ...)

The anonymous collector of *Iggeret ha-Kodesh* has rightly found this provocative passage worthy of inclusion (Warsaw, 1879, p. 6a). The text of the passage as given in the *Iggeret ha-Kodesh* differs only slightly from that in the *Likkutei Amarim*.

15. לספר בכל פעם לפני המורה לו דרך השם ואפי׳ לפני חבר נאמן, כל המחשבות והרהורים רעים אשר הם נגד תורתינו הקדושה אשר היצר הרע מעלה אותן על מוחו ולבו. הן בשעת התורה ותפלה הן בשכבו על מיטתו והן באמצע היום. ולא יעלים שום דבר מחמת הבושה. ונמצא ע״י סיפור הדברים המוציא מכח אל הפועל משבר את כח היצר הרע שלא יוכל להתגבר עליו כל כך בפעם אחרת. חוץ מעצה הטובה אשר יוכל לקבל מחבירו שהוא דרך השם והוא סגולה נפלאה. (צעטיל קטן לר׳ אלימלך מליזנסק.)

16. See *Avaneha Barzel*, ed. Samuel ben Isaiah ha-Levi Horovitz (Jerusalem, 1935), p. 9.

17. Teitelbaum, *Ha-Rav mi-Ladi*, Warsaw, 1910, vol. 1, p. 111. The practice seems to have started after the death of the Maggid. It is worth noting that Salomon Maimon, who gave us the most plastic description of the "court" of the Great Maggid, still stresses the fact that the initiated were not required to confess to the *Ṣaddik*: "Jeder Mensch . . . haette nichts mehr noetig, als sich an die hohen Obern zu wenden und *eo ipso* gehoerte er schon als Mitglied zu dieser Gesellschaft. Er habe nicht einmal noetig (wie es sonst mit Medizinern der Fall ist), diesen hohen Obern von seinen moralischen Schwaechen, seiner bisher gefuehrten Lebensart und dergleichen etwas zu melden, indem diesen hohen Obern nichts unbekannt sei" (*Lebensgeschichte*, ed. Fromer [Munich, 1911], p. 198).

The Authorship and Literary Unity of the *Darkhei Yesharim*

In the year 1805 (תקס"ה) a little booklet of twenty-four small pages was printed in Zhitomir bearing the title *Darkhei Yesharim*. Its author was, according to the title page, which will be examined in the present note, Menaḥem Mendel Premyslaner.

The book itself is a manual of contemplative life, containing a series of injunctions, admonitions, and practical advice on how to attain *devekuth*, the mind's sustained attachment to God, which should become a habit through Hasidic practice. The tract consists of short literary units varying in length from two lines to a page or two. There is no comprehensive pattern discernible among the tiny literary sections, no logical development of a theme. Even an arrangement of the material according to subject matter seems not to have been attempted by the author or the compiler, whichever the case may be.

The literary style of the book is not markedly original or obviously distinguished by individual idiosyncrasies of expression. Its vocabulary is limited and presents very few exceptional features. The grammar appears to be that of the usual clumsy Hasidic Hebrew of the time. The writer certainly lacks the aristocratic literary elegance of *Ḥabad* or indeed even a basic awareness of literary style. Idiomatic expressions are rare and the author sticks tenaciously to a very limited number of phrases generally current in early Hasidic writing. A noticeable stylistic feature is the author's predilection for certain phrases. The most striking of these is לעשות נחת רוח ל-, which he uses repeatedly.[1] Another stylistic phenomenon is the use of מכוח as almost the only causal conjunction. Though this clumsy construction is now and again used in other early Hasidic texts, the frequency with which it recurs on nearly every page of the book appears to be a stylistic idiosyncrasy of the author. Other stock phrases are לנוח and לנוח עצמו or שכל חזק, שכל חלש. Admittedly data of such minor significance as these cannot be taken as established criteria of Menaḥem Mendel's literary style, particularly as no other literary work attributed to him has come down to us.

A good test of the individual identity of a religious text is its choice of synonyms for the name of God. The favorite expression for God in our text is הבורא, which occurs fifty-four times, whereas the name ה׳, ה׳ ית׳ is not used more than nine times, הקב״ה is used only three times, יוצר once and אלקים once. The unusually high incidence of הבורא for God in these few pages and the frequent recurrence of the idiomatic phrase לעשות נחת רוח would seem to be disproportionate for any Hasidic text of established authorship, and are some indication that the tract is not a random collection of passages but one literary unit written by one author. Indeed, this is the main bibliographical thesis of the present paper. The stylistic oddities of the tract run through the whole of the text.

The title page is written in a clumsy Hebrew style, in which subjects, objects, or finite verbs are confidently omitted and anacoluthic constructions abound:

ספר דרכי ישרים והוא הנהגות ישרות מר׳ מענדיל מפרעמשליין. אלו דברים הנחמדים והנעומים [sic!] מפז ומפנינים יקרים אשר איזן ותיקן ועשה אזניים לתורה מלוקט מפי קדושי׳ עמודי העולם, ה״ה בוצינא קדישא חסידא ופרושא מו׳ ישראל בעש״ט זלל״הה ומהרב המגיד בוצינא קדישא מו׳ דוב בער. מ״מ דק״ק מעזיריטש. וגם הוסיף נופח [sic!] מדליה אשר עד הנה לא עלו על משבח הדפוס. שנמצא ת״י [תחת יד] הרבני... מוהר״ר אברהם אבלי מטשודנוב [Cudnów, county of Kiev] שהיה מקדם מ״צ ומ״מ בק״ק וויטקאב ובהגהת נכונת [sic!] וישרות שמבאר כל סתום באר היטב. וקראנו הספר הזה בשם דרכי ישרים כי הוא מורה לבני אדם את הדרך אשר ילכו בה ואת המעשה אשר יעשה אותו האדם וחי בהם. וכדי לזכות את הרבים קמו הני שותפי ה״ה ... יוסף בן ציון בנו של ... מוה׳ אברהם אבלי הנ״ל והרבני מוה׳ דוב במוהר״ר חיים והעלו את זה הספר על משבח הדפוס. נדפס בזיטאמיר ... בשנת וידריכם בדרך ישרה ... לפ״ק.

This is certainly a title page that bibliographers and literary historians would find difficult to sort out. Let us start at a point where we are on firm ground: the date of publication.

The numerical value of the year of publication adds up to

תקס״ה[2] and the same year appears in the last line of the last page.[3] There are two approbations (*haskamoth*), both given in the month of the second *Adar* of that year. Consequently, the actual time of publication must have been between spring and autumn in 1805.

In spite of the grammatical and syntactical confusion of the title page, a few facts transpire from it:

(1) The name *Darkhei Yesharim* was given by the printer or by the two publishers, the original name having been simply *Hanhagoth Yesharoth*; therefore

(2) the original heading must have been something like:

הנהגות ישרות מר״ מענדיל מפרעמישליין;

(3) the manuscript of the little tract was in the possession of Abraham Abele, whose son Joseph is one of the two partners endeavoring to publish the work.

In order to establish authorship, the approbations should be scrutinized in their relationship to the title page. Both *haskamoth* were given in Zhitomir. No doubt the two "publishers" explained the nature of the manuscript to the two authorities granting the *haskamoth* or even showed the manuscript to them. The first of the two approbations, given by R. Michael ben Jacob Kopel of Zhitomir, is rather vague. It describes the efforts of the two partners in the publishing venture in the following way:

... ומגילת ספר בידם כתבי קדש והנהגות ישרות מהרב בוצינא קדישה חסידא ופרישא מוה׳ מנחם מענדיל מפרעמישליין אשר ליקט ואסף אסיפת [sic!] הרבה מעמודי עולם:...

This amounts to plain copying from the title page, which was possibly already formulated for the layout. Or the other way round: the printer may have used the wording of the approbation for the title page. In any event, we do not have two *independent* testimonies as to the authorship of the tract since one of these two derives directly from the other. The second approbation, by R. Isaac Eisik of Zhitomir, is of a more definite kind in stating the authorship of the booklet, which is here unequivocally ascribed to R. Menaḥem Mendel Premyslaner. R. Isaac does not employ vague terms such as איזן ותיקן or ליקט ואסף but uses the definite *ḥibber*.

The tract is thus prima facie ascribed to R. Menaḥem Mendel, who must be regarded as the author unless proved otherwise. And only very strong evidence to the contrary would carry sufficient weight to undermine R. Menaḥem Mendel's claim to authorship stated on the title page and corroborated by the approbation of R. Isaac Eisik of Zhitomir[4].

Even if the booklet originates with R. Menaḥem Mendel, in what sense is he its author? The crucial point in our inquiry into the authorship of the tract must now be whether the correct term describing R. Menaḥem Mendel's literary activity is the *ḥibber* of one approbation or the *asaf ve-likket* of the other.

An additional description of the tract given on the title page by the printer (or by the two editors) does more to obscure the issue than to clarify it.

אלו דברים ... אשר איזן ותיקן ועשה אזניים לתורה מלוקט מפי קדושי׳ ... מו׳
ישראל בעש״ט ... ומהרב המגיד ... מו׳ דוב בער

The tendency of this *meliṣah* style to indicate rather than to state clearly is well known to students of this branch of literature. Grammatically, the subject of the clause אשר איזן ותיקן ועשה אזניים לתורה is R. Menaḥem Mendel. His responsibility for the literary document in our hands is thus admitted, but the admission of his authorship is qualified by the statement that the דברים נחמדים contained in the tract are מלוקט [for מלוקטים] from the mouth of Israel Baalshem and the Great Maggid.

What is meant by this in terms of textual criticism? Does it mean that R. Menaḥem Mendel collected the sayings of Israel Baalshem and the Great Maggid that had come into his possession in a literary i.e., written form? Or does it mean rather that R. Menaḥem Mendel gave literary form to *hanhagoth* that, the printer or the editors thought, originated in some undefined manner in the teachings of Israel Baalshem and the Great Maggid and had come to R. Menaḥem Mendel's knowledge in oral form (מפי קדוש׳)? Is the bulk of the booklet Menaḥem Mendel's own teaching or is he echoing the teachings of Israel Baalshem and the Great Maggid?

One thing must be borne in mind. The sentence on the title page naming Israel Baalshem and the Great Maggid greatly enhances the importance of the tract, as well as its commercial value, by linking it up with the by then legendary founder of Hasidism and with R. Dov Baer, another great name in the movement. Should this fact not have a bearing on our inquiries into the provenance of the booklet in the strict literary sense of authorship? Perhaps R. Menaḥem Mendel is not the author after all. His contribution may have been limited to collecting the written or oral sayings of two earlier teachers? If this be the case, R. Menaḥem Mendel's status would be reduced to that of a mere compiler, and the tract would have to be considered as his anthology.

I do not believe this to be so. As to the appearance of the two great names on the title page, the solution I would put forward for consideration is as follows. Israel Baalshem is indeed mentioned twice in the tract in the third person, and his teachings are quoted as scattered paragraphs within the tract.[5] This would account perfectly well for Israel Baalshem's name appearing on the title page, particularly as the printer must have been anxious to mention it for commercial reasons. As to the name of R. Dov Baer, he is not quoted in the tract in a similar fashion. There is reason to believe that Dov Baer and Menaḥem Mendel, both disciples of Israel Baalshem, did not see eye to eye.[6] Yet immediately after the end of the tract the printer published four of R. Dov Baer's then unpublished homilies (*Derushim*), apparently, though this is not stated explicitly, in order to make up the full twenty-four pages of the booklet, or to use the customary Hebrew typographical phrase שלא להוציא את הנייר חלק (in order not to leave the pages blank). The provenance of these homilies is clearly stated by the printer as Maggidic:

עוד הצגנו פה דברים נחמדים דרושים נאים מלוקטים שנמצא[ים ב]כתבי קדש עדיין לא היה לעולמים מהרב המגיד דק״ק מעזיריטש.

Whether these homilies were found at the end of the manuscript copy of the *hanhagoth* of R. Menaḥem Mendel and were simply taken over from there by the printer, or whether he used other independent manuscripts of the Maggid's teachings, cannot be decided.

Though it has no direct bearing on the question of the authorship of the tract we are discussing, it is interesting to note that the homilies published here "for the first time" were not really unpublished in 1805 since in the Maggidic collection *Or Torah* (Korzecz תקס״ד) all four homilies had appeared, one year prior to the publication of the *Darkhei Yesharim:*

וידע אלקים = *Or Torah*	p. [35b] in the section פ׳ שמות
נגד שמיה = ibid.	p. [132b] in על אגדות חז״ל
וחנה מדברת על לבה = ibid.	p. [112b] in פסוקים מלוקטים

ופדויי ה' = ibid. p. [112b–13a] ibid.

Since all four *Derushim* attached to the *Darkhei Yesharim* are in *Or Torah*, one might reasonably conclude that the printer of *Darkhei Yesharim* simply copied them from the printed edition of *Or Torah*, published one year earlier. However, a minute collation of both texts clearly shows that the printer of *Darkhei Yesharim* did not use the text published a year earlier, but printed the homilies from an independent manuscript, although he might possibly but not necessarily have known that the homilies he described in his edition of 1805 as שלא היה לעולמים had actually been included in the collection of the Great Maggid's homilies printed under the title *Or Torah* in Korzecz in 1804. We have to bear in mind that the accepted methods of Hasidic publishing and republishing were not violated by this procedure; in fact, this is a pattern that can be observed in Hasidic publishing throughout, in particular where manuscript copies were legion and their literary units short. It happened quite frequently that parts of books already published were subsequently republished by another printer and—as the textual analysis will nearly always show—not from the first print, the existence of which would be sometimes genuinely unknown to the second printer, but from another manuscript copy of the text that happened to be available to him. Many a bibliographical riddle can be solved in this way, and more than one of Dubnow's severely critical bibliographical remarks about fakes, forgeries, and falsifications in certain Hasidic books could in all fairness have been omitted if he had understood the Hasidic habits of publication.[7]

In any event, the four homilies printed at the end of *Darkhei Yesharim* sufficiently justify the insertion by the printer of the name of R. Dov Baer on the title page. This does not, of course, indicate that the tract itself originated from Dov Baer and not from Menaḥem Mendel. On the contrary, the printer's dividing line between the text of the short tract and the accompanying homilies of the Great Maggid is clear enough. The tract itself is a distinct literary unity, and its author is to the best available testimony, i.e., the title-page, Menaḥem Mendel himself.

Perhaps one more point ought to be mentioned. Some parts of the tract occur also in the volume *Or ha-Emeth*, a collection of Maggidic material published in Zhitomir in 1900. Does this indicate that Menaḥem Mendel borrowed at least some material from the Great Maggid?

This possibility is greatly minimized by the fact that the passages in the tract *Darkhei Yesharim* identical with the Maggidic material can be found only in this one book, published from a manuscript collectanea of the Maggid's homilies that had experienced a number of perilous adventures (see the preface). This collection published as late as 1900 though not a "forgery" as Dubnow holds,[8] does contain material of dubious provenance and was copied at a time when the various texts had already been confused. Rather than claim the authorship of certain paragraphs of *Darkhei Yesharim* for the Great Maggid, I would suggest that paragraphs of the *Darkhei Yesharim* found their way into manuscripts containing genuinely Maggidic material and were incorporated there. The existence of some paragraphs of the *Darkhei Yesharim* in the later collection of *Or ha-Emeth* should therefore not unduly influence our deliberations.

The whole question can perhaps be simplified in the following manner: Have we any reason to believe that the text of the tract *Darkhei Yesharim* is a homogeneous literary document *ab initio*? If the basic unity of the text of the whole tract can be proved, the emergence of isolated paragraphs of the tract in other texts should not worry us; the text of the *Darkhei Yesharim* will have to be considered the primary one from which the borrowing took place and not the other way around.

But can the basic unity of the tract be established? I think it can. Every aspect of the tract's literary features shows that it has an original, not a composite unity. In other words, the tract was written out as a whole and not pieced together. The main reasons for this are as follows:

(1) The writer refers several times to earlier passages in the tract, e.g., רק מכל מקום צריך לישב עצמו ... כמו שכתבתי לעיל, where he refers to 3b; and again in 4a, ולא יחשוב במחשבתו מחשבות רבות רק מחשבה אחת כמו שכתבתי לעיל , where he patently refers to the very beginning of the tract:

וכלל זה יהיה בידך שיהיה לאדם תמיד רק מחשבה אחת בעבודת הבורא... שמכח רבות מחשבות האדם מתבלבל בעבודתו (2b).

The writer refers to his previous כללים on page 5b

וכל מה שכתבתי הם כללים גדולים ונחמדים מפז רב כל דבר ודבר הוא כלל

גדול ובזכות כללים אלו יזכה האדם לדבק Finally, he concludes with a eulogy: את עצמו מן העולם ועד העולם ברוך י״י לעולם אמן ואמן באלקי ישראל
These cross-references surely testify to the original unity of the work.

(2) This original unity is conclusively substantiated by the uniformity of the literary structure of the separate paragraphs. We have in our tract a series of short pieces of spiritual advice on contemplative conduct. The author himself refers to these frequently as כלל or כלל גדול:

p. 2b	וכלל [כצ״ל] זה יהיה בידך
p. 4a	ועוד כלל אחר שלא להרבות בלימוד
p. 4b	עוד כלל שאל ירבה בדקדוקים יתרים
p. 5b	ועוד כלל גדול כשיחרפו אותו בני אדם
p. 5b	וכל מה שכתבתי הם כללים גדולים... כל דבר ודבר הוא כלל גדול
p. 6b	וזהו יהי׳ בידך לכלל גדול
p. 8a	וזה כלל גדול שיזכה לדביקות
p. 8b	זה כלל גדול לפעמים יעמוד בתפלה
p. 8b	זה כלל גדול לדביקות
p. 9a	הבעל שם טוב אמר כלל גדול הוא השתוות
end).	ובזכות כללים אלו . . .

Our tract thus largely consists of what the author calls כללים The tract's dissimilarity from the traditional literary forms of Hasidic teaching is patent from a comparison of the literary genre of the paragraphs of the tract with that of the authentic dicta of the great Hasidic teachers. The latter usually commence with a biblical, sometimes Talmudic or Cabbalistic, quotation that serves as the basis of a short discussion. In other words, theirs is the literary pattern of a homily.

In contrast, the paragraphs of our tract usually start with a short piece of advice, and this in an apodictic fashion, rarely in the form of exegesis but more often in the form of indirect commands in the third person of the imperfect (e.g., יחשוב), a kind of jussive form though not in the strict grammatical sense. Proof texts are quoted from time to time, but the basic fact remains that the advice is not generally deduced by way of exegesis but boldly stated in jussive form.

The genre of the *hanhagah* has become a favorite literary form in Hasidism. Several minor tracts of the size and form of *Darkhei Yesharim* were written and published subsequently to the publication of R. Menaḥem Mendel's work. Perhaps the most important of these is an anonymous tract, *Darkhei Ṣedek*, first published in 1796, which patently imitates our tract, not only in the title given to the work but also in style, arrangement, and structure.[9]

A similar ramification of this literary genre is the extensive *hanhagoth* literature written by various *Ṣaddikim*, printed not independently but as appendices to Hasidic works. Among the most important, mention should be made of הנהגות אדם מהרב המגיד מוהר"ר אלימלך and of the famous צעטיל קטן מרבינו אלימלך מליזענסק

The development of the genre of *Hanhagah* is unexplored, and even a bibliography of these is still a desideratum. For a preliminary characterization, it will be sufficient to say at present that in the latter examples the Halakhic element appears to prevail over Hasidic teaching.[10]

Besides the problem of the literary authorship of the tract proper, another question emerges: that of the authorship of the *Hagahoth* or marginal notes. These appear either (1) with the heading *Hagahah* scattered throughout the text, or (2) interwoven in the text without heading, but separated from the text by brackets. Occasionally they are longish interpolations, e.g., on page 3b. The two kinds of marginal notes take up a considerable proportion of the twenty-four small pages. They do not usually offer additional ideas or advice, but rather add quotations as additional proof texts, mainly biblical ones, ushering them in by introductory formulae such as:
כמו שאמר הכתוב, וזה שאמר הכתוב, נ"ל ז"ס [נראה לי זה סוד], וז"ס [וזה סוד]

Our first question regarding these marginal notes is whether both kinds of notes, those headed *hagahah* and the bracketed ones, derive from the same author or not. Why do two kinds of notes exist at all? Does this necessarily imply two different authors for the two types of notes? Perhaps the solution is a simple one: both types of notes derive from one author, who copied the whole text of the tract interpolating his own additional notes and distinguishing these latter by the use of brackets. Once this copy was made, he continued annotating his own private copy of the tract in the margin. As the literary style in the two sets of notes appears to be similar and the introductory formulae are the same, one is led to eliminate the possibility of two authors. As there is no philological indication to the contrary, to ascribe them to one single author is amply warranted.

The next step in the literary examination of the notes—taking both types as deriving from one hand—is to identify their author. In other words: Was it R. Menaḥem Mendel, the author of the tract himself who jotted down in the margin of his own manuscript copy some additional scriptural references or some cognate ideas and associations that occurred to him later? Prima facie, there is nothing from the doctrinal, terminological, and stylistic point of view that would absolutely rule out this possibility. An author adding marginal glosses to his own manuscript from time to time seems pretty reasonable. It was not uncommon for an author of a Hebrew work to write marginal notes on his own manuscript in order to amplify some of his previous statements and to call these later notes *hagahoth*.

On the other hand, the alternative, i.e., that the *hagahoth* were added by a later student of the manuscript text, as distinct from the author, has something to be said for it. What is the relationship between the text proper and the notes, and is there anything that would warrant ascribing them to two different authors?

Certain significant features emerge when one compares the text and the marginal glosses in detail. The notes are on the whole heavy with exegetical zeal; scriptural and other quotations abound, including later *Musar* literature (Elijah Vidal's *Reshith Ḥokhmah* is quoted there twice, Moses Cordovero's *Tomer Devorah* once). Because of this, the structure of some of the longer notes becomes too complex, and the use of the exegetical method contrasts with the simplicity of expression characteristic of the text of the tract proper. Again, a rare idiomatic coinage, for example, the beautiful expression נשר מן in respect of the awareness of God, possibly unique in the whole Hasidic literature, occurs in the glosses in two different passages,[11] though it does not occur in the text of the tract itself.

Remarkable as all this may be, the absence in the tract proper of a favorite expression in the glosses or the subtle differences in exegetical orientation are too vague as literary criteria to establish conclusively the independent authorship of the marginal notes.

The suggestion as to two different authors, one for the tract proper and one for the marginal notes, could be more firmly substantiated only if some of the marginal notes could be shown to have misunderstood the text of the tract or to be in open disagreement with it.

Generally, one cannot discover in the *hagahoth* any misunderstanding of the original text. This is not surprising since the main aim of notes is usually to supply more references and proof texts. Nevertheless, there is one single passage (pp. 9–10 of the first edition) in which the marginal note appears to be dissatisfied with the advice given in the text of the tract on the very significant theme of silence. The original text advises silence for the attainment of *devekuth* because silence is more helpful than talk. The formulation of the idea is without reservations:

כל המרבה דברים מביא חטא ר״ל חסרון, שאפילו כשמדבר דברים עם בני אדם בחכמת התורה כידוע לנו, מ״מ השתיקה היא טוב׳ יותר והטע׳ שיכו׳ בשתיק׳ לחשו[ב] בגדולתו יתברך ולקש[ר] עצמו בו ית׳ משיקשו[ר] עצמו בע[ת] הדיבו[ר].

Here the marginal note appears to challenge this unqualified advocacy of silence which is said to be preferable even to the communication of דברי תורה to others—a radical position indeed. The dissatisfaction of the bracketed note is slightly concealed:

ומכלל זה נשמע אם הוא אינו במדריגה זו יותר טוב לו לדבר דברי תורה והבן

Not only the tone and content of the note but also its wording, ומכלל זה נשמע imply that the two statements are not by the same person, and that the author of the note is anxious to reverse the somewhat disturbing statement made by the author of the original text on the primacy of silence over *divrei Torah*. This would tentatively point to a separate author for the *hagahah*. If this is so one could go a step further and ascribe the responsibility for the marginal notes to R. Abraham Abele, since the title page makes mention of him as the owner of the manuscript, and seems to indicate, at least in the printer's or editors' very vaguely expressed opinion, that he was also the author of the marginal notes שנמצא ת״י... מוהר״ר אברהם אבלי... ובהגהת נכונת וישרות שמבאר כל סתום באר היטב...

The wording as it stands is such as not to commit the printer to the view that the *hagahoth* stem from the pen of R. Abraham Abele, and yet it gives the impression that it was intended to mean that. But this may be only the printers' ambiguous formulation, which by no means would commit the bibliographer to follow suit.

The result of the above textual analysis, viz, that the author of the notes is not the author of the basic text of the tract, is thus corroborated and amplified by the title page, which implies that R. Abraham Abele was the author of the marginal notes while R. Menaḥem Mendel of Premyslan must be credited with the authorship of the main text of the tract.

NOTES

1. Eight times in the sixteen pages of the main text of the tract. The variations of the idiomatic expression are: לעשות נחת רוח לבורא; — לשכינה; — ליוצרו; see pp. 3a, 5a, 5b, 7a, 8a, 8b, 9a–9b.

2. בשנת וידריכם בדרך ישרה

3. ובאו לציון הזה ברנה בשמחה

4. I understand that there exists a manuscript copy of *Hanhagoth Yesharoth* in the National and University Library in Jerusalem in which the tract is attributed to R. Dov Baer, the Great Maggid of Mesritz. I shall endeavor to show in a forthcoming analysis of this tract that its author had distinct ideas about the nature and methods of contemplation and that these are at variance with those current in early Hasidism. In an earlier paper, "Torah study in early Ḥasidism," above, pp. 56–68, I tried to show that R. Menaḥem Mendel's little tract constituted a radical deviation from the accepted norms regarding the possibility of contemplative study. The possibility and desirability of such double activity—I mean contemplation and study carried out simultaneously—was accepted and indeed was hailed as a lofty ideal in early Hasidism both by R. Israel Baalshem and the Maggid Dov Baer. In contrast, our tract takes it for granted that study and contemplation are mutually exclusive, in other words, that the two cannot be carried out simultaneously. Since the author has no doubts that *devekuth* is the cardinal duty, Talmud Torah was necessarily relegated in his tract to a propaedeutic function of *devekuth*.

5. As we know, Menaḥem Mendel was a disciple of Israel Baalshem (Rubinstein, "A possibly new fragment of Shivḥei Ha-Besht" (Heb.) *Tarbiz* 35 (1966): 180, 184.

6. Rubinstein, *ibid.*, p. 180, n. 24.

7. I drew attention to at least one case of Dubnow's unjustified criticism, regarding a book by R. Jacob Joseph of Polonnoye, in my note "Is the Hasidic Book *Kethoneth Passim* a Literary Forgery?," *Journal of Jewish Studies* 9 (1958): 81–83.

8. *Toledoth ha-Ḥasiduth* (Tel Aviv, 1931), 3:396, n. 142.

9. The author of the work *Darkhei Ṣedek* is far from being established; the manuscript itself was in the possession of R. Menaḥem Mendel of Lisko. According to the preface, it was considered by many, though not all, to have come from the pen of R. Zechariah Mendel of Jaroslaw, a disciple of R. Elimelekh of Lizensk. (An epistle by him is printed at the end of R. Elimelekh's *Noam Elimelekh*.) Whatever the case—research has not even started on this other tract—it is clearly of later origin than our *Darkhei Yesharim*, on which it is modeled from the literary point of view, and from which its anonymous

author has not only drawn his literary inspiration but has borrowed quite substantially. An inquiry into the authorship and literary sources of *Darkhei Ṣedek* is much needed.

10. The genre of *Hanhagah* is certainly not a Hasidic literary innovation. One might suggest that its pre-Hasidic literary antecedents are to be found in the צוואה literature of the great rabbis and in the vast literature of אזהרות תיקונים וסייגים e.g. by R. Joseph Karo printed in his *Maggid Mesharim*.

11. כעלה הנושר מן האילן (p. 3a) ; ולהיות נושר ונפסק מיראה (p. 4a).

The Ṣaddik—Altering the Divine Will

The most original and significant contribution of the Great Maggid in his Ṣaddikology is undoubtedly his stress on the magical aspect of the *Ṣaddik*'s powers. This is the essential innovation of R. Dov Baer. These magical powers do not have the same meaning for him as for the "circle of Maggidim" contemporaries of the Baalshem. The latter's powers consisted of magical means of purifying the community, procedures that equip the preacher with new devices for saving his flock from spiritual peril by means of contemplative techniques for bringing them to repentance, and when need arises for forcing "remedies" upon them.

All these ideas of spiritual regeneration, i.e., redemption on a small scale, are far from the theories of the Maggid. His image of the figure of the *Ṣaddik* is not that of a leader who redeems or cleanses his followers in a spiritual sense. The *Ṣaddik*'s magical powers, according to the Maggid, are related to the material world. The aim here is not the magical saving of souls, but a simpler, more primary magic, working in stark physical reality. This object is formulated in the dicta that sum up his Ṣaddikology, such as "the *Ṣaddik* rules through the fear of the Lord" or: "the Holy One, blessed be He, decrees—the *Ṣaddik* cancels the decree"[1]: and last but by no means least, "the *Ṣaddikim* overthrow the Divine attribute of Judgment [*Middath ha-Din*] and replace it with the attribute of Mercy [*Middath ha-Raḥamim*)."[2]

What is the nature of these magical activities? Our object is to see whether it is possible to explain all the texts in nonmagical terms so as to show the *Ṣaddik*'s intervention as merely an act of God or a prayer to God. If such an interpretation were possible, we could remove the Maggid's doctrine from its magical context. Such an exegesis is, however, impossible. The historian of religions is not the only one confronted by this problem for it evidently haunted the Maggid himself. There are passages in his writings that appear to apologize for his own theories and methods. The basic conflict of religion and magic has found explicit and implicit utterance in the Maggid's writings. How is it possible for the human to compel the Will of God? How can His Will be changed? Or, the same question in a more extreme form, how is it possible to annul His Will? Traditional religious sensitivity recoils from the suggestion. Such an arrogant assertion as "the Holy One blessed be He decrees—the *Ṣaddik* cancels the decree" puts the fine edge of the Maggid's understanding to a severe trial: he cannot silently pass over this statement in the manner of the original Midrash, which fails to pose the question. It is precisely because magical techniques had been developed by the Maggid that he is obliged to account in religious terms for a rabbinic dictum as audacious as this one, according to which the *Ṣaddik* can cancel the divine decree. Thus, a statement that in the world of the Midrash had been but a bold saying without any practical implications became a saying heavily weighted with institutionalized practical consequences in the world of the Maggid. We shall therefore not be surprised to find the Maggid going back to and struggling with this fundamental problem of religion versus magic—a conflict no less central for the Maggid than, for instance, the conflict of religion and philosophy for the medieval philosopher.

The Maggid indicated the way of escape from this dilemma in an easy solution that by no means faces the problem in its entirety. God is portrayed in a most anthropomorphistic manner. He is personalized in order that He may smile approvingly at the magical activities of His creatures. The line of defense the Maggid takes up with regard to the practice of thaumaturgy is that this practice does not conflict with the Will of God at all. Man is capable of the Divine Will. There is, however, a deeper level of affective life in God beyond or behind the volitional lurch. The Will of God as expressed in His decrees is not identical with His innermost Will, for the personal God has an affective aspect that transcends His volitional aspect and it is precisely with a consent operating at this level of His nature that He awaits the active intervention of the *Ṣaddik*, or indeed, of man in general. One could go further and say that His highest satisfaction is obtained when man changes His Will! The Maggid is here exploring the problems and solutions that, in the Midrash, found expression in the formula, "The Holy One, blessed be He, craves after the prayer of the righteous [*Ṣaddikim*]."[3] It is no part of my task here to analyze this saying in order to discover whether it was originally devised as an apologetic answer to the problem of prayer; it seems to me that this is hardly possible, for the whole concept of a theory of prayer did not arise in Judaism until the time of medieval philosophy. However that may be as far as the original Midrash is concerned, the Maggid for his part uses the Midrashic expressions as the solution of his central problem. The Maggid transfers the viewpoint of the *Gemara* regarding the authority of the rabbis to decide legal questions by a majority decision even against the declared Divine Will as voiced by the *bath kol* (heavenly voice), to the thaumaturgic realm peculiar to his own system, and concludes that God consents to, and even takes pleasure in, the victory of His children over Himself:

> What triumph can there be in his victory over others? Even if he triumphs over the high world [of Divinity] what fresh achievement does the Holy One gain thereby? But the victory [signified by the text] is when one triumphs over God, blessed be He. For instance, when He makes a decree, and the *Ṣaddik* cancels it, then it transpires that God consents in the victory gained over Him—that is to say [He does so] from the love He bears His child.[4]

The idea that God permits the *Ṣaddik* to act, gives him authority so to do and, what is more, takes pleasure in the dominion exercised by the *Ṣaddikim* in the world—all this is a powerful theme in the Maggid's system of thought and one that recurs repeatedly as an accompaniment to his discussion of the nature of magic. It still remains for us to consider this theme where it appears in his writings.

> "He performs the will of those who fear Him" (Psalm 145:19). He does not mean to say (literally) that the Holy One blessed be He fulfils the will of the righteous and the God-fearing [as such]; for will [*raṣon*] has the meaning of desire [*ta'avah*], and the will of man proper may long for anything; and this verse does not mean to suggest that the righteous and the God-fearing may long for material benefits [and God will accordingly grant them]. But prayer [also] is called *raṣon* as it is written, "and as for me, my prayer to you is a time of *raṣon*" (Psalm 69:14). And behold the Holy One, blessed be He, craves the prayers of the *Ṣaddikim*, and He Himself imparts to them the will to pray—in

accordance [with that scriptural verse] "From man are the orderings of the heart and from God the answer of the tongue . . ." (Proverbs 16:1)—and then is his prayer acceptable. The latter phrase means as our teacher has written, "if my prayer flows readily from my mouth." And this is the meaning of the verse, "He does the will of those who fear Him." It means to say that his prayer is performed and accepted and all this arises for the one to whom the Holy One blessed be He sends "the tongue's answer" and He does this because he was a righteous and God-fearing man prior to that; therefore He sent him a "will" [prayer] which should be proper and acceptable.[5]

In this extract a radical analysis serves to take the sting out of the idea of change in the Divine Will brought about through the instrumentality of the *Ṣaddik*. The *Ṣaddik* does not change the Will of God; but rather does God provoke the prayer of the *Ṣaddik*. There is a circular chain of impulses here, commencing not with the *Ṣaddik* but with God. The solution that emerges from the passage clearly indicates that the problem here was not the philosophical problem posed by an anthropomorphism that represents a change of mind within God, but rather the religious problem created by God's supposed dependence on man, however righteous and God-fearing he might be. The Maggid sometimes is aware of a further problem even if he does not always apply himself seriously to it, viz., that of the pervading shadow of magic. Sometimes the very attempt to overcome a problem reveals that problem most clearly. What then should we say of a teaching in which all contradictory motives are interwoven and show the Maggid's real point of view to have been—in spite of his recognition of the underlying problems—unquestionably magical?

The magical activity of the *Ṣaddik* becomes sharply visible at the point where the *Ṣaddik* rules by means of the Divine Will. But according to the Maggid, this is not strictly a Divine Will, but the creation of the *Ṣaddikim* themselves, the projecting of their will into the divine sphere. It is easy to demonstrate on Cabbalistic premises that the *En Sof* is by definition without will. What we call "will" or "Divine Will" is merely what is thrown up by the delight of the *Ṣaddikim*, who run the affairs of the world after the manner of children enjoying a game.

"God will rejoice in His works" (Psalm 104:31). [This means] that God desires to rejoice in His works. Let us take as a parable a father who has a little son who wishes to take a stick and ride on it like a horse. And although it is the way of a horse to guide a man, whereas he [the child] here guides—nevertheless he [the father] takes pleasure in this. And he helps [the game along] and gives him the stick. Thus the *Ṣaddikim* wish to control the [higher worlds] in order that they may be governed at their behest. And we do not hereby infringe the honor of His blessed essence but only the Glory [*kavod*] dispersed in the [higher] worlds. To this end, He contracted Himself in the worlds in order that He might be amused by the pleasure of the *Ṣaddikim* who receive delight from those worlds. And that is [the meaning of the verse] "He performs the will of those who fear Him." For the term *raṣon* does not belong to the *En Sof*, but it means, "those who fear Him—viz., the *Ṣaddikim*—may perform the Will."[6]

This parable of the *Ṣaddik* as a *homo ludens* and of God as the onlooker who takes pleasure in his game apparently does not describe a magical situation at all. The relationships are human and the figures the Maggid employs are not so far removed from the naïve pictorial description of the prayer of Onias, the circle maker, in the Talmud tractate *Ta'anit*. But here in the words of the Maggid we are not dealing with a childlike prayer of a "son who importunes his father to perform his request."[7] The I/Thou relationship vanishes in the Maggid's parable, and the father is presented as a mere onlooker. The *Ṣaddikim* act in the world as in their own domain. We have here a far-reaching autonomy in the force exercised by the *Ṣaddikim* through the circumvention of the direct and personal relation of dependence between themselves and God. God has His place in the parable, but a verbal analysis does not reveal any essential part for Him in the actual work. The miracle or the control of events in the world is done by the *Ṣaddikim*, as it were, over God's head, even, we might almost say, behind His back! God's tender and affectionate observation of His children—the *Ṣaddikim*—at their game of running the world by the authority of the King does not prejudice the near-magical character of this "game," although this gratified observation on the part of God is invoked to ease the theological difficulties involved in a situation that can only half belong to the realm of religious experience proper: its other half is clearly thaumaturgical. The fact that the Maggid brings into his parable the theme of the Higher Will, which is stimulated by means of the will of the *Ṣaddikim*, almost tips the balance over toward the thaumaturgical, and so the exact determination of the place and tone of the parable in the no-man's-land between magic and religion is left to the discretion of the judicious reader.

"And all Thy children are taught of the Lord" (Isaiah 54:13). This applies to the prayer of Onias the circle maker, who, as one might say, *changed* the will of the Creator, blessed be His Name. And also Moses, our teacher, peace be upon him, as it is stated in the *Zohar*,[8] [on the verse] "Remember to Abraham, Isaac, and Jacob" (Exodus 32:13 misquoted), he seized Him by the arm and body as [to take a parable] one should take one's friend by the hand and not suffer him to go, and so *alter* his will—in the same way, as one might say, he seized the Almighty and altered His Will, blessed be His Name, and thus R. Joshua declares, "We do not heed the *bath kol*," and the Holy One blessed be He has said, "My children have overcome Me."[9] And this is the meaning of the verse "Thy children are taught [*limmude*] of the Lord." [Take this to mean] that they, as it were, teach [*lomedim*] the Lord, blessed be His name.[10]

This extract does not explicitly legislate for the *Ṣaddik*, but the examples quoted of Onias the circle maker and Moses are hints that the author has in mind the function of the *Ṣaddik*. The parable in which a man forces his friend by the pressure of his arm does not correspond perfectly to the language of the prayer mentioned in connection with Onias the circle maker. And if we are concerned here with the force of the human hand, that is to say, not supplication and entreaty but impulsion, then we are once again in the no-man's-land between prayer and magic and, moreover, the nature of the parable indicates that we have, if anything, moved nearer to the sphere of magic. The figure used—that of influencing someone by physical means—intimates that a personal relationship still subsists between the two partners, the one who impels and the other who suffers himself to be impelled; here we do not yet have the pure magic that consists of a depersonalized technology operating by automatic means, working *ex opere operato*. But the more we approach the central nerve of the Great Maggid's doctrine of the *Ṣaddik*, the further we depart from the element of personal theology in his magical conceptions that appears, as we have seen, in some of his parables. Moreover, the nearer we get to his more systematic doctrines, the more purely and unambiguously magical do they appear.

Any mystical doctrine declaring the oneness of God and the world, or of God and man, or of all three, may constitute the essential basis for a magical theory that envisages the possibility of man's producing changes either in the world or in the sphere of the Divinity. Here we confine our attention to the unity of God and man, as the basis for a speculative magical theory in early Hasidism. A monistic doctrine such as this serves to resolve the inherent contradiction in the Maggid's theological system of two opposite ideas: (*a*) that of man's dependence on God and (*b*) that of man's magical influence over God. The idea of oneness reconciles these ideas: according to this view, both man and God are parts of one single organism.

The most cautious delineation of magical unity is to be found in the utterances of the Great Maggid. To be more precise, the theoretical basis is not that of the *Ṣaddik*'s oneness with God but a slightly more acceptable notion: the correspondence or parallelism between God and the *Ṣaddik*. This constitutes a common ground, tenuous but nevertheless sufficient for the purpose of facilitating thaumaturgical activity. The image of two identically tuned harps, one of which can set up an answering resonance in the other, is used to explain the influence of man (or more specifically of the *Ṣaddik*) over God. The image came to the Maggid from popular Hebrew encyclopedic handbooks:

> "The Seraphs stood above Him" (Isaiah 6:2). This means those who worship the Lord, blessed be His Name, with devotion. [And] how do they come to occupy this station? By virtue of the fact that they always range their thoughts above the whole [cosmos. Hence] as things happen with him, so they happen on high in accordance with the saying, "Know what is above thee."[11] If we stir up love in the heart of the *Ṣaddik*, then love is stirred, so to speak in Him also, may He be blessed: and if it be fear, then likewise. And this is the meaning of the verse: "I will open my dark saying with the harp" (Psalm 49:5). As for the Holy One blessed be He, the heaven and the heavens above the heavens cannot contain Him, and yet He has confined [*ṣimṣem*] his *Shekhinah* within man. And the philosophers have said that when one makes a small harp to exactly the same scale as a large one, when one sounds the small one, then the large one sounds its note also. And the Lord, blessed be His Name, created man in His likeness, and so he is like a small harp and can stir up the *Shekhinah* by all his actions. And therefore everything must needs be done for the sake of heaven so that we do not, heaven forbid, rouse up the *Shekhinah* in vain.[12]

Within the context of a scriptural formula, the Maggid introduces the idea of correspondence between man and God (which he moreover relates to the concept of man's being created in the image of God), together with the idea of the contraction of the *Shekhinah* within the bounds of the human being. The analysis of the concept of *ṣimṣum* (contraction) in the system of the Maggid would reveal that this does not imply simply *concentration*, but rather a *transforming emanation*. That means to say that the actual "essence" of the *Shekhinah* is not concentrated within the human being, but only its qualified essence. At any rate, the idea of the *ṣimṣum* of the divine nature within man—or within the *Ṣaddik*—even if it does not entirely correspond with the image of the two harps, means that the true import of the Maggid's teaching is considerably nearer to the notion of the union of man and God than would appear from the image of the harp itself. The homily thus already conveys the lesson of magic based upon the union of existences, though this meaning is camouflaged by the imagery.

The aforementioned passage by the Maggid on the subject of the *Ṣaddik*'s magical power has a significant parallel, which agrees at all points, with his following exegesis on that selfsame verse where the Maggid now expounds his doctrine as to the ability of the *Ṣaddik* to *know* what is done above. The corresponding passage, accordingly, does not speak of the *Ṣaddik*'s influence and power, but of his *knowing* what is done in the higher sphere. And this is the other side of the same coin—namely, of the union of man and God—but here the conclusion drawn is the opposite from that drawn in the magical part of his philosophy. Here the *Ṣaddik* does not exert his influence on the higher spheres but receives knowledge from them; nonetheless, this capacity of his to receive higher knowledge is grounded on that same crucial principle of union with God. Even the details of the earlier formulation recur in the corresponding passage and confirm the interpretation proposed above:

> "The Seraphs stand above Him" (Isaiah 6:2). This refers to the *Ṣaddikim* whose hearts burn [seraphim = "burning angels"] with love for the Creator—that is on account of His being above them—in conformity with that saying "Know what is above thee." Know then that *man is a part of God above*. And when he attaches his thought to what is above, he may come to know what is done on high, for all the events on high pass through his thought. As R. Simeon ben Yohai said, "I am a sign in the world"[13] which means, all the [Divine] properties which are aroused on high are aroused below in the *Ṣaddik*.[14]

Contemplative thinking, which according to the Maggid is the authentic means by which man may be joined with the powers above, corresponds to the minor harp in the earlier-quoted allegory, while the Divine thought or the "world of thought proper" (*Olam ha-Maḥashavah*), as the Maggid designates elsewhere this higher metaphysical sphere, corresponds to the larger harp. The harp image is not strictly necessary to the Maggid here, for in place of the cautious homology implied by the correspondence between the spheres of man and God, he expresses here in unambiguous terms a more radical concept of unity. "Man is a part of God above." The link between what is above and what is below is founded on this kind of unity, whether in its more cautious or its more extreme form. Moreover, from the point of view of the Maggid's basic philosophy, there is great significance in the fact that we have here a two-way traffic, from above downward, and from below upward. There is no better proof of the integrated nature of the Maggid's thought on this subject.

The new propaganda slogans the Great Maggid introduced into Ṣaddikology may be brought together to form one consistent explanation of the activities of the *Ṣaddik* based on the reality of his intrinsic oneness with God. This unity is sometimes apprehended as an organic consubstantiality of body—a concept certainly far removed from the imagery of the two harps, and far more radical.

> "The *Ṣaddik* rules by means of the fear of God: the *Ṣaddikim* convert the Divine attribute of justice [*Middath ha-Din*] to that of mercy." As, to take a parable, when a child desires to have something that he takes pleasure in, his father on account of his love for the child has pleasure also in seeing him enjoy it. So the child occasions his father's love. Similarly, when a man has a pain in his foot, it produces a desire in his mind that he should bid his hand remove the pain, for the *hand and foot form one entity*. Likewise, when the *Ṣaddik* cleaves to the Creator, blessed be He, anything that he lacks gives rise, as it were, to [the same] desire in the Creator, may He be blessed, and this just comparison fits in with the saying of the sages that it is a *miṣvah* [pious duty] to eat and drink on the Sabbath. Evidently, we may ask what the supplementary soul [*neshamah yetherah*][15] [which inheres within us on the Sabbath] gains from this. But according to this parable, it well appears that the supplementary soul has also its delights from this [enjoyment of our lower soul].[16]

Examination of this extract shows that the two parables it contains, namely, that of the child and his father and that of the parts of the body working together—do not exactly correspond. Only the parable of the parts of the body expresses the idea of oneness—and that in a most extreme form; whereas the parable of the father and child scarcely implies oneness at all, unless we enlarge the concept of unity to include a unifying bond of emotion. The first parable is indeed subsidiary to the second. Even the motivation behind the first is different, for its purpose is not to explain the system of assumptions that make possible the magical work of the *Ṣaddikim*, that is to say, how they come to bring about a change in the Divine Will; rather does it aim to show that this process does not displease God's spirit, but that, on the contrary, He takes pleasure in it, in the same way as the supplementary soul takes pleasure in the enjoyment of the body. Like many others of these unintegrated parables, it comes basically not as an illustration of the essential possibility of magic and its precise modes of operation, but rather as a justification for it *as an admitted phenomenon*, and as a means of showing that there is no religious danger in the thaumaturgical practice whereby the *Ṣaddik* presumes to govern the realm of reality at his pleasure.

The apologetic strain serves to emphasize that God smilingly consents to this activity and even takes pleasure in it. Even the parable of the father enjoying the child's game of riding horseback on the stick had hinged, as it were, on this same apologetic intention. This does not, however, apply to the parable of the parts of the body, which contains the essential concept of union between God and the *Ṣaddik* as the fundamental ground of the *Ṣaddik's* actual thaumaturgical activities, though it is likely that the apologetic strain is not entirely lacking there either.

The theoretical basis of divine monism comes out clearly in other formulae of the Maggid. Union with God is understood in the above-quoted passage as a state achieved by man or, more specifically, by the *Ṣaddik* on account of his congenital nature. The *Shekhinah*, which in normal conditions contracts itself within man, constitutes the basis of this unity. But sometimes this coherence (or inherence) is not thought of as the essential and continuing status of a man, but rather as a transitory condition following upon a heightened emotional state. Unity with God is thus achieved at moments of supreme religious enthusiasm, at a time when the soul is filled with love and fear of God, etc., always in accordance with those positive states of the soul valued by Hasidism, i.e., love, fear, humility, enthusiasm, etc. This kind of union with God is not a permanent state or a quality of human nature, but a fleeting one occurring only in moments of profound emotional experience. The possibility of magical deeds is limited according to this variation of the theory to certain fixed times, those moments of supreme devotional fulfilment.

"For My thoughts are not your thoughts" (Isaiah 55:8), for there are men who always walk in the ways of the Lord but without attaining Him, may He be blessed, because they do good deeds without the fear and love; then one is caught up with Him, in total unity, and then He, as it were, changes His will. According to what he desires, so the Holy One blessed be He desires, and this is what is meant by saying, the *Ṣaddik* rules [the world] by the fear of God, like the pinch of yeast which leavens the dough, so [variant reading, "there"] he alters His will, for he has become one unity with Him, blessed be He.[17]

NOTES

1. [B. T. *Mo'ed Katan*, 16b.]
2. [See *Or Torah* (Lublin, 1884), pp. 19 and 25.]
3. [B. T. *Yevamot*, 64a.]
4. [*Or ha-Emet* (Zhitomir, 1900), 21a.]
5. [*Or Torah*, p. 85.]
6. [*Maggid Devarav le-Ya'akov*, ed. Rivka Schatz-Uffenheimer (Jerusalem, 1976), p. 21, no. 7.]
7. [B. T. *Ta'anit*, 19a.]
8. [*Tikkunei ha-Zohar* (Jerusalem, 1978), no. 21, f. 54b.]
9. [B. T. *Baba Meṣi'a*, 59b.]
10. [*Or Torah*, p. 110.]
11. *Mishnah, Avot*, 2:1.
12. [*Or Torah*, p. 96.]
13. [*Zohar, Va-yeḥi*, 225a.]
14. [*Or Torah*, p. 104.]
15. [See B. T. *Beṣah*, 16a.]
16. [*Maggid Devarav le-Ya'akov*, pp. 42–43, no. 21.]
17. [*Or ha-Emet*, p. 12a.]

The Hasidic Way of Ḥabad

It is open to doubt whether the application of such popular definitions as "the priority of the intellect over the heart" or vice versa can give any idea of the essence of Hasidism in general or of any of its movements in particular. These pseudo-concepts tend to confuse more than clarify. The difficulties of defining the Ḥabad movement within Hasidism are particularly abundant because the material under discussion does not consist in this case of parables, proverbs, and anecdotes; it constitutes a whole body of literature written by systematic thinkers who make use of conceptual and symbolical language. The language of these books can only be deciphered by reference to the Cabbalistic writings (especially those coming from the circle of Isaac Luria) that the chief Ḥabad writers set out to continue and to develop, finding themselves in the process originators of complicated new systems of their own. As most of the Ḥabad books are arranged according to subjects, in a systematic way, and not as commentaries on the scriptures (this applies at least to the *Tanya* by Shneur Zalman of Ladi, which is the central work of the Ḥabad movement), it was tempting to dub Ḥabad "the philosophical movement in Hasidism." This label was used together with the one that attributed to Ḥabad the "priority of the intellect over the heart" as against other Hasidic movements that allegedly preferred the heart to the intellect.

It is perhaps not entirely superfluous to emphasize that even the use of the awe-inspiring word *philosophy* does not make this definition any better than those which use *intellect*, *heart*, and *sentiments* as terms of reference. If the Ḥabad movement has any specific character of its own, it has to be defined by the aid of concepts used for the analysis of religious phenomena and by statements that have a fairly definite and concrete meaning accepted by those who deal with the history of religions.

A concept of this kind with quite a substantial amount of definite meaning is "mysticism." Insofar as its meaning is not sharply and unequivocally clear, one can make it more pointed by comparing it with its opposite, by putting the religious life of mysticism, with its central themes of meditation, ecstasy, self-annihilation, etc., in opposition to the religious life of faith, the prominent themes of which are faith and man's clinging to it, trust, hope, etc. The question whether Hasidism is a mystical movement at all is still under debate, perhaps precisely because it is a movement that embraces various fields each with its own distinct character. A multicolored map of Hasidism has not yet been drawn; but the Ḥabad movement, it seems, can actually be defined by its purely mystical character.

After a short period of development marked by great intellectual progress during which many new ideas were introduced, all the mystical elements, already latent in the beginning of Hasidism, crystalized and developed toward pure mysticism, unadulterated by any mixture of non-mystical elements. It is possible to establish a straight line of development leading without deviations to its goal, the rigorously pure mysticism of Ḥabad. The mixture of different elements that marks the religious character of Hasidism at its beginning is no longer found in Ḥabad. In this progress toward pure mysticism the doctrine of the Maggid of Mesritz constitutes an important milestone. From there a straight path leads directly to the doctrine of Shneur Zalman, the founder of Ḥabad. Even this direct line of development is full of many transformations and surprises. We shall here specify only one point, selected from many, which testifies to the deepening of the mystical tendency and the development of an exceedingly austere mystical world view.

It is possible to say that an important, if not decisive, transformation in the Hasidic attitude to the world came about with the rise of Ḥabad. This transformation was not expressed in open ideological debate by the representatives of the new line against the old doctrine; it was not even made manifest by exegetical efforts through which the old ideas could give way to the new outlook. But whoever has access to the sermon books of

Dov Baer, the Great Maggid of Mesritz, and compares them to the books written by his disciple Shneur Zalman of Ladi, known as the Old Master, founder of the Ḥabad school (or those written by the latter's son, Rabbi Dov Baer, known as the Middle Rabbi), will inevitably reach the conclusion that from a certain point of view, and a very important one at that, the master and his disciple did not share the same spiritual atmosphere. It is true that their closeness to each other can be demonstrated in many matters, especially in one most central doctrine: they both agree that the idea that the world is permeated with divine sparks is a fundamental principle. They share the view that it is this divine vitality which sustains the world, and that this vitality has very real presence even in the lowest regions of the worlds. Not only is this doctrine not alien to the spirit of Ḥabad; one can even go further and say that Ḥabad added new depth and fresh boldness to the discussion of this focal problem, and even carried it considerably beyond the doctrine of the Maggid of Mesritz. The manner in which Ḥabad continued the work of its predecessors is in this case visible and manifest with great clarity and intensity.

This, however, is not all. There are two aspects, theoretical and practical, to the continuity of the doctrine of divine immanence in the world, which is regarded, not without justice, as the central theme of Hasidic thinking. The practical aspect is very closely connected with the exercises in meditation that form part of the doctrine of the Great Maggid of Mesritz. The problem of this connection between the contemplative exercises and the ideas of immanence arises with regard to the Ḥabad movement as well. Did this combination of the theoretical and the practical aspects persist, or did it break down, causing the two tendencies to separate? Or else, did they perhaps become united again in a new and different way? Is there a clearly distinct division between the Maggid's way and that of Ḥabad? Can one possibly prove that at precisely that point where these two Hasidic movements come closest to each other they also separate and take different routes?

In the world view of the Maggid of Mesritz's school, the individual objects of the physical world exist and indeed play a major part in the contemplative awakening of the devout. It is a basic principle in the Great Maggid's Hasidism that contemplative exercises are not performed in the void, with one's eyes shut; contemplation, on the contrary, arises out of man's encounter with those objects in the world which come his way. The contemplative awakening of a follower of the Maggid would be caused by the discovery of the divine spark that is within things, in all those physical objects that happen to confront him at any given moment. One can label this approach as "contemplation within the world," because it is essentially a way of exposing the lofty root of things, of presenting any particular mixture as *the* unique manifestation. The turning point toward spiritual ascent in contemplative exercises is not brought about by the doctrine of divine life penetrating the objects of the world; contemplation according to the Maggid begins, rather, by opening one's eyes to the world. The following example is the Maggid's favorite commentary on the verse in the Song of Solomon (3:11), which he repeats more than once in various places:

> "Go forth and look, daughters of Zion"; this means: "Go forth"—out of the material, "look"—one should always regard the inner meaning of everything, and not its material aspect; therefore it is written: "look daughters of Zion," meaning: behold, for example, the beauty of a material woman, which he calls "the daughters of Zion," which is no more than a mark [*ṣiyyun*] and symbol of the divine beauty which dwells in her, a spark of beauty, as it were, from the realm of *Tiferet*. No man is allowed to attach himself to that earthly beauty, but if a woman suddenly crosses his path, he has to attach himself, through this beauty, to the heavenly beauty. That is what is meant in the verse: "Go forth and look daughters of Zion at King Solomon"; that beauty which is in woman is but a mark and symbol of what is *at* King Solomon, i.e., God [Who is called the King to whom peace [*shalom*] belongs].[1]

Our purpose is to elucidate here the structure of that form of contemplative meditation which begins from within the objects of the physical world and proceeds through them.

At this point the way of Ḥabad parts company with the methods current in the school of the Maggid of Mesritz. In the Ḥabad way the objects of the physical world cease to serve as a starting point for the contemplative elevation of the spirit. It is obvious that the differences between the two forms of spiritual exercises are greater and cannot be restricted to this point alone. Considering the variety of shades and emphases in the interrelationship between the different elements in spiritual awakening, it is certainly possible to point out important distinctions between the characters of these two Hasidic ways. But the point that has been raised is particularly important when the specific structure of these two ways is discussed: whether the world and its objects exist and have a bearing on these spiritual exercises, or whether they are absent from them; whether it is a contemplative awakening brought about by keeping one's eyes open or by keeping them shut. These distinctions are not just trivial differences, they are decisive in defining the very structure of these systems, so that we are bound to say that we deal here with two distinct types of mystical paths and methods. Now if, in Ḥabad, the spiritual awakening is not taken out of the multitude of concrete realities in the world, if it is not caused by the ever-recurring experiences that cross man's path, what then is its origin? The answer to this question is clear enough if one reads through the descriptions and instructions of Ḥabad spiritual experiences; it must, however, be noted that this question is not explicitly discussed by Ḥabad writers, and that one must be content with discovering the implicit assumptions upon which the whole theoretical structure is based.

In Ḥabad writings one no longer reads descriptions, parables, and examples such as those found in the sermons of the Maggid. The eyes of the devout no longer wander about the universe in order to see and discover the divine vitality in things. This change is not due to the fact that the idea of divine immanence was discarded; on the contrary, it occurs in the sharpest and most extreme forms. But it is no longer the things of the world that remind the devout of the doctrine of immanence and engender contemplative states of mind. This is no longer necessary, because the ways of contemplation in Ḥabad Hasidism are no longer dependent on this world and its realities; it is possible to go through this world with one's eyes shut, and it may even be preferable to keep one's eyes shut.

Two small but significant books that describe Ḥabad exercises in meditation in a systematic way were written by Dov Baer, Shneur Zalman's son. Despite the changes Dov Baer introduced into Ḥabad doctrines, these two books of his give an exceptionally clear idea of Ḥabad methods in general, and it would be useful to study them precisely because of their systematic arrangement. One of them has the title "Treatise on Ecstasy" (*Kunteres ha-Hitpa'aluth*) and is mainly devoted to an accurate description of the ways of Ḥabad ecstasy.

The reading of this small book is not encumbered by difficult terminology; it is in fact a book even laymen can understand. The primary aim of this short treatise is to present Ḥabad ecstasy in terms of contemplative mystical experience at its purest. It strives to make a clear-cut distinction between "pure" experience, which is entirely spiritual, and the elementary vital ecstasy of blind sensual excitement, "drunkenness," which does not start in meditation. In the course of this discussion on the distinction between a higher and a lower type of ecstasy, we come across remarks that allude to the origin of Ḥabad ecstasy, and illuminate the problem of whether it is affected by the things of the world, as it is in the system of the Maggid of Mesritz. "It is plainly visible that every man, even one who is lowest in qualities, whose soul is mean and base as regards understanding and virtues, when he hears anything relating to divine contemplation his soul becomes exceedingly ecstatic."[2]

We hear even more explicit words on the spiritual exercises being divorced from the affairs of this world in the other book of the Middle Rabbi, "The Chapter on the Unity of God," which is generally known under the title of the "Treatise on Contemplation" (*Kunteres ha-Hitbonenuth*). This small but difficult book brings us into the innermost chambers of Ḥabad contemplation. It is a detailed itinerary, one might say, of the soul's travels during contemplation. It is possible roughly to define the difference between the Ḥabad way and that of the Maggid of Mesritz by saying that the direction of meditation in Ḥabad is not one of ascent but of descent. Thought does not rise gradually by passing through one realm after the other, beginning with that of the phenomenal world and ending in the highest of worlds, as is the case with the Maggid's contemplation. Meditation according to the new ways of Ḥabad is the process in which one imagines in one's soul the chain of emanation of the worlds from the highest to the lowest, coming finally to the lowest of all, our own phenomenal world. The pure idealism of meditation constructs in pure thought the way in which the worlds descended. No longer does thought rely on phenomena; everything remains within the limits of the activity of consciousness that accompanies the emanation of the worlds with all their ramifications, following the method by which these processes were explained in later Cabbala. When mind imagines to itself these processes, it does not depend on the sensual world of phenomena. Only, perhaps, toward the end of contemplative thought, at the final stage of the voyage, when meditation reaches the last link in the chain of emanation, the world of concrete phenomena, only there can the question arise as to the relationship between thought and our sensory world with its physical objects. But even here, at this point, the relationship is no more than incidental; when thought pours out into individual phenomena, it simply comes to its end; it is merely terminated; it does not reach the aim and purpose it originally set out to achieve. It is perfectly possible, of course, to envisage a downward direction in meditation whose termination, in the world of phenomena, would be a kind of magnet, a goal toward which everything is directed. However, such a function is never assigned to the world of phenomena in the system of Ḥabad. Our world has no impelling function whatsoever in the spiritual exercises of Ḥabad Hasidism.

The present discussion had to be based mainly on the words of the Middle Rabbi, not on those of his father, Shneur Zalman, the founder of Ḥabad. The reason for this is that the attitude of the Old Master on this point is much too complicated and elaborate to present within such a short space, and it requires additional analysis. Incidentally, however, a conversation between father and son on this very question has been preserved. From this conversation we might conclude that Shneur Zalman still held to the way of his master, the Maggid of Mesritz, at least in practice. The representative of the new way in this conversation is the son. This is the text of the conversation: "The Old Master once asked his son, the Middle Master: 'With what [i.e., with what kind of meditation] do you pray?' The son answered: 'With [meditation on] the commentary to the prayer: "and every stature bows down before Thee"'; the son then asked his father: 'And with what do you pray?' The answer was: 'With the floor and the bench.' "[3] It is true that material of this kind should not normally be used when the actual doctrines are available, and for this reason no firm conclusion concerning the Old Master's attitude can be drawn from this conversation alone; but it does at least show that the problem presented here regarding contemplation, its release from the objects of the physical world and its being diverted from them into the individual and his inner meditative concentration, was already the subject of discussion in the Ḥabad school itself.

This process of interiorizing the contents and methods of meditation, removing them from the outside world into the consciousness of the contemplative himself could be compared, though without stretching the analogy too far, to the change in approach between Platonism and Neoplatonism toward the same subject. In Greek thought as here, the change was expressed by an intensification of the mystical character and by a determined emphasis on pure mysticism.

NOTES

1. [*Maggid Devarav le Ya'akov*, ed. Rivka Schatz Uffenheimer (Jerusalem, 1976), p. 29, no. 15.]
2. [*Tract on Ecstasy*, trans. L. Jacobs (London, 1963), p. 66.]
3. [H. M. Heilmann, *Sefer Bet Rabbi* (Berdyczów, 1903), part 1, p. 89.]

Some Notes on Ecstasy in Ḥabad Hasidism

The small book, *Tract on Ecstasy*, written by the Middle Rabbi, Dov Baer, son of Shneur Zalman, will certainly be of interest to students of religion in general and of mysticism in particular. Over eighty years ago, a Westerner, Aaron Marcus, who had arrived at Hasidism by unusual paths, attempted to translate this work into German, as he realized that it was worth a wider public than Hebrew readers and students of Hasidism alone. Marcus, who was then living in Cracow, began to translate the work into German and to publish it in German in his *Krakauer Juedische Zeitung*, 1898–99.

But only a few instalments of the translation were published, and the experiment, for some unknown reason, failed, perhaps due to the perverse nature of the translator, who was a highly interesting man, a sort of fantast who attempted many things beyond his capacity.[1]

Now we have the first English translation of this small book, by Rabbi Dr. Louis Jacobs.[2] He has also added a useful introduction summarizing the conceptual patterns of the work. It serves as an Ariadne's thread through the labyrinth of the cluttered sentences of the tract, for it is written in the style typical of Ḥabad literature created by the Old Rabbi, the father of our author. Rabbi Shneur Zalman of Ladi, the Old Rabbi, was the pupil of Rabbi Dov Baer of Mesritz, who was himself the pupil of Israel Baalshem Tov. R. Shneur Zalman was thus a third-generation Hasidic leader, and became the founder of a new school, called Ḥabad, which flourished in Lithuania for many generations, and is today the strongest and most vital

Hasidic school in the United States, where it was relocated during the war.

Rabbi Shneur Zalman of Ladi initiated a new Hebrew literary style, which his pupils and pupils' pupils inherited. It is easy to recognize this style after reading only a few lines of any Ḥabadic text. It is marked by long sentences, extremely condensed in character, with the main and subordinate clauses often mixed up, and frequent anacoluthic constructions. As for the lexicographic elements, abstract nouns abound largely taken from medieval philosophical literature, translated from Arabic into Hebrew by the Tibbon family.

As far as I can see, little attention has been paid to the stylistic and lexicographic provenance of Rabbi Shneur Zalman's writings. If changes in the literary style of Ḥabad have occurred in the course of its development, only a rigorous examination of vocabulary and syntax could demonstrate these changes. The reader does not notice any essential difference between the style of the Old Rabbi in the first generation and that of the Middle Rabbi in the second. They are almost identical, which is an indication of the stylistic (and perhaps also conceptual) dependence of the Middle Rabbi on his father.

It is evident that this involved style of long sentences, where nouns predominate over verbs, and where abstract nouns and phrases are joined together within subordinate clauses, could be conveyed more adequately in German than in English, and that the translator must needs adapt his translation to the characteristics of the language into which he is translating it. I want here to draw certain conclusions that arise from the translator's notes, and from the extensive apparatus that he has appended to his translation, and in so doing, hope to solve the literary problem raised by the book.

The similarity apparent between the style of the Old Rabbi and the style of the Middle Rabbi, his son, affords no room for doubts concerning the authorship of the *Tract on Ecstasy*. The book was published as the work of the Middle Rabbi, and there is nothing in the manuscript tradition to invalidate this. It is beyond all doubt that the book was written by Dov Baer, the son of Rabbi Shneur Zalman from Ladi, as stated in the title pages of the printed editions as well as in the manuscripts.

But there is another question altogether: Whose ideas are

contained in the book? Rabbi Dov Baer incessantly emphasizes that all the ideas he has written down are those of his late father, Rabbi Shneur Zalman, and that he has not added to them or altered them. In other words, from the point of view of the history of ideas, we would have here the conceptual heritage of the Old Rabbi and not the original notions of his son, the Middle Rabbi. The latter merely edited and put in order what his father had said: perhaps reorganized the material—not more. This is what the Middle Rabbi says in the *Tract on Ecstasy*:

> So it is with regard to all the true doctrine on contemplation and knowledge of the divine to which his honor, our master and father, our teacher and instructor, of blessed memory, his soul is in Eden, has made us his heir, each in accordance with his capacity. . . . It is, therefore, most essential to expound and explain everything in order that they do not "hang empty pitchers on me" etc. The main object is to establish and secure the chief intention of our master and father, our teacher and instructor, of blessed memory, his soul is in Eden, in the light of the doctrine he revealed to us these past thirty years. My whole aim from youth, on behalf of my beloved friends, who seek the words of the living God in truth, is for the light of eternal life to be fixed firmly in their soul to the full extent intended. This is the matter of the revelation of the divine in their soul, each according to his capacity, as is well-known [trans. Jacobs pp. 59–61.]

One thing is clear: we have here not just the humility of a son toward a great father. It is indeed true that remarks such as this, where a certain book includes the literary inheritance of someone else, of the author's teacher or father, and is not the author's own original thought—that such typical expressions of modesty find their place in every culture built on tradition rather than on admiration of originality. From this point of view the historian of ideas should be warned not to accept the words of the Middle Rabbi as they stand, and would be advised to reexamine the testimony of the author.

Moreover, everyone reading the letter at the head of the book will understand that the original problem concerned the time of the composition of the book. These were days brimming with the quarrel and struggle between Rabbi Dov Baer, son of the Old Rabbi, and Rabbi Aaron of Staroshelye, each of them maintaining that the spiritual inheritance of the Old Rabbi was in his own and not in his rival's possession. The struggle was not without personal motivation, but this fact should not obscure the far-reaching differences that existed between the attitudes of the two rivals. From the letter attached to the *Tract on Ecstasy*, it clearly emerges that the disciples of Rabbi Aaron of Staroshelye and perhaps he himself argued against the Middle Rabbi that he had invented elements that were not found in his master's teaching. In a culture built on the admiration of tradition, and particularly in circles whose religious adoration of the departed charismatic leader knew no limit, this charge of inventing is sufficient to invalidate the whole.

It is clear that in the reiterated emphases of the Middle Rabbi, there is, apart from the motive of humility, an element of defense against the charges then current against him. The background of his declaration is the argument that took place between him and Rabbi Aaron of Staroshelye, or, more accurately, between the camps of Ḥabad disciples in the second generation after the departure of the Old Rabbi. The fact that we have found individual motivation (humility) and even historical motivation (the dispute with Rabbi Aaron) for the fact that the Middle Rabbi stressed the dependence of all his material on his father is interesting in itself. But it is very possible that, in spite of all this, the words of the Middle Rabbi are aimed at historical truth! It is actually possible that he did not invent his teaching but got it from his father, even though he repeatedly stresses this fact for other, tangential reasons. What can the historian of Hasidic ideas say after an examination of the sources?

Whoever wants to consider the historical problem of the place of the *Tract on Ecstasy* in the thought of Ḥabad and to answer the question of whether there is something new here or whether the words of the Middle Rabbi are correct (that he added nothing of his own and that everything came from the original thought proceeding from the array of religious experiences of the Old Rabbi) will have to examine the works of the Old Rabbi and compare them to the ideas and formulations of the Middle Rabbi. Whoever does this is in for a surprise. The only book by the Old Rabbi published in his lifetime is nowadays called the book of the *Tanya*[3] and is considered to be a summary of the Old Rabbi's thought. If one looks for the central term of our tract, "ecstasy," one is surprised to find that the doctrine of ecstasy does not appear anywhere in the *Tanya* and the word *ecstasy* appears only a few times with no terminological weight.

This silence about the doctrine of ecstasy in the texts of the Old Rabbi, and even about its central word, might lead us to the notion that there is indeed something new here, and that the whole *Tract on Ecstasy* is the massive invention of the Middle Rabbi. It seems historically that the Old Rabbi knew nothing of ecstatic practices, but that the Middle Rabbi invented the whole theory from the start.

But this explanation of the fact is unlikely. Both the two main pupils of the Old Rabbi, the Middle Rabbi and his rival, Rabbi Aaron, invoke the theory of ecstasy, and there is no quarrel between them except as to the exact method of ecstasy. Rabbi Aaron is lenient regarding the severity of the idea of ecstasy, whereas the Middle Rabbi is most strict, and is not prepared for compromise on the matter. Therefore it is difficult to suppose that the doctrine of their teacher included no elements of ecstatic doctrine and that the term *ecstasy* was not one frequently on the lips of the Old Rabbi. From the terminological point of view as well, the two pupils of the Old Rabbi see eye to eye, and there is no controversy between them as to what term should be used to designate the ecstatic experience, whose existence they both accept. The two do indeed argue over details, but there is no argument between them about the fundamental principle.

The question of the provenance of the doctrine of ecstasy and its terminology becomes complicated still further when we examine not only the *Tanya* of the Old Rabbi (where, as mentioned above, we have found no hint of the technical term and very little of the doctrine), but also the large volumes of the Old Rabbi's sermons, volumes almost unreadable because they are so vast. To our astonishment, we find in these sermons both the doctrine of ecstasy and its terminology, and in abundance. In the light of this situation, we should ask what has happened here. Should we assume that the sermons of the Old Rabbi, which were first published a long time after their author died, were textually forged in the spirit of the teaching of the Middle Rabbi? Whoever knows the state of the manuscripts of the Old Rabbi's compositions will hesitate to make such an assumption. One other possibility presents itself as a likely hypothesis.

The strange silence in the *Tanya* relating to the whole matter of ecstasy, including the term for it, may be explained with greater probability by these considerations: the Old Rabbi edited the *Tanya* for publication when the dispute over his system was at its height. We must assume then that such a delicate historical situation compelled him to take care with the material that was to appear in published form. Any incautious word was liable to have calamitous consequences for himself and his followers.

Jewish mysticism is not rich in descriptions of ecstatic experiences, and there is no doubt that ecstasy played a much less important part in Jewish mysticism than, for example, in Christian mysticism. The very few examples that do exist of descriptions of ecstatic experiences have not been published till this day and have remained in manuscripts, as the greatest of scholars in this field, Gershom Scholem, has pointed out with special emphasis. That ecstasy was part, however, of the authentic doctrine of the Old Rabbi no one who troubles to read his thick volumes of sermons can doubt. The origin of the doctrine of ecstasy, together with the term for it, are to be found in the religious thinking of the Old Rabbi. Ecstatic elements were incorporated into his sermons, but he took particular care to omit every mention of ecstasy from the *Tanya* when he was preparing it for publication during his own lifetime. The omission of whole themes, whether for esoteric or for tactical reasons, is a common practice of all mystics of all times and in all religions. In the sermons that the Old Rabbi delivered to his followers by word of mouth, things were said that were too extreme to be written down and published during the controversy over Hasidism in general, and over the Ḥabad school in particular.

This seems the most likely explanation of the strange discrepancy between the *Tract on Ecstasy* and the *Tanya*, and it is also the most likely explanation of the no less strange affinity between the *Tract on Ecstasy* and the Old Rabbi's sermons.

We may infer that, when the Middle Rabbi repeatedly stresses that his whole doctrine is derived from his father, there may be real evidence for what he says, and the historian must take account of it.

NOTES

1. See Scholem's remarks in his Hebrew article on Marcus, *Beḥinoth* 7 (Summer 1954): 3–8.

2. [*Dobh Baer of Lubavitch*, *Tract on Ecstasy*, translated from the Hebrew with an introduction and notes by Louis Jacobs (London, 1963).]

3. For bibliographical notes on the *Tanya*, see A. M. Habermann, *Alei Ayin*, *The Schocken Jubilee Volume* (Jerusalem, 1951), pp. 307–9.

A Late Jewish Utopia of Religious Freedom

A problem much discussed in the field of the history of religion is whether the mystic must conflict with religious authority; the well-known thesis of Rufus Jones, that almost all mystics are anarchists, is in direct contradiction to the historical facts. Several years ago Gershom Scholem drew a balanced picture of the relationship between religious authority and mysticism. He demonstrated that the socioreligious possibilities of mystical attitudes could range from pronounced conservatism to extreme anarchism. From this standpoint, he attempted to define the position of Jewish mysticism on the general map of religious history.[1] His researches confirmed that Jewish mystics, not unlike those of other religions, had a beneficial influence on conservative, traditional forces, and that the relationship in Judaism between recognized religious authorities and those who practiced mysticism was almost invariably serene.

My present exposition is concerned with the *Ṣaddik* Mordecai Joseph Leiner, the charismatic leader of a small Hasidic group in Izbica (Poland). He was a pupil of Simcha Bunam of Pzysha, and later of the well-known Kotzker *Ṣaddik* Menaḥem Mendel, that tragic figure on the fringes of Polish Hasidism, whom he openly opposed. Mordecai Joseph died in 1853 after acting for a mere thirteen years as leader of the small Hasidic group[2] from which there came, admittedly generations later, certain developments—they could be called retrogressions—derived from his religious teachings.[3]

Comparatively little is known about his life; his isolation within a confined personal circle may have been due more to his rebellion against his master than to his own radical lines of thought.[4] Indeed, when his grandson, Gershon Chanoch Leiner, collected the sayings of Mordechai Joseph after the latter's death and published them in the form of a book entitled *Mei ha-Shiloaḥ*, the book had to be printed in far-off Vienna, where there was a press that also had facilities for printing Hebrew texts. It seems to me that the reason for this highly uncharacteristic action was that in Poland and Russia, where all Hasidic books had been published up to this point, there was no Jewish printer prepared to accept the work for publication.[5] As was to be expected, the book was burned as heretical.[6]

It seems characteristic of the position of Izbican Hasidism within the Hasidic world that in the famous bibliographical dictionary produced by Aaron Walden of Warsaw in 1864, a rabbinical and Hasidic *Who's Who* entitled *Shem ha-Gedolim he-Ḥadash*, both Mordecai Joseph and his book, published only a few years previously, are passed over in silence.[7] The publication of the second portion of Mordecai Joseph's sermons only followed in 1922, by which time his dynasty formed part of the Hasidic establishment.

By family tradition, the biography of Mordecai Joseph is expressed apologetically. The long introduction by his grandson to the first edition of *Bet Ya'akov* (vol. 1, Warsaw, 1890) describes him as a pupil of Simcha Bunam of Pzysha and says that, after the death of the master (1827), he wavered for thirteen years before feeling entitled to head a Hasidic community. A casual sentence describes those thirteen years as a period of self-examination, which he undertook out of humility, feeling that he was not yet ready. He only started to establish his own "circle" in 1839, a date his grandson attempts to determine by means of messianic calculations.

The historical truth is, however, less straightforward than that described in the authorized family biography. During the thirteen years between the death of Simcha Bunam and Mordecai Joseph's own assumption of office, he underwent a second "apprenticeship," under his former fellow student, the Kotzker rabbi, who was established as the Hasidic leader in Kotzk after Simcha Bunam's death.[8] His attendance upon the Kotzker rabbi, which is evidence of his "apprenticeship," was a voluntary act on his part. But a secret rivalry must have gnawed at his breast.[9] The precise development of the relationship between the two in this period is not known to us. However, the latent tension eventually culminated in an open break during the Feast of Tabernacles in 1839, when Mordecai Joseph, who was younger than his master, left the town ostentatiously, without the master's permission, accompanied by a group of Jewish students. This scandal caused an uproar in the whole world of Hasidism. The Kotzker rabbi was then fifty-three years of age and Mordecai Joseph forty. Amazingly, neither his apprenticeship nor the conflict is mentioned in the biographical particulars prepared by his grandson. The latter does not try, even apologetically, to gloss over the behavior of his grandfather (as was sometimes attempted in later Hasidic literature), but ignores the matter completely. The family records merely purport to show that Mordacai Joseph was the pupil of R. Simcha Bunam.[10]

In the mid-nineteenth century, when the first part of the *Mei ha-Shiloaḥ* was published, the Hasidic movement, which had never attempted to break with the religious law and its representatives and had used every means to avoid a rupture if conflict did arise, attained a high degree of cooperation with the rabbis, the institutional guardians of the religious law, especially in those Hasidic circles from which Mordecai Joseph came. Nevertheless, Mordecai Joseph Leiner, the most radical of the Jewish mystics, raised in its most acute form the problem of the relationship between personal illumination as the source for religious behavior and the ever-enduring Jewish law.

The question we must now put is: What is the form and nature of divine illumination? In what aspects does it appear? Does it come through physical manifestations, visions, or voices? Is it ecstasy or rapture? Is excitement or violent agitation associated with the appearance of illumination or an accompaniment to it, as is often the case with similar phenomena in religious history? Is the technical Hebrew expression for illumination, *ha'arah* (from *or*, light), as found in these texts, a descriptive term for what happens? And what was the word for "illumination" in Yiddish, the language in which Mordecai Joseph's sermons were originally delivered, before his grandson transcribed them into Hebrew? This is a fascinating question both for philologists and for students of the history of religion.[11] The question here is, however, limited to the following: Is the reality of this illumination experienced in exceptional physical or spiritual circumstances; is it the fruit of long, contemplative seclusion; or is it a sudden certainty, totally unprepared for, which fills the consciousness of the person illuminated as if in a flash?

It is well known that mystics struggle with language to express their innermost experiences in words. Mordecai Joseph, who always appears to have been very reticent in personal matters, and who would never state whether he himself had undergone such an experience as he described, is also silent about the manner in which such an illumination appears. Nevertheless, it seems that the experience of illumination does not occur in exceptional circumstances, but more often in banal, everyday experiences. We read, for instance, "that the Will of God can be ascertained from the speech of man." Such a statement must mean that a sentence, a clause, or even a single word can be isolated from the context of an utterance—we do not even know whether the person so illuminated makes the utterance himself or simply hears it—and the word so isolated can be elevated into the absolute and become the basis of an illuminating experience.

I

Direct guidance of one kind or another applies to each individual. According to Mordecai Joseph's conception, each individual is summoned to his directing illumination from above; he alone is its sole recipient and no one can transfer to someone else the illumination allocated to him. This, of course, implies the total liquidation of the system of commands and prohibitions; the doors to religious anarchy stand wide open.

Each man can receive illumination only for himself, directly into the heart, and only from God the Illuminator. This implies that illumination proceeds in *one* direction only, vertically, and excludes horizontal communication between individuals. Thus, every man is merely entitled to an illumination of his own being; according to Mordecai Joseph, divine illumination bestowed upon a whole people, as understood in transmitted Jewish theology by the collective revelation at Mount Sinai, has in the final analysis no real function. Extreme religious individuality is the first consequence of the concept of illumination.

It would never have occurred to that radical individualist,

Mordecai Joseph, to ask, let alone to answer, the question of how a religious community can be based on divine guidance rather than on generally applicable laws. He never appreciated the inadequacy within a community of personal guidance of the individual and the chaos that must necessarily arise from it. Individual guidance is, indeed, not compatible with the formation of a community; it is, in fact, a disruptive element because of the possible contradictory aspects of individual illuminations.

The text nowhere states explicitly that the personal illumination of members of a community can and perhaps must give rise to conflict, but this is tacitly assumed since Mordecai Joseph eliminates from religious practices the concept of the mutual responsibility of the community for the exhortation of its members. Among other things, he attempts to prove the sheer impossibility of complying with the biblical commandment "Thou shalt surely rebuke thy neighbour, and not bear sin because of him" (Leviticus 19:17), when he says: "There may be something not permitted to one person which is permitted to another, since there are many things permitted to one person and forbidden to others."[12] The universal application of law and religion within Jewish tradition is thus shattered, with fragments split up among individuals, each concerned with his own commandments.

A further question now arises: Is the divine illumination a unique experience for an individual? If someone has experienced it, is he bound from that time onwards to comply with the specific act of illumination he has been privileged to receive on one particular day of his life? Must he keep this illumination always in the forefront of his mind because he has, as it were, sworn an oath of obedience? Is man not entitled to ever-renewed illumination? Can he remain obedient to the voice of illumination granted to him on a single occasion and should he be guided by it for the remainder of his life? Is the religious anarchist still able to attribute religious value to an illumination years after the immediacy of the vision has faded? In other words, is it not to be expected that attachment to a unique act of divine guidance would gradually weaken and finally, perhaps, entirely disappear? Or, since divine illumination is considered here not as a matter of systematic speculative thought, but as practical help in the requirements of everyday life, does the fragmentation of a recognizable continuity of life not become inevitable? Direct divine guidance can only be followed in this way. Constant guidance at the present moment, not the recollection of previous guidance, becomes the maxim of the consistent anarchist and thus of Mordecai Joseph, since he knows that illumination must not age by a single day, even at the price of later theological confusion.

The religious anarchy of Mordecai Joseph is not based on the concept of the individuality of differing natures, but on the concept of the Divine Will. An antinomianism more assertive of the individual could be satisfied with a single, eternally valid occurrence if it were personal revelation that formed the zenith of the life of the individual so favored, a moment not followed by some other immutable truth in relation to the same experience and in relation to obedience to the voice in that unique individual revelation. Mordecai Joseph, however, takes no account of this concept or of that of the highly personal disposition of mankind, his "inner form," the "roots of his soul," as expressed in Cabbalistic terms, essentially logical concepts from which antinomian propositions can, indeed, easily be derived.[13] Although the concept of personality as setting a rhythm for individual lifelong acts is not elaborated in the teachings of Mordecai Joseph, nevertheless he does not entirely exclude this as one element within his works. This is shown by the emphasis laid on the personal *miṣvah*, the personal religious duty laid on each and every individual—a view that does occur within our author's books, although it does not stem from him.[14]

Mordecai Joseph basically anchors his teachings to divine, not human initiative. His main doctrine is the Will of God as an irrational phenomenon, moving in a frequently changing, irrational and arbitrary manner: the "innermost" Will of God cannot be laid down in the Torah. What emerges from this concept of an inconstant Divine Will is that there is no certainty of determining whether the Divine Will of yesterday will be the same as that of tomorrow.

This is, in fact, the ultimate conclusion of this process of thought. All traditional affirmations about the eternal nature of the Divine Will are entirely lost in Mordecai Joseph's teachings.

The Divine Will is in no way exalted above the realm of time, nor is it by any means eternal.[15]

In this respect Mordecai Joseph differs from the doctrine of relative finality, which is the basis of a number of earlier Jewish heretical viewpoints. The "uneternal" quality of the Will of God in the doctrine we are attempting to clarify here implies its absolute finiteness, i.e., a particularised uniqueness that knows of no greater unit of time than the passing moment. Medieval and Sabbatian heretical or semiheretical doctrines divide time up into great world periods in which the passage of time fulfills the function of a changing backcloth for the Will of God. Divine Will expresses itself in the variation of legal standards, changing throughout history.[16] Mordecai Joseph does not adopt this concept of time as a passing sequence of great epochs that follow one another according to a predetermined plan. Every philosophy of history, even the most confused, gives an impression of grand order, not disorder.

However, there is no hard and fast element in the teachings of Mordecai Joseph. Time breaks up into innumerable minute units. There is, essentially, no longer such a thing as "time," but only the highly questionable concept of the "moment." "At that precise moment each soul in Israel,[17] from the least to the greatest, will recognize what God requires at that very moment. And in the understanding of their hearts [*binat levavam*], they will appreciate that at that particular moment God's Will desires such and such, and that they should not act according to general basic principles [*kelalim*]."[18]

According to the internal logic of this brand of thinking, at least ideally, each single action would require an act of guidance and illumination specifically determined for it. Such a requirement would lead to the complete fragmentation of the Divine Will or reduce it and divine leadership to absurdity, since fresh divine illumination would be awaited in respect of each fresh action undertaken by man.

Occasionally, however, Mordecai Joseph adopts a democratic attitude, whereby each individual is provided illumination through divine guidance in respect of every action and at every moment, as, for example, in the above quotation. Yet he is not consistent about this for he often says that such a need is met only for an elect category of individuals. Who are the elect? He gives no criteria by which such election can be recognized, but it is almost inconceivable, psychologically speaking, that he did not reckon himself among the elect.

Although the empirical role played by the *Ṣaddikim*, the leaders of Hasidism, still applied and even became stronger, the *Ṣaddik* as the central concept of Hasidic theory gradually diminished in the middle period of Polish Hasidism of the nineteenth century, and its complete effacement is the general characteristic of the spiritual atmosphere in which Mordecai Joseph was active. One thing is clear: the elect are not unquestioningly to be identified with the *Ṣaddikim*.

Mordecai Joseph once said that of the three patriarchs only Jacob, but not Isaac and Abraham, attained the level of complete enlightenment. Abraham and Isaac had to rationalize and elaborate the enlightenment bestowed upon them. "For they [Abraham and Isaac] were possessed in high degree of wisdom [*ḥokhmah*], and understanding [*binah*], so that they were able to extend [their knowledge of] the Will of God from their own resources; and even if He [God] merely opened a very small chink for them, they extended and elaborated it by means of their wisdom [*ḥokhmah*], so as to carry out the Will of God. Hence they were also capable of understanding matters about which God had granted them no explicit illumination [*she-lo he'ir la-hem ha-shem yitbarakh meforash*]."[19]

This was not so with Jacob, who was subject to continuous and ever-renewed guidance. "[Thus sayeth Jacob] . . . as for me, the Lord has tended me all my life unto this day,[20] which implies that I need God to enlighten my eyes so as to know His Will before even the smallest action that I propose to undertake. I need illumination to know whether it still conforms to His Will, or whether He wants me to alter it [the act].[21] In this respect Jacob was, really, the greatest of the patriarchs, for it is an exceptionally exalted situation for God to direct a human being so continuously."

This homily, accordingly, offers the following classification: there is one type of revelation that is unique, which therefore needs further elaboration of a rational and discursive kind. Against this limited revelation, Mordecai Joseph sets a pure revelation devoid of rational elements and not dependent upon elaboration, which must be considered superior for that reason.

With this, the process of fragmentation is complete; in the higher spheres there is no longer any trace of continuity—and in this context continuity means rationality.

It is this "pure" form of guidance and revelation which Mordecai Joseph sets against the rational system of ordained duties, against the idea of a fundamental accountability for acts required in accordance with the general rules (*kelalim*) of Jewish religious law, the Halakhah. He stresses continually the contrast between "general principles," that is to say, standardized sets of duties, on the one hand and, on the other, specific revelation for each and every action. It is the contrast between divine rule, which is continuously in operation, and rational action resulting from logical conclusions drawn by human beings—the whole unique logic of Jewish religious law.

What Mordecai Joseph means is that in certain circumstances the institutional world of Judaism, based on the Sinaitic revelation and its traditional interpretation, can be set aside for individuals as a result of direct "personal illumination." When so illumined, man should, must in fact, prevail over the shrewdness of the Halakhah. Of course, this does not imply a general abandonment of the law: God does not release man or the community from the divine requirements contained in the laws revealed in the Bible. Nevertheless, for the elect there is another, even higher duty: to hold themselves open to illumination and then to comply. In principle, surprises are impossible within the confines of the rational arrangement of the Halakhah, for everything contained within it has been derived from what already exists and the generality is arrived at from all logically possible and specific conclusions. Illumination is quite different: it is full of surprises. It is in this sense that Mordecai Joseph explains the well-known Talmudical passage[22] dealing with the Hanukkah lights. The sages disagreed as to whether the essence of the ordinance lay in the kindling of the lights or in the duty of setting the lamp in position. Mordecai Joseph allegorizes the Talmudic discussion as follows: "And this is the point of their query, whether it is the positioning [*hanaḥah*] of the lights that constitutes the religious duty, i.e., whether one should follow the general rules that are fixed [*munaḥim*] and 'rigid' [*kevuim*], . . . or whether it is the kindling of the lights that constitutes the *miṣvah*, religious duty. The latter would mean that one must not rely upon general rules, but carry out each individual act in accordance with the illumination vouchsafed by God. This [second possibility] is the intended meaning of the Talmudic passage, 'It is the act of kindling that constitutes the *miṣvah.*' This means the light that God must send forth in connection with every act, and it is this view that has prevailed."[23]

Mordecai Joseph produces a further proposition from this. He maintains that the specific reason for the primacy of illumination over defined religious law is that, as opposed to rational thought, the former is incapable of error. The discursive method of deducing the particular from the general, which is the essential function of rational thinking, leaves a wide margin for the introduction of logical errors, whereas unquantifiable illumination, in which there is no place for rational steps, is in his view incapable of error and consequently more reliable. This is a conclusion, however surprising it may appear to us, that is fully endorsed by the inner logic of its premises. "In connection with each and every action, step or transaction, man needs divine illumination. He must not rely on general principles, for sometimes he may not derive the particular from the general and thus fall into error."[24]

A classical example of continually self-renewing divine guidance is to be found in the typological interpretation of Isaiah 11:13. According to Mordecai Joseph, Ephraim and Judah, the two kingdoms, reflect two human types. The one embodies the man who bases his concept of the Divine Will on general principles. He acts in accordance with the existing laws, with the Halakhah, from which he never departs. However, the other man, symbolized by Judah, is the religious anarchist, whose attitude is entirely orientated to the ever-changing Divine Will. Two life-styles are contrasted here. By typifying the two figures, Judah and Ephraim, each with a different inner rhythm, the claim to exclusiveness in spiritual matters is removed, hence avoiding an outright attack on the religious code. The two types, as we shall see below, are originally presented in a typological manner. Ephraim represents today, whereas Judah represents Utopia. Typology in history and human nature are closely coordinated by Mordecai Joseph and the one can easily merge into the other in the course of one of his expositions: "Ephraim shall not envy Judah, and Judah shall not vex Ephraim" (Isaiah 11:13). Actually these two tribes were constantly in conflict. For the type of life implanted by God in the tribe of Ephraim is a type that considers the law and the Halakhah on every issue so as never to depart from it. On the other hand, the root principle (*shoresh ha-ḥayyim*) of Judah's life is always to look to God Himself. Even though he knows perfectly well the direction in which the law is pointing, Judah always looks to God in order to be shown the profundity of the truth (*omek ha-emet*) appropriate to the situation. This is the basic principle of Judah's life, to look to God in every situation and not to behave in accordance with the precepts laid down by men. Even though he may have performed a similar act yesterday, such a man will nevertheless be reluctant to rely on yesterday's experience, but will entreat God for a renewed illumination of His Will. Such action will sometimes compel him to break the religious law. "For it is time for the Lord to work; they have made void Thy law" (Psalm 119:126).[25]

The existence of the spiritual Judah figure does not, however, negate the right to existence of the other type, who invariably acts in accordance with the law. The Ephraim figures and their code of behavior are legitimate, since He Who breathes breath into our nostrils cannot demand exclusiveness and must therefore recognize the coexistence of both types.

The antinomian effects of the concept of divine illumination now become manifest. Illumination, which apparently precedes each and every act, can be contrary to the law; and one is tempted to add that such acts must be contrary to the law if they are not essentially merely a repetition of the established code of religious laws.

Mordecai Joseph, who repeatedly compasses his theories with the aid of typology, representing Ephraim as the traditional law abider and Judah as the spiritual type, does not mention to which group he himself belongs. Unlike other Hasidic *Ṣaddikim* as, for example, Naḥman of Brazlav (d. 1811), no "I" sentences have been transmitted to us. We also do not find within him any superelevation of his own person, unlike Naḥman, who seems to stand at the other extreme in many respects. No reader can fail to notice the anonymity and complete lack of awareness of personal mission in Mordecai Joseph. There is a clear supposition that in his proposed typological division he recognized himself as a Judah type and as a member of the future with its new religion of promise, but this supposition is merely supported by the general psychology of "election" and cannot be proven. What was Mordecai Joseph's attitude to Messianic self-awareness? The two aspects of his attitude to personality that we have touched upon here are closely related. In its Jewish framework messianic self-awareness is the supreme awareness of personal election. Undoubtedly it was not an altogether secret ambition of many *Ṣaddikim* in the nineteenth century, if not to be the Messiah themselves, at least to exercise a function in the history of salvation.

The tribe of Judah (David's tribe) always had a strong messianic association in Jewish history, based on the text (Genesis 49:10) "The sceptre shall not depart from Judah, nor the ruler's staff from between his feet." Mordecai Joseph is particularly attracted to the kingship figure of Judah. Surely it is not coincidental that, among the most important ancient sources from which he derives his anarchistic theories, there appears a quotation from the Talmud, *Pesaḥim* 110a: *melekh poreṣ gader*, "the king breaks through the hedge."[26] This and other quotations are intended to prove that the king is above the law. But in Jewish tradition the kingship figure is often identical with the messianic figure, and Mordecai Joseph's derivation of his anarchistic teachings from the ancient pronouncements about kingship is, therefore, just as significant as its divergence from messianic views. The legitimate anarchists of history accordingly belong to a metaphysical race of premature Messiahs: an explosion of the late Jewish messianic concept and the splitting of the single messianic figure into many such figures.

It is worth noting that Mordechai Joseph's ancestral tree, prepared by his grandson Gershom Chanoch Leiner (printed in R. Jacob Leiner's *Bet Ya'akov* (Warsaw, 1890), 1:22) ends with the words: "I am descended from the seed of David." (This significant final sentence is, however, lacking in the ancestral tree reproduced in the two volumes of Gershon Chanoch's *Sidrei Taharoth* [Jozefow, 1873, Pietrokow, 1903].)

Why did R. Gershon Chanoch Leiner compose the *Sidrei Taharoth*, two enormous folio volumes dealing with the levitical laws of purity supplemented by copious commentaries? The author's expectation that the messianic age was near may have played an important role in this since, traditionally, the messianic age would be accompanied by the restoration of the sacrifices and the reintroduction of the laws of purity.[27]

In this connection mention must be made of R. Gershon Chanoch Leiner's well-known but abortive attempt to reintroduce the so-called sky-blue coloring (*tekheleth*) obtained from a certain type of ink fish (more precisely, snail, *ḥilazon*). According to the commandment (Numbers 15:37–41), a sky-blue thread should be introduced between the white fringes of the four-cornered garment. For many centuries this commandment had fallen into disuse because the species of snail (*ḥilazon*) mentioned in the Talmud could no longer be identified. R. Gershon Chanoch Leiner wrote a number of missives in which he announced his rediscovery of the *ḥilazon* and proposed a practical method of dyeing with it (*Sefunei temunei ḥol* [Warsaw, 1887], *Pethil tekheleth* [Warsaw, 1888], *Ein ha-tekheleth* [Warsaw, 1891]). His eagerness to revive this forgotten ritual commandment was received defensively by his contemporaries. His suggestion was taken up by just a few, but on the whole ignored. What interests us here is the messianic anticipation from which the search for the *ḥilazon* must have been derived. The sky-blue coloring is not only prescribed for the fringes, but also for certain cultic appurtenances needed for the sacrificial ceremonies that were to be reintroduced. Behind his apparent concern for the perfect execution of an obscure commandment there lies R. Gershon Chanoch Leiner's abolute readiness for the approach of the messianic age. Admittedly this does not go so far as to imply his readiness to assume the role of the Messiah, but it seems to me more than likely that R. Gershon Chanoch Leiner saw himself in that light.[28]

When R. Gershon Chanoch Leiner published the verbally transmitted sermons of his grandfather in 1860, he entitled the book *The Waters of Shiloah*. This title is taken from Isaiah 8:6. The verse speaks of the waters of Shiloah "that go softly," a description that can hardly be applied to the theories of Mordecai Joseph.[29] But the secret of the title seems to lie in the traditional interpretation of this biblical verse, which has been transmitted in the Aramaic paraphrase of the prophetic book. This exposition of the verse was so well known that it even found its way into the classical medieval commentaries: it identifies "the waters of Shiloah" with the royal house of David. But this is the messianic royal house. Whether the grandson's messianic secret was, indeed, a carefully preserved family tradition, originating from his grandfather, is not a matter that can be investigated here.

However, it is worth mentioning that Mordecai Joseph constantly repeats that all matters in the House of David were conducted in an antinomian manner (he uses the present tense: are conducted). "All the public buildings of the kingdom of the House of David were arranged by God in such a way that at the final hour they would appear to be sinful, since Judah considered her [Tamar] to be a whore since she kept her face concealed. But this means that this was a divine secret. . . . Even before the prophets it was conceded that the rise of the kingdom would be undertaken by the House of David."[30]

The social implications of the antinomian way of life are indicated by this comment. There are two kinds of behavior: "One kind is action undertaken by man that finds favor in the eyes of his fellowmen, and there is another kind of action that is good in the deepest recesses of his being [*be-omek u-ma'amakei ḥayyim shelo*], and that is the inner form of mankind [*ṣurat ha-adam*]. One must take great care to ensure that one's actions are clarified [*mevorarim*] in both ways."[31]

A similar question, again referring to the royal House of David, is raised in another homily. Even more radical conclusions are drawn this time from the incongruity between the inner and the outer value of a deed. This incongruity, indeed contradiction, between the external ugliness and internal beauty of certain deeds, was one of the main teachings of the Sabbatian heresy almost from its start. The historical persistence in Hasidic thinking of this religious paradox has not as yet been clarified, but Mordecai Joseph's ideas about the esoteric effect of appearances in assessing sin are dangerously close to heretical religious thinking. "Azariah, king of Judah, had defeated Edom and cast down ten thousand from the top of the rock so that they all were broken into pieces . . . and later he served the gods of Edom, and he sent to Joash, the king of Israel: 'come, let us test our strength in battle' (2 Chronicles 25:17). The point is that Edom is the start of *kelipah*, uncleanliness, and more important than all other peoples. . . . Immediately after this *kelipah* comes Israel. Today Israel is not the more powerful, but will be in the future."[32] Amaziah thought that "after he had defeated them, the *kelipah*, his heart would rest with God and would continue to do so, and that no evil would be able to overcome him. . . . He therefore deliberately *attempted* to serve the god of Edom and sent an envoy to Joash, king of Israel: 'Come, let us test our strength in battle.' This means, however, that 'although I have performed a deed which appears to be bad, I am nevertheless closer to God than you.' But this was not the Will of God and he was punished: Joash captured him. Nevertheless, it is recorded that Amaziah lived on for fifteen years after the death of Joash, so as to show that Amaziah was greater than Joash and that his sin related merely to the limitations of human understanding. He who appreciates the doings of the royal House of David and those of the kings of Judah, whom God loved so dearly, [knows] that their deeds could not be judged in their simplest form [*ki-feshutam*]".[33]

Mordechai Joseph's paraphrases when recapitulating the biblical account need further consideration. Edom plays an important part as far as Mordechai Joseph is concerned. Amaziah, king of Judah, had "attempted" to serve Edom and, nevertheless, to cleave to God. That was not the Will of God. But there can be no doubt that this transgressor was more God-fearing than his opponent, Joash. It is worth noting that for almost the last 2,000 years Edom has been identified in Jewish tradition with Christianity. The king of Judah who "attempted" to serve the gods of Edom could, by Mordechai Joseph's terminology, be taken as an allusion to Jacob Frank and his open apostasy. If this textual interpretation is correct, it would mean that almost a century after Frank's conversion to Christianity, one single figure among the Hasidic leaders was still brooding over this apostasy.

Even if Mordechai Joseph does not draw the ultimate conclusions from the antinomian vindication of Frank, the historian of ideas must ask how far Hasidic thought was influenced by Sabbatian and Frankist heretical thinking. The words *ḥayyim* (life) or *shoresh ha-ḥayyim* (the root of life)[34] appear very frequently in quotations. The connection between the passages in which the words are repeated almost as a *terminus technicus* makes it clear that they refer specifically to the anarchic life-style of Judah and those like him: the concept of life is to be appreciated in all its significance. In this sense one can refer to the extraordinary biblical commandment concerning the red heifer in the book of Numbers (19:2) "a red heifer without spot wherein is no blemish and upon which never came yoke." Mordecai Joseph interprets this as: "the red heifer represents the midpoint of life (*nekudat ha-ḥayyim*) which makes fruitful and multiplies; the redness implies strength and happiness and the biblical phrase 'which never came under yoke' implies freedom from any yoke."[35] Does not this definition of life echo the similar definition of the concept of life by Jacob Frank? Six years ago Scholem investigated Frank's definition of this passage. This "life," according to Frank, does not mean the harmonious fulfillment of all things in compliance with God's own laws, i.e., a picture of a well-ordered and eternally constructive authority; on the contrary, this concept of life means a life not bound by laws and enchained by authority, but freely developing and changing, flowing along without confining barriers. Such a life is represented as not determined by law, but by the anarchic element of submersion into the freedom of restraint from all barriers and in the promiscuity of all beings.[36]

It is highly instructive that the libertine apostate Jacob Frank and the Hasidic *Ṣaddik*, who used all his endeavors to remain within the confines of orthodox Jewry and who nevertheless entered into the fascination of anarchism, should have had an important section of their esoteric language in common.

Mordecai Joseph finds it possible to mitigate the contradiction between orthodox and spiritual codes of behavior and to treat them as complementary. Our author says about the verse in Psalm 119:126 that is even referred to in the Talmud with a whisper of an antinomian tendency[37]: "If it is clear [*mevorar*] to someone that it is time for the Lord to act, as for instance Elijah on Mount Carmel, then it is necessary to tear up the general principles of the Torah and to act in accordance with the 'spiritual' understanding [*binah*] that God bestows on man . . . but if the understanding [*binah*] does not provide a clear [*meforeshet*] answer, man is obliged to follow the general laws of the Torah so as not to cause a breach in the fence round the Halakhah. . . . In Aaron's time the Jews in the wilderness followed the understanding of their own hearts which provided a clear [*meforeshet*] answer and they wandered in compliance[38] with the pillars of cloud of the Almighty. But when the pillars of cloud of the Almighty withdrew, the Jews began to follow the general laws of the Torah: as it is today, now that the Temple has been destroyed, God has nothing in His world but the four cubits of the Halakhah alone."[39]

The relationship between recognition through illumination of "the profundity of the Divine Will" [*omek reşon ha-shem yitbarakh*] and the generally applicable religious laws [*kelalei divrei Torah*] is not something that Mordecai Joseph is able to answer clearly, especially since he is anxious to accept that the relationship between the two sources of religion is complementary, not antithetical. In this context, the "profundity of the Divine Will" simply seems to be a deepening of the laws of the Torah. On this assumption it can be said that rabbinic law submitted the original laws of the Torah to the profound Will of God. "It is acknowledged that there is a profundity [*omek*] in the words of the Torah, more profound than appears on the surface [*al ha-levush*]. And God has enlightened [*he'ir*] our sages concerning this law with the profundity of His Will [*omek reşono*] so that here (Leviticus 26:3) an expression of doubt can be used. Thus, however careful a man may be in complying with the *Shulḥan Arukh*,[40] he is still in doubt as to whether he has acted in accordance with the profundity of the divine Will, *im kivven le-omek reşon ha-shem*, for the Will of God is 'exceeding deep, who can find it out?'" (Ecclesiastes 7:24).[41]

But if there were to be open conflict, how is one to decide? What should one do if the divine illumination were to demand that one should eat a piece of pork, something forbidden to Jews, or lay hands on a forbidden woman—and both Jewish and general histories of religion demonstrate that antinomian or anarchic trains of thought lead into the area of sex? Should one comply with the illumination that guides us or with the book of laws? The theoretician of religious anarchy is far more hesitant than we would have expected in converting such illumination into action.

II

The conflict between the power to break or comply with the law, which perhaps reflects certain personal traits in Mordecai Joseph's religious character, is again clearly expressed in his teachings about criteria. In his opinion anarchistic behavior is not only permissible but even obligatory; he is unequivocal and holds no reservations about this. Nevertheless, at this point he introduces a security device so as not to open all the floodgates to instinctive passions. He demands a critical self-appraisal prior to action so as to clarify the inner motives that give rise to the urge. Such examination is to allow the waverer to decide whether to obey the command of the illumination, which may be in open conflict with the law, or to resist it. He appreciates that the problem for all mystics is to make sure that the illumination is real, since there is a danger of irrational behavior arising out of pure illusion.[42] He is fully aware that sentimental and illegitimate illumination must be avoided at all costs. A test must be established to distinguish true from false illumination. How is the authenticity of divine illumination to be established? What signs are to be looked for to prove its truth? How is one to know that the illumination is a meeting with the divine and not with the demonic world? There is always a danger of being led astray; but one searches in vain for a theoretical basis in Mordecai Joseph's works. He is aware of the danger of acting in accordance with inspiration or illumination, yet does not characterize this danger; the figure of the devil as a tempter or deceiver is not mentioned in his writings.

Before proceeding to a more detailed analysis of the rationally conditioned and, hence, retarding process of the self-examination required, for which various categories of criteria can be distinguished in the two volumes of *Mei ha-Shiloaḥ*,[43] we must first give a broad outline of the character of this self-examination.

It is obvious that the required self-examination constitutes a strange element for the illuminee, since it brings rational consideration into contact with his intuitive individualistic behavior. Surely this self-examination, which itself implies a mistrust of the illumination, must influence the spontaneity of the act? Yet Mordecai Joseph's concern is with untrammeled spontaneity of action and self-assurance in performing the act.

In all the many ways in which it is formulated, the test reveals an atomistic character. That is to say, the self-analysis is solely concerned with a particular act confronting a man at a specific moment. It has no applicability to future similar acts or to any longer period of time. A single act of self-examination does not give a man the assurance that he can be certain of the authenticity of any future illumination. The atomistic character of such self-examination corresponds in every way with the atomistic nature of divine guidance. Atomization remains the essential feature and implies the suspension of the continuity and coherence of conscious thinking.

It always comes back to the particular act of the person concerned. It is merely a fraction, not the whole, of humanity that is subjected to the test: the test is whether the isolated act conforms to the Divine Will. To some extent, all this is contrary to the typological ideas of Judah and Ephraim. A man who knows that he belongs to the metaphysical tribe of Ephraim has no reason to test himself again and again before each separate act, for the law is binding upon him; whereas a man of the Judah type, if he is certain that he is of that type, should not find it necessary to reactivate the criteria repeatedly.

A further point must be added. The object of the test is invariably the man who has the urge to undertake a particular act. The test is not applied to the act itself, but to the man who is preparing to carry out the act. The description of such self-examination given by Mordecai Joseph in various passages in his writings is not uniform. In one passage, for instance, the man is obliged to test his inner disposition, in another to examine the motivation of his urge to perform the act concerned. In either case, it is clear that this is a form of psychological self-analysis and not the objective examination of the act itself.

Loss of free will is the surest sign of the divine origin of the urge within the human soul. The traditional Jewish picture of man shows him as a creature forever distracted from his continuous religious obligations. Nevertheless, postbiblical teaching speaks of two inclinations[44] that dwell within the human heart, evil and good, *yeṣer ha-ra* and *yeṣer ha-tov*, which shows that man has the strength to resist the blandishments of his evil inclinations. According to the fundamental concept contained in the traditional idea of free will, no one is exposed to temptation that he is unable to resist.

Mordecai Joseph advances beyond this thesis by recognising the possibility of a significant denial of the power of resistance. A situation in which a man is unable to overcome his natural inclination should not be counted as a moral lapse but, in such a case of a man's failure to resist, as the supreme victory of Almighty God. On the text: "And [if thou] seest among the captives a beautiful woman, etc. . . . she shall be thy wife" (Deuteronomy 21:11 ff.), the Talmud comments that the Torah here has the evil inclination in mind.[45] Mordecai Joseph's own comment on this is: "The reason why the Torah exceptionally grants the evil inclination an indulgence at this moment is simply because a man can be so overcome by his evil inclination as to be unable to tear himself away. It is then clear [*barur*] that the matter has been ordained by God, just as in the case of Judah [and Tamar].[46] The Torah makes reference here to this fact in order that a person who acts in this way should not feel utterly despondent about his sin."[47]

In Mordecai Joseph's view, an insuperable urge, treated as a psychological criterion, is an objective indication of the Divine Will. On such empirically established occasions, the voice of the urge must be recognized as the divine voice. The chapter of the Torah relating to the sight of a beautiful woman captive is chosen by Mordecai Joseph as a classical case of passionate longing, the intensity of which overcomes man's power of free choice. The sacrifice brought about by the perpetration of the act as a result of the overwhelming strength of his desire is not condemned by Mordecai Joseph as a transgression of the Divine Will of God, but praised as the fullfilment of the Divine Will. He not only implies by this that a man is not liable to punishment if, from time to time, he acts according to his irrestible inclinations,[48] but that, in having given reign to his inclinations whose intensity robbed him of his freedom of choice, the concealed Will of God has become manifest.

The examples quoted by the author as biblical proof of his paradoxical doctrine indicate that sexual temptation is at the forefront of his imagination. His most important illustrations, apart from the laws regarding the beautiful female captive, are the history of Judah and Tamar (Genesis 28) and Zimri's encounter with the Midianite woman (Numbers 25:6 ff). "And in truth regarding both Judah's relationship with Tamar and all other relationships of a similar nature in the tribe of Judah, God infused them with such intense desire that it was impossible for them to exercise self-control; it was the angel of desire that compelled them to act in this way. Consequently there was no guilt attached to him, since he was incapable of overcoming his desire."[49]

The second classical example of the annihilation of free will that indicates an identification of human desire with Divine Will is furnished by what Mordecai Joseph has to say about the relationship between Zimri and the Midianite woman.[50] Here, too, it was divine power at work, not human (decision).

The new light that he throws on the dispute between Phineas and Zimri fundamentally alters the biblical evaluation of these two characters. The biblical text is examined so intensely that, at the critical moment, everything depends on the question of freedom of will. He gives a detailed description of the events that finally caused Zimri to lose his freedom of will. The representation of the ten stages of asceticism appearing here in Mordecai Joseph's teachings serves a dual purpose. First, no man achieves anarchistic maturity in the biographical sense until he has passed through the school of strict asceticism. Zimri maintains that he has done so. But schooling in asceticism acts as the dam holding back the overwhelming power of lust. The unique character of irresistible desire can be shown to be a true criterion of the Divine Will only if it is based on such ascetic schooling.

> God forbid that man should ever for a moment believe that Zimri was just an ordinary sensualist. God would never have devoted a whole chapter of the Torah to a sensualist! No, there is a secret embedded in this biblical passage. For there are in fact ten grades of harlotry. The first is concerned with a person who bedecks himself and sallies forth with every intention of sinning. He who does this is seeking the evil inclination within himself. Beyond this, there are nine further stages of harlotry. Finally, at the ultimate stage, a man can lose the power of free will, so that it becomes impossible for him to avoid the sin however much he tries. He no longer has the power to restrain himself. If his evil propensity overcomes him at this stage and he does perform the act, then it is surely God who is exercising His will upon him. As in the affair between Judah and Tamar where, quite unknown to him, she became his predestined partner, so it was here between Zimri and the Midianite woman]. In truth Zimri had been restraining himself from all evil passions, but it turned out that she [the Midianite woman] was his predestined partner. It no longer lay within his power to avoid being entrapped by the sin. But Phineas said that this was not so, and that he might well have been able to restrain himself.[51]

The slaying of Zimri by Phineas in punishment would appear from the biblical text to be the well-merited victory of moral indignation over unbridled lust, but that is not Mordecai Joseph's opinion. According to the interpretation in *Mei ha-Shiloaḥ*, we find, amazingly, that Phineas is never excluded from the confines of anarchistic teachings. Mordecai Joseph considers that both of them, Phineas as well as Zimri, were protagonists of the theory and practice of religious anarchy. The conflict between them is reduced to the mere question of the criteria regarding the obligatory length of ascetic study. Phineas's main argument is not against Zimri's behavior, but he complains that Zimri's preparatory asceticism had not been carried to the point where the successful exponent of its highest school could justifiably apply the anarchistic principles. For both Zimri and Phineas are convinced that the annihilation of free will is the determining criterion in relation to the divine origin of illumination. According to Mordecai Joseph, Zimri claimed that he had already passed through all the stages of asceticism. If his lust overwhelmed him despite this, the criterion of compulsion had been fulfilled and, in accordance with the definition, had been identical with the Divine Will. Phineas counters this by asserting that Zimri could have mastered his inclinations by applying the utmost resolution, and that the prior stipulation of compulsion had not yet been completely fulfilled. Consequently Zimri should not have listened to the inner voice of his inclination, nor should he have accepted it as the Divine Will.[52]

Mordecai Joseph's treatment of the story of Zimri and Phineas concludes with a further explanation of the great mistake that Phineas made in assessing the moral character of Zimri. It is clear that Mordecai Joseph's anarchistic rehabilitation of Zimri is incomplete until the source of Phineas's passionate eagerness can be explained.

His error, which Moses arbitrarily describes as praiseworthy in the historical account—Mordecai Joseph attempts to deny Phineas any justification for his eagerness—must have been based on ancestral considerations. Such considerations could explain Phineas's bias against Zimri, for Zimri was a descendant of Joseph the chaste.[53]

It should be mentioned here that the gruesome encounter

between Phineas and Zimri did not arise from an action about to be performed, but from an action that had already been completed. The fatal discussion between them was a retrospective evaluation of a sin that had already been committed. The retrospective character of this is an important aspect of this train of thought and will be discussed later.

It is an open question whether self-analysis before an action is at all possible in such circumstances. The unique character of acting in accordance with illumination received lies in its compulsive uninterrupted spontaneity, in the dreamlike confidence by which man is entirely liberated from any reflective misgivings about his actions. This freedom from concern as to the truth of the illumination also implies unrestrained power of action in the given situation. The texts describe such human idealistic behavior by the word *tekufot* or *bi-tekufot*, often used adverbially, which means "powerful, mighty, overpowering." Mordecai Joseph does not attempt to span the gap between such reflective and spontaneous elements. He does not say how illumination, impulse, self-analysis, and deed are to be reconciled, and it is possible that he never consciously appreciated the dissimilarity within such situations.

Despite the superficial similarity between the systematic antinomianism of the heretical strains in Judaism in the seventeenth and eighteenth centuries, and the anarchistic antinomianism of Mordecai Joseph, there are important differences between the two schools of thought. In Sabbatianism the breaking of the law was celebrated on specified days. It became a festive act. In Mordecai Joseph's fantasies of freedom, the law was abjured at unspecified moments and, apparently, as a result of inescapable and hence divinely recognized compulsion. The supreme act is the romantic "premise" that is contained in the assumed identity between "God" and "I" at a level where arbitrary action by God imposed on man encounters the absolute law. The inner meaning of the law lies in spiritual certainty, individual passivity, and devotion to what must be. The Sabbatians were fully aware of their sinful behavior, undertaken with full ceremony, form, and ritual, but in Mordecai Joseph's world mankind is overpowered by the inalienable, instant, and spontaneous action of higher powers.

III

The Utopian vision of our author is based not so much on traditional Jewish, i.e., biblical, rabbinic, or mystical ideas about the End of Days, as on the antinomian message he preached to his followers in an impassioned and emotional fashion. His Utopian dreams revealed a religious order, perhaps better described as "disorder," based entirely upon the principle of direct divine guidance. In the face of this guidance, the whole elaborate system of positive and negative commandments still applicable to the Jewish religion today is liable to total collapse with the advent of the messianic age. Eschatological illumination will fill the vacuum left by the messianic atrophy of the traditional form of Jewish life.[54] Mordecai Joseph is thinking of the final "clarification" (*berur*) of the Utopian age, a central feature of Lurianic doctrine, and indeed he is looking to a future in which all Jews will have attained religious maturity, that is to say, anarchic maturity.

In the present, premessianic order, the message of anarchism is directed only to a small spiritual elite who must exclusively comprise Judah types. Even among them, legitimate disorder cannot operate without that rigorous self-examination whose function it is to examine the divine origin of the impulses in the depths of the human soul. The practices now performed by this Jewish elite, insofar as they are admissible in face of their understandable rejection by the equally legitimate Jewish community abiding by the Halakhic laws, are exclusively aimed at the establishment of a life in a Utopian community. The powerful inclination, even if self-contradictory, that has hitherto stirred within but a few will then be manifest in its true dimensions. These messianic stages will form the basis for the new "disorder." The Halakhah with its laws and prohibitions will be abandoned in its entirety and the world will be bathed in the light of direct and continuous illumination.

Utopian freedom, as taught by anarchistic theologians in respect of the messianic future, cannot appear without historical preparation, and such preparation goes on in the lives of the spiritual minority who even now let themselves be guided by the principles of the Utopian age. Their way of life is a guide to the messianic state of affairs, where religious behavior will no longer be determined by the unique revelation at Sinai and the hallowed formulation of the commandments.

In the Utopian age this existence, controlled directly by divine authority, which is now only permissible to a few, will be the form of life applicable to each and every one. Thus this way of life can be followed, in some elements at least, in premessianic times, in particular by people of the Judah type who are anxiously concerned not to let it become publicly available. This means, however, that the messianic age will not be an absolute novelty. Thus the unattainable Utopia that has never been experienced turns into a sporadic Utopia where true revelation can occur in exceptional circumstances.

In Mordecai Joseph's Utopian vision there are two conflicting tendencies, one destructive and the other constructive. The tendency that seeks to set aside the law banishes religious life from the innermost recesses of the human heart (*ma'amakei ha-lev*), according to Mordecai Joseph's phrase for the Utopian localization of the religious spirit. In this dual concept, which integrates a religious rebirth in the innermost recesses of the heart with the tearing down of the old framework, Utopia appears as the continuation and realization of the semi-failures and successes of premessianic attempts. Similarly, we find the same two components in the theory that indicates sporadic religious anarchy in the present age, the abolition of the existing legal system on the one hand and the establishment of direct contact with God on the other.

At this point it might be helpful to take another brief look at the Sabbatian movement. The Sabbatians lived in the awareness of an eschatology already established within themselves, since they believed that the messianic age had secretly been established in the year 1666. This had resulted not only in the nullification of important sections of the law, but, in particular, to a change in religious values.

Even the religious nihilist Jacob Frank, the most extreme of all the heretical exponents of Sabbatianism, could not entirely free himself from the eternal fascination of the might of the law. Although he changed the values of Jewish tradition, the specifically Jewish element, though negative both in theory and practice, still remained alive. The conversion of positive commandments into transgressions and vice versa in his doctrine merely exchanged one framework for another. According to the eschatological scheme of Sabbatian teaching, the new order will replace its predecessor, the order based upon the Torah, at the dawn of the apocalyptic era. On the other hand, Mordecai Joseph's doctrine is the only one that contains the new principle of religious spontaneity, which will be introduced in place of the existing order despite the chains of the religious law. This is not merely a deviation from an existing legal system, but a revolution that attacks the roots of Judaism.

Among Jewish mystics Mordecai Joseph adopts a unique position, advancing beyond the bounds of a legally determined Utopia. Every definition of what is Utopian is to be derived from a positive or negative attitude to the Torah. Only in this way will the Utopian law become "absolute," that is to say, divorced from any relationship, including negative relationships, with history and its inherent norms. According to anarchist theory, Judaism is destined to cease as a closed religious system with its unique and eternal revelation of texts, a religion revealed by written codes and laws. It will reemerge as messianic religion open only to direct injunction. The content of Judaism will not only be turned topsy-turvy, as in Sabbatianism, but the source of religion will change: the religion of compliance with the written law will become the religion of the free spirit.

In describing the relationship between messianic and premessianic times, Mordecai Joseph adopts the exegetical method he used in all his homilies about the form of the existing religion, totally comprised in his view in the word *ḥokhmah*, wisdom. Then there follows a description of the establishment of the Utopian, completely spontaneous religion, which he characterizes by the word *tevunah*, understanding. He concludes with the organization of the Utopian religion, which, once again, reveals the unmistakable characteristics of *tevunah*. "At first there will be brought upon Israel the total transfiguration that God desires to bring to the world, which is a long Sabbath. This will clear the sediment and froth from the wine, which is the explanation of the Talmudic phrase, that the Torah will one day be entirely forgotten by Israel,[55] meaning that the Will of God will be shrouded in such a mysterious way that it will not be possible to obtain wisdom or advice from the Torah. This will complete the purging. Israel will divine the Will of God solely from within its heart."[56]

This formulation uses the word *berur*, divination, which is the Lurianic concept of the messianic differentiation between good and evil. According to Mordecai Joseph, this messianic divination has become an inner divination of hallowed certainty that justifies Israel's trust in the inspiration of its heart.

IV

In traditional Judaism the concept of penitence is developed from regret, contrition, and the desire never to repeat the action.[57] Totally unexpectedly, Mordecai Joseph associates this with the concept of illumination: "And if, God forbid, a complaint were to be made and it so appeared that a man had sinned from a sense of deliberate masterfulness, God will provide him with illumination [*ya'ir ha-shem yitbarakh*] so as to demonstrate that the deed was performed only out of the fear of God."[58] Retrospectively, the sin has become the true implementation of the Divine Will as a result of illumination.

Deformation always requires rehabilitation. What has illumination to offer in this respect? It is an experience by which the sinner is freed from the phantom of his guilt. It is a therapeutic process during which the sinner is restored to his entirety, since he can view a guilt-ridden episode in his life in a new and positive light. His failings are reinterpreted, thus saving him from despair. The possibility of such reevaluation is the stamp of the retrospective approval of the act by God.

The function of such illumination is, therefore, retrospective and serves to relieve a devout person from a sin he has committed. This illumination looks into the past, but does not work in it; it converts the sin, as it were, into an optical illusion. What previously appeared mistakenly to be a sin can be viewed as a worthy act, as a result of an illumination that corrects the original picture. Mordecai Joseph has to amass all his theological arguments to prove his thesis that in fact no sin has ever been committed in Israel. Everything contrary to this teaching, including the literal sense of biblical accounts, comes from misunderstandings and mistakes and requires radical reinterpretation.

Divine atonement is optical, not ontological, by nature. Through it the sin is not converted into a positive *mişvah*, for the *mişvah* was not initially conceded when the apparently sinful act was performed. The most important point is the fact that not merely society, the "public world", had suffered the apparently negative character of the act, but the sinner himself was deluded to his own disadvantage into thinking that he was a sinner. Illumination, however, reveals the true situation to the perpetrator of the act and, by revealing the optical illusion, brings him unexpected relief. After true penitence, divine illumination puts the sin into inverted commas.

What is the effect of this relief-bearing illumination? Mordecai Joseph's teaching rests on the radical theological basis that the activity of divine power is exclusive. The essential passivity of mankind is the other side of the same coin. The illumination resulting from penitence expresses the ultimate religious truth, which reveals that in the final analysis each human action is exercised by God alone. This brings us to the following conclusion: the actual sin that caused the sinner so many pangs of conscience was an act performed by God, not by the man himself.

The eternal symbol of liberation from the oppressive burden of sin is the figure of Adam. "After his repentances Adam appreciated that man alone can do nothing in this world, but that all is performed by God. It therefore follows that his own 'sin' was carried out in accordance with the Divine Will, but this transcended Adam's understanding."[59]

According to Hasidic tradition, the concept of repentance is closely linked with rehabilitation (*tikkun*). Once mystical literature had recognized in sin a real and even metaphysical quality the classical Jewish concept of the annulment of sin through active repentance was shown to be inadequate. The teaching that repentance annuls sin becomes most complicated in later mystical systems.[60] The mystic demands that, in addition to repentance, which takes place between the penitent and God, the metaphysical impression the sin has left behind should be expiated. In this connection, it is irrelevant whether the impression is stamped upon the soul of the perpetrator or on the mystical zones, the divine *sefirot*, which, in Cabbalistic terms, are highly sensitive to human influences. This idea is not to be found in Mordecai Joseph's teachings. Since, according to him, sin is only apparently committed and is in fact an impossibility, there is no point in penitence and it is contrary to his teaching. Since sin lacks reality and the awareness of sin has no existence in real terms, God's reply to the despairing cry of the presumed sinner must also be placed upon the same subjective level. This is a new interpretation of life, shown only to the sinner; it consists of the illuminating gift of being able to recognize divine overlordship of the sin that has been committed. This satisfying insight constitutes man's rehabilitation. His rehabilitation is no longer the responsibility of the repentant sinner, as in the Cabbala, but of divine action. It is in this light that the following passage can be understood: "'The Lord will enlighten my darkness' (Psalm 18:29). This means that once a man has acknowledged his sin and retrospectively has come to reproach himself with it, he is thereby graced with the favor of knowing that God beams forth in rehabilitation after his sin [*me'ir tikkun al ḥeto*]. That is the meaning of the word *yaggiah*, 'He will enlighten'—the word is used in connection with the rising of the sun—'my darkness' means that the powers of darkness, that is, the regret and self-reproach that he experiences as a result of his false action, will be granted a recognition of the light in which his rehabilitation [*tikkun*] will be simultaneously revealed. That is the meaning of the adage[61] 'darkness at first, thereafter light.'"[62] The sudden illumination is followed by relief from the burden of responsibility because the responsibility for the sin and the absolution are fully borne by God.

What is the relationship between the doctrine of rehabilitation in the life of the individual and the doctrine of messianic rehabilitation? It is hardly surprising that in the homilies of Mordecai Joseph both types of rehabilitation frequently run in parallel and are often interwoven. Utopian rehabilitation, too, implies the exposure of an error in evaluating a past act. Eschatological *tikkun* shows that all the sins of Israel in premessianic history were merely misconceptions and hallucinations. In both instances the essence of rehabilitation is not the correcting of what is past, for it does not need correcting. This is classically formulated in a passage in which the aspects of personal repentance and eschatological ages are intermingled. "In the [messianic] future when [earlier] behavior arising from presumptuous sins are converted into meritorious deeds,[63] God will make the soul of the sinner realize that at the time [of committing the sin] he had plumbed depths more profound than human understanding can reach [*omek mi-kol da'at*]. And he [the penitent] will bring all this about through his cry in the midst of his regret."[64] According to Lurianic Cabbala, the sin of Adam will be healed in future aeons by eschatological rehabilitation. But what Mordecai Joseph means by *tikkun* is made clear by the following: "When the sin of Adam is set aright in the [messianic] future, there will be a re-rendering [of the passage in Genesis 2:16–17][65] in the following sense: 'of every tree in the garden thou mayest freely eat, and of the tree of the knowledge of good. But evil thou shalt not eat,' which means that he may eat of the good of the tree, but not of its evil. And God will make it clear that in fact he [Adam] ate only from the good, so that sin did not occur except subjectively, *le-fi da'ato*, and then only very slightly[66] and no more."[67]

Adam's rehabilitation implies the correction of a historical astigmatism. It will "become clear" (*yitbarer*) that in fact Adam ate only of the good. The central sin upon which the whole of human history depends appears, from the Utopian point of view, to have been an act that Adam erroneously thought of as his own. The motive for divine rule over sin is lacking here, but the Utopian state of salvation is nevertheless mandatory, since all historical reality experiences the correction of optical astigmatism retrospectively.

A similar formulation of eschatological awareness is found in another passage, which deals with the sinful acts performed by Israel in the course of its long history. Such acts, which are described by our author as overstepping the bounds, or unbridled expansion of human activity (*hitpashetut*), are shown in the Utopian future to have been undertaken in accordance with the Will of God. "For in time to come God will clarify and purify [*yevarer vi-yṣaref*] the acts of Israel, in which there was not the slightest element of sin. . . . Therefore the text reads (Ecclesiastes 11:9): 'Rejoice, O young man, in thy youth,' which means: in your acts of expansion [*hitpashetut*]. For all acts of expansion reach ultimate rehabilitation and all [that is past] will be seen to have been in accordance with the Will of God."[68]

The Utopian age will therefore be a time for taking a new look and a period of liberation from oppressive optical illusion—and this does not refer exclusively to the rich history of Israel's sins. From an eschatological point of view, the crucial errors of Jewish historiography will have to be corrected, namely, that the Jews were in exile and in slavery to other peoples. All the paradoxes of the Utopian age that we have encountered in connection with the sins of Israel are repeated word for word in what Mordecai Joseph has to say about the inversion in the world to come of what appears to have been the Exile. It is not merely that Israel is destined to exchange bondage for freedom—that was always an inalienable feature of the traditional eschatological picture[69]—but that the entire premessianic history of Jewry will retrospectively require a new interpretation. It will become manifest that the enslavement of Israel among the nations was nothing more than a delusion. "One must understand that God intended to establish [the people of] Israel in eternal freedom and to make it known that they were never in exile or subject to any [rule] other than God's rule."[70] And again: "In times to come, God will save and deliver us, He will show that we were never in exile, and that no one, other than God Himself, has ruled over us."[71] Life in exile means life in the shadow of imaginary oppression itself, and the relief of those supposedly oppressed from their sick delusions will only come to pass through messianic therapy.

These theses are by their nature based on religious and not on inspirational theories and are derived from the radical nature of the concept of the exclusive power of God in both space and time. But if God is the sole active agent in history and none other holds sway over Israel but Him, then every historical fact that appears to contradict this fundamental religious truth is not only a deception but also a kind of divine disguise concealing the ultimate truth. This ultimate, illuminating revelation is itself a divine act. With all its attributes, it must be attributed not to the Messiah, but to God Himself, for the personified Messiah has no function of his own accord.

We cannot part from this subject without at least considering an important inner inconsistency in Mordecai Joseph's teachings. His description of the divine act of illumination as a consequence of repentance or at the Utopian End of Days does not make any clear distinction between sins of various categories. Apparently he intends to say that the retrospective divine act of redemption includes all sins, whatever their nature: they all reveal themselves as *miṣvot* in disguise. The inconsistency is that Mordecai Joseph, in his practical teaching of anarchy as described above, lays great stress on elaborating the specific criteria of legitimate sins. He draws a sharp distinction between a "correct" and a "false" sin. "Correct," that is to say, anarchistically legitimate, sins are those which are undertaken through the exuberance of life in conformity with anarchistic criteria. The other category includes those sins where such conditions have not been fulfilled, probably sins arising out of human weakness. In such cases it is assumed that the urge toward a sin of that nature is not an expression of the Divine Will. The practical rules of anarchistic doctrine draw a hard and fast distinction between these two categories, but in the Utopian doctrine of retrospective illumination and rehabilitation, this classification of sins is ignored. There, all sins, without distinction, are promised *post hoc* a happy conversion into the positive.

V

The conflict of religious motivation in Mordecai Joseph's thinking is demonstrated most clearly in his vain attempts to distinguish between the historical present and the Utopian future on the level of reality. This distinction is a cornerstone of the Jewish religion, and a radical and real differentiation between the unredeemed world of history and the world of messianic redemption has been one of the main themes of the Jewish religion throughout the centuries.

Jewish Utopians believe in a messianic transformation on the flatbed of reality. On this point Scholem remarked some years ago how important it was for the peculiar position of Judaism in religious history that it does not recognize a purely inner redemption that is not manifested externally as well.[72]

From this angle the feebleness of Mordecai Joseph's pronouncements about the difference between the historical present and the Utopian future is particularly striking. Inasmuch as he recognizes the distinction at all, it remains purely spiritual. The distinction between the historical and eschatological worlds is based by Mordecai Joseph on the principle of the exclusive activity of God in the Utopian world, whereby man forfeits his power of decision. The Talmudic basis for religious freedom of choice: "Everything, except the fear of Heaven, is in the hands of Heaven,"[73] is accepted, but at the same time taken as a maxim of determinism in the extrareligious spheres. This aspect is particularly stressed by Mordecai Joseph. Of more importance, however, is the fact that the author limits the application of the Talmudic maxim about religious freedom to historical times. Thereafter, he teaches, total determinism will rule the world. He assumes that the spheres of determinism, which do not at present include religious decisions and acts, will embrace all these remaining aspects of human free will in the Utopian world. In messianic terms, acts of religious significance, sins or good deeds, will remain firmly in the divine hand. He propounds a doctrine, unique in Jewish theology, that at the time of the redemption: "Everything, including the fear of Heaven, will be in the hands of Heaven." In this reversed form the Talmudic saying becomes the expression of absolute religious determinism in the Utopian world.[74]

The relationship between the historical and Utopian worlds is symbolized in this respect by Mordecai Joseph by the Utopian right to pronounce the now ineffable name of God.

> 'In that day there shall be upon the bells of the horses: Holiness unto the Lord' (Zechariah 14:20). This world is unlike the world to come. In this world the ineffable Name [of God] is written in the form of the Tetragrammaton, but in its place the surrogate *Adonai*, my Lord, is now pronounced.[75] But in the world to come it will be pronounced as it is written. For in truth the Tetragrammaton YHWH means that everything lies in the hands of God, even the fear of Heaven. Nevertheless, [at the present time] in place of the divine Name we say *the Lord, my God* and thereby indicate that He is the Lord and we His slaves. That is why our sages explained[76]: "Everything, except the fear of Heaven, is in the hands of Heaven," but that only applies to this world. So long as the difference between good and evil is not clarified, commandments and good deeds, as well as their converse [transgressions], must be spoken of [*nikraim*] in relation to human endeavor, that is to say, that they are inconceivable without human endeavor. But in the world to come, when all has been clarified, *there shall be one Lord, and His name one* (Zechariah 14:9), and all will lie in the hands of Heaven.[77]

It is impossible not to recognize that Mordecai Joseph's eschatological concepts run parallel to his general anarchistic doctrine. In respect of the latter, the determining criterion, as far as he is concerned, is the subjective sensation of empirical necessity that man experiences before an act. This sensation is a sign that the act is to be carried out since it signals the Will of God. However, this criterion is not the same as the determinative basis of Utopia, as translated into psychological terms: "Everything, including the fear of Heaven, will be in the hands of Heaven," a principle that will be given unqualified validity in the eschatological world.[78] The breakthrough of divine action becomes manifest in the untrammeled power of absolute compulsion. Human salvation begins when man is rendered defenseless before the divine power and thus embodies within himself complete lack of guilt for his actions.

The principle of messianic determinism is therefore structurally identical with normal anarchism, which may only become operative on select occasions in this historical world. In other words, religious anarchism in pre-eschatological history can be defined, as to its psychological character, as the occasional inroad of the absolute determinist character of the messianic age into the present premessianic world. That which is called sin reveals itself from this standpoint as anticipation of the situation in the messianic future. The messianic order must be an anarchistic disorder, a disorder that will be maintained by continuous divine guidance, a disorder in which God alone moves men like puppets on a string. Viewed in this light: "Israel's sins were that they sensed the illumination of God which was intended for the future. . . . Verily, all Israel's sins can be likened to the eating of unripe fruit and the absorption of light before the appropriate hour."[79]

This is sufficiently clear as to the eschatological order. It is a future condition dependent entirely upon the actions of God. But what Mordecai Joseph has to say about the present pre-eschatological situation is by no means as clear. Human actions, meritorious acts as well as sins, have to be "pronounced" (*nikraim*) in relation to human endeavor. The same Hebrew word (*nikraim*) that can be translated here as *pronounced* or *spoken of* is also used in relation to the pronouncing of the ineffable Name. Mordecai Joseph emphasizes the difference between the messianic age when the ineffable Name is pronounced as written, and the present world in which the pronounciation of the ineffable Name is not yet permitted—and it is a grave theological error to mix the two ages. It is precisely this that constituted the sin of Nadab and Abihu (Leviticus 10) "who believed that in the present world all is [already] in the hands of God."[80] But in reality, what is the situation in the existing, unredeemed world? Was the error of the sinners really so great?

At one point Mordecai Joseph remarks that the Talmudic saying concerning the freedom of man in the religious sphere "was only said in relation to the bounds of human understanding. But in truth [*be-emet*] everything, including the fear of Heaven, lies in the hands of Heaven . . . and the particular attribute of our father Isaac was to clarify and show that the fear of Heaven also lay in the hands of Heaven and that all the sins of Israel were exercised under divine providence, and for that reason His great Name is glorified and hallowed. And understand this, for it is very profound."[81] Here, too, a relationship is established between the concept of sin and determinism. Absolute determinism is not described here as the future achievement of the Utopian age, but as the concealed truth of the present.

The two ages, pre- and post-redemption, are therefore not absolute opposites, since the Utopian state of the world is already present but concealed in the pre-redemption period. Both sinner and penitent probably foresee this and their deep penitence is a partial anticipation of Utopia. Nothing real can happen in redemption since, at least since Adam's remorse, the Utopian state of the world has always been present, if latent, as the fundamental Utopian situation. Thus Utopia will allow the joyful and free recall of what was already there before. Such a conciliatory retrospective view of the past produces nothing new; raised into the spheres of the All-containing and All-embracing, it repeats the attitude of all individual penitents.

This view of Utopia does not promise to create a new heaven and a new earth, as does the apocalyptic doctrine. It merely promises a change of viewpoint by which all incidental iniquity will be seen ultimately, that is to say, in Utopia, as divinely ordained necessity. Utopia itself is not the illusion; the previous false reality will come to seem illusory through Utopia. This is important as a profound inner intensification of the Jewish conception of redemption. Redemption is an incident in man's concept of himself, an incident in religious awareness, not of outer reality. Those steeped in guilt will be freed from an awareness of their guilt in the messianic state of the world. Only in this way will they be redeemed.

The various, sometimes contradictory attitudes adopted by Mordecai Joseph to the problem of freedom from sin can be summarized in the following way:

1. The antinomian cry for *peccare fortiter*.

2. This is, however, counterbalanced by criteria that allow the sin to take place under conditions practically impossible to fulful and that virtually exclude legitimate freedom from sin.

3. A promise is made of general freedom from sin, but only in the future Utopia.

4. The whole doctrine is thus reduced to the removal of sins already committed.

We may conclude then that Mordechai Joseph's anarchistic thoughts move in contradictory directions on the axis of time, looking both forward and backward. Looking backward, Mordecai Joseph offers open-handed redemption for all past sins, that is to say, those committed both by the individual and collectively. According to his interpretation of history, there is nothing to prevent this, whether it concerns the life of the individual or the people as a whole. In his total picture of the past, sins are converted by the divine Almighty, removing all human autonomy.

This overwhelming concept of the Divine Will is found in the Utopian doctrine, too, which also depends on the basic concept of absolute divine intervention and the consequent religious irresponsibility of mankind. The certainty of the absolute infallibility of all human activities is common both retrospectively to the past and to the Utopia that will be established in the future.

But Mordecai Joseph's negative attitude to the present brings him to the conclusion that anarchism is premature and inappropriate to the present day. He cannot recognize any validity in the irrationality of what makes up the present day and, in practice, antinomian action is at present impossible. So a revolution cannot occur and all these wild thoughts must remain a fantastic incursion into the unreal and a hopeless attempt to establish new values for what has already gone before: this is what makes Mordecai Joseph so exceptional. It is his rare capacity for suffering the chaotic without perishing within it.

NOTES

1. Gershom Scholem, "Religiöse Autorität und Mystik," *Eranos-Jahrbuch* 26 (1957), 243–78.

2. The so-called Izbica-Radzin dynasty, about which there has now appeared a short Hebrew account, which includes the most important biographical details, by S. Z. Shragai (in *Sefer ha-Baal Shemtov*, ed. J. Maimon, [Jerusalem, 1960], pp. 153–201). The author is in possession of many oral traditions, which he has used all too sparingly. The essay is dependent for many of its details on Hayyim Simcha Leiner's dynastic sketch *Dor Yesharim* (Lublin, 1909). This book is difficult to obtain today, but a second, expanded edition was published (Lublin, 1924) from which the compromising Izbica-Kotzk affair has been omitted.

3. The works of Jacob Leiner (d. 1878), son of Mordecai Joseph, already show a marked departure from the radical ideas of his father. The briefly formulated, keen lines of thought of the father are elaborated and embedded in endless quotations from the *Zohar* and related literature. There is, in general, a noticeable tendency to tone down the more radical expressions to make them more acceptable. Mordecai Joseph's terminology, however, is essentially retained in his son's books. Certain lines of thought are still kept alive, although often somewhat tempered, in the rich literary remains of Zadok Rabinowitz ha-Kohen, one of Mordecai Joseph's pupils. Nevertheless, he often deletes the specific terminology of the master. I understand from reliable sources that at least one work of the rich literary remains of Zadok ha-Kohen, *Ṣidkat ha-Ṣaddik* (Lublin, 1902), was censored by a Hasidic committee before publication. Well-informed Hasidim today should be able to say whether certain parts of *Ṣidkat ha-Ṣaddik* were suppressed. In fact, the following paragraphs are lacking in the printed version: 54, 69, 74–75, 105, 146, 162–63. I do not know whether his other works were also censored. The small popular biography of Zadok ha-Kohen by A. J. Bromberg (Jerusalem, 1954) does everything possible not to damage its hero.

4. See, for example, *Siaḥ Sarfei Kodesh* by Y. K. Kadish, (Lodz, 1928), 4:84.

5. There can be hardly any doubt that the book was in fact printed by the well-known Viennese printer Adalbert della Torre, as shown on the title page. We are familiar with this printer's other works. Vienna also appears as the town of origin in M. Steinschneider's *Hebräische Bibliographie* (1863), 6:59, reference note 170. In order to explain the book's unusual place of origin, which must have puzzled Hasidic circles, it has been suggested that the printing was actually done in Jozefow and that Vienna appears on the title page simply to deceive the Russian censorship (see Shragai, *op. cit.*, p. 167). The assumption made in the text of my lecture that the reason for the choice of this unusual place of printing is to be sought in the refusal of the Jewish printers in the East is merely a conjecture I cannot substantiate from any oral or written tradition.

6. See Shragai in the paper mentioned above, with his euphemistic formulation, *danuhu bi-serefah*.

7. In this connection it must be freely recognized that Walden was an enthusiastic supporter of Menaḥem Mendel Kotzker, as is repeatedly emphasized in the pages

devoted to the latter; see also I. Alfasi, *Ha-Rabbi mi-Kotzk* (Hebrew) (Tel Aviv, 1952), p. 65.

8. *Siaḥ Sarfei Kodesh* (Lodz, 1928), 3:15, contains a remark by Mordecai Joseph that he was (a pupil) with the Kotzker for seven years.

9. M. Buber, *Schriften zum Chassidismus*, Munich, 1963, p. 145.

10. The original edition of Hayyim Simcha Leiner's *Dor Yesharim* (1909) describes the Izbica-Kotzk conflict, though it is generally softened down. The two heroes part in mutual forgiveness, according to Shragai. On the other hand, voluminous Kotzk tradition speaks much more openly about the matter.

11. The Hebrew translations also use verbal forms formed from the same root, such as *or*, light, as for example, *meir*, literally "(God) will illuminate."

12. *Mei ha-Shiloaḥ* (Vienna, 1860), 1:43b.

13. These were not lacking in middle Hasidism: see the polemical utterances of R. Hayyim of Volozhin in his book *Nefesh ha-Ḥayyim* (Vilna, 1824), 14a.

14. Each individual soul has a duty, *avodah*, that is personal to him (*Mei ha-Shiloaḥ* [Lublin, 1922], 2:97, 120); man should be prepared to sacrifice his life for this individual *miṣvah*, although, according to the general legal decisions about martyrdom, this should not be undertaken except in the case of compulsion to serve false gods, fornication, or murder (1:57b, 62a). The author's views about a man's vows are an essential part of his individualism; he counsels personal vows. Whereas the laws of the Torah are of general application and unalterable (*niṣrakhim be-khol et be-khol zeman le-khol adam*), vows are individual, conditioned by time and place (*mekkabelim shinnui le-fi ha-et ve-ha-zeman*), (1:54b). Both methods of compliance with duty, laws and vows, are not assumed to be antithetical, but complementary (ibid).

15. The idea of the Divine Will being conditioned by time and place is brought out strongly in Mordecai Joseph's attitude to prophecy. All prophets were conditioned by time (*ke-fi ha-et ve-ha-zeman*), and "Moses fully understood that prophecy was only (valid) for a certain period and that God will determine otherwise in the future" (1:54b).

16. See G. Scholem, *Ursprung und Anfänge der Kabbala* (Berlin, 1962), pp. 407–19.

17. The theory of religious anarchism is invariably limited solely to the Jews as a people: see 1:32a.

18. Ibid., f. 53b.

19. Ibid., f. 17b.

20. Gen. 48:15.

21. The sense of the passage is no longer entirely clear even in the Hebrew text.

22. B. Shabbat 22b.

23. Vol. 1, second foliation, f. 12b.

24. Ibid.

25. 1:14b–15a. A typological trisection of the tribe of Israel in 1:47a.

26. *Gader* and *seyag*, i.e., fence, do not mean for Mordecai Joseph a fence around the law, as in rabbinic terminology, but more frequently self-identification with the law, because of an interpretation of the law that stresses its restrictive function. The other versions of the saying, B. T. *Bava Kamma* 60b, *Bava Bathra* 100b and *Yevamoth* 76b, are ignored by Mordecai Joseph. For Mordecai Joseph's regal anarchy, see also 1:60a and, especially, 2:36 and 46.

27. The motivation for this is perhaps indicated in the introduction and approbation of R. Jacob Leiner's *Sidrei Taharoth*, the work of his son.

28. On many of the points dealt with here, Shragai refers to his paper quoted above. As opposed to this useful summary, his essay "Redemption in Izbica-Radzyn Hasidism" (which appeared in Hebrew in *Chassidismus und Zion*, ed S. Federbusch [Jerusalem, 1963], pp. 88–92) must be regarded as a failure, since the author analyzes the idea of redemption practically exclusively from a geographical viewpoint (Palestine, Zion). This narrowing of the eschatological perspective is most unfruitful in relation to the

Izbica Hasidic attitude, since the geographical aspect of Jewish redemption plays no role in it.

29. Compare, however, this reason for the title in *Bet Ya'akov* (Warsaw, 1890), 1:92: "the waters of Shiloah that go softly, but are deep."

30. 1:16a.

31. Ibid., f. 15b.

32. Ibid., f. 33a.

33. Ibid.

34. For instance, *keviut beli ḥayyim* (2:57), "determining (or deciding upon) without living." *Omek raṣon* is identical with *shoresh ha-ḥayyim* (2:53); see also 1:25b.

35. 1:52a.

36. Scholem, "Religiöse Autorität und Mystik," *Eranos-Jahrbuch* 26 (1957): 275; an earlier formulation by Scholem in his "Le mouvement sabbataïste en Pologne," *Revue de l'Histoire des Religions*, 164 (1953): 61.

37. See Bab. Talmud, *Berakhot* 63a; the antinomian tendency is remarked upon very acutely by Rashi in his commentary on this passage.

38. *Hevinu*, which is used as a *terminus technicus* for *binah*, spiritual understanding.

39. 1:52a; the Talmud quotation at the end: B. *Berakhot* 8a.

40. [The authoritative legal code of the Jews.]

41. 2:54.

42. On this problem, see E. Benz, "Vision und Führung," *Eranos-Jahrbuch* 31 (1962): 117–69.

43. The fourfold self-examination (1:17b) or the two- or threefold (1:25b) cannot be described here. A touchstone mentioned frequently in Mordecai Joseph's writings is that the content of the illumination brings with it neither advantages nor desire on the part of the illuminee, so that (in the Kantian sense) the individual remains uninterested (1:38a, 7b). The detailed process of the method of self-examination, known in the sources as "the three points of the Torah" (1:6b, 37b, 45b, 62a), which also form an exceptional element in the historical development of Mordecai Joseph's teachings, must await further detailed investigation.

44. See F. C. Porter, "The Yecer Hara," *Yale Biblical and Semitic Studies*, 1901, pp. 91–156; S. Schechter, *Some Aspects of Rabbinic Theology* (London, 1909), pp. 242–92; Strack-Billerbeck, *Kommentar zum Neuen Testament aus Talmud und Midrasch* 3:330 ff, 4 (i): 466; R. J. Z. Werblowsky in the collected volume *Das Gewissen*, Studies by the C. J. Jung Institute (Zürich, 1958), pp. 104–10.

45. B. *Kiddushin* 21b.

46. Gen. 38.

47. 1:62a.

48. As Zadok ha-Kohen, Mordecai Joseph's pupil, writes in *Ṣidkat ha-Ṣaddik* (Lublin, 1902), p. 61, in reference to the Talmudic saying: "God spared [from punishment] those acting under compulsion," B. *Bava Kamma* 28b.

49. 1:14b.

50. Num. 25:1–4.

51. 1:54a.

52. Ibid.

53. Ibid. Joseph is contrasted with Judah by Mordecai Joseph (1:14b).

54. In the sense of the Talmudic expression (B. *Niddah* 61b): "The commandments will become untenable in the [messianic] future," a phrase Mordecai Joseph often quotes.

55. B. *Shabbat* 138b. The sentence has no eschatological meaning in the Talmudic context, but was later applied messianically.

56. Vol 1, second foliation, fol. 13b.

57. See, inter alia, F. G. Moore, *Judaism* (Cambridge, Mass., 1927), 1:507–34; E. K.

Dietrich, *Die Umkehr im Alten Testament und im Judentum* (Stuttgart, 1936), especially pp. 350–427. The classical concept of reversal in postbiblical Judaism is codified in Maimonides' *Hilkhot Teshuvah* (in his *Mishneh Torah*). The further development, in the later Middle Ages, of the concept of reversal and the practices of repentance, are essentially of a mysterious character; see: Scholem, *Jüdische Mystik*, pp. 113 ff. A milder protest against the mystical changes in the practice of repentance is to be found in a halakhic responsum by Ezekiel Landau (d. 1793), which is printed in his *Noda bi-Yehuda* (first version, *Oraḥ Ḥayyim*, para. 35).

58. 2:10.

59. 2:9.

60. See Scholem, *Jüdische Mystik*, pp. 113 ff.

61. B. *Shabbat* 77b.

62. Vol 1, second foliation, ff. 12b–13a.

63. See B. *Yoma* 86b. This Talmudic passage merely says that action arising from rash sin is turned into a praiseworthy deed by the repentance of the perpetrator; the original Talmudic passage does not refer to the messianic future.

64. 2:111.

65. [The biblical text reads: "But from the tree of knowledge of good and evil thou shalt not eat."]

66. [Literally: "as the scales peel off garlic," *ki-kelipot ha-shum*.]

67. 1:4a.

68. Vol. 1, second foliation, f. 1b.

69. Even in the classical minimal program of the Babylonian teacher Mar Samuel (of the third century), who saw that the sole difference between historical and messianic times lay in the relief of Israel in the future from enslavement among foreign powers (see B. *Berakhot* 34a).

70. Vol 1, second foliation, f. 17b.

71. 1:16b.

72. "Zum Verständnis der messianischen Idee im Judentum," *Eranos-Jahrbuch* 28 (1959): 212–14.

73. B. *Berakhot* 33b.

74. See further my Hebrew essay: "The Religious Determinism of Mordecai Joseph Leiner," in the *Y. F. Baer Jubilee Volume* (Jerusalem, 1960), pp. 431–46.

75. [In rabbinic Judaism the biblical name of God, YHWH, is no longer pronounced and *Adonai* is used instead. Hence, the resulting ineffable name of God became a favorite subject for mystical contemplation. In order to make things clear in this translation, I have paraphrased into the third person the personified and "I" form of the divine Name in the original text (even in a quotation from the Babylonian Talmud, *Pesaḥim*, 50a).]

76. *Berakhot* 33b.

77. Vol. 1, second foliation ff. 14a and 14b.

78. Both criteria are mentioned as identical theses in one sentence in 2:130.

79. 2:9; regarding the Sabbatian precursor of this idea, see Scholem's remark in "Gut und Böse in der Kabbala", *Eranos-Jahrbuch* 30 (1961): 59, n. 24.

80. 1:14b.

81. 1:8a.

Sense and Nonsense in Defining Judaism—The Strange Case of Naḥman of Brazlav

The theologian, be he Jewish or Christian, perhaps even the agnostic philosopher, will be strongly inclined to define the phenomenon of Judaism in the singular, so as to enter into conceptual abstractions; he may be professionally obliged to do so. But the historian will prefer using the plural and talk of the phenomena of Judaism, thus remaining within the domain of strictly descriptive scholarship.

In the last analysis, any attempt to define that elusive "essence of Judaism" that Jews and Gentiles, philo-Semites and anti-Semites have tried long to establish is doomed to failure if it takes as its starting point anything other than the fullness of all available historical phenomena. The historian, as distinct from the theologian, has a powerful case against overhasty generalizations. He will claim not to know the full facts. The fullness of Judaism, he says, has not realized itself. His argument will be a double one: Against the Christian theologian he will argue that there occurred no noticeable end of Judaism with the birth of Christianity. Jewry still remained a changing, developing entity whose totality had not been exhausted with the emergence of the daughter religion. And the historian will have to argue against the Jewish theologian that he (the historian) cannot easily assimilate into his empirical method the concept of a revelation as a supernatural act that embraced once and for all the totality of all correct Jewish views and practice, and from which every Jewish phenomenon will have to be derived in order to be justified. The historian will therefore find no sense in a definition of Judaism that arrogates that totality. He will instead insist on the obligation of the historian to assemble the facts without imposing on them any grandiose, monolithic scheme. His main concern will remain at the level of empirical phenomena—facts, views, happenings—which he will attempt to analyze in their ordinary operation of cause and effect. He will then readily confess his failure to discover a totality of Jewish phenomena, and will be glad to hand over the material he established to theologians and philosophers for free use by them. But he will be reluctant to attempt to do their job and define Judaism *in toto.*

The historian, without the dramatic beginning of a revelation and without the crowning act of a redemption, is by definition doomed to have no guide in his quest for the essence of Judaism but the empirical existence of the Jewish people, and what is inherent in this existence. Since historical prediction is precluded for him, he will find no justification for the superimposition in advance of any definition or any scheme of Jewish history. For him there will be only piecemeal meaningfulness in Jewish history and this piecemeal meaningfulness is likely to defy any definition of Judaism as it is likely to defy any philosophical construction in history.

As Professor Katz of the Hebrew University of Jerusalem has said, modern generalizations regarding various religions as the "essence" of Christianity, the "essence" of Judaism, the "essence" of Buddhism or of Zen do reveal certain insights into some characteristics of the religions in question. Penetrating as these insights may be, they hardly enlighten anyone who is interested not in understanding the respective religions, but in deciding which one to believe in, like the heathen king in Yehuda Ha-Levi's medieval *Kuzari*. Summoned before such a heathen king to present their case, the modern protagonists of the "essences" of various religions would no doubt be dismissed with some such pronouncement as "You have said many nice things about your own religion and some nasty things about other religions, but you have not touched upon what I should like to know—which of the religions is the true religion?" Indeed, one cannot help feeling that the "essences" of Judaism, Christianity, etc., were invited in order to hide the embarrassment caused by the fact that no one seemed to care any more for the real medieval question: which one is the true religion? I would hasten to add that this was already the case in the nineteenth and early twentieth centuries and the imaginary conversation made up by Katz is thus the superb summary of the "Essence of Judaism" period, of which Leo Baeck was an eloquent speaker and my own late teacher, Julius Guttmann, an outstanding scholarly representative. Baeck's generation—perhaps with the exception of Ahad Haam—was German-oriented, and most of its literary output was written in that language.

The quest for a general understanding of the essence of Judaism seems strange to a generation brought up to be specialists in the various branches of Jewish studies. Our own generation does not find it easy to understand the tenor of that "Essence of Judaism" period.

It is characteristic that when Guttmann's magisterial German work *Philosophie des Judentums* was published in an English translation some years ago—a book that, in spite of its title, is not a philosophical tract, but a historical survey of Jewish philosophical literature—the subject in its title was slightly changed, presumably by the editor. The title is no longer *Philosophy of Judaism*, but *Philosophies of Judaism*, in the plural. The editor, Professor Werblowsky of Jerusalem, explains in his introduction that Guttmann had nowhere explicitly stated his own views regarding a definition of Judaism; as a historian rather than a systematic thinker, he preferred his "phenomenology of Judaism" to remain implicit in his work. But Guttmann was far from being a historical relativist and firmly believed in an essence of Judaism, the proper understanding of which would be not merely descriptive but normative. It would provide a yardstick by which to measure the essential Jewishness or, alternatively, the degree of un-Jewish deviation in ideas, doctrines, and acts of Jews over the millenia.

This change of the singular *philosophy* into the plural *philosophies*, which remains unmentioned in the otherwise full introduction, is a typical example of the influence of the new school. Whereas the previous generation that found so much sense in defining Judaism wrote in German, the post–"Essence of Judaism" school writes in Hebrew and lives predominantly in Israel. It has no theoreticians like Leo Baeck of the previous generation. Its adherents are all practicing historians of the Jewish people, and their greatest representative is perhaps

Scholem, who is miles away from anything like an attempt to define Judaism as a philosophical abstraction.

Guttman's editor, Werblowsky, hints at his own and his generation's position when he writes that philosophers and historians may be at variance on the question of the nature, or even the very existence, of constant factors or structures making up an "essence" of Judaism. The new historical consciousness that holds that defining Judaism is a hopeless operation will particularly flourish in Israel far away from the apologetical necessities of a diaspora on the defensive. It is by no means confined geographically to Israel, nor are all Israeli historians of the Jewish people committed to the views of the new school. For instance, Baer, one of the leading historians of our generation, now a professor emeritus in Jerusalem, who probably shared for some time, at least theoretically, the relativism of the new generation, became a refugee from the more violent shores of the new school in order to retire in old age to his own image of Judaism, which he defined and redefined.

Notwithstanding such important defections from the new way of thinking about Judaism, the post-"Essence" school thinks in terms of historical, psychological, and sociological relativism. Its yardstick is no longer the concept of doctrinal Judaism but the living reality of the Jewish people with its thousand faces. Its motto is *nihil Judaicum a me alienum puto*, which one could freely translate by saying that "nothing Jewish is un-Jewish for us."

Naḥman of Brazlav would have been eminently ineligible for the "Essence of Judaism" school. The difficulty is the following: In the Middle Ages, the conflict between Church and Synagogue was partly concentrated in the argument about the advent of the Messiah: whether the event had already occurred or was expected to take place at some future date. When, with the waning of the dogmatic attitude, the "Essence of Judaism" attitude came to replace it, the futuristic Messiah expectation in Judaism remained axiomatic. Of course, the messianic movements of the Sabbatian type could be taken as a strong argument against the generalization that the grammatical form of all Jewish Messianic manifestations must inevitably be in the future tense. The counterargument of the "Essence of Judaism" school to this is that the Sabbatian type of Messianic movement did not remain within the Jewish fold. After Scholem's researches, this statement is only partly true. Naḥman of Brazlav exhibits a clear case of nonfuturistic messianic consciousness within the Jewish fold. Of course, his was a borderline case, but borderline cases are notoriously instructive.

Naḥman of Brazlav was born in 1772 in Podolia as the great-grandson of Israel Baalshem, the founder of the Hasidic movement. Thus his family background could not have given him a better chance for a successful leadership role within Hasidism, but he made a mess of it and never achieved celebrity in his lifetime. His life was a failure: the number of his followers remained a trickle when Hasidism in general went from strength to strength and rapidly conquered the Jewish population in Podolia and the Ukraine.

He settled in a small town, Zlatopolia, which he had to flee in view of the incessant maltreatment of himself and his followers by a social campaign organized against him by a competitor, another Hasidic leader, Aryeh Leib the so-called Old Man of Shpola. Eventually Naḥman settled in Brazlav, whose Jewish population either followed him or was favorably inclined toward him. Significantly, the rabbi of Brazlav was also a follower of Naḥman. Naḥman died of consumption in 1810, at the age of thirty-eight. My task here is not to summarize his biography, but rather to analyze his indebtedness to his possible literary sources, disentangle the complexities of his thought, and to survey the most intense inner conflicts of this remarkable Hasidic leader: his partial solutions in those moments when he saw himself in messianic garb—only the next moment to mock himself and the fantasies of his most imaginative mind in an abysmal torment darkened by self-suspicion. He remained sensitive to this self-suspicion till the end and continued to argue about it with himself all his life. This is the most painful element in Naḥman's whole cast of mind, a character trait that endears him to us more than his messianic delusions of grandeur.

His work is that of a considerable genius, and he is one of the most conspicuous and impressive figures among the host of theologically displaced persons who found a precarious refuge in the emergency camp of Hasidism. And he is a man of fierce intelligence, persistently responsive to the endless challenges of an unconventional religious urge.

This controversial *Ṣaddik*, whose alleged blasphemies horrified the Hasidic establishment, had a rarefied nervous sensitivity that one is tempted to call metaphysical sensitivity, coupled with the sense of being an outsider, which he no doubt was nearly everywhere. A lack of emotional reticence gave his thought and writing an unmistakably autobiographical or rather confessional character. One would venture the statement that whatever Naḥman says or writes, he says and writes about himself—so endless is his introspective self-centeredness. Even in middle age, Naḥman often seemed touchingly immature, like a defiant schoolboy surrounded by disapproving grown-ups. Perhaps even his nearest, most devoted, and most obstinate followers became alarmed sometimes by the occasional capriciousness of his life. He would suddenly go, on the spur of the moment, on long journeys, in absolute incognito.

His passion was to read and interpret the temperatures of his own mind; and in doing so he drew the fever chart of the Jewry of an epoch. It indicates a panorama of restless Judaism, of philosophical and rationalistic scepticism on the one hand (in which the medieval rationalists have as great a share as the "Enlightened" of the eighteenth century), and of turbulent religious crisis on the other, in which in the aftermath of heretical Sabbatianism, suspected and half-admitted ultrairrationalist heresies raise their heads. Indeed, much of Naḥman's work reads like the self-diagnosis of a desperate physician who, suffering the disease on his patients' behalf, comes to prescribe a cure that he himself cannot accomplish: to live by paradoxical faith. But we shall come to that later.

Naḥman made frequent remarks to his disciples and followers about his emotional, religious, and sexual predicament with a frankness clearly denoting a need to share intimacies. Thus it is quite likely that his religious ruminations were intensified by sexual fantasies. An old, by now dead, member of the Brazlav sect in Jerusalem told me, some twenty years ago, that there was a manuscript in his hands—its authorship unclear—describing Naḥman's sexual temptations. This manuscript has never been published, but from some passages in the printed books of Brazlav, all of them heavily censored by an internal, Brazlavic censorship, we are able to reconstruct the types of temptation, though not their details or the degree of Naḥman's success in resisting them. We realize, of course, that Naḥman is quoted as having said: "There are many wagons full of women. And they are all my portions of cohabitation."

His inquiring mind looked for new symbols for expressing his amazement about his own behavior and he stumbled on the mythical stone called, in Hebrew, *even shethiyah*, which was, according to Talmudic tradition, the foundation stone of the universe. According to the rabbinic view, this stone, though the Jerusalem sanctuary was built upon it, was neither stable nor stationary, but would sometimes move upward, sometimes downward. What better symbol for Naḥman's own unstable mind than this mythical stone? And even more, traditional mystical literature had seen in the stone the keyword for the tenth *Sefirah*, with which Naḥman came to identify himself. His own psychological drama could be explained in terms of the ascending and descending movements of the Jerusalem stone. Even the messianic aspect of his own elevated status could be hinted at since the last *Sefirah* is also called "kingdom," David's kingdom, which, of course, invites messianic associations.

The life story of Naḥman of Brazlav as told in Nathan Sternherz's *Ḥayyei Moharan*, exhibits some features of the biographical pattern found in hagiological literature about many of the *Ṣaddikim*, the charismatic leaders of the Hasidic movement. It differs strikingly from the stereotypical biography of the rabbi or rabbinical scholar of the period. The rabbi's life, as depicted in the typical biography, develops in an uninterrupted ascending line of increasing knowledge and fame—fame representing the social recognition of his scholastic eminence. According to their biographers, rabbis begin their careers as child prodigies and their subsequent rise is rapid. Their later scholastic distinction is already latent in the achievement of the child of tender age who arouses shame in his schoolmates and amazement in his teachers. According to this pattern, the great rabbi, after having exhausted the scholarly resources of his home environment, usually migrates in search of further knowledge from one famous academy to another still more famous. The career of a rabbi in this literature is the spectacular, though unsurprising, unfolding of his inherent intellectual capacity, which was never in doubt from the very beginning.

By contrast, the element of surprise is one of the most

significant motifs in the biographical literature dealing with the Hasidic leaders. While in the biography of the rabbinical scholar the point of departure is early childhood and there is then a steady development and gradual fulfilment of the confident expectation of his family and his early environment, the fundamental fact about the life of the great *Ṣaddikim* is that they have a turning point. Their partly legendary biographies often represent them as leading a kind of double life until the great day of their self-revelation, the technical term for which is *gilluy* or *hithgalluth*. Usually this self-revelation is not conceived as a sudden event, happening overnight or in one single day, but as a process that takes place in a comparatively short period. Prior to this change in their lives, the *Ṣaddikim* are conscious of their latent value, but refuse to divulge it; and following some inner compulsion, they don the mask of the common man in order to cover up the hidden life within them. Neither in the legendary biography of Israel Baalshem nor in later Hasidic hagiography do we find the radical form of the saint's religious double life as it occurs in some Christian, mainly Russian Orthodox, hagiographical literature, where sometimes the saint poses as a sinner in order to conceal his spirituality, and thus avoids public adulation—a well-known type of hidden saintliness that has countless variations in Christian tradition. The Hasidic *Ṣaddik* shuns actual sin but deliberately shrouds himself in commonness in order to deceive his potential admirers: for instance, he decides not to go regularly to synagogue, or to neglect some of his religious studies. This course of action successfully accomplishes the aim of avoiding social acclaim. The virtue of self-concealment (*hester*) is thus not simply the practice of the religious virtue of humility: the *Ṣaddik-to-be* harbors a hidden arrogance and a vague sense of expectation. The psychological dialectics of humility and pride are here at work.

The *hester* (or self-concealment) of Israel Baalshem, which led to his self-revelation at the age of thirty-six, consisted of accepting menial tasks that led him to the utter seclusion of the Carpathian mountains or to the common jobs of a religious vagabond life. At the age of thirty-six he lets fall the mask and the second part of his life commences in unexpectedly sharp contrast to the first. The turning point, however, is not an absolute break followed by a completely new beginning, but the continuation of his earlier, hidden spiritual life now revealed to the public and thus fully recognized and appreciated. His social position is reversed after the termination of the *hester*. He becomes a central figure of the community in which he had hitherto figured, not as a sinner, but as a rather despised marginal member. He can now trade isolation and obscurity for fully acknowledged charismatic leadership.

Many *Ṣaddikim* who attempted to repeat the biographical pattern of Israel Baalshem, the founder, were to have his socioreligious experience and they sharply divided their lives into the two periods of *hester* and *gilluy*, or concealment and revelation. After the period of isolation and self-engineered social rejection, there follows the period of public acceptance on a level commensurate with the real religious standing of the hitherto misunderstood, erroneously undervalued *Ṣaddik*, who himself had quite deliberately caused the misunderstanding.

I would emphasize that I can see no connection between the dichotomous life of the Hasidic *Ṣaddik* as outlined here and the earlier folkloristic pre-Hasidic concept of the so-called thirty six hidden *Ṣaddikim* on whom the fate of the world is supposed to rest. Saints of this type live incognito all their lives. Their full-time concealment to the very end is an essential feature of their calling. The religious idea of the "hidden" or "concealed" *Ṣaddik* of Jewish folklore does not involve voluntary self-concealment transformed into public recognition, which is so characteristic of the typical biography of the Hasidic *Ṣaddik* from Israel Baalshem onwards. The element of public surprise is entirely lacking in the concept of the hidden *Ṣaddik* of pre-Hasidic folklore. Moreover, in many variations on the theme the hidden *Ṣaddikim* are themselves not aware of their special status. They may lead their simple lives as shoemakers or tailors without ever discovering that they are of the elect. The hidden arrogance of the self-concealing *Ṣaddik* in the first phase of his life is absent in the folkloristic concept. This, together with the fact that the folklore's hidden *Ṣaddik* never reaches a second phase of public acknowledgment, makes it quite obvious that the two religious types, the thirty-six hidden *Ṣaddikim* of folkloristic origin and the self-concealed young *Ṣaddikism* of the Hasidic hagiographical tradition, are not to be identified with one another.

How would Naḥman of Brazlav fit into the pattern of the dichotomous life of the typical Hasidic leader? Are we permitted to pose this question at all?

Although the legendary biography of Israel Baalshem did not appear in print until 1815, five years after Naḥman of Brazlav's death, we certainly must assume that at least the general pattern of his great-grandfather's life was not unfamiliar to him. The *hester/gilluy* dichotomy of his great-grandfather's life must have been passed on to him through family traditions. Indeed, he habitually alluded to himself as *Ṣaddik nistar* or *Ṣaddik ne'elam*: a concealed *Ṣaddik*. Although the term does occur occasionally in the plural (*Ṣaddikim nistarim*), one could make out a good case that the plural is employed in order to mislead. The undiluted Brazlavic doctrine is mono-Ṣaddikism, i.e., that there exists only one true *Ṣaddik nistar* who is Naḥman himself. This, he thought, was generally true, with the exception, perhaps, of Levi Yitzḥak of Berdyczów, his lifelong friend in nearly all his adversities. All the other *Ṣaddikim* were in his view either downright fakes, *Ṣaddikim shel skeker*, false *Ṣaddikim*, anti-*Ṣaddikim*, or at best, sparkling distortions of the one brilliant image, minor half-truths, irrelevant exaggerations, mere shadows or poor substitutes of the one real *Ṣaddik*, Naḥman, who lives incognito. Whether the nature of his self-concealment was voluntary or involuntary is a pivotal question in Brazlav theology. The light of Naḥman has to remain hidden and many a good reason is adduced in Brazlavic thought why this should be so.

The temporary concealment will be replaced by a second phase, the phase of *gilluy*, fully in accordance with the biographical pattern he inherited from his great-grandfather. But a remarkable point is added in Brazlav to the commencement of the second phase, namely, that this will coincide in time with the advent of the Messiah. The hidden *Ṣaddik* remains in his paradoxical situation, a misunderstood and therefore even persecuted man, until the day breaks and his true character can be revealed within the framework of the all-inclusive messianic revelation. This messianic timing for the start of the second phase in Naḥman's life is most significant. Is it simply coincidence in time? One cannot help thinking that the coincidence in time represents coincidence in person and that Naḥman will in fact be identical with the long-awaited Messiah. During the period of concealment he kept hidden his most important characteristic: Naḥman's secret messianic nature. His rehabilitation at the end of the *hester* will be part of total world rehabilitation. (Significantly, the messianic times, according to Brazlav, include the total resolution of all logical contradictions.)

Here we come to another Brazlavic departure from the well-established Hasidic idea of the *Ṣaddik*'s self-concealment. In the first phase of his life, in the *hester*, the *Ṣaddik* appears to be somewhat careless regarding his religious duties, in order to create a smoke screen around himself, but he never actually sins in order to make others believe that he is the sinner. Only in Brazlavic thought does actual sin seem to belong to the qualifications of successful self-concealment: there is no better incognito for a real *Ṣaddik* than to appear a sinner, or, better still, there is no safer concealment than the incognito of actual sin.

This is how sin became in Brazlav as among the Sabbatian heretics, a necessary accompaniment of the hidden Messiah, who is the true, the only true *Ṣaddik* long before his final revelation as the messianic redeemer. His sin does not remain undiscovered and he has to go through the calvary of persecution, abandonment, and social ostracism. He becomes the center of violent controversy in every social sphere. His unpopularity is but another aspect of his self-concealment, his avoidance, for a time, of being celebrated as the true Messiah.

As in all matters of importance, Naḥman maintained a strange ambivalence toward himself: he alternated between extreme self-abhorrence and unbelievable self-esteem. He said with no little self-irony of his own charismatic power and its apparent dialectics: "If I had a Master like you have, I would go to him, even if I had to walk on my own two legs. But as to the return journey from him—I would run!" We have to assume that many of his followers could not have agreed with him more, to judge from the frightening dimensions of their defection from the fold. Thus the Master alternates between calling himself the lowest of sinners and alluding to himself with messianic imagery. This in itself may be a symptom of his own—as it is called nowadays in psychological parlance—unsolved identity crisis. Was he really the Messiah? Could he be the Messiah in spite of everything that points so poignantly against this possibility?

Regarding his messianic role too, Naḥman oscillates between despondency and irrational optimism. His followers may dwindle, but his automessianic allusions multiply and he attempts to establish for his followers what he cannot establish for himself: the certainty of his own messianic calling. He would not settle for less, and he, therefore, urgently demands of his followers absolute faith in the paradox of his messianic vocation, grossly disfigured by the critical objections to him, all of them so painfully valid. It is an enigmatic state of affairs, to say the least, it is a mock order for the world, a caricature of logic and consistency to believe in a Messiah such as Naḥman. And yet he made his total claim by persistently alluding to himself as holding the monopoly of salvation, as being the only true *Ṣaddik*, whose messianic function was above reasonable doubt, but who hoped against hope that his own doubt in himself could be counterbalanced by his followers' faith in him. The mortal vulnerability of the potential Messiah has thus become the very backbone of the paradoxical faith in his spiritual strength and ultimate truth. The dialectician of faith is different from the simple believer: the latter is unconscious of any possible alternative, and therefore cannot doubt. The dialectician, on the other hand, is conscious of the fact that alternatives do exist or might exist, so that even if what he believes happens to be true, he cannot avoid the realization that he does not believe it for this reason, but because of his free choice unsupported by evidence; since there are as many valid arguments against it as there are for it. Therefore, the dialectician's faith in anything—including himself—is a composite one: it is a blend of utter logical barbarity and of endless religious refinement. It takes a great deal of sophistication to achieve that. The generous tributes to the simple, naïve, and unsophisticated believers whom Naḥman admired not for their affinities with himself, but for being utterly different from him illuminate his own complicated, despairingly complicated, religious predicament.

Naḥman was not unique among contemporary Hasidic leaders in assuming messianic postures. In its first half-century or so Hasidism was blissfully unaware of the messianic potential of its leaders, the *Ṣaddikim*. But by the beginning of the nineteenth century the messianic competition among a variety of *Ṣaddikim* started and may have well colored or even triggered off the fight between the Old Man of Shpola and Naḥman of Brazlav. The price paid for the messianic race of the *Ṣaddikim* was the splintering of the image of the one Messiah into many minor facets, producing a whole galaxy of candidates for messianic office. Take Israel of Rizhin, for instance, a later contender for the messianic title, of whom Scholem wrote that he was nothing but another Jacob Frank in his quest for power who had achieved the miracle of remaining an orthodox Jew. I may add: Doesn't Israel of Rizhin, in turn, strike us, with his golden throne, his royal household, his transparent messianic allusions to himself, as an extrovert parody of Naḥman of Brazlav? But neither he nor any of the others fought more desperately for the messianic crown than Naḥman and none with less self-confidence.

The following nightmare was related by Naḥman about a year before his death:

Kislev 1809, here at Brazlav; a dream: I was in my house and no one came to see me. As this seemed strange to me, I went into the second room but there, too, there was not a soul. I went to the big house and to the *Beth ha-midrash*, the house of study, but no one was there either. I made up my mind to go out. I went and saw that people were standing there in circles, whispering together; some were mocking me, others laughing at me, and some just being rude. Even my own men were against me, whispering secrets, being rude and so on. I called one of my men and asked him: "What is this all about?" And he replied: "How could you have done such a thing? Is it possible that you have committed such a monstrous sin?" But I had no idea why they were mocking me. I asked that person to assemble some of my men. He went away and I never saw him again.

I asked myself what I ought to do and decided to journey to some other country. When I arrived there, people were standing together talking, for there too, they knew about it. So I decided to stay in a forest. With five of my men who had joined me, I went to the forest and we stayed there. Whenever we needed food we would send one of the men to buy for us what we wanted. And I used to ask him if the turmoil had died down and he would answer no, for it was still raging. While we were staying there, an old man called for me and said that he had something to talk over with me. I went with him and he started speaking to me. "Would a man like you do such a thing?" he said. "How is it that you are not ashamed before your ancestors, before your grandfather Naḥman of Horodenka and your great-grandfather, Israel Baalshem, blessed be his memory; and how is it that you are not ashamed before the Law of Moses and the holy Patriarchs, Abraham, Isaac and Jacob. Do you think that you can just stay here? Can you really stay here for ever? Would you not run short of money, and, since you are a delicate man, what could you do? Sailing away to some other country is no answer, no matter how you look at it. If they [in another country] don't know who you are, you will not be able to stay because they would not give you money; and if they *do* know who you are, you will not be able to stay because there, too, they would know about it!" (Thus spoke the Old Man.)

"Since this is so," I said, "that I am an outcast, I shall [at least] have a share in the World to Come." And he replied: "A share in the World to Come! Even in Hell there would be no place for you to be buried, because you have committed such a profanation of the Divine Name!" "Please go," I said, "I had thought you would console and ease me but now I see that you are tormenting me. Please go." And the Old Man departed.

While I was sitting there I thought: As I am to stay here for such a long time, I might entirely forget my studies. I ordered the man whom we used to send to town for our needs to look for a book there and bring it to us. He went to town but did not bring a book, saying that it was impossible to get one because he could not disclose for whom the book was required, and it was impossible to find a book secretly. I was greatly distressed by this, because I had to wander as an outcast from place to place, and without a book I might entirely forget my studies.

Later the Old Man returned, carrying a book in his arms. "What are you carrying?" I asked. "A book," he said. "Give it to me," I said, and he gave me the book. I took it, but did not even know how to put it down. I opened the book and could not understand it at all. It appeared to me as if it was written in a different script and in another language, because I could not understand it at all, not at all. I was greatly distressed by this and feared that when the people who were still with me found this out, they might leave me too.

Once again, the Old Man came to speak to me. I went with him and he went on as before: "How could you have done it? Have you no shame? Even in Hell there will be no place for you to be buried." And I said: "Had a man from Heaven said this to me I would have believed him." And he replied: "That is where I come from." And he showed me something to prove that he had come from there. I recalled the well-known story of Israel Baalshem, blessed be his memory, who had also thought at the time that he would have no share in the World to Come. And I threw my head backward with great bitterness. And as I did so, my ancestors, the Patriarchs and all the others before whom the Old Man had said I should be ashamed, gathered around me, and recited to me the biblical verse from Isaiah, "And the fruit of the earth shall be excellent and comely" (4:2), and they said: "We shall take pride in you!" And they summoned all my men and my children (for my children, too, had parted from me at first), and they eased me with such things which were the very opposite of what the Old Man had said. And as to when I threw my head backward [they said] that even a man who had transgressed the Torah eight hundred times, if he had cast his head back with such bitterness, his sins would certainly have been forgiven him. The rest of the good things I do not wish to tell you, for they were certainly good.

The confessional importance of this dream—or rather nightmare—is enhanced by the fact that Naḥman used the first person singular in telling it. He usually alludes to himself in stories told about "a *Ṣaddik*" in the third person. The use of the first person here must be read as an additional pointer to the confessional aspect.

With this Kafkaesque confession, Naḥman summed up the interpretation of his own life less than a year before its end, in which there are two central emotions: shame and guilt. Both these components had joined and perhaps struggled with one another in Naḥman's psyche, molding his complex personality. Indiscretion about the self speaks from the nightmare, exposing a sensitive aspect, an exceedingly vulnerable side of his life and personality. No enemy, however cunning, could have set Naḥman's life as a target for attack; but his guilty conscience was violently alive long before attack from outside.

The sense of shame and the sense of guilt are by no means identical but they are interwoven here into one intricate web. Shame is a feeling engendered by other human beings, whereas the consciousness of sin, being entirely religious, points to a disrupted relationship between God and man. Rumors spread about an unutterable sin in Naḥman's life, and his nightmare reflects his own fear of isolation as well as the actual isolation that followed this fear.

One cannot tell any more whether the isolation is the result of the bottomless fear or of the unspeakable sin, whether it is a punishment for the fear or a punishment for the sin. The destructive mental experience of being silently branded, of considering oneself an outcast, as well as being considered one by others, this experience itself is isolating and turns one into an outcast.

Psychologists may maintain that the consciousness of sin and the consciousness of shame are closely related through a deep conflict of the personality, and that this conflict manifests in the two basic feelings. However, I am not here concerned with psychology, but with the various notions and ideologies put forward by this morbidly vulnerable man about himself.

The crisis of his own identity emerges from the outcast's preoccupation with the forms of social blemish and religious sin. While his shame is thus exposed, he stands abashed among his contemporaries as well as before his ancestors in the past and descendants in the future. He knows the hidden aspects of his personality that call for criticism and attack, better than any of his critics and opponents. Here is the inner dialectics of a man who, prone to self-criticism, later fell victim inevitably to the attack of his enemies. He cannot escape them because his own self-criticism is reinforced by their criticism, and as a leader, he is particularly vulnerable to the attacks of his opponents.

A boundless awareness of his guilt is revealed in this nightmare, and its articulation is partly a social one: the man who had done what is unmentionable, who had committed the nameless sin, finds himself cut off from his social environment, which threatens him with hints and endless whispering. In vain does he try to escape, migrate to another country—his reputation precedes him, and nowhere on earth can he find refuge. His friends desert him in silence, his followers are reduced to a few men. Even to them he cannot confide his secret: he has forgotten the Hebrew language! There is no more forceful expression of the alienation in which he finds himself, an exile within exile. The Hebrew book, standing for Jewish law and religion, has become a strange script to him, which he is unable to decipher. The social estrangement is thus but an external anticipation of his own alienation, unknown to all except himself and stands like an iron wall between him and the tradition of his ancestors.

The identity of the man in the nightmare becomes clear. Who is this outcast whose grandfathers were Naḥman of Horodenka and Israel Baalshem? The answer is self-evident: Naḥman of Brazlav speaks in his own name of his own religious and social predicament. There emerge three powerful themes: the problem of guilt, which is religious, that of shame, which is social, and that of the succession of generations, which is genealogical. The three are so closely related in the nightmare that it is hardly possible to disentangle them.

Three times during the nightmare a curious or, perhaps, wondrous personality makes his appearance—the one referred to as "the Old Man." He is not the one who had stirred up the turmoil in the first place, for the whispering and sneering in Naḥman's closest circle of friends and followers had started before the Old Man ever appeared on the scene. Even Naḥman's migration to another country as a result of the indirect, ambiguous hints at his guilt took place before the Old

Man arrived. Who is this Old Man, who, although he does not cause the trouble to break out, speaks almost directly to Naḥman, telling him to his face about an unmentionable sin that the others only hint at? The expression "Old Man" is common throughout Brazlav literature as the nickname of Naḥman's fiercest opponent—Aryeh Leib, the Old Man of Shpola. He was an aged man of considerable popular following at the time when Naḥman was still a young competitor. The Old Man of Shpola had become Naḥman's mortal enemy and had been the organizing spirit of the campaign against him at least ever since 1800. There is no doubt that this is also the case in Naḥman's nightmare, and the Old Man stands for Aryeh Leib. In a number of utterances scattered in Brazlav literature Naḥman refers to him as the messenger of Satan, or as Satan himself. The diabolical preoccupation of Naḥman found a center of gravity in the person of his archenemy, the Old Man of Shpola. In the nightmare, this relationship is greatly mitigated: the Old Man is not portrayed with hatred. His image in the story is not satanical. He does not seek maliciously to harm the persecuted, and he does not seem to be motivated by prejudice. He is not ill-disposed or ill-intentioned. He appears as the true Reprover, who speaks on behalf of the Patriarchs, and it is from his very call for a confrontation between the defendant and his ancestors that the Old Man derives some of his authority. Naḥman could even think for a while that the Old Man had come to console him. On the other hand, he does not promise the accused forgiveness; on the contrary, he promises him shame both in this world and in the world to come. He threatens that "even in Hell there will be no place for you, because you have committed such a profanation of the Divine Name." In his second appearance, the Old Man carries a book in his arms—a much coveted object that Naḥman had for some time desired to see, but that his few remaining companions were unable to obtain for him. It is in this connection that the outcast makes his most painful self-discovery—he has completely lost his Hebrew, the most elementary contact with his ancestors' tradition. He himself was unaware of this until his confrontation with the open book—the symbol of law, tradition, his ancestors, Israel Baalshem, the Patriarchs. His astonishment and dismay are very great and he contrives to conceal his frightening discovery from the few who had remained loyal to him through sheer ignorance of his condition.

The Old Man again appears, once more not as a slanderer but as a true Reprover. He might almost seem to be the outcast's own conscience, except that the Old Man always addresses himself to Naḥman's social sense of shame rather than to his religious sense of guilt. Only the people who whispered and sneered at him before the Old Man had appeared spoke about sin. One of them had said to Naḥman: "How could you have done *it*? Is it possible that you have committed such a monstrous sin?" This anonymous man was more penetrating, more religious than the Old Man, whose questions were not concerned with sin, but merely with shame.

The Kafkaesque strangeness of the story is that the sin allegedly committed is nowhere specified. Its nature remains vague, but there can be no doubt as to its seriousness. A second Kafkaesque feature of the story is that the occurrence of the alleged sin is neither confirmed nor denied by the accused, but by his very silence and going into exile one gets the impression that his genuine guilt has driven him into tacitly accepting the inarticulate challenge of the many. At first, he claims he does not know what it is all about, but his final movement, the last desperation and the remark that the violent throwing back of his head in despair would atone even for having transgressed the whole law 800 times leave no doubt that the sin was in fact committed. The nightmare is about an actual sin, not about one made up in the hothouse of guilt feelings. But we still lack the slightest clue as to the nature of the sin concerned.

The nightmare is dated 1809, about a year before his death. But two years earlier, he had been panic-stricken when the doctors in Lemberg—he had traveled there from the depths of Podolia—told him that his illness was fatal.

His predicament in Lemberg confronts him with a quite personal decision. Guilt-ridden about his views as formulated in a secret manuscript, in terror and anxiety over his precarious health, he overcomes one of his severest temptations: to keep his manuscript intact.

He decides, after prolonged hesitation, to destroy both existing copies of his handwritten book, toward whose doctrines he must have harbored a highly ambivalent attitude for some time. The manuscript was destroyed at his order by a disciple and friend of his, whom he sent home urgently from Lemberg to Brazlav with the one task of burning this dangerous work. If the book burned, he would get at least another lease of life, a short moratorium before having to die. Thus ran the confused ideas of sin and punishment in his mind, seized by the terror of a period in his life when he realized that death was impending. We do not need to discuss in detail the circumstances leading to this perception and to this auto-da-fé of esoteric texts that has the deplorable consequence for us that Naḥman's most intimate ideas are lost forever. Needless to say, it can be no more than speculation that the destroyed book contained unorthodox lines of thought whose doctrinal deviation was fully known to their author; this would explain, for instance, why the original copy of the book was *not* dictated to Nathan, the literary secretary, as all his other texts, but was written by Naḥman's own hand. When some years before the final destruction Naḥman had ordered his secretary to make a copy of the esoteric handwritten book, the secretary, who should have known better, was patently horrified by what he copied. "I was shocked though I did not understand what I was copying," confessed the secretary disarmingly in his autobiography, although in the climate of Brazlav he must have been used to being shocked for no apparent reason. Nevertheless, we have no direct proof for the assumption that the secret manuscript contained unorthodox theology.

Was this destruction of his own manuscript necessary? I would propose presenting it as an acute crisis of identity in Naḥman's life. All that was contained in the manuscript presumably constituted a threat to Naḥman's identity as conceived by his group and as conceived by himself. It had to be burned at a crucial point in his life when he felt that the time had come for his life to be terminated immediately.

His hardly disguised hesitation and ambivalence between orthodoxy and heterodoxy, his indecision, all this dialectical exercise was remorsefully revoked in a moment of personal crisis.

Whether or not he was able to make a full recantation of the theological positions put forward in the burned manuscript is another question, which I cannot discuss here. But if theology is an attitude of mind, it becomes very hard to believe that the return to orthodox theories could be completely satisfactory.

Did Augustine fully recover after his youthful delectations in Manichean heterodoxy? Did Yehuda Ha-Levi abandon Aristotelian and Neo-Platonic philosophy without leaving a trace in the texture of the new antiphilosophical Judaism he formulated in his *Kuzari*? Did Rosenzweig's infatuation with Christianity not leave any permanent marks in his post-Christian, apparently fully Jewish thought? The answer in all these cases is in the negative; hardly anyone can reject his own heterodox past with impunity.

No doubt Naḥman was both horrified and fascinated by heresy, by *all* heresy. His attraction to the two heresies of the day, the rational heresy of the Enlightenment and the irrational heresy of the Sabbatian-Frankist tradition, left some permanent traces on his work. No one knew the taste of these two heresies better than Naḥman himself, who experienced their seductive power firsthand. One of Naḥman's specific terrors was his apocalyptic vision of universal atheism inundating everything and everybody—and particularly the mind of the Messiah, who will in this way be put to the supreme test. This is again, of course, the romantic indiscretion of a lonely man, hopelessly struggling against the destructive ghosts of his own personal unbelief. This is Naḥman's fight against himself, or rather against his own mortal fascination with the two heresies, the rational and the irrational, which he experienced as the two great doctrinal temptations of his age, as the eighteenth moved into the nineteenth century. Both of them, in Naḥman's penetrating vision, would lead relentlessly to the total disintegration of Jewish religion and law, and of the Jewish people. This morbid fixation on two opposite movements within the context of contemporaneous Jewish society, the emerging rational Enlightenment and the declining irrational Sabbatian heresy, make Naḥman the most representative speaker of his century. He confronted both great heresies of his age, looked into their eyes, drew the logical conclusions from their premises, and examined his own ambiguity toward them. The traces of this inner struggle against rejected doctrines are noticeable in his writings. His own image of himself is of a messianic figure destined to be despised and to die, and to return later on the occasion of his parousia in power and glory. In all this he is largely indebted to Sabbatian theories, whose dogmas he certainly rejected. His indebtedness to his unorthodox sources must not be interpreted as his own final theological position.

For those who are adamant on the cut-and-dried definitions of an "Essence of Judaism" school, Naḥman of Brazlav must pose some deeply disturbing questions. To the unbiased historian, who takes delight in the endless accumulation of nonidentical Jewish experiences and in the richness of Jewish phenomena, and wishes to draw upon a wide canvas, Naḥman will prove an unexpected witness.

Index